THE ROUGH GUIDE TO

Bangkok

Written and researched by

Paul Gray and Lucy Ridout

This sixth edition updated by

Paul Gray

ROUGH GUIDES

roughguides.com

Contents

WITHDRAWN

Introduction to

Bangkok

The headlong pace and flawed modernity of Bangkok match few people's visions of the capital of exotic Siam. Spiked with scores of high-rise buildings of concrete and glass, it's a vast flatness that holds an estimated population of nearly fifteen million, and feels even bigger. But under the shadow of the skyscrapers you'll find a heady mix of chaos and refinement, of frenetic markets and hushed golden temples, of early-morning alms-giving ceremonies and ultra-hip designer bars.

Bangkok is a relatively young capital, established in 1782 after the Burmese sacked Ayutthaya, its predecessor. A temporary base was set up on the western bank of the Chao Phraya River, in what is now Thonburi, before work started on the more defensible east bank, where the first king of the new dynasty, Rama I, built his fabulously ornate palace within a protective ring of canals. Around the temples and palaces of this "royal island", there spread an amphibious city of shops and houses built on bamboo rafts moored on the river and canals.

Ever since its foundation, but with breakneck acceleration in recent years, Bangkok has attracted internal migration from all over Thailand, pushing the city's boundaries

---

RAT OR RAJA?

There's no standard system of transliterating Thai script into Roman, so you're sure to find that the Thai words in this book don't always match the versions you'll see elsewhere. Maps and street signs are the biggest sources of confusion, so we've generally gone for the **transliteration** that's most common on the spot; where it's a toss-up between two equally popular versions, we've used the one that helps best with pronunciation. However, sometimes you'll need to do a bit of lateral thinking, bearing in mind that a classic variant for the town of Ayutthaya is Ayudhia, while among street names, Thanon Rajavithi could come out as Thanon Ratwithi – and it's not unheard of to find one spelling posted at one end of a road, with another at the opposite end. See the Language section of this book for an introduction to Thai.

ever outwards in an explosion of modernization that has seen the canals on the east side of the river concreted over and left the city without an obvious centre. The capital now sprawls over 330 square kilometres and, with a population forty times that of the second city, Chiang Mai, and four-fifths of the nation's automobiles, it's far and away the country's dominant metropolis. In the make-up of its population, however, Thailand's capital supports world trends – over half of its inhabitants are under thirty, a fact that helps to consolidate Bangkok's position as one of the liveliest and most fashionable cities in Asia.

What to see

Rama I named his royal island **Ratanakosin**, and this remains the city's spiritual heart, not to mention its culturally most rewarding quarter. No visit to the capital would be complete without seeing the star attractions here – if necessary, the dazzling ostentation of **Wat Phra Kaeo** and the **Grand Palace**, lively and grandiose **Wat Pho** and the **National Museum**'s hoard of exquisite works of art can all be crammed into a single action-packed day.

One of the other great pleasures of the city is a ride on its remaining waterways; the majestic **Chao Phraya River** is served by frequent ferries and longtail boats, and is the

CENTRAL CHAO PHRAYA EXPRESS-BOAT PIERS

N15	◁▲▶	Thewet (all boats)
N14	◁▲▶	Rama VIII Bridge (no flag)
N13	◁▲▶	Phra Arthit (no flag and orange flag)
N12	◁▲▶	Phra Pinklao Bridge (all boats)
N11	▶	Thonburi Railway Station (no flag and orange flag)
N10	◁▲▶	Wang Lang (all boats)
N9	▲▶	Chang (no flag, green flag and orange flag)
N8	▶	Thien (no flag and orange flag)
N7		Ratchini (no flag)
N6	▶	Saphan Phut (no flag and orange flag)
N5	◁▲▶	Rachawongse (all boats)
N4	▶	Marine (Harbour) Department (no flag and orange flag)
N3	◁▲▶	Si Phraya (all boats)
N2		Wat Muang Kae (no flag)
N1	▶	Oriental (no flag and orange flag)
Central	◁▲▶	Sathorn (all boats)

▶ All-day	◁ ▲ Rush hour only (Mon–Fri)
Rush-hour no-flag boats stop at all piers (Mon–Fri)	

backbone of a network of old canals, stilted houses and lovely waterside temples – including the striking five-towered **Wat Arun** – that remains fundamentally intact in the west-bank **Thonburi** district. Inevitably the waterways have earned Bangkok the title of "Venice of the East", a tag that seems all too apt when you're wading through flooded streets in the rainy season.

FACT FILE

- Bangkok (**Krung Thep** in Thai) is the capital of Thailand, which was known as **Siam** until 1939 (and again from 1945 to 1949); some academics feel changing the name back again would better reflect the country's Thai and non-Thai diversity.

- Buddhism is the national **religion**, Islam the largest minority religion, but nearly all Thais also practise some form of animism (spirit worship).

- Since 1932 the country has been a **constitutional monarchy**. King Bhumibol, also known as Rama IX (being the ninth ruler of the Chakri dynasty), is the world's longest-ruling head of state, having been on the throne since 1946. Prince Vajiralongkorn is the heir to the throne, while his younger sister, the popular Princess Sirindhorn, is also often seen in public.

- **Tourism** is the country's main industry, and its biggest **exports** are computers and components, vehicles and vehicle parts, textiles and rubber.

- Bangkok has only 0.4 square metres of public parkland per inhabitant, the lowest figure in the world, compared, for example, to London's 30.4 square metres per person. Meanwhile, over two million of the city's inhabitants live in two thousand areas of the city that are classified by the Bangkok Metropolitan Administration as slums.

Bangkok began to assume its modern guise at the end of the nineteenth century, when the forward-looking Rama V relocated the royal family to a neighbourhood north of Ratanakosin called **Dusit**. Here he commissioned grand European-style boulevards, built the new Chitrlada Palace (still used by the royal family today), had his charming summer palace – the teakwood **Vimanmek Palace** – reconstructed nearby, and capped it all with the erection of a sumptuous new temple, **Wat Benjamabophit**, which was built from Italian marble. When political modernization followed in 1932, Dusit was the obvious choice of home for Thailand's new parliament, which now sits in Parliament House.

Bangkok's commercial heart lies to the southeast of Dusit, where sleek glass towers and cool marble malls lend an air of energy and big-city drama to the districts of **Silom**, **Siam Square** and **Sukhumvit**. These areas shelter a few noteworthy tourist sights, too, best of which is **Jim Thompson's House**, a small, elegant and very personal museum of Thai design. **Shopping** downtown varies from touristic outlets selling Thai silks and handicrafts to international fashion emporia and boutiques showcasing the country's home-grown contemporary designs. For livelier scenes, explore the dark alleys of the bazaars in **Chinatown** or the Indian district, **Pahurat**, or head out to the enormous, open-air **Chatuchak Weekend Market**. Similarly, the city offers wildly varied entertainment, ranging from traditional dancing and the orchestrated bedlam of Thai boxing, through hip bars and clubs both downtown and in the backpackers' enclave of **Banglamphu**, to the farang-only sex bars of the notorious Patpong district.

FROM TOP AYUTTHAYA; LONGTAIL BOAT, THONBURI

CITY OF ANGELS

When Rama I was crowned in 1782, he gave his new capital a grand 43-syllable name to match his ambitious plans for the building of the city. Since then 21 more syllables have been added.

Krungthepmahanakhornboworn-ratanakosinmahintarayutthayamahadilokpopnopparat-ratchathaniburiromudomratchaniwetmahasathanamornpimanavatarnsathitsakkathattiyavisnu-karprasit is Guinness-certified as the longest place name in the world and roughly translates as "Great city of angels, the supreme repository of divine jewels, the great land unconquerable, the grand and prominent realm, the royal and delightful capital city full of nine noble gems, the highest royal dwelling and grand palace, the divine shelter and living place of the reincarnated spirits". Fortunately, all Thais refer to the city simply as Krung Thep ("City of Angels"), though plenty can recite the full name at the drop of a hat. Bangkok – "Village of the Plum Olive" – was the name of the original village on the Thonburi side of the Chao Phraya; with remarkable persistence, it has remained in use by foreigners since the 1660s, when the French built a short-lived garrison fort in the area.

North and west of the city, the unwieldy urban mass of Greater Bangkok peters out into the vast, well-watered central plains, a region that for centuries has grown the bulk of the nation's food. The atmospheric ruins of Thailand's fourteenth-century capital **Ayutthaya** lie here, ninety minutes' train ride to the north of Bangkok and, together with the ornate palace at nearby **Bang Pa-In**, make a rewarding excursion from the modern metropolis. Further west, the massive stupa at **Nakhon Pathom** and the floating markets of **Damnoen Saduak** are also easily manageable as a day-trip, and combine well with a visit to the historic town of **Phetchaburi**, famous for its charming old temples. Riverside **Amphawa** is similarly evocative and makes a perfect

Author picks

Having finally settled down in Thailand after twenty years of toiling and froing, our author, Paul, has plenty to write home about. Here are some of his personal faves.

Aroy aroy "Delicious, delicious" food is always at hand in the city of fifty thousand restaurants. Try the house deep-fried fish salad at *Taling Pling* (see p.167) or sample the meticulously authentic dishes at *Bolan* (see p.165). The area south of Democracy Monument is a fruitful hunting ground for traditional restaurants such as *Krua Apsorn* (see p.162).

Oishi aroy Perhaps surprisingly, Bangkok is a great place for delicious Japanese food, too, at lower prices than in Japan or the West. The sushi at *Hinata* (see p.163) is superb while the miso ramen at *Ramentei* (see p.167) and just about anything at all-rounder *Aoi* (see p.166) always hit the spot.

Bangkok de luxe The Thai capital's hotels do luxury extremely well so, if you can, push the boat out at the riverside *Peninsula* (see p.155), the elegant *Sukhothai* (see p.155) or the graceful *Anantara Siam* (see p.152).

Kneads must A good pummelling at the massage pavilions amid the historic, kaleidoscopic architecture of Wat Pho is one of Bangkok's unbeatable experiences (see p.182).

Khon Soak up the haunting music, beautiful costumes and exquisite gestures of Thailand's highest dramatic art (see p.177).

On the river Catch one of the express boats on the Chao Phraya whenever you can (see p.28): they're cheap, faster than road transport and open a window on the river's teeming life, set against a backdrop of temples, skyscrapers and colonial-style villas.

> Our author recommendations don't end here. We've flagged up our favourite places – a perfectly sited hotel, an atmospheric café, a special restaurant – throughout the guide, highlighted with the ★ symbol.

OPPOSITE CHINATOWN **RIGHT FROM TOP** PRAWN WITH NOODLES AND SHREDDED MANGO; WAT PHO; PART OF *KHON* COSTUME

escape from the bustle of the city, with its genuine floating markets and traditional canalside neighbourhoods. An overnight stay at **Kanchanaburi** is also well worth the effort: impressively sited on the River Kwai, it holds several moving World War II memorials, including the notorious Death Railway.

When to go

Bangkok's climate is governed by three seasons, though in reality the city sits firmly within the tropics and so enjoys warm days and nights year-round. The so-called **cool season**, which runs from November to February, is the most pleasant time of year to visit; days are invariably bright and clear, and temperatures average a manageable 27°C (though they can still reach a broiling 31°C at noon). This is high season for the tourist industry, so rooms and flights are at a premium and well worth booking in advance; prices shoot up further for the Christmas and New Year period.

March sees the beginning of the **hot season**, when temperatures can rise to 36°C, and continue to do so beyond the end of April. During these sweltering months you may find yourself spending more money than at other times, simply in order to secure the benefits of air-conditioning, whether in hotel rooms, restaurants, taxis or buses. Come in mid-April and you'll also find the city in full swing as it celebrates Songkhran, the Thai New Year (see p.36), filling the streets with raucous waterfights.

The daily downpours that characterize the **rainy season** can come as a welcome relief, though being hot and wet is a sensation that doesn't necessarily appeal to everyone. The rainy season varies in length and intensity from year to year, but usually starts with a bang in May, gathers force between June and August, and comes to a peak in September and October, when whole districts of the capital are flooded. Rain rarely lasts all day however, so as long as you're armed with an umbrella there's no reason to reschedule your trip – come during the rainy season and you'll get more for your money, too, as many hotels and airlines drop their prices right down at this time of year.

AVERAGE DAILY TEMPERATURES AND RAINFALL IN BANGKOK

	Jan	Feb	Mar	Apr	May	Jun	Jul	Aug	Sep	Oct	Nov	Dec
Max/min (°C)	28/21	28/21	29/21	30/22	31/23	31/23	30/23	31/23	31/23	30/23	29/23	28/22
Max/min (°F)	82/70	82/70	84/70	86/72	88/73	88/73	86/73	88/73	88/73	86/73	84/73	82/72
Rainfall (mm)	11	28	31	72	190	152	158	187	320	231	57	9

19

things not to miss

It's not possible to see everything Bangkok has to offer on a short trip – and we don't suggest you try. What follows is a selective taste of the city's highlights, from extravagant palaces and frenetic markets to tranquil neighbourhoods and cutting-edge shopping, plus great day-trip destinations out of the city. All entries have a page reference to take you straight into the guide, where you can find out more. Coloured numbers refer to chapters in the Guide section.

3

4

6 JIM THOMPSON'S HOUSE
Page 94

A very personal museum of Thai crafts and architecture.

7 SONGKHRAN
Page 36

Thai New Year is the excuse for a national water fight – don't plan on getting much done if you come in mid-April, just join in the fun.

8 THANON KHAO SAN
Page 65

Legendary hub for Southeast Asian backpackers: the place for cheap sleeps, baggy trousers and tall tales.

9 THAI BOXING
Page 178

Nightly bouts at the national stadia are accompanied by live music and frenetic betting.

10 TRADITIONAL MASSAGE
Page 180

Combining elements of acupressure and yoga, a pleasantly brutal way to help shed jet lag or to end the day.

11 NATIONAL MUSEUM
Page 60

The cornucopia of Thailand's artistic heritage, ranging from sculptural treasures to royal funeral chariots.

12 MUANG BORAN ANCIENT CITY
Page 112

Escape from the city to this attractively landscaped open-air museum, which features beautiful replicas of Thailand's finest monuments.

9

10

11

12

17

18

19

TUK-TUK IN BANGKOK

Basics

Getting there

Nearly all international flights into Bangkok use Suvarnabhumi Airport (see p.24); a few flights from other Asian countries, low-cost flights, and many domestic services, use the old Don Muang Airport (see p.25).

Air fares to Bangkok generally depend on the **season**, with the highest being from approximately mid-November to mid-February, when the weather is best (with premium rates charged for flights between mid-December and New Year), and in July and August to coincide with school holidays. You will need to book several months in advance to get reasonably priced tickets during these peak periods.

Flights from the UK and Ireland

The fastest and most comfortable way of reaching Bangkok **from the UK** is to fly nonstop from London with Thai Airways (Wthaiairways.com), British Airways (Wba.com) or Eva Airways (Wevaair.com), a journey of about eleven and a half hours. These airlines sometimes have special promotions, but a typical fare in high season might come in at around £800–900. Fares on indirect scheduled flights to Bangkok are always cheaper than nonstop flights – starting at about £450 in high season if booked well in advance with Qatar Airways (Wqatarairways .com), for example – though these journeys can take anything from two to twelve hours longer.

There are no nonstop flights from any **regional airports** in Britain or from any **Irish airports**, but rather than routing via London, you may find it convenient to fly to another hub such as Frankfurt (with Lufthansa; Wlufthansa.com), Zurich (with Swiss; Wswiss.com), Abu Dhabi (with Etihad; Wetihadairways.com) or Istanbul (with Turkish Airlines; Wturkishairlines.com), and take a connecting flight from there. Return flights from Newcastle upon Tyne with Emirates (Wemirates.com), for example, currently start at around £500 in high season if booked far in advance, and from Dublin via Copenhagen with Emirates, at around €650.

Flights from the US and Canada

Thai Airways (Wthaiairways.com) offers convenient flights from LA to Bangkok, with a ninety-minute stop in Seoul, charging from US$1100 in high season if booked well in advance. Plenty of other airlines run to Bangkok from East and West Coast cities with one stop en route; it's generally easier to find a reasonable fare on flights via Asia than via Europe, even if you're departing from the East Coast – if you book far in advance, you can get a flight from New York for as little as US$850 return in high season, including taxes. Air Canada (Waircanada .com) has the most convenient service to Bangkok from the largest number of Canadian cities; from Vancouver, expect to pay from around Can$1200 in high season; from Toronto, Can$1350. Cheaper rates are often available if you're prepared to make two or three stops and take more time.

Minimum **flying times** are twenty hours from New York or Toronto (westbound or eastbound), including stopovers, seventeen hours (nonstop) or nineteen and a half hours (with one stop) from LA, and eighteen hours from Vancouver.

Flights from Australia and New Zealand

There's no shortage of **scheduled flights** to Bangkok **from Australia**, with direct services from major cities operated by Thai Airways (Wthaiair ways.com), Qantas (Wqantas.com.au) and half a dozen others (around 9hr from Sydney and Perth), and plenty of indirect flights via Asian hubs, which take at least eleven and a half hours. There's often not much difference between the fares on nonstop and indirect flights with the major carriers, nor between the fares from the major eastern cities. From Sydney, if you book far in advance, you can get a ticket to Bangkok in high season for around Aus$800, on a low-cost carrier such as Jetstar or through a special promotion with one of the major airlines; nonstop flights with the major airlines more typically cost around Aus$1200. Fares from Perth and Darwin are up to Aus$200 cheaper.

A BETTER KIND OF TRAVEL

At Rough Guides we are passionately committed to travel. We believe it helps us understand the world we live in and the people we share it with – and of course tourism is vital to many developing economies. But the scale of modern tourism has also damaged some places irreparably, and climate change is accelerated by most forms of transport, especially flying. All Rough Guides' flights are carbon-offset, and every year we donate money to a variety of environmental charities.

From **New Zealand**, Thai Airways runs nonstop twelve-hour flights between Auckland and Bangkok, costing from around NZ$1250 (including taxes) in high season with advanced booking. British Airways/Qantas flights from Auckland make brief stops in Sydney, adding about three hours to the trip, and other major Asian airlines offer indirect flights via their hubs (from 13hr, but more typically 17hr); fares for indirect flights can start as low as NZ$1100 in high season.

Flights from South Africa

Thai Airways' nonstop, code-sharing flights with South African Airways (W flysaa.com) from Johannesburg to Bangkok have been discontinued, so you'll be making a stop in East Africa, the Middle East, Singapore or Hong Kong, with fares starting at around ZAR8000 for an advance booking in high season, and a journey time of fourteen hours or more.

TRAVEL AGENTS AND TOUR OPERATORS WORLDWIDE

Creative Events Asia Thailand W creativeeventsasia.com. Wedding specialists for everything from paperwork to the ceremony and guest accommodation.

Flight Centre Australia ☎ 13 31 33, Canada ☎ 877 967 5302, New Zealand ☎ 0800 243 544, South Africa ☎ 0877 405000, UK ☎ 0800 678 1134, US ☎ 877 409 7018; W flightcentre.com. Australian company offering cheap international air fares.

Grasshopper Adventures Australia ☎ 03 9016 3172, Thailand ☎ 02 280 0832, UK ☎ 020 8123 8144, US ☎ 818 921 7101; W grasshopperadventures.com. Cycling day-tours and two-day trips around Bangkok.

North South Travel UK ☎ 01245 608 291, W northsouthtravel .co.uk. Friendly, competitive travel agency, offering discounted fares worldwide. Profits are used to support projects in the developing world, especially the promotion of sustainable tourism.

Origin Asia Thailand W alex-kerr.com. Cultural programmes lasting from half a day to a week that teach and explain living Thai arts such as dance, music, martial arts, textiles, flower offerings and cooking.

STA Travel UK ☎ 0333 321 0099, US ☎ 800 781 4040, Australia ☎ 134 782, New Zealand ☎ 0800 474 400, South Africa ☎ 0861 781 781; W statravel.co.uk. Worldwide specialists in independent travel; also student IDs, travel insurance, car rental and more. Good discounts for students and under-26s.

Trailfinders UK ☎ 0207 368 1200, Ireland ☎ 021 464 8800, W trailfinders.com. One of the best-informed and most efficient agents for independent travellers.

Travel CUTS Canada ☎ 800 667 2887, US ☎ 800 592 2887, W travelcuts.com. Canadian youth and student travel firm.

USIT Ireland ☎ 01 602 1906, Australia ☎ 1800 092 499, W usit.ie. Ireland's main student and youth travel specialists, with a branch in Sydney.

TRAVEL AGENTS AND TOUR OPERATORS IN BANGKOK

Asian Trails 9th Floor, SG Tower, 161/1 Soi Mahadlek Luang 3, Thanon Rajdamri ☎ 02 626 2000, W asiantrails.travel. Sells flights, tours and airport transfers.

Educational Travel Centre (ETC) 180 Thanon Khao San, Banglamphu ☎ 02 629 1885; and inside ETZ Hostel, off Thanon Rama IV (see p.154). Sells air and bus tickets, and Thailand tours.

New Road Guest House 1216/1 Thanon Charoen Krung, between sois 34 and 36 ☎ 02 630 9371, W newroadguesthouse.com. Thai headquarters of Danish backpacker tour operator, Visit Beyond, New Road Guest House is a reliable agent for train and bus tickets, as well as their own unusual tours.

Olavi Travel 53 Thanon Chakrabongse, Banglamphu ☎ 02 629 4710, W olavi.com. Sells air, train and bus tickets opposite the west end of Thanon Khao San.

STA Travel Viengtai Hotel, Thanon Ram Bhuttri, Banglamphu ☎ 098 284 6163; and 14th Floor, Wall Street Tower, 33/70 Thanon Suriwong ☎ 02 236 0262; W statravel.co.th. The Bangkok branches of the worldwide STA Travel are reliable outlets for cheap international flights and local tours.

Travelling from neighbouring countries

Sharing land borders with Myanmar, Laos, Cambodia and Malaysia, Thailand works well as part of many overland itineraries, both across Asia and between Europe and Australia. Bangkok is also one of the major regional flight hubs for Southeast Asia, with flights to and from all four neighbouring countries. As part of plans for the ASEAN (Association of South East Asian Nations) Economic Community, which at the time of writing was soon to be launched, cross-border links in Southeast Asia have improved considerably recently and are likely to continue to do so in the next few years.

The main restrictions on overland routes in and out of Thailand are determined by where the permitted land crossings lie and by **visas** – all **Asian embassies** are located in Bangkok (see p.44). Many Khao San tour agents offer to get your visa for you, but beware: some are reportedly **faking the stamps**, which could get you into pretty serious trouble, so it's safer to go to the embassy yourself.

Myanmar

There are now four overland access points between **Myanmar (Burma)** and Thailand that are open to

Westerners: at Thachileik opposite Mae Sai; at Myawaddy near Mae Sot; at remote Htee Khee opposite Phu Nam Ron in Kanchanaburi province, a crossing that's being developed to facilitate transport between the major new port at Dawei on the Bay of Bengal and Bangkok; and at Kaw Thaung (Victoria Point) near Ranong. At these borders Western tourists can enter Myanmar either forearmed with a Burmese **tourist visa**, or on a temporary US$10 (or B500) **border pass**, which will allow you to make limited-distance trips into Myanmar, usually just for the day.

Cambodia

At the time of writing, six overland crossings on the **Thai-Cambodian border** were open to Westerners. The most commonly used land crossing is at **Poipet**, which lies just across the border from the Thai town of **Aranyaprathet** and has public-transport connections with Sisophon, Siem Reap and Phnom Penh. There are now direct public buses that run all the way between Bangkok's Northern Terminal (Mo Chit) and Siem Reap and between Mo Chit and Phnom Penh, which should help you dodge the scams and touts at this frontier post, as well as the scams operated by travel agents selling through tickets in Banglamphu. The second most popular route is from Sihanoukville in Cambodia via Koh Kong (Cham Yeam) and Hat Lek to Trat, which is near Ko Chang on Thailand's east coast.

Tourist **visas** for Cambodia are issued to travellers **on arrival** at all the overland border crossings. If you want to buy an **advance** thirty-day visa, you can do so online at ⓦ evisa.gov.kh, which should help you to avoid the more excessive scams at Poipet and Koh Kong.

Laos

There are five main points along the **Lao border** where tourists can cross into Thailand: Houayxai (for Chiang Khong); Vientiane (for Nong Khai); Khammouan (aka Thakhek, for Nakhon Phanom); Savannakhet (for Mukdahan); and Pakse (for Chong Mek). Increasing numbers of direct, long-distance public buses, such as those between Bangkok's Northern (Mo Chit) Bus Terminal and Vientiane and between Bangkok and Pakse, use these crossings to link major towns in the two countries; all five of the Thai border towns mentioned above also have direct bus connections with Bangkok. All these borders can also be used as exits into Laos; tourist **visas** are available **on arrival** at all of the above-listed land borders, or you can buy one in **advance** from the Lao Embassy in Bangkok.

Malaysia

Travelling between Thailand and **Malaysia** has in the past been a straightforward and very commonly used overland route, with plentiful connections by bus, minibus, share-taxi and train, most of them routed through the southern Thai city and transport hub of Hat Yai. However, because of the ongoing **violence in Thailand's deep south**, all major Western governments are currently advising people not to travel to or through Songkhla, Pattani, Yala and Narathiwat provinces, unless essential (and consequently most insurance companies are not covering travel there). This encompasses Hat Yai and the following border crossings to and from Malaysia: at Padang Besar, on the main rail line connecting Butterworth in Malaysia (and, ultimately, Kuala Lumpur and Singapore) with Hat Yai and Bangkok; at Sungai Kolok, terminus of a railway line from Hat Yai and Bangkok, and at adjacent Ban Taba, both of which are connected by road to nearby Kota Bharu in Malaysia; and at the road crossings at Sadao, south of Hat Yai, and at Betong, south of Yala. (The routes towards Kota Bharu and Betong pass through particularly volatile territory, with martial law declared in Pattani, Yala and Narathiwat provinces; however, martial law is not in effect in Hat Yai itself.)

Nevertheless, the provinces of Trang and Satun on the west coast are not affected, and it's still perfectly possible to travel **overland via Satun**: by ferry between Satun's Thammalang pier and the island of Langkawi, or overland by a/c minibus between Satun and Kangar; or by boat between Ko Lipe and Langkawi. For up-to-the-minute advice, consult your government travel advisory (see p.38).

Most Western tourists can spend thirty days in Malaysia without having bought a visa beforehand, and there are Thai embassies or consulates in Kuala Lumpur, Kota Bharu and Penang (see p.43).

Arrival and departure

Unless you arrive in Bangkok by train, be prepared for a long trip into the city centre. Suvarnabhumi Airport and Don Muang airports are both 25km out, and the three long-distance bus stations are not much closer in, though at least the Northern Terminal is fairly near the Skytrain and subway, while the Eastern Terminal is close to a Skytrain station.

By plane

When departing from Bangkok, leave plenty of time to get to Suvarnabhumi or Don Muang, as getting there by road can be severely hampered by traffic jams.

Suvarnabhumi airport

Suvarnabhumi, Bangkok's main airport (coded "BKK" and pronounced "soo-wanna poom"; W suvarna bhumiairport.com) is situated 25km east of central Bangkok between highways 7 and 34. The large airport is well stocked with 24hr exchange booths, ATMs, places to eat, pharmacies and a post office. The airport authority operates no fewer than ten generally helpful information counters and there's a tourist police booth in the arrivals hall on Floor 2; there are 24hr left-luggage depots (B100/item/day) in arrivals and in the departures hall on Floor 4. There are a number of accommodation options near Suvarnabhumi (see p.155).

Situated on the other side of the huge airport complex from the terminal building, the **Public Transportation Centre** is reached by a free, 10min ride on an "Express" shuttle bus (every 15min) from Gate 5 outside arrivals or Gate 5 outside departures – be sure not to confuse these with the much slower "Ordinary" shuttle buses, which ferry airport staff around the complex.

Airport transport

The high-speed **Suvarnabhumi Airport Rail Link** (SARL; W srtet.co.th; daily 6am–midnight) from the basement of Suvarnabhumi is generally the quickest means of getting downtown, though it also serves as an important link for commuters and can get very crowded (the pricier express trains have recently been discontinued). There's only one set of elevated tracks, ending at Phaya Thai station, with trains running roughly every 12–15min (26min; B45), stopping at Makkasan, Ratchaprarop and four other stations. Phaya Thai is an interchange with the Skytrain system, and is served by a/c and non-a/c #59 buses (heading south on Thanon Phrayathai) to Thanon Rajadamnoen Klang, for Banglamphu.

Taxis to the centre are comfortable, a/c and reasonably priced, although the driving can be hairy. Walk past the pricey taxis and limousines on offer within the baggage hall and arrivals hall, and ignore any tout who may offer a cheap ride in an unlicensed and unmetered vehicle, as newly arrived travellers are seen as easy prey for robbery and the cabs are untraceable. Licensed and metered public taxis are operated from clearly signposted and well-regulated counters, outside Floor 1's Gates 4 and 7. Including the B50 airport pick-up fee and around B70 tolls for the overhead expressways, a journey to Thanon Silom downtown, for example, should set you back around B300–400, depending on the traffic. Heading back to the airport, drivers will nearly always try to leave their meters off and agree an inflated price with you – say "*poet meter, dai mai khrap/kha?*" to get them to switch the meter on. If you leave the downtown areas before 7am or after 9pm you can get to the airport in half an hour, but at other times you should set off about an hour and a half before you have to check in.

The most economical way of getting into the city is by public **a/c bus or a/c minibus** operated by the Bangkok Mass Transit Authority, but they're designed for airport staff and only a couple of minibus routes are likely to be useful to visitors: #551 to Victory Monument (every 20min; B40); and #552 to On Nut Skytrain station (every 20min; B20).

BANGKOK ADDRESSES

Thai **addresses** can be immensely confusing, mainly because property is often numbered twice, first to show which real-estate lot it stands in, and then to distinguish where it is on that lot. Thus 154/7–10 Thanon Rajdamnoen means the building is on lot 154 and occupies numbers 7–10. However, neither of these numbers will necessarily help you to find a particular building on a long street; when asking for directions or talking to taxi drivers, it's best to be able to quote a nearby temple, big hotel or other landmark. There's an additional idiosyncrasy in the way Thai roads are sometimes named: in large cities a minor road running off a major road is often numbered as a soi ("lane" or "alley", though it may be a sizeable thoroughfare), rather than given its own street name. Thanon Sukhumvit for example – Bangkok's longest – has minor roads numbered Soi 1 to Soi 103, with odd numbers on one side of the road and even on the other; so a Thanon Sukhumvit address could read something like 27/9–11 Soi 15, Thanon Sukhumvit, which would mean the property occupies numbers 9–11 on lot 27 on minor road number 15 running off Thanon Sukhumvit.

ORIENTATION

Bangkok ("Krung Thep" in Thai) can be a tricky place to get your bearings as it's huge and ridiculously congested, with largely featureless modern buildings and no obvious centre. The boldest line on the map is the **Chao Phraya River**, which divides the city into Bangkok proper on the east bank, and **Thonburi**, part of Greater Bangkok, on the west.

The historical core of Bangkok proper, site of the original royal palace, is **Ratanakosin**, cradled in a bend in the river. Three concentric canals radiate eastwards around Ratanakosin: the southern part of the area between the canals is the old-style trading enclave of **Chinatown** and Indian **Pahurat**, connected to the old palace by Thanon Charoen Krung (aka New Road); the northern part is characterized by old temples and the **Democracy Monument**, west of which is the backpackers' ghetto of **Banglamphu**. Beyond the canals to the north, **Dusit** is the site of many government buildings and the nineteenth-century Vimanmek Palace, and is linked to Ratanakosin by the three stately avenues, Thanon Rajdamnoen Nok, Thanon Rajdamnoen Klang and Thanon Rajdamnoen Nai.

"New" Bangkok begins to the east of the canals and beyond the main rail line and Hualamphong Station, and stretches as far as the eye can see to the east and north. The main business district is south of **Thanon Rama IV**, with the port of Khlong Toey at its eastern edge. The diverse area north of Thanon Rama IV includes the sprawling campus of Chulalongkorn University, huge shopping centres around **Siam Square** and a variety of other businesses. A couple of blocks northeast of Siam Square stands the tallest building in Bangkok, the 84-storey **Baiyoke II Tower**, whose golden spire makes a good point of reference. To the east lies the swish residential quarter of **Thanon Sukhumvit**.

These public minibuses start at the Public Transportation Centre and pick up outside the terminal's Floor 1 (Gates 1 and 8, with an information counter inside near Gate 8); however, if they fill up at the Public Transportation Centre, there'll be no pick-up at the terminal. On departure, many travellers opt for one of the private minibus services to Suvarnabhumi (B130–150) organized through guesthouses and travel agents in Banglamphu and elsewhere around the city.

Car-rental companies in the arrivals hall (Floor 2) near Gate 8 include Avis and Budget (see p.31), though you'll have to pick your car up from the Public Transportation Centre.

Don Muang

The old Don Muang Airport (coded "DMK"; W donmueangairportthai.com), 25km north of the city, is now Bangkok's main base for low-cost airlines. It shelters currency exchange booths, ATMs and a limited choice of places to eat.

Airport transport

The easiest way to get into the city centre is by licensed, metered **taxi** from the desk outside Arrivals, costing about B300–400, including B50 airport fee and expressway fees (B110 to Banglamphu, for instance). There are also **shuttle buses** from outside Arrivals (roughly every 15min; B30) that run to Mo Chit Skytrain and Chatuchak

Park subway stations and the nearby Northern Bus Terminal (Mo Chit). Operating between every 30min and every hour (see W suvarnabhumiairport .com for times), an a/c **transfer bus** that's free to passengers runs between Don Muang and Suvarnabhumi airports; at Suvarnabhumi, it picks up outside Gate 3, Floor 2, and drops off outside Gate 5, Floor 4. Meanwhile, the #59 **city bus**, stopping on the main highway that runs north–south in front of the airport buildings, will drop you off on Thanon Rajdamnoen Klang in Banglamphu. On departure, many travellers choose to use one of the **private minibus services** to Don Muang (B130–150) organized through guesthouses and travel agents in Banglamphu and elsewhere around Bangkok.

By train

Travelling to Bangkok by **train** from Malaysia and most parts of Thailand, you arrive at **Hualamphong Station**. Centrally located at the edge of Chinatown, Hualamphong is at the southern end of the subway line and is connected to Banglamphu by bus #53 (see box, p.27).

Station facilities include an exchange booth, several ATMs, a left-luggage office at the front of the main concourse (daily 4am–11pm; B20–80/ day) and a 24-hour State Railways (SRT) information booth in the main concourse, on the right.

Beware, the station area is fertile ground for con-artists who are looking to prey on new arrivals. Anyone who comes up to you in or around the station concourse and offers help/ information/transport or ticket-booking services is probably a scammer, however many official-looking ID tags are hanging round their neck. Hualamphong also nurtures plenty of dishonest tuk-tuk drivers – take a metered taxi or public transport instead.

By bus

Bangkok's three main bus terminals, all of which have left-luggage facilities of some kind, are distributed around the outskirts of town. If you happen to need to buy a ticket out of Bangkok, this can most easily be done at the ATS office (Advanced Technology Systems; Mon–Fri 9am–5pm) near the *Royal Ratanakosin Hotel* on Thanon Rajdamnoen Klang in Banglamphu, the official seller of government bus tickets, or by checking out Ⓦ thaiticketmajor.com.

All services from the north and northeast terminate at the **Northern and Northeastern Bus Terminal (Mo Chit)** on Thanon Kamphaeng Phet 2 (though a move even further into the northern suburbs is being talked about); some east-coast buses and a few from the south also use Mo Chit. The quickest way to get into the city centre from Mo Chit is to hop onto the Skytrain at Mo Chit Station on Thanon Phaholyothin, or the subway at the adjacent Chatuchak Park Station or at Kamphaeng Phet Station (at the bottom of Thanon Kamphaeng Phet 2), all of which are about a 15min walk from the bus terminal, then change onto a city bus if necessary. Otherwise, it's a long bus or taxi ride into town: city buses from the Northern Bus Terminal include ordinary and a/c #3, and a/c #509 to Banglamphu (see box opposite).

Most buses to and from east-coast destinations such as Pattaya, Ban Phe (for Ko Samet) and Trat (for Ko Chang) use the **Eastern Bus Terminal** (Ekamai) between sois 40 and 42 on Thanon Sukhumvit. This bus station is right beside the Ekamai Skytrain stop and is also served by lots of city buses, including a/c #511 to and from Banglamphu and the Southern Bus Terminal. Alternatively, you can use the Khlong Saen Saeb canal-boat service, which runs westwards almost as far as Banglamphu (see p.29); there's a pier called Tha Charn Issara, near the northern end of Sukhumvit Soi 63 (Soi Ekamai), which is easiest reached from the bus station by taxi.

The huge, airport-like **Southern Bus Terminal**, or Sathaanii Sai Tai, handles transport to and from Malaysia and all points south of the capital, including Hua Hin, Chumphon (for Ko Tao), Surat Thani (for Ko Samui), Phuket and Krabi, and buses for destinations west of Bangkok, such as Amphawa, Nakhon Pathom and Kanchanaburi. The terminal lies at the junction of Thanon Borom Ratchonni and Thanon Phutthamonthon Sai 1 in Taling Chan, an interminable 11km west of the Chao Phraya River and Banglamphu, so access to and from city accommodation can take an age, even in a taxi. City buses serving the Southern Bus Terminal include #124 for Banglamphu, #511 for Banglamphu, Thanon Sukhumvit and Ekamai, and #516 for Banglamphu and Thewet, but note that when arriving in Bangkok most long-distance bus services make a more convenient stop before reaching the terminus (via a time-consuming U-turn), towards the eastern end of Thanon Borom Ratchonni, much nearer Phra Pinklao Bridge and the river; the majority of passengers get off here, and it's highly recommended to do the same rather than continue to the terminal. The above-listed city buses all cross the river from this bus drop, as do many additional services, and this is also a faster and cheaper place to grab a taxi into town.

City transport

Transport can undoubtedly be a headache in a city where it's not unusual for residents to spend three hours getting to work – and these are people who know where they're going.

The main form of transport is **buses**, and once you've mastered the labyrinthine complexity of the route maps you'll be able to get to any part of the city, albeit slowly. Catching the various kinds of **taxi** is more expensive – though a/c metered taxis are surprisingly good value – and you'll still get held up by the daytime traffic jams. **Boats** are obviously more limited in their range, but they're regular and as cheap as buses, and you'll save a lot of time by using them whenever possible – a journey between Banglamphu and Saphan Taksin, for instance, will take around 30min by water, half what it would usually take on land. The **Skytrain** and **subway** each have a similarly limited range but are also worth using whenever suitable for all or part of your journey; their networks roughly coincide with each other at the east end of Thanon Silom, at the corner of Soi Asoke and Thanon Sukhumvit, and on

Thanon Phaholyothin by Chatuchak Park (Mo Chit), while the Skytrain joins up with the Chao Phraya River express boats at the vital hub of Sathorn/ Saphan Taksin (Taksin Bridge). At each Skytrain and subway station, you'll find a useful map of the immediate neighbourhood. Also under construction in the north of the city are the elevated metro lines known as the SRT Red Lines from Bang Sue (to connect with the subway), one of which will (eventually) stop at Don Muang Airport. **Walking** might often be quicker than travelling by road, but the heat can be unbearable, pavements are poorly maintained and the engine fumes are stifling.

Buses

Bangkok has reputedly the world's largest bus network, on which operate two main types of bus

---

USEFUL BUS ROUTES

In addition to those listed below, there are also bus routes from Suvarnabhumi Airport (see p.24) and Don Muang (see p.25). In Banglamphu, finding the right bus stop can sometimes be tricky (see p.65).

#3 (ordinary and a/c)
Northern Bus Terminal–Chatuchak Weekend Market–Thanon Phaholyothin–Thanon Samsen–Thanon Chakrabongse/Thanon Phra Arthit (for Banglamphu guesthouses)–Thanon Sanam Chai (for Museum of Siam)–Thanon Triphet–Memorial Bridge (for Pak Khlong Talat)–Taksin Monument (for Wongwian Yai) –Khlong San.

#15 (ordinary)
The Mall Tha Pra–Krung Thep Bridge–Thanon Charoen Krung (for Asiatique and Tha Sathorn)–Thanon Silom–Thanon Rajdamri–Siam Square–Thanon Lan Luang–Democracy Monument–Thanon Phra Arthit/Thanon Chakrabongse (for Banglamphu guesthouses)–Sanam Luang.

#16 (ordinary and a/c)
Northern Bus Terminal– Chatuchak Weekend Market–Thanon Samsen–Thewet (for guesthouses)–Thanon Phitsanulok–Thanon Phrayathai–Siam Square–Thanon Suriwong.

#25 (ordinary)
Pak Nam (for Ancient City buses)–Thanon Sukhumvit–Eastern Bus Terminal–Siam Square–Hualamphong Station–Thanon Yaowarat (for Chinatown)–Pahurat–Wat Pho–Tha Chang (for the Grand Palace).

#53 circular (also anticlockwise; ordinary)
Thewet–Thanon Krung Kasem– Hualamphong Station–Thanon Yaowarat (for Chinatown)–Pahurat–Pak Khlong Talat–Thanon Maharat (for Wat Pho and the Grand Palace)–Sanam Luang (for National Museum)–Thanon Phra Arthit and Thanon Samsen (for Banglamphu guesthouses)–Thewet.

#124 (ordinary)
Sanam Luang–Thanon Rajinee (for Banglamphu guesthouses)–Phra Pinklao Bridge–Southern Bus Terminal–Mahidol University.

#503 (a/c)
Sanam Luang–Democracy Monument (for Banglamphu guesthouses)–Thanon Rajdamnoen Nok (for TAT and boxing stadium)–Wat Benjamabophit–Thanon Sri Ayutthaya–Victory Monument–Chatuchak Weekend Market–Rangsit.

#508 (ordinary and a/c)
Sanam Luang–Grand Palace–Siam Square–Thanon Sukhumvit–Eastern Bus Terminal–Pak Nam (for Ancient City buses).

#509 (a/c)
Northern Bus Terminal–Chatuchak Weekend Market–Victory Monument–Thanon Rajwithi–Thanon Sawankhalok–Thanon Phitsanulok–Thanon Rajdamnoen Nok (for TAT and boxing stadium)–Democracy Monument–Thanon Rajdamnoen Klang (for Banglamphu guesthouses)–Phra Pinklao Bridge–Thonburi.

#511 (a/c)
Southern Bus Terminal–Phra Pinklao Bridge (for Banglamphu guesthouses)–Democracy Monument–Thanon Lan Luang–Thanon Phetchaburi–Thanon Sukhumvit–Eastern Bus Terminal–Pak Nam (for Ancient City buses).

TOURS OF THE CITY

Unlikely as it sounds, the most popular organized **tours** in Bangkok for independent travellers are by bicycle, heading to the city's outer neighbourhoods and beyond; these are an excellent way to gain a different perspective on Thai life and offer a unique chance to see traditional communities close up. In addition to those listed below, other tour options include Thonburi canal tours (see p.81), Chao Phraya Express tourist boats (see below), boat tours to Ko Kred (see p.109) and dinner cruises along the Chao Phraya River (see p.159).

ABC Amazing Bangkok Cyclist Tours 10/5–7 Soi Aree, Soi 26, Thanon Sukhumvit ☎ 02 665 6364, Ⓦ realasia.net. ABC's are the most popular and longest-running bicycle tours, starting in the Sukhumvit area and taking you across the river to surprisingly rural khlong and riverside communities (including a floating market at weekends); they also offer cycle-and-dine tours in the evening. Tours operate every day year-round, cover up to 30km depending on the itinerary, and need to be reserved in advance (B1300–2400 including bicycle).

Bangkok Bike Rides (Spice Roads) 45 Soi Pannee, Soi Pridi Banomyong 26, Soi 71, Thanon Sukhumvit ☎ 02 381 7490, Ⓦ bangkokbikerides.com or Ⓦ spiceroads.com. Bangkok Bike Rides runs a programme of different day and half-day tours within Greater Bangkok (B1200–3850/person, minimum two people), including Ko Kred, as well as to the floating markets and canalside

neighbourhoods of Damnoen Saduak and to Ayutthaya. Also offers multi-day trips out of the city.

Real Asia 10/5–7 Soi Aree, Soi 26, Thanon Sukhumvit ☎ 02 665 6364, Ⓦ realasia.net. Part of the same company as ABC, Real Asia does full-day canal and walking tours through Thonburi and a "Backdoors to Bangkok" half-day tour, as well as leading outings by train to the historic fishing port of Samut Sakhon (all B2400, including lunch and boat trips).

Velo Thailand Soi 4, Thanon Samsen ☎ 02 628 8628, Ⓦ velothailand.com. Velo Thailand runs half a dozen different bike tours of the capital (and further afield) out of its cycle shop on the edge of Banglamphu, including an after-dark tour (6–10pm; B1100) that takes in floodlit sights including Wat Pho, Wat Arun and the Pak Khlong Talat flower market.

service. On ordinary (non-a/c) buses, which are mostly red and white or blue and white, fares range from B6.50 to B8.50 (though some are currently free); most routes operate from about 5am to 11pm, but some maintain a 24hr service. Air-conditioned buses are either blue, orange or yellow (some are articulated) and charge between B10 and B34 according to distance travelled; most stop in the late evening, but a few of the more popular routes run 24hr services. As buses can only go as fast as the car in front, which at the moment is averaging 4km/h, you'll probably be spending a long time on each journey, so you'd be well advised to pay the extra for cool air – and the a/c buses are usually less crowded, too. For a comprehensive roundup of bus routes in the capital, buy a bus map (see p.32) or try logging onto the Bangkok Mass Transit Authority website (Ⓦ bmta.co.th), which gives hard-to-follow details of all city-bus routes.

Boats

Bangkok was built as an amphibious city around a network of canals – or **khlongs** – and the first streets were constructed only in the second half of the nineteenth century. Many canals remain on the Thonburi side of the river, but most of those on the Bangkok side have been turned into roads. The Chao Phraya River itself is still a major transport route for residents and non-residents alike, forming

more of a link than a barrier between the two halves of the city.

Express boats

The Chao Phraya Express Boat Company operates the vital **express-boat** (*reua duan*; Ⓦ chaophraya expressboat.com) services, using large water buses to plough up and down the river, between clearly signed piers (*tha*), which appear on all Bangkok maps. Tha Sathorn, which gives access to the Skytrain network, has been designated "Central Pier", with piers to the south of here numbered S1, S2, etc, those to the north N1, N2 and so on (see box opposite). Boats do not necessarily stop at every landing – they only pull in if people want to get on or off, and when they do stop, it's not for long – so when you want to get off, be ready at the back of the boat in good time for your pier. No-flag, local-line boats call at every pier between Nonthaburi and Wat Rajsingkorn, 90min away to the south beyond Sathorn, but only operate during rush hour (Mon–Fri, departing roughly 6.45–7.30am & 4–4.30pm; B10–14). The only boats to run all day, every day, are on the limited-stop orange-flag service (Nonthaburi to Wat Rajsingkorn in 1hr; roughly 6am–7pm, every 5–20min; B15). Other limited-stop services run during rush hour, flying either a yellow flag (between Nonthaburi and Rajburana, far downriver beyond Krung Thep Bridge, via Tha Sathorn, in about 50min; Mon–Fri roughly 6.15–8.20am & 4.45–8pm; B20–29) or a green flag (Pakkred to Tha Sathorn Mon–Fri 6.10–8.10am, Tha Sathorn to Pakkred Mon–Fri 4.05–6.05pm; about 50min; B13–32). Tickets can be bought on board; don't discard your ticket until you're off the boat, as the staff at some piers impose a B1 fine on anyone disembarking without one.

Tourist boats

The Chao Phraya Express Boat Company also runs tourist boats, distinguished by their light-blue flags, between Sathorn (every 30min; 9.30am–4pm) and Phra Arthit piers (every 30min; 10am–5pm). In between (in both directions), these boats call in at Oriental, Si Phraya, Rachawongse, Thien, Maharat (near Wat Mahathat and the Grand Palace) and Wang Lang. On-board guides provide running commentaries, and a one-day ticket for unlimited trips, which also allows you to use other express boats within the same route on the same day, costs B150; one-way tickets are also available, costing B40.

Cross-river ferries

Smaller than express boats are the slow cross-river ferries (*reua kham fak*), which shuttle back and forth between the same two points. Found at or beside every express-boat stop and plenty of other piers in between, they are especially useful for exploring Thonburi. Fares are generally B3–4, payable at the entrance to the pier.

Canal boats

Longtail boats (*reua hang yao*) ply the canals of Thonburi like commuter buses, stopping at designated shelters (fares are in line with those of express boats), and are available for individual rental here and on the river (see box, p.81). On the Bangkok side, **Khlong Saen Saeb** is well served by passenger boats, which run at least every 20min during daylight hours (eastbound services start and end a little later; Ⓦ khlongsaensaep .com). They start from the Phan Fah pier (Panfa Leelard) at the Golden Mount (handy for Banglamphu, Ratanakosin and Chinatown), and head way out east to Wat Sribunruang, with useful stops at Thanon Phrayathai, aka Saphan Hua Chang (for Jim Thompson's House and Ratchathevi Skytrain stop); Pratunam (for the Erawan Shrine); Soi Chitlom; Thanon Witthayu (Wireless Road); and Soi Nana Nua (Soi 3), Thanon Asok Montri (Soi 21, for TAT headquarters and Phetchaburi subway stop), Soi Thonglo (Soi 55) and Charn Issara, near Soi Ekamai (Soi 63), all off Thanon Sukhumvit. This is your quickest and most interesting way of getting between the west and east parts of town, if you can stand the stench of the canal.

You may have trouble actually locating the piers as few are signed in English and they all look very unassuming and rickety; keep your eyes peeled for a plain wooden jetty – most jetties serve boats running in both directions. Once on the boat,

---

CENTRAL STOPS FOR THE CHAO PHRAYA EXPRESS BOATS

N15 Thewet (all express boats) – for Thewet guesthouses.
N14 Rama VIII Bridge (no flag) – for Samsen Soi 5.
N13 Phra Arthit (no flag and orange flag) – for Thanon Phra Arthit, Thanon Khao San and Banglamphu guesthouses.
N12 Phra Pinklao Bridge (all boats) – for Royal Barge Museum.
N11 Thonburi Railway Station (or Bangkok Noi; no flag and orange flag) – for trains to Kanchanaburi.
N10 Wang Lang (aka Siriraj or Prannok; all boats) – for Wat Rakhang.
N9 Chang (no flag, green flag and orange flag) – for the Grand Palace, Sanam Luang and the National Museum.
N8 Thien (no flag and orange flag) – for Wat Pho, and the cross-river ferry to Wat Arun.
N7 Ratchini (aka Rajinee; no flag).
N6 Saphan Phut (Memorial Bridge; no flag and orange flag) – for Pahurat, Pak Khlong Talat and Wat Prayoon.
N5 Rachawongse (aka Rajawong; all boats) – for Chinatown.
N4 Harbour (Marine) Department (no flag and orange flag).
N3 Si Phraya (all boats) – walk north past the *Sheraton Royal Orchid Hotel* for River City shopping complex.
N2 Wat Muang Kae (no flag).
N1 Oriental (no flag and orange flag) – for Thanon Silom.
Central Sathorn (all boats) – for the Skytrain and Thanon Sathorn.

state your destination to the conductor when he collects your fare, which will be between B10 and B20. Due to the construction of some low bridges, all passengers change onto a different boat at Tha Pratunam – just follow the crowd.

The Skytrain

Although its network is limited, the **BTS Skytrain**, or *rot fai faa* (Ⓦ www.bts.co.th), provides a much faster alternative to the bus, and is clean, efficient and over-vigorously air-conditioned. There are only two Skytrain lines, which interconnect at Siam Square (Central Station). Both run every few minutes from around 6am to midnight, with fares of B15–52/trip depending on distance travelled. You buy tickets from machines that accept only coins, but you can change notes at staffed counters. You'd really have to be motoring to justify buying a day pass at B130, while the various multi-trip cards are designed for long-distance commuters.

The **Sukhumvit Line** runs from Mo Chit (stop N8) in the northern part of the city, via the interchange at Phayathai (N2) with the airport rail line, to Bearing (Soi 105, Thanon Sukhumvit; E14) in around 40min. The **Silom Line** runs from the National Stadium (W1) via Saphan Taksin (Taksin, or Sathorn, Bridge; S6), to link up with the full gamut of express boats on the Chao Phraya River (though there are plans to close down Saphan Taksin Station and build a moving walkway between the river and Surasak Station), to Bang Wa (S12) in Thonburi (on Thanon Phetkasem, Highway 4).

The subway

Bangkok's underground rail system, the **MRT subway** (or metro; in Thai, *rot fai tai din*; Ⓦ www .bangkokmetro.co.th), has similar advantages to the Skytrain, though its current single line connects few places of interest for visitors. It runs every few minutes between around 6am and midnight from Hualamphong train station, via Silom (near Sala Daeng Skytrain station), Sukhumvit (near Asoke Skytrain) and Chatuchak Park (near Mo Chit Skytrain), to Bang Sue train station in the north of the city. Building work is under way to continue the line westwards from Hualamphong to Wat Mangkon Kamalawat in Chinatown, Pahurat, Thanon Sanam Chai in Ratanakosin, then across to Thonburi (currently due for completion in 2017); the eventual plan is to complete a loop back to Bang Sue. Pay your fare (B16–42) at a staffed

counter or machine, where you'll receive a token to put through an entrance gate (the various day-passes and stored-value cards available are unlikely to be worthwhile for visitors).

Taxis

Bangkok taxis come in three forms, and are so plentiful that you rarely have to wait more than a couple of minutes before spotting an empty one of any description. Neither tuk-tuks nor motorbike taxis have meters, so you should agree on a price before setting off, and expect to do a fair amount of haggling.

Metered taxis

For nearly all journeys, the best and most comfortable option is to flag down one of Bangkok's metered, a/c taxi cabs; look out for the "TAXI METER" sign on the roof, and a red light in the windscreen in front of the passenger seat, which means the cab is available for hire. Starting at B35, fares are displayed on a clearly visible meter that the driver should reset at the start of each trip (say *"poet meter, dai mai khrap/kha?"* to ask him to switch it on), and increase in stages on a combined distance/time formula; as an example, a medium-range journey from Thanon Ploenchit to Thanon Sathorn will cost around B50 at a quiet time of day. Try to have change with you as cabs tend not to carry a lot of money; tipping of up to ten percent is common, though occasionally a cabbie will round down the fare on the meter. If a driver tries to quote a flat fare (often the case with taxis that park outside tourist hotels waiting for business) rather than using the meter, let him go, and avoid the now-rare unmetered cabs (denoted by a "TAXI" sign on the roof). Getting a metered taxi in the middle of the afternoon when the cars return to base for a change of drivers can sometimes be a problem. If you want to book a metered taxi (B20–50 surcharge), try Siam Taxi Co-operative on ☎1661 or Taxi Radio on ☎1681.

Tuk-tuks

Somewhat less stable though typically Thai, tuk-tuks in Bangkok have very little to recommend them. These noisy, three-wheeled, open-sided buggies, which can carry three medium-sized passengers comfortably, fully expose you to the worst of Bangkok's pollution and weather. You'll have to bargain very hard to get a fare lower than the taxi-cab flagfall of B35; for a longer trip, for example from Thanon Convent to Siam Square, drivers will ask for as much as B200. Be aware, also, that tuk-tuk drivers tend to speak less English than taxi drivers – and there have been cases of robberies and attacks on women passengers late at night. During the day it's quite common for tuk-tuk drivers to try and con their passengers into visiting a jewellery, tailor's or expensive souvenir shop with them (see p.37).

Motorbike taxis

Motorbike taxis generally congregate at the entrances to long sois – pick the riders out by their numbered, coloured vests – and charge from B10

for short trips down into the side streets. If you're short on time and have nerves of steel, it's also possible to charter them for hairy journeys out on the main roads (a short trip from Sanam Luang to Thanon Samsen will cost around B40). Crash helmets are compulsory on all main roads in the capital (traffic police fine non-wearers on the spot), though they're rarely worn on trips down the sois.

Car and bike rental

You'd need to be a bit mad to rent a self-drive car for getting around Bangkok, especially as taxis are so cheap. Theoretically, foreigners need an inter-

---

BTS SKYTRAIN & SUBWAY

- (S)— BTS Skytrain and station
- (M)·· Subway and station
- (A)— Suvarnabhumi Airport Rail Link and station
- ☆ Khlong Saen Saeb boat stop

Northern Bus Terminal ★
Bangkok Butterfly Garden
Don Muang Airport
(M) Phahon Yothin
(M) Lat Phrao
(M) Chatuchak Park
Bangsue (M)
Chatuchak Weekend Market
(S) Mo Chit
(M) Ratchadapisek
Kamphaeng Phet (M)
(S) Saphan Kwai
PRADIPHAT
(M) Sutthisan
Chao Phraya River
Samsen Station
(S) Ari
(M) Huai Khwang
THANON RAJWITHI
(S) Sanam Pao
Siam Niramit
Lao Embassy (E)(E)
Khlong Krung Kasem
Chitrlada Palace
Thailand Cultural Centre (M)
Cambodian Embassy
Victory Monument
Chinese Embassy (E)
Thailand Cultural Centre
mocracy (i) TAT
nument
Victory Monument (S)
Phaya Thai
Phaya Thai
(S)(A)
Rama IX (Phra Ram 9) (M)
Tha
han
Fa
☆ Golden Mount
Ratchaprarop (A)
Budget
Tha Saphan Hua Chang ☆(S)
Ratchathevi (S)
Makkasan (A) EXPRESSWAY
Bangkok Hospital
Tha Nana Nua
Tha Pratunam
Tha Chit Lom
☆ ☆ ☆
TAT HQ
(i) Phetchaburi (M)
THANON PHETCHABURI
House Cinema
National Stadium (S)
Siam (Central Station)
Chit Lom (S)
Tha Witthayu
Tha Asoke (A)
Khlong Saen Saeb
Hualamphong Station
Hua Lamphong (M)
Siam
Ratchadamri (S)
Phloen Chit (S)
Nana (S)
Sukhumvit (S)(M)
Samitivej Hospital
Tha Charn Issara
Wat Traimit ▲
Asok
(M) Sam Yan
Lumphini Park
(S) Si Lom
Phrom Pong (S)
Chao Phraya River
Sala Daeng (S)
THANON SILOM
(S) Chong Nonsi
Lumphini (M) RAMA-IV
Thong Lo (S)
SATHORN
Khlong Toei
Queen Sirikit National Convention Centre (QSNCC) (M)
Ekamai (S)
Eastern Bus Terminal ★
Phra Khanong
Saphan Taksin (S)
(S) Surasak
On Nut (S)
BTS Bearing (S)

1 kilometre

N

national driver's licence to rent a car, but most companies accept national licences. Prices for a small car start at about B1000 per day; for **petrol**, most Thais use gasohol, which can generally be used in rental cars (though it's worth checking) and currently costs around B28 a litre. Thais drive on the left, and the speed limit is 60km per hour within built-up areas and 90km per hour outside them.

CAR AND BIKE RENTAL AGENCIES

Avis Branches are at 40 Thanon Sathorn Nua (delivery and collection anywhere in Bangkok), as well as Suvarnabhumi and Don Muang airports (☎ 02 251 1131–2, ⓦ avisthailand .com).

Budget Branches can be found at the following locations: 19/23 Building A, Royal City Avenue, Thanon Phetchaburi Mai; Suvarnabhumi Airport; and Don Muang Airport (☎ 02 203 9222, ⓦ budget.co.th).

Velo Thailand Soi 4, Thanon Samsen (☎ 02 628 8628, ⓦ velothailand.com). Offers good-quality bikes for B300/day to brave/ foolhardy souls.

Information and maps

The Tourism Authority of Thailand, or TAT (ⓦ www.tourismthailand.org), maintains offices in several cities abroad, where you can pick up a few glossy brochures and get answers to pre-trip questions. More comprehensive local information is given at the TAT offices in Bangkok and at booths run by the city's Bangkok Tourism Division. You can also contact the helpful TAT tourist assistance phoneline from within Thailand for free on ☎ 1672 (daily 8am–8pm).

The **Bangkok Tourism Division** is the official source of information on the capital, whose head office is currently next to Phra Pinklao Bridge at 17/1 Thanon Phra Arthit in Banglamphu (Mon–Fri 8am–7pm, Sat & Sun 9am–5pm; ☎ 02 225 7612–4, ⓦ bangkoktourist.com); however, it's slated to move to an inconvenient location on the west side of Rama VIII Bridge over in Thonburi, though an information booth may be left in its place. The head office is supported by about twenty strategically placed satellite booths around the capital; most open Mon–Sat 9am–5pm, though some open Sunday too, including in front of the

Grand Palace, at Paragon and Mah Boon Krong shopping centres, and in front of Banglamphu's Wat Bowoniwes.

The city's branches of the nationwide **Tourism Authority of Thailand** can also be useful. TAT maintains tourist information counters (both open daily 8.30am–4.30pm) at its head office, which is rather inconveniently located at 1600 Thanon Phetchaburi Mai, and, within walking distance of Banglamphu, at the Ministry of Tourism and Sports, 4 Rajdamnoen Nok – it's a 20min stroll from Thanon Khao San, or a short ride in a/c bus #503.

It's worth noting, however, that the many travel agents, shops and private offices across the capital displaying signs announcing "TAT Tourist Information" or similar are **not official Tourism Authority of Thailand centres** and will not be dispensing impartial advice (they may be licensed by TAT to run their business, but that doesn't make them government information offices). The Tourism Authority of Thailand never uses the acronym "TAT" on its office-fronts or in its logo, and none of its offices offers accommodation, tour or transport booking.

TAT OFFICES ABROAD

Australia and New Zealand Suite 2002, Level 20, 56 Pitt St, Sydney, NSW 2000 ☎ 02 9247 7549, ⓦ thailand.net.au.
South Africa Contact the UK office.
UK and Ireland 1st Floor, 17–19 Cockspur St, London SW1Y 5BL ☎ 020 7925 2511, ⓔ info@tourismthailand.co.uk.
US and Canada 61 Broadway, Suite 2810, New York, NY 10006 ☎ 212 432 0433, ⓔ info@tatny.com; 611 North Larchmont Blvd, 1st Floor, Los Angeles, CA 90004 ☎ 323 461 9814, ⓔ tatla@tat.or.th.

Maps and listings magazines

To get around Bangkok on the cheap, you'll need to buy a bus **map**. Thinknet's regularly updated *Bangkok Bus Guide*, which charts a/c and non-a/c buses, with close-up maps of Banglamphu and Victory Monument, is the most widely available. Bangkok Guide's *Bus Routes & Map* also charts all major a/c and non-a/c bus routes, as well as carrying detailed written itineraries of some two hundred routes, but is more difficult to come across these days. For a personal guide to Bangkok's most interesting shops, markets, restaurants and backstreets, look for the famously idiosyncratic hand-drawn *Nancy Chandler's Map of Bangkok* and *Nancy Chandler's Map of Khao San and Old Bangkok*. Both carry a mass of annotated recommendations, are impressively accurate and regularly reissued; they're sold in most tourist areas, and copies and interim updates are also available at Ⓦ nancychandler.net.

Listings magazines rise and fall with confusing rapidity in Bangkok; the best of the current publications is the free, weekly *Bk Magazine*, and its online counterpart, Ⓦ bk.asia city.com, which gives a decent rundown of the art and drama scenes, live music and club nights for the week ahead.

If you're interested in Bangkok's contemporary art scene, pick up a copy of the free, monthly **Bangkok Art Map** for exhibition listings (Ⓦ facebook.com /bangkokartmap).

Health

Although Thailand's climate, wildlife and cuisine present Western travellers with fewer health worries than in many Asian destinations, it's still good to know in advance what the risks might be, and what preventive or curative measures you should take.

For a start, there's no need to bring huge supplies of non-prescription medicines with you, as Thai **pharmacies** (*raan khai yaa*; typically open daily 8.30am–8pm) are well stocked with local and international branded medicaments, and of course they are generally much less expensive than at home. Nearly all pharmacies – including the city-wide branches of the British chain, Boots (see p.185) – are run by trained English-speaking pharmacists, who are usually the best people to talk to if your symptoms aren't acute enough to warrant seeing a doctor.

MEDICAL RESOURCES

Canadian Society for International Health ☎ 613 241 5785, Ⓦ csih.org. Extensive list of travel health centres.

CDC ☎ 800 232 4636, Ⓦ cdc.gov/travel. Official US government travel health site.

Hospital for Tropical Diseases Travel Clinic UK Ⓦ thehtd.org.

International Society for Travel Medicine US ☎ 404 373 8282, Ⓦ istm.org. Has a full list of travel health clinics.

MASTA (Medical Advisory Service for Travellers Abroad) UK Ⓦ masta-travel-health.com.

NHS Travel Health Website UK Ⓦ fitfortravel.scot.nhs.uk.

The Travel Doctor – TMVC ☎ 1300 658 844, Ⓦ tmvc.com.au. Lists travel clinics in Australia, New Zealand and South Africa.

Tropical Medical Bureau Ireland ☎ 1850 487 674, Ⓦ tmb.ie.

Inoculations

There are no compulsory **inoculation** requirements for people travelling to Thailand from the West, but you should consult a doctor or other health professional, preferably at least four weeks in advance of your trip, for the latest information on recommended immunizations. In addition to making sure that your recommended immunizations for life in your home country are up to date, most doctors strongly advise vaccinations or boosters against tetanus, diphtheria, hepatitis A and, in many cases, typhoid, and in some cases they might also recommend protecting yourself against Japanese encephalitis, rabies and hepatitis B. If you forget to have all your inoculations before leaving home, or don't leave yourself sufficient time, you can get them in Bangkok at, for example, the Thai Red Cross Society's Queen Saovabha Institute or Global Doctor (see p.34).

Mosquito-borne diseases

Only certain regions of Thailand are now considered malarial, and **Bangkok is malaria-free**, so if you are restricting yourself to the capital you do not have to take malaria prophylactics. Bangkok does however have its fair share of **mosquitoes**; though nearly all the city's hotels and guesthouses have screened windows, you will probably need to have mosquito repellent containing the chemical compound DEET. Supermarkets and pharmacies in Bangkok stock it, but if you want the highest-strength repellent, or convenient roll-ons or sprays, it's probably best to do your shopping before you leave home – or at a branch of Boots in Bangkok (see p.185). DEET is strong stuff, and if you have sensitive skin, a natural alternative is citronella (available in the UK as Mosi-guard), made from a blend of eucalyptus oils; the Thai version is made with lemon grass. Plug-in insecticide vaporizers, insect room sprays and mosquito coils – also widely available in Thailand – help keep the insects at bay; electronic "buzzers" are useless. If you are bitten, applying locally made "yellow oil" is effective at reducing the itch.

A further reason to protect yourself is the possibility of contracting **dengue fever**, a debilitating and occasionally fatal viral disease that is particularly prevalent during and just after the rainy season. It's on the increase throughout tropical Asia, and is endemic to many areas of Thailand (including Bangkok), with over 150,000 reported cases in 2013. Unlike malaria, dengue fever is spread by mosquitoes that can bite during daylight hours, so you should also use mosquito repellent during the day. Symptoms may include fever, headaches, fierce joint and muscle pain ("breakbone fever" is another name for dengue), and possibly a rash, and usually develop between five and eight days after being bitten.

There is no vaccine against dengue fever; the only treatment is lots of rest, liquids and paracetamol (or any other acetaminophen painkiller, not aspirin), though more serious cases may require hospitalization.

Digestive problems

By far the most common travellers' complaint in Thailand, **digestive troubles** are often caused by contaminated food and water, or sometimes just by an overdose of unfamiliar foodstuffs.

Stomach trouble usually manifests itself as simple **diarrhoea**, which should clear up without medical treatment within three to seven days and is best combated by drinking lots of fluids. If this doesn't work, you're in danger of getting **dehydrated** and should take some kind of rehydration solution, either a commercial sachet of ORS (oral rehydration solution), sold in all Thai pharmacies, or a do-it-yourself version, which can be made by adding a handful of sugar and a pinch of salt to every litre of boiled or bottled water (soft drinks are not a viable alternative). If you can eat, avoid fatty foods.

Anti-diarrhoeal agents such as Imodium are useful for blocking you up on long bus journeys, but only attack the symptoms and may prolong infections; an antibiotic such as ciprofloxacin, however, can often reduce a typical attack of traveller's diarrhoea to one day. If the diarrhoea persists for a week or more, or if you have blood or mucus in your stools, or an accompanying fever, go to a doctor or hospital.

Other diseases

Rabies is endemic in Thailand, mainly carried by dogs (between four and seven percent of stray dogs in Bangkok are reported to be rabid), but also cats and monkeys. It is transmitted by bites, scratches or even occasionally licks. Dogs are everywhere in Thailand and even if kept as pets they're often not very well cared for; hopefully their mangy appearance will discourage the urge to pat them, as you should steer well clear of them. Rabies is invariably fatal if the patient waits

until symptoms begin, though modern vaccines and treatments are very effective and deaths are rare. The important thing is, if you are bitten, licked or scratched by an animal, to vigorously clean the wound with soap and disinfect it, preferably with something containing iodine, and to seek medical advice regarding treatment, at the Thai Red Cross Society, for example (see below), right away.

HIV infection is widespread in Thailand, primarily because of the sex trade. **Condoms** (*meechai*) are sold in pharmacies, convenience stores, department stores, hairdressers and even street markets. Due to rigorous screening methods, Thailand's medical blood supply is now considered safe from HIV/AIDS infection.

Medical and dental treatment

Hospital (*rong phayaabahn*) cleanliness and efficiency vary, but generally hygiene and healthcare standards are good, the ratio of medical staff to patients is considerably higher than in most parts of the West, and the doctors speak English. In the event of a major health crisis, get someone to contact your embassy (see p.44) and insurance company.

HOSPITALS AND CLINICS

Bangkok Hospital Medical Centre, 2 Soi Soonvijai 7, Thanon Phetchaburi Mai ☎ 02 310 3000 or ☎ 1719, ⓦ bangkokhospital .com. Another highly rated hospital.

BNH (Bangkok Nursing Home) Hospital 9 Thanon Convent ☎ 02 686 2700, ⓦ bnhhospital.com. Well regarded by expats.

Bumrungrad International Hospital 33 Sukhumvit Soi 3 ☎ 02 667 1000, emergency ☎ 02 667 2999, ⓦ bumrungrad.com. Most expats rate this private hospital as the best and most comfortable in the city.

Global Doctor Ground Floor, Holiday Inn Hotel, 981 Thanon Silom (corner of Thanon Surasak) ☎ 02 236 8442–4, ⓦ globaldoctorclinic .com. Among general clinics, Global Doctor is recommended.

Thai Red Cross Society's Queen Saovabha Memorial Institute (QSMI) and Snake Farm on the corner of Thanon Rama IV and Thanon Henri Dunant; Mon–Fri 8.30am–4.30pm, Sat 8.30am–noon; ☎ 02 252 0161–4 ext 125 or 132, ⓦ saovabha .com. A good place to get travel vaccinations, as well as rabies advice and treatment.

DENTISTS

Bumrungrad Hospital's dental department ☎ 02 667 2300.

Dental Hospital 88/88 Sukhumvit Soi 49 ☎ 02 260 5000–15, ⓦ dentalhospitalbangkok.com.

Siam Family Dental Clinic 209 Thanon Phrayathai, opposite MBK ☎ 081 987 7700, ⓦ siamfamilydental.com.

The media

To keep you abreast of world affairs, there are several English-language newspapers in Thailand, though relatively mild forms of censorship (as well as some self-censorship) affect all newspapers and the predominantly state-controlled media.

Newspapers and magazines

Of the hundreds of **Thai-language newspapers and magazines** published every week, the sensationalist daily tabloid *Thai Rath* attracts the widest readership, with circulation of around a million, while the moderately progressive *Matichon* is the leading quality daily, with an estimated circulation of 600,000.

Alongside these, two daily **English-language papers** – the *Bangkok Post* (Ⓦbangkokpost.com) and the *Nation* (Ⓦnationmultimedia.com) – are capable of adopting a fairly critical attitude to political goings-on and cover major domestic and international stories as well as tourist-related issues. The *Post's Spectrum* supplement, which comes inside the Sunday edition, carries investigative journalism. Both the *Post* and *Nation* are sold at many newsstands in the capital as well as in major provincial towns and tourist resorts; the more isolated places receive their few copies one day late. Details of local English-language publications are given in the relevant Guide accounts.

You can also pick up **foreign** magazines such as *Newsweek* and *Time* in Bangkok, Chiang Mai and the major resorts. English-language bookshops such as Bookazine and some expensive hotels carry air-freighted, or sometimes locally printed and stapled, copies of foreign national newspapers for at least B50 a copy; the latter are also sold in tourist-oriented minimarkets in the big resorts.

Television

There are six government-controlled, terrestrial **TV channels** in Thailand: channels 3, 5 (owned and operated by the army), 7 and 9 transmit a blend of news, documentaries, soaps, sports, talk and quiz shows, while the more serious-minded PBS and NBT are public-service channels, owned and operated by the government's public relations department. **Cable** networks – available in many guesthouse and hotel rooms – carry channels from all around the world, including CNN or Fox News from the US, BBC

World News from the UK and sometimes ABC from Australia, as well as English-language movie channels and various sports, music and documentary channels. Both the *Bangkok Post* and the *Nation* print the daily TV and cable **schedule**.

Radio

Thailand boasts over five hundred **radio stations**, mostly music-oriented, ranging from Eazy (105.5 FM), which serves up Western pop, through *luk thung* on 95 FM, to Fat Radio, which plays Thai indie sounds (104.5 FM). Chulalongkorn University Radio (101.5 FM) plays classical music from 9.35pm to midnight every night. Net 107 on 107 FM is one of several stations that include English-language news bulletins.

With a **shortwave radio** or by going **online**, you can listen to the BBC World Service (Ⓦbbc.co.uk /worldserviceradio), Radio Australia (Ⓦradio australia.net.au), Voice of America (Ⓦvoanews.com), Radio Canada (Ⓦrcinet.ca) and other international stations right across Thailand. Times and wavelengths change regularly, so consult the websites for frequency and programme guides.

Festivals

Nearly all Thai festivals have a religious aspect. The most theatrical are generally Brahmin (Hindu) or animistic in origin, honouring elemental spirits with ancient rites and ceremonial costumed parades. In Buddhist celebrations, merit-making plays an important role and events are usually staged at the local temple, but a light-hearted atmosphere prevails, as the wat grounds are swamped with food- and trinket-vendors and makeshift stages are set up to show likay folk theatre, singing stars and beauty contests; there may even be funfair rides as well.

Few of the dates for religious festivals are fixed, so check with TAT for specifics (Ⓦtourismthailand.org). Some of the festivals below are designated as national holidays (see p.46).

JANUARY– MARCH

Chinese New Year (Truut Jiin) New moon of the first lunar month, some time between mid-Jan and late Feb. Even more food stalls than usual in Chinatown (Thanon Yaowarat and Charoen Krung) and plenty to feast your eyes on too, including Chinese opera shows and jaunty parades led by traditional Chinese dragons and lions.

Maha Puja On the day of full moon in Feb. A day of merit-making marks the occasion when 1250 disciples gathered spontaneously to hear the Buddha preach. Best experienced at Wat Benjamabophit, where the festival culminates with a candlelit procession round the temple.

Kite fights and flying contests Late Feb to mid-April. Sanam Luang (Ratanakosin) next to the Grand Palace is the venue for demonstrations and competitions of kite-flying and fighting (see p.58).

APRIL

Songkhran: Thai New Year April 13–15. The Thai New Year is welcomed in with massive waterfights, and no one, least of all foreign tourists, escapes a good-natured soaking. Trucks roam the streets spraying passers-by with hosepipes and half the population carry huge water pistols for the duration. Don't wear your favourite outfit as water is sometimes laced with dye. Celebrated throughout the city but famously raucous on Thanon Silom and, especially, on Thanon Khao San, which also stages special organized entertainments.

MAY AND JUNE

Raek Na (Royal Ploughing Ceremony) Early in May. To mark the beginning of the rice-planting season, ceremonially clad Brahmin leaders parade sacred oxen and the royal plough across Sanam Luang, interpreting omens to forecast the year's rice yield (see also p.59).

Visakha Puja May/June; on the day of full moon of the sixth lunar month. Temples across the city are the focus of this holiest day of the Buddhist calendar, which commemorates the birth, enlightenment and death of the Buddha. The most photogenic event is the candlelit evening procession around the wat, particularly at Wat Benjamabophit in Dusit.

OCTOBER–NOVEMBER

Chulalongkorn Day October 23. The city marks the anniversary of the death of the widely loved Rama V, King Chulalongkorn (1868–1910), by laying offerings around the famous equestrian statue of the king, at the Thanon U-Thong-Thanon Sri Ayutthaya crossroads in Dusit.

Awk Pansa On the day of full moon. Devotees at temples across the city make offerings to monks and there's general merrymaking to celebrate the Buddha's descent to Earth from Tavatimsa heaven and the end of the Khao Pansa retreat.

Thawt Kathin Oct–Nov; the month between Awk Pansa and Loy Krathong. During the month following the end of the monks' rainy-season retreat, it's traditional for the laity to donate new robes to the monkhood. Occasionally, when it coincides with a kingly anniversary, this is celebrated with a spectacular Royal Barge Procession down the Chao Phraya River in Bangkok.

Loy Krathong On the full moon day of the twelfth lunar month, in late Oct or Nov. Wishes and prayers wrapped up in banana-leaf baskets full of flowers and lighted candles are released on to the Chao Phraya River and Thonburi canals in this charming festival that both honours the water spirits and celebrates the end of the rainy season.

Vegetarian Festival (Ngan Kin Jeh) Oct/Nov; held over nine days during the ninth lunar month in the Chinese calendar. Many Chinese people become vegetarian for this annual nine-day Taoist detox, so most food vendors and restaurants in Chinatown, and many outlets in other parts of the city, turn veggie too, displaying a yellow pennant to alert their customers (see p.158).

Ngan Wat Saket First week of Nov. Probably Thailand's biggest temple fair, held around Wat Saket (near Democracy Monument) and the Golden Mount, with funfairs, folk theatre, music and tons of food.

DECEMBER

Trooping the Colour Dec 2. An extraordinary array of sumptuous uniforms makes this annual marshalling of the Royal Guards a sight worth stopping for. Head to Suan Amporn in Dusit.

King's Birthday Dec 5. In the evening thousands of people gather in Sanam Luang (Ratanakosin) to light candles and sing the king's anthem, after which there's free entertainment into the night from pop stars and folk theatre troupes, capped by a huge fireworks display. Nearby Rajadamnoen Klang is prettily decorated with special lights and portraits of the king.

Western New Year's Eve Dec 31. The new year is greeted with fireworks along the river and at Sanam Luang, and huge crowds gather for a mass countdown around the Central World and Siam Square area, which is usually pedestrianized for the night.

Crime, safety and the law

As long as you keep your wits about you, you shouldn't encounter much trouble in Bangkok. Pickpocketing and bag-snatching are two of the main problems – not surprising, considering that a huge percentage of the local population scrape by on under US$10 per day – but the most common cause for concern is the number of con-artists who dupe gullible tourists into parting with their cash. There are various Thai laws that tourists need to be aware of, particularly regarding passports, the age of consent and smoking in public.

Theft

To **prevent theft**, most travellers prefer to carry their valuables with them at all times, but it's often possible to use a safe in a hotel or a locker in a guesthouse – the safest lockers are those that require your own padlock, as there are occasional reports of valuables being stolen by guesthouse staff. **Padlock your luggage** when leaving it in storage or taking it on public transport. Padlocks also come in handy as extra security on your room.

Personal safety

Be wary of accepting food and drink from strangers as it may be drugged. This might sound paranoid, but there have been enough **drug-muggings** for TAT to publish a specific warning about the problem. Drinks are sometimes spiked in bars and clubs, especially by sex-workers who later steal from their victim's room.

Violent crime against tourists is not common, but it does occur, and there have been several serious attacks on women travellers in the last few years. However, bearing in mind that 25 million foreigners visit Thailand every year, the statistical likelihood of becoming a victim is extremely small. **Obvious precautions** for travellers of either sex include locking accessible windows and doors at night (with your own padlock in the simpler guest-houses), taking care at night, especially around bars, and not travelling alone at night in a taxi or tuk-tuk. Nor should you risk jumping into an unlicensed taxi at the airport in Bangkok at any time of day: there have been some very violent robberies in these, so take the well-marked licensed, metered taxis instead.

Unfortunately, it is also necessary for female tourists to think twice about spending time alone with a **monk**, as not all men of the cloth uphold the Buddhist precepts and there have been rapes and murders committed by men wearing the saffron robes of the monkhood (see p.208).

Though unpalatable and distressing, Thailand's high-profile **sex industry** is relatively unthreat-ening for Western women, with its energy focused exclusively on farang men; it's also quite easily avoided, being contained within certain pockets of the capital. As for **harassment** from men, it's hard to generalize, but most Western women find it less a problem in Thailand than they do back home.

For advice on safe travelling in Thailand, consult your government's travel advisory.

Scams

Despite the best efforts of guidebook writers, TAT and the Thai tourist police, countless travellers to Thailand get scammed every year. Nearly all **scams** are easily avoided if you're on your guard against anyone who makes an unnatural effort to befriend you. We have outlined the main scams in the relevant sections of this Guide, but con-artists are nothing if not creative, so if in doubt walk away at the earliest opportunity.

Many Bangkok **tuk-tuk drivers** earn most of their living through securing **commissions** from tourist-oriented shops and will do their damnedest to get you to go to a gem shop (see p.190). The most common tactic is for drivers to pretend that the Grand Palace or other major sight you intended to visit is closed for the day – they usually invent a plausible reason, such as a festival or royal occasion (see p.49) – and to then offer to take you on a round-city tour instead, perhaps even for free. The tour will invariably include a visit to a gem shop. The easiest way to avoid all this is to take a **metered taxi**; if you're fixed on taking a tuk-tuk, ignore any tuk-tuk that is parked up or loitering and be firm about where you want to go.

Self-styled **tourist guides**, **touts** and anyone else who might introduce themselves as **students** or **businesspeople** and offer to take you somewhere of interest, or invite you to meet their family, are often the first piece of bait in a well-honed chain of con-artists. If you bite, chances are you'll end up either at a gem shop or in a gambling den, or, at best, at a tour operator or hotel that you had not planned to patronize. This is not to say that you should never accept an invitation from a local person, but be extremely wary of doing so

---

REPORTING A CRIME OR EMERGENCY

For all emergencies, contact the English-speaking **tourist police**, who maintain a 24-hour toll-free nationwide line (☎1155).

Getting in touch with the tourist police first is invariably more efficient than directly contacting the local police, ambulance or fire service. The tourist police's job is to offer advice and tell you what to do next, but they do not file crime reports, which must be done at the nearest police station. The tourist police are based on the grounds of Suvarnabhumi Airport (☎02 134 0521, ✆tourist.police.go.th), or drop in at the more convenient Chana Songkhram Police Station at the west end of Thanon Khao San in Banglamphu (☎02 282 2323). The **British Embassy** in Bangkok provides advice for British victims of crime in Thailand and also posts practical tips and a list of useful contacts on its website (☎02 305 8333, ✆ukinthailand .fco.gov.uk/en/help-for-british-nationals).

GOVERNMENTAL TRAVEL ADVISORIES

Australian Department of Foreign Affairs Ⓦ dfat.gov.au.
British Foreign & Commonwealth Office Ⓦ www.gov.uk/government/organisations
/foreign-commonwealth-office.
Canadian Department of Foreign Affairs Ⓦ international.gc.ca.
Irish Department of Foreign Affairs Ⓦ dfa.ie.
New Zealand Ministry of Foreign Affairs Ⓦ mfat.govt.nz.
South African Department of Foreign Affairs Ⓦ dfa.gov.za.
US State Department Ⓦ state.gov.

---

following a street encounter in Bangkok. Tourist guides' ID cards are easily faked.

For many of these characters, the goal is to get you inside a dodgy **gem shop** (see box, p.190), but the bottom line is that if you are not experienced at buying and trading in valuable gems you will definitely be ripped off, possibly even to the tune of several thousand dollars.

A less common but potentially more frightening scam involves a similar cast of warm-up artists leading tourists into a **gambling** game. The scammers invite their victim home on an innocent-sounding pretext, get out a pack of cards, and then set about fleecing the incomer in any number of subtle or unsubtle ways. Often this can be especially scary as the venue is likely to be far from hotels or recognizable landmarks, and there have been stories of visitors being forced to withdraw large amounts of money from ATMs. You're unlikely to get any sympathy from police, as gambling is **illegal** in Thailand.

Age restrictions and other laws

Thai law requires that tourists **carry their original passports** at all times, though sometimes it's more practical to carry a photocopy and keep the original locked in a safety deposit. The **age of consent** is 15, but the law allows anyone under the age of 18, or their parents, to file charges in retrospect even if they consented to sex at the time. It is against the law to have sex with a prostitute who is under 18. It is illegal for under-18s to **buy cigarettes** or **to drive**, and you must be 20 or over to **buy alcohol** or be allowed into a **bar or club** (ID checks are sometimes enforced in Bangkok). It is illegal for anyone to **gamble** in Thailand (though many do).

Smoking in public is widely prohibited. The ban covers all public buildings (including restaurants, bars and clubs) and trains, buses and planes and can even be extended to parks and the street; violators may be subject to a B2000–5000 fine.

Dropping cigarette butts, **littering** and spitting in public places can also earn you a B2000–5000 fine. There are fines for **overstaying your visa** (see p.43), **working without a permit**, **not wearing a motorcycle helmet** and violating other **traffic laws**.

Drugs

Drug-smuggling carries a maximum penalty in Thailand of death, and **dealing drugs** will get you anything from four years to life in a Thai prison; penalties depend on the drug and the amount involved. Travellers caught with even the smallest amount of drugs at airports and international borders are prosecuted for trafficking, and no one charged with trafficking offences gets bail. Heroin, amphetamines, LSD and ecstasy are classed as Category 1 drugs and carry the most severe penalties: even **possession** of Category 1 drugs for personal use can result in a **life sentence**. Away from international borders, most foreigners arrested in possession of small amounts of cannabis are released on bail, then fined and deported, but the law is complex and prison sentences are possible.

Despite occasional royal pardons, don't expect special treatment as a farang: you only need to read one of the first-hand accounts by foreign former prisoners (see p.218) or read the blogs at Ⓦ thaiprisonlife.com to get the picture. The **police** actively look for tourists doing drugs, reportedly searching people regularly and randomly on Thanon Khao San, for example. They have the power to order a urine test if they have reasonable grounds for suspicion, and even a positive result for marijuana consumption could lead to a year's imprisonment. Be wary also of **being shopped** by a farang or local dealer keen to earn a financial reward for a successful bust, or having substances slipped into your luggage (simple enough to perpetrate unless all fastenings are secured with padlocks).

If you are arrested, ask for your embassy to be contacted immediately (see p.44), which is your right under Thai law, and embassy staff will talk you through procedures; the website of the British Embassy in Thailand also posts useful information, including a list of English-speaking lawyers, at ⓦ ukinthailand.fco.gov.uk/en/help-for-british-nationals. The British charity Prisoners Abroad (ⓦ prisonersabroad.org.uk) carries a detailed survival guide on its website, which outlines what to expect if arrested in Thailand, from the point of apprehension through trial and conviction to life in a Thai jail; if contacted, the charity may also be able to offer direct support to a British citizen facing imprisonment in a Thai jail.

Culture and etiquette

Tourist literature has marketed Thailand as the "Land of Smiles" so successfully that a lot of farangs arrive in the country expecting to be forgiven any outrageous behaviour. This is just not the case: there are some things so universally sacred in Thailand that even a hint of disrespect will cause deep offence.

The monarchy

It is both socially unacceptable to many Thais and a criminal offence to make critical or defamatory remarks about the **royal family**. Thailand's monarchy might be a constitutional one, but most households display a picture of King Bhumibol and Queen Sirikit in a prominent position, and respectful crowds mass whenever the royals make a public appearance. The second of their four children, Prince Vajiralongkorn, is the heir to the throne; his younger sister, Princess Sirindhorn, is often on TV and in the English-language newspapers as she is involved in many charitable projects. When addressing or speaking about royalty, Thais use a special language full of deference, called *rajasap* (literally "royal language").

Thailand's **lese-majesty laws** are among the most strictly applied in the world, increasingly invoked as the Thai establishment becomes ever more uneasy over the erosion of traditional monarchist sentiments and the rise of critical voices, particularly on the internet (though these are generally quickly censored). Accusations of lese-majesty can be levelled by and against anyone, Thai national or farang, and must be investigated by the police. As a few high-profile cases involving foreigners have demonstrated, they can be raised for seemingly minor infractions, such as defacing a poster or being less than respectful in a work of fiction. Transgressions are met with jail sentences of up to fifteen years for each offence.

Aside from keeping any anti-monarchy sentiments to yourself, you should be prepared to stand when the **king's anthem** is played at the beginning of every cinema programme, and to stop in your tracks if the town you're in plays the **national anthem** over its public address system – many small towns do this twice a day at 8am and again at 6pm, as do some train stations and airports. A less obvious point: as the king's head features on all Thai currency, you should never step on a coin or banknote, which is tantamount to kicking the king in the face.

Religion

Almost equally insensitive would be to disregard certain **religious** precepts. **Buddhism** plays a fundamental role in Thai culture, and Buddhist monuments should be treated with respect – which basically means wearing long trousers or knee-length skirts, covering your arms and removing your shoes whenever you visit one.

All **Buddha images** are sacred, however small, tacky or ruined, and should never be used as a backdrop for a portrait photo, clambered over, placed in a position of inferiority or treated in any manner that could be construed as disrespectful. In an attempt to prevent foreigners from committing any kind of transgression the government requires a special licence for all Buddha statues exported from the country (see p.42).

Monks come only just beneath the monarchy in the social hierarchy, and they too are addressed and discussed in a special language. If there's a monk around, he'll always get a seat on the bus, usually right at the back. Theoretically, monks are forbidden to have any close contact with women, which means that, as a female, you mustn't sit or stand next to a monk, or even brush against his robes; if it's essential to pass him something, put the object down so that he can then pick it up – never hand it over directly. Nuns, however, get treated like ordinary women.

See "Contexts" for more on religious practices in Thailand (see p.206).

The body

The Western liberalism embraced by the Thai sex industry is very unrepresentative of the majority Thai attitude to the body. **Clothing** – or the lack of it – is what bothers Thais most about tourist behaviour. You need to dress modestly when entering temples (see p.51), but the same also applies to other important buildings and all public places. Stuffy and sweaty as it sounds, you should keep short shorts and vests for the real tourist resorts, and be especially diligent about covering up and, for women, wearing bras in rural areas. Baring your flesh on beaches is very much a Western practice: when Thais go swimming they often do so fully clothed, and they find topless and nude bathing offensive.

According to ancient Hindu belief, the **head** is the most sacred part of the body and the **feet** are the most unclean. This belief, imported into Thailand, means that it's very rude to touch another person's head or to point your feet either at a human being or at a sacred image – when sitting on a temple floor, for example, you should **tuck your legs beneath you** rather than stretch them out towards the Buddha. These hierarchies also forbid people from wearing **shoes** (which are even more unclean than feet) inside temples and most private homes, and – by extension – Thais take offence when they see someone sitting on the "head", or prow, of a boat. **Putting your feet up** on a table, a chair or a pillow is also considered very uncouth, and Thais will always take their shoes off if they need to stand on a train or bus seat to get to the luggage rack, for example. On a more practical note, the **left hand** is used for washing after going to the toilet, so Thais never use it to put food in their mouth, pass things or shake hands – as a farang, though, you'll be assumed to have different customs, so left-handers shouldn't worry unduly.

Social conventions

Thais rarely shake hands, instead using the **wai** to greet and say goodbye and to acknowledge respect, gratitude or apology. A prayer-like gesture made with raised hands, the *wai* changes according to the relative status of the two people involved: Thais can instantaneously assess which *wai* to use, but as a farang your safest bet is to raise your hands close to your chest, bow your head and place your fingertips just below your nose. If someone makes a *wai* at you, you should generally *wai* back, but it's safer not to initiate.

Public displays of **physical affection** in Thailand are more common between friends of the same sex than between lovers, whether hetero- or homosexual. Holding hands and hugging is as common among male friends as with females, so if you're caressed by a Thai acquaintance of the same sex, don't assume you're being propositioned.

Finally, there are three specifically Thai **concepts** you're bound to come across, which may help you comprehend a sometimes laissez-faire attitude to delayed buses and other inconveniences. The first, **jai yen**, translates literally as "cool heart" and is something everyone tries to maintain: most Thais hate raised voices, visible irritation and confrontations of any kind, so losing one's cool can have a much more inflammatory effect than in more combative cultures. Related to this is the oft-quoted response to a difficulty, **mai pen rai** – "never mind", "no problem" or "it can't be helped" – the verbal equivalent of an open-handed shoulder shrug, which has its basis in the Buddhist notion of karma (see p.207). And then there's **sanuk**, the wide-reaching philosophy of "fun", which, crass as it sounds, Thais do their best to inject into any situation, even work. Hence the crowds of inebriated Thais who congregate at waterfalls and other beauty spots on public holidays (travelling solo is definitely not *sanuk*), the reluctance to do almost anything without high-volume musical accompaniment, and the national waterfight which takes place during Songkhran every April on streets right across Thailand.

Thai names

Although all Thais have a first **name** and a family name, everyone is addressed by their first name – even when meeting strangers – prefixed by the title **"Khun"** (Mr/Ms); no one is ever addressed as Khun Surname, and even the phone book lists people by their given name. In Thailand you will often be addressed in an anglicized version of this convention, as "Mr Paul" or "Miss Lucy" for example. Bear in mind, though, that when a man is introduced to you as Khun Pirom, his wife will definitely not be Khun Pirom as well (that would be like calling them, for instance, "Mr and Mrs Paul"). Among friends and relatives, **Phii** ("older brother/sister") is often used instead of Khun when addressing older familiars (though as a tourist you're on surer ground with Khun), and **Nong** ("younger brother/sister") is used for younger ones.

Many Thai **first names** come from ancient Sanskrit and have an auspicious meaning; for example, Boon means good deeds, Porn means blessings, Siri means glory and Thawee means to increase. However, Thais of all ages are commonly known by the **nickname** given them soon after birth rather than by their official first name. This tradition arises out of a deep-rooted superstition that once a child has been officially named the spirits will begin to take an unhealthy interest in them, so a nickname is used instead to confuse the spirits. Common nicknames – which often bear no resemblance to the adult's personality or physique – include Yai (Big), Uan (Fat) and Muu (Pig); Lek or Noi (Little), Nok (Bird), Nuu (Mouse) and Kung (Shrimp); and English nicknames like Apple, Joy or even Pepsi.

Family names were only introduced in 1913 (by Rama VI, who invented many of the aristocracy's surnames himself), and are used only in very formal situations, always in conjunction with the first name. It's quite usual for good friends never to know each other's surname. Ethnic Thais generally have short surnames like Somboon or Srisai, while the long, convoluted family names – such as Sonthanasumpun – usually indicate Chinese origin, not because they are phonetically Chinese but because many Chinese immigrants have chosen to adopt new Thai surnames and Thai law states that every newly created surname must be unique. Thus anyone who wants to change their surname must submit a short list of five unique Thai names – each to a maximum length of ten Thai characters – to be checked against a database of existing names. As more and more names are taken, Chinese family names get increasingly unwieldy, and more easily distinguishable from the pithy old Thai names.

Travel essentials

Charities and volunteer projects

Reassured by the plethora of well-stocked shopping plazas, efficient services and abundance of bars and restaurants, it is easy to forget that life is extremely hard for many people in Bangkok. Countless **charities** work with Thailand's many poor and disadvantaged communities: listed below are a few that would welcome help in some way from visitors.

CHARITABLE AND VOLUNTEER ORGANIZATIONS

Human Development Foundation Klong Toey, Bangkok Ⓦ mercycentre.org. Founded in 1973, Father Joe Maier's organization provides education and support for Bangkok's street kids and slum-dwellers. It now runs two dozen kindergartens in the slums, among many other projects. Contact the centre for information about donations, sponsoring and volunteering. Father Joe's books, *The Slaughterhouse: Stories from Bangkok's Klong Toey Slum* and *The Open Gate of Mercy*, give eye-opening insights into this often invisible side of Thai life.

The Mirror Foundation Ⓦ themirrorfoundation.org. NGO working mainly with the hill tribes in Chiang Rai province, with a branch in Bangkok dealing with urban problems; volunteers, interns and donations sought.

The Students' Education Trust (SET) Ⓦ thaistudentcharity .org. High-school and further education in Thailand is a luxury that the poorest kids cannot afford so many are sent to live in temples instead. The SET helps such kids pursue their education and escape from the poverty trap. Some of their stories are told in *Little Angels: The Real-Life Stories of Twelve Thai Novice Monks* (see p.218). SET welcomes donations.

Costs

Bangkok can be a very cheap place to visit. At the bottom of the scale, you can just about manage on a **daily budget** of around B750 (£15/US$25) if you're willing to opt for basic accommodation and eat, drink and travel as the locals do. With extras like air conditioning, taxis and a meal and beer in a more touristy restaurant, a day's outlay would be at least B1000 (£20/US$30). Staying in well-equipped, mid-range hotels and eating in the more upmarket restaurants, you should be able to live comfortably for around B2000 a day (£40/US$60).

Bargaining is expected practice for a lot of commercial transactions, particularly at markets and when hiring tuk-tuks and motorbike taxis (though not in supermarkets or department stores). It's a delicate art that requires humour, tact and patience. If your price is way out of line, the vendor's vehement refusal should be enough to make you increase your offer: never forget that the few pennies or cents you're making such a fuss over will go a lot further in a Thai person's hands than in your own.

Shoppers who are departing via an international airport can save some money by claiming a **Value Added Tax refund** (Ⓦ www.rd.go.th/vrt), though it's a bit of a palaver for seven percent (the current rate of VAT, though at the time of writing this was due to increase to ten percent). The total amount of your purchases (gems are excluded) from participating shops needs to be at least B2000 per person. You'll need to show your passport and fill in an application form (to which original tax invoices need to be attached) at the shop. At the airport, you'll need to show your form and purchases to customs officers before checking in, then make your claim from VAT refund officers – from which fees of at least B100 are deducted.

Customs regulations

The **duty-free** allowance on entry to Thailand is 200 cigarettes (or 250g of tobacco or cigars) and a litre of spirits or wine (see Ⓦ customs.go.th for more information).

To **export antiques** or newly cast **Buddha images** from Thailand, you need to have a licence granted by the Fine Arts Department (the export of religious antiques, especially Buddha images, is forbidden). Licences can be obtained for example through the Office of Archeology and National Museums, 81/1 Thanon Si Ayutthaya (near the National Library), Bangkok (☎02 628 5032). Applications take at least three working days and need to be accompanied by the object itself, some evidence of its rightful possession, two postcard-sized colour photos of it, taken face-on and against a white background, and photocopies of the applicant's passport; furthermore, if the object is a Buddha image, the passport photocopies need to be certified by your embassy in Bangkok. Some antiques shops can organize all this for you.

Electricity

Mains **electricity** is supplied at 220 volts AC. If you're packing phone and camera chargers, a laptop or other appliance, you'll need to take a set of travel-plug adaptors as several plug types are commonly in use, most usually with two round pins, but also with two flat-blade pins, and sometimes with both options.

Entry requirements

There are three main entry categories for visitors to Thailand; for all of them, under International Air Travel Association rules, your passport should be valid for at least six months. As visa requirements are subject to frequent change, you should always consult before departure a Thai embassy or consulate, a reliable travel agent, or the Thai Ministry of Foreign Affairs' website at Ⓦ mfa.go.th. For further, unofficial but usually reliable, details on all visa matters – especially as the rules are not consistently enforced across all Thai border checkpoints and immigration offices – go to the moderated forums on Ⓦ thaivisa.com.

Most Western passport holders (that includes citizens of the UK, Ireland, the US, Canada, Australia, New Zealand and South Africa) are allowed to enter the country for short **stays** without having to apply for a visa – officially termed the **tourist visa exemption** (not to be confused with "visas on arrival", another category of entry that's not available to citizens of the countries listed above). You'll be granted a thirty-day stay at an international airport, while at an overland border, most visitors are given fifteen days, but citizens of G7 countries, including the UK, US and Canada, are allowed thirty days; the period of stay will be stamped into your passport by immigration officials upon entry. You're somehow supposed to be able to show proof of means of living while in the country (B10,000 per person, B20,000 per family), and in theory you may be put back on the next plane without it or sent back to get a sixty-day tourist visa from the nearest Thai embassy, but this is unheard of. You are also required to show proof of tickets to leave Thailand again within the allotted time, though the Thai immigration authorities do not appear to be consistent about checking this (it seems to be more likely at land borders). However, if you have a one-way air ticket to Thailand and no evidence of onward travel arrangements, it's best to buy a tourist visa in advance: many airlines will stop you boarding the plane without one, as they would be liable for flying you back to your point of origin if you did happen to be stopped.

If you're fairly certain you may want to stay longer than fifteen/thirty days, then from the outset you should apply for a **sixty-day tourist visa** from a Thai embassy or consulate, accompanying your application – which generally takes several days to process – with your passport and one or two photos. The sixty-day visa currently costs B1000 or rough equivalent; multiple-entry versions are available, costing B1000 per entry, which may be handy if you're going to be leaving and re-entering Thailand. Ordinary tourist visas are valid for three months; ie you must enter Thailand within three months of the visa being issued by the Thai embassy or consulate, while multiple-entry versions are valid for six months. Visa application forms can be downloaded from, for example, the Thai Ministry of Foreign Affairs' website.

Thai embassies also consider applications for **ninety-day non-immigrant visas** (B2000 or rough equivalent for single entry, B5000 for multiple-entry) as long as you can offer a reason for your visit, such as study, business or visiting family (there are different categories of non-immigrant visa for which different levels of proof are needed). As it can be a hassle to organize a ninety-day visa, it's generally easier to apply for a thirty-day extension to your sixty-day visa once inside Thai borders.

It's not a good idea to **overstay** your visa limits. Once you're at the airport or the border, you'll have to pay a fine of B500 per day before you can leave Thailand (and there is talk, at the time of writing, of stiffening the sanctions). More importantly, however, if you're in the country with an expired visa and you get involved with police or immigration officials for any reason, however trivial, they are obliged to take you to court, possibly imprison you, and deport you.

Extensions, border runs and re-entry permits

Tourist visa exemptions, as well as sixty-day tourist visas, can be **extended** within Thailand for a further thirty days, at the discretion of immigration officials; extensions cost B1900 and are issued over the counter at immigration offices (*kaan khao muang* or *taw maw*; ☎1111 for 24hr information in English, ⓦimmigration.go.th). You'll need to bring one or two photos, one or two photocopies of the main pages of your passport including your Thai departure card, arrival stamp and visa; you may be asked for proof of tickets to leave Thailand again within the proposed time and evidence of where you're staying, and it's possible though unlikely that you'll be asked for proof of means of living while in Thailand. Many Khao San tour agents offer to get your visa extension for you, but beware: some are reportedly faking the stamps, which could get you into serious trouble. In 2014, the Thai immigration authorities started clamping down again on foreigners who stay in Thailand long-term by doing back-to-back **border runs** for tourist visa exemptions; however, it's still possible for ordinary travellers to get one new fifteen/thirty-day tourist visa exemption by hopping **across the border** into a neighbouring country and back. Immigration offices also issue **re-entry permits** (B1000 single re-entry, B3800 multiple) if you want to leave the country and come back again while maintaining the validity of your existing visa.

Bangkok immigration office

The **immigration office** is north of the centre off Thanon Wiphawadi Rangsit at Floor 2, B Building, Government Complex, Soi 7, Thanon Chaeng-wattana (Mon–Fri 8.30am–noon & 1–4.30pm; ☎02 141 9889, ⓦbangkok.immigration.go.th, which includes a map). When trying to extend your **visa**, be very wary of any Khao San tour agents who offer to organize a visa extension for you: some are reportedly faking the relevant stamps and this has caused problems at immigration.

THAI EMBASSIES AND CONSULATES ABROAD

For a full listing of Thai diplomatic missions abroad, consult the Thai Ministry of Foreign Affairs' website at ⓦmfa.go.th/web/2712.php; its other site, ⓦthaiembassy.org, has links to the websites of most of the offices below.

Australia 111 Empire Circuit, Yarralumla, Canberra ACT 2600 ☎02 6206 0100; plus consulate at 131 Macquarrie St, Sydney, NSW 2000 ☎02 9241 2542–3.

Cambodia 196 Preah Norodom Blvd, Sangkat Tonle Bassac, Khan Chamcar Mon, Phnom Penh ☎023 726306–8.

Canada 180 Island Park Drive, Ottawa, ON, K1Y 0A2 ☎613 722 4444; plus consulate at 1040 Burrard St, Vancouver, BC, V6Z 2R9 ☎604 687 1143.

Laos Vientiane: embassy at Avenue Kaysone Phomvihane, Saysettha District ☎021 214581–2, consular section at Unit 15 Bourichane Rd, Ban Phone Si Nuan, Muang Si Sattanak ☎021 453916; plus consulate at Khanthabouly District, Savannakhet Province, PO Box 513 ☎041 212373.

Malaysia 206 Jalan Ampang, 50450 Kuala Lumpur ☎03 2148 8222; plus consulates at 4426 Jalan Pengkalan Chepa, 15400 Kota Bharu ☎09 748 2545; and 1 Jalan Tunku Abdul Rahman, 10350 Penang ☎04 226 9484.

Myanmar 94 Pyay Rd, Dagon Township, Rangoon ☎01 226721.

New Zealand 110 Molesworth St, Thorndon, Wellington ☎04 476 8616.

Singapore 370 Orchard Rd, Singapore 238870 ☎6737 2158.

South Africa 428 Pretorius/Hill St, Arcadia, Pretoria 0083 ☎012 342 5470.

UK and Ireland 29–30 Queens Gate, London SW7 5JB ☎020 7589 2944. In Ireland, visa applications by post can be sent to the consulate in Dublin (ⓦthaiconsulateireland.com).

US 1024 Wisconsin Ave NW, Suite 401, Washington, DC 20007 ☎202 944 3600; plus consulates at 700 North Rush St, Chicago, IL 60611 ☎312 664 3129; 611 North Larchmont Blvd, 2nd Floor, Los Angeles, CA 90004 ☎323 962 9574; and 351 E 52nd St, New York, NY 10022 ☎212 754 1770.

Vietnam 63–65 Hoang Dieu St, Hanoi ☎04 3823-5092–4; plus consulate at 77 Tran Quoc Thao St, District 3, Ho Chi Minh City ☎08 3932-7637–8.

FOREIGN EMBASSIES AND CONSULATES IN BANGKOK

Australia 37 Thanon Sathorn Tai ☎ 02 344 6300, ⓦ thailand.embassy.gov.au.

Cambodia 518/4 Thanon Pracha Uthit (Soi Ramkamhaeng 39) ☎ 02 957 5851–2.

Canada 15th floor, Abdulrahim Place, 990 Thanon Rama IV ☎ 02 646 4300, ⓦ thailand.gc.ca.

China 57 Thanon Rajadapisek ☎ 02 245 7033 or ☎ 02 245 7036.

India 46 Sukhumvit Soi 23 ☎ 02 258 0300–6, ⓦ indianembassy.in.th.

Indonesia 600–602 Thanon Phetchaburi ☎ 02 252 3135–9, ⓦ kemlu.go.id/Bangkok.

Ireland Floor 23, Athenee Tower, 63 Thanon Witthayu ☎ 02 126 8092.

Laos 502/1–3 Soi Sahakarnpramoon, Thanon Pracha Uthit ☎ 02 539 6667–8 ext 106, ⓦ laoembassybkk.gov.la.

Malaysia 35 Thanon Sathorn Tai ☎ 02 629 6800.

Myanmar (Burma) 132 Thanon Sathorn Nua ☎ 02 234 4789.

New Zealand 14th Floor, M Thai Tower, All Seasons Place, 87 Thanon Witthayu ☎ 02 254 2530, ⓦ nzembassy.com/Thailand.

Singapore 129 Thanon Sathorn Tai ☎ 02 286 2111.

South Africa Floor 12A, M Thai Tower, All Seasons Place, 87 Thanon Witthayu ☎ 02 659 2900, ⓦ www.dirco.gov.za/Bangkok.

UK 14 Thanon Witthayu ☎ 02 305 8333.

US 120 Thanon Witthayu ☎ 02 205 4000.

Vietnam 83/1 Thanon Witthayu ☎ 02 650 8979.

For further details about Bangkok's diplomatic corps, go to ⓦ mfa.go.th /main/en/information on the Thai Ministry of Foreign Affairs' website.

Insurance

Most visitors to Thailand will need to take out **specialist travel insurance**, though you should check exactly what's covered.

Internet

Internet access is now almost ubiquitous in Thailand. As well as 4G (see p.46), there's free wi-fi in nearly all hotels and guesthouses (though in cheaper places, the signal may not stretch to all bedrooms) and most cafés, restaurants and bars in Bangkok. Given all this, internet cafés are inexorably disappearing. If you want to use high-speed computers or print, you could head for *True*, housed in an early twentieth-century villa in a courtyard off the western end of Thanon Khao San, where you also can sip coffee (daily 9.30am–8pm); or *True Urban Park* on Floor 3 of Siam Paragon shopping centre, Thanon Rama I (daily 10am–10pm), which also sells coffee and mobile phone packages.

Laundry

Guesthouses and cheap hotels run low-cost, same- or next-day **laundry** services, though in luxury hotels, it'll cost an arm and a leg. In some places you pay per item, in others you're charged by the kilo (generally around B30–50/kg); ironing is often included in the price.

Left luggage

Luggage can be left at Suvarnabhumi Airport (B100/day); Don Muang Airport (B75/day); Hualamphong train station (B20–80/day); the bus terminals and most hotels and guesthouses.

Living in Bangkok

The most common source of **employment** in Bangkok is **teaching English**. You can search for openings at schools on ⓦ ajarn.com (*ajarn* means "teacher"), which also features extensive general advice on teaching and living in Bangkok. Another useful resource is the excellent ⓦ thaivisa.com, whose scores of well-used forums focus on specific topics that range from employment in Thailand to legal issues and cultural and practical topics. Guesthouse noticeboards occasionally carry adverts for more unusual jobs, such as playing extras in Thai movies.

A tourist visa does not entitle you to work in Thailand, so, legally, you'll need to apply for a **work permit**.

Language classes

The most popular place to **study Thai** is Bangkok, and there's plenty of choice, including private and group lessons for both tourists and expats; note, however, that some schools' main reason for existence is to provide educational visas for long-staying foreigners. The longest-running and best-regarded courses and private lessons are provided by AUA (American University Alumni; Ⓦauathailand.org).

Mail

Overseas airmail usually takes around seven days from Bangkok (it's worth asking at the post office about its express EMS services, which can cut this down to three days and aren't prohibitively expensive). **Post offices** in Thailand (Ⓦthailandpost.com) have recently been quite successfully privatized, and many now offer money-wiring facilities (in association with Western Union), parcel packing, long-distance bus tickets, amulets, whitening cream, you name it. They're generally open Monday to Friday 8.30am to 4.30pm, Saturday 9am to noon; some close Monday to Friday noon to 1pm and may stay open until 6pm, and a few open 9am to noon on Sundays and public holidays. Almost all post offices operate a **poste restante** service and will hold letters for one to three months. Mail should be addressed: *Name* (family name underlined or capitalized), Poste Restante, GPO, *Town or City*, Thailand. It will be filed by surname, though it's always wise to check under your first and middle names as well; you need to show your passport. Post offices are the best places to buy **stamps**, though hotels and guesthouses often sell them too.

If you're staying in Banglamphu, it's probably most convenient to use the local postal, packing and poste restante services at Banglamphubon PO, Soi Sibsam Hang, Bangkok 10203 (daily 8am–5pm). Downtown, Prasanmit PO, 12/3–4 Soi 23 (Soi Prasanmit), Thanon Sukhumvit, Bangkok 10110 (Mon–Fri 8.30am–5.30pm, Sat 9am–noon), is handy for both the BTS and the subway.

Money and banks

Thailand's unit of currency is the **baht** (abbreviated in this guide to "B"), divided into 100 satang – which are rarely seen these days. Coins come in B1 (silver), B2 (golden), B5 (silver) and B10 (mostly golden, encircled by a silver ring) denominations, notes in B20, B50, B100, B500 and B1000 denominations, inscribed with Western as well as Thai numerals, and generally increasing in size according to value.

At the time of writing, **exchange rates** were around B30 to US$1, B35 to €1 and B50 to £1. A good site for current exchange rates is Ⓦxe.com. Note that Thailand has no black market in foreign currency.

Banking hours are generally Monday to Friday from 8.30am to 3.30 or 4.30pm, though branches in shopping centres and supermarkets are often open longer hours and at weekends. Streetside exchange kiosks run by the banks in the main tourist areas are always open till at least 5pm, sometimes 10pm, and upmarket hotels change money (at poor rates) 24 hours a day. The Suvarnabhumi Airport exchange counters also operate 24 hours, while exchange kiosks at overseas airports with flights to Thailand usually keep Thai currency.

Travellers' cheques are accepted by banks and exchange booths; everyone offers better rates for cheques than for straight cash. Generally, a total of B153 in commission and duty is charged per cheque, so you'll save money if you deal in larger cheque denominations. Note that Scottish and Northern Irish sterling notes may not be accepted in some places.

Visa and MasterCard **credit and debit cards** are accepted at upmarket guesthouses and hotels as well as in posh restaurants, department stores, tourist shops and travel agents; American Express is less widely accepted. It's common for smaller businesses to add on a surcharge of three percent, which amounts to the fee that Visa and Mastercard charge them for the privilege. Beware theft and forgery – try not to let the card out of your sight, and never leave cards in baggage storage. With a debit or credit card and personal identification number (PIN), you can also withdraw cash from hundreds of 24hr **ATMs** around the city, including a huge number of standalone ATMs in shopping malls and on the streets, often outside supermarkets and post offices. However, Thai banks now make a charge of B150–180 per ATM withdrawal (on top of whatever your bank at home will be charging you); to get around this, go into a bank with your card and passport instead and ask for a cash advance, or check with your bank before you come to Thailand – some overseas banks will not pass on to customers the B150–180 levied at Thai ATMs.

Opening hours and public holidays

Most **shops** open at least Monday to Saturday from about 8am to 8pm, while department stores and shopping malls operate daily from around 10am to 9pm. Private office hours are generally Monday to Friday 8am to 5pm and Saturday 8am to noon, though in tourist areas these hours are longer, with weekends worked like any other day. Government offices work Monday to Friday 8.30am to 4.30pm (often closing for lunch between noon and 1pm). Temples generally open their gates every day from dawn to dusk.

Many tourists only register **national holidays** because trains and buses suddenly get extraordinarily crowded, especially if the holiday is moved from a Saturday or a Sunday to a Monday or a Friday as a substitution day, thus creating a long weekend: although government offices shut on these days, most shops and tourist-oriented businesses carry on regardless, and TAT branches continue to hand out free maps. (Bank holidays vary slightly from the government office holidays given below: banks close on May 1 and July 1, but not for the Royal Ploughing Ceremony nor for Khao Pansa.) Some national holidays are celebrated with theatrical festivals (see p.35). The only time an inconvenient number of shops, restaurants and hotels do close is during **Chinese New Year**, which, though not marked as an official national holiday, brings many businesses to a standstill for several days in late January or February.

Thais use both the Western Gregorian **calendar** and a Buddhist calendar – the Buddha is said to have died (or entered Nirvana) in the year 543 BC, so Thai dates start from that point: thus 2016 AD becomes 2559 BE (Buddhist Era).

NATIONAL HOLIDAYS

Jan 1 Western New Year's Day.

Feb (day of full moon) Makha Puja. Commemorates the Buddha preaching to a spontaneously assembled crowd of 1250.

April 6 Chakri Day. The founding of the Chakri dynasty, the current royal family.

April (usually 13–15) Songkhran. Thai New Year.

May 5 Coronation Day.

May (early in the month) Royal Ploughing Ceremony. Marks the traditional start of the rice-planting season.

May (day of full moon) Visakha Puja. The holiest of all Buddhist holidays, which celebrates the birth, enlightenment and death of the Buddha.

July (day of full moon) Asanha Puja. The anniversary of the Buddha's first sermon.

July (day after Asanha Puja) Khao Pansa. The start of the annual three-month Buddhist rains retreat, when new monks are ordained.

Aug 12 Queen's birthday and Mothers' Day.

Oct 23 Chulalongkorn Day. The anniversary of Rama V's death.

Dec 5 King's birthday and Fathers' Day. Also now celebrated as National Day (instead of Constitution Day).

Dec 10 Constitution Day.

Dec 31 Western New Year's Eve.

Phones

Most foreign **mobile-phone** networks have links with Thai networks, but you need to check on roaming rates, which are often exorbitant, before you leave home. To get round this, most travellers purchase a Thai pre-paid SIM card (providers include AIS, DTAC and True Move) either for their mobile phone (*moe thoe*), for an old phone brought from home or for a new set cheaply purchased in Thailand (which can most easily be done in a shopping centre, especially Mah Boon Krong – see p.185). Thai SIM cards are available for as little as B50 (sometimes free at the airport) and can be topped up at 7-Elevens around the city; they offer very cheap calls, both domestically and internationally (especially if you use low-cost international prefixes such as 008, 009 or 1-2-Call's 005 or 00500, rather than the standard 001 or 007 prefixes). They also offer data packages (4G is now available in Bangkok), very cheap texting, and are, of course, free of charge for all incoming calls. A data package or wi-fi on your own mobile device will

---

INTERNATIONAL DIALLING CODES

Calling from abroad, the international **country code** for Thailand is **66**, after which you leave off the initial zero of the Thai number.

Calling from Thailand, you'll need the relevant country code (see "Phones", opposite for information on prefixes):

Australia 61
Canada 1
Ireland 353
New Zealand 64
South Africa 27
UK 44
US 1

For **international directory enquiries** and operator services, call ☎ 100.

also allow you to make free or very cheap video or voice calls via Skype or a similar service.

When **dialling** any number in Thailand, you must now always preface it with what used to be the area code, even when dialling from the same area. Where we've given several line numbers – eg ❶02 431 1802–9 – you can substitute the last digit, 2, with any digit between 3 and 9. For **directory enquiries** within Thailand, call ❶1133.

Mobile-phone numbers in Thailand have ten digits, beginning "08" or "09". Note, however, that Thais tend to change mobile-phone providers – and therefore numbers – comparatively frequently, in search of a better deal.

One final local idiosyncrasy: Thai phone books list people by their first name, not their family name.

Time

Thailand is in the same time zone year-round, with no daylight savings period. Bangkok is five hours ahead of South Africa, seven hours ahead of GMT, twelve hours ahead of US Eastern Standard Time, three hours behind Australian Eastern Standard Time and five hours behind New Zealand Standard Time.

Tipping

It is usual to **tip** hotel bellboys and porters B20–40, and to round up taxi fares to the nearest B10. Most guides, drivers, masseurs, waiters and maids also depend on tips. Some upmarket hotels and restaurants will add an automatic ten percent service charge to your bill, though this is not always shared out.

Travellers with disabilities

Thailand makes few provisions for its disabled citizens and this obviously affects **travellers with disabilities**, but taxis, comfortable hotels and personal tour guides are all more affordable than in the West and most travellers with disabilities find Thais only too happy to offer assistance where they can. Hiring a local tour guide to accompany you on a day's sightseeing is particularly recommended: government-licensed tour guides can be arranged through any TAT office.

Most **wheelchair-users** end up driving on the roads because it's too hard to negotiate the uneven pavements, which are high to allow for flooding and invariably lack dropped kerbs. Crossing the road can be a trial in Bangkok, where it's usually a question of climbing steps up to a bridge rather than taking a ramped underpass. Few buildings, buses and trains have ramps but some Skytrain stations and all subway stations have lifts.

Several **tour companies** in Thailand specialize in organizing trips featuring adapted facilities, accessible transport and escorts. The Bangkok-based Help and Care Travel Company (❶081 375 0792, ⓦwheelchairtours.com) designs **accessible holidays** for slow walkers and wheelchair-users, as well as offering airport transfers, personal assistants and many other services.

THE GRAND PALACE

Ratanakosin

The only place to start your exploration of Bangkok is Ratanakosin, the royal island where the city's most important sights are located. When Rama I developed Ratanakosin for his new capital in 1782, after the sacking of Ayutthaya and a stay in Thonburi, he paid tribute to its precursor by imitating Ayutthaya's layout and architecture. Like Ayutthaya, Ratanakosin was sited beside a river and turned into an artificial island by the construction of defensive canals, with a central Grand Palace and adjoining royal temple, Wat Phra Kaeo, fronted by an open field, Sanam Luang; the Wang Na, now the National Museum, was also built at this time. Wat Pho, which predates the capital's founding, was further embellished by Rama I's successors, who also built several European-style palaces: Wat Mahathat, the National Theatre, the National Gallery, and Thammasat and Silpakorn universities.

Bangkok has expanded eastwards away from the river, leaving the Grand Palace a good 5km from the city's commercial heart, and the royal family has long since moved its residence to Dusit, but Ratanakosin remains the ceremonial centre of the whole kingdom – so much so that it feels as if it might sink into the boggy ground under the weight of its own mighty edifices. The heavy, stately feel is lightened by traditional shophouses selling herbal medicines, pavement amulet-sellers and studenty canteens along the riverside road, **Thanon Maharat**; and by Sanam Luang, still used for cremations and royal ceremonies, but also functioning as a popular open park and the hub of the modern city's bus system. Despite containing several of the country's main sights, the area is busy enough in its own right not to have become a swarming tourist zone, and strikes a neat balance between liveliness and grandeur.

ARRIVAL AND DEPARTURE   RATANAKOSIN

Ratanakosin is within easy walking distance of Banglamphu, but is best approached from the river, via the **express-boat piers** of Tha Chang (the former bathing place of the royal elephants, which gives access to the Grand Palace) or Tha Thien (for Wat Pho). An extension of the **subway** line from Hualamphong is being built (its opening currently proposed for 2017), with a new station at the Museum of Siam, 5min walk from Wat Pho, 10min from Tha Thien express boat pier and 15min from the entrance to the Grand Palace.

Wat Phra Kaeo and the Grand Palace

Thanon Na Phra Lan • Daily 8.30am–4pm, last admission 3.30pm (weapons museum, Phra Thinang Amarin Winichai and Dusit Maha Prasat interiors closed Sat & Sun) • B500, including a map and admission, within 7 days, to Dusit Park (see p.88) or Sanam Chandra Palace in Nakhon Pathom (see p.128); 2hr personal audioguide B200, with passport or credit card as deposit • ⓦ palaces.thai.net

Hanging together in a precarious harmony of strangely beautiful colours and shapes, **Wat Phra Kaeo** is the apogee of Thai religious art and the holiest Buddhist site in the country, housing the most important image, the **Emerald Buddha**. Built as the private royal temple, Wat Phra Kaeo occupies the northeast corner of the huge **Grand Palace**, whose official opening in 1785 marked the founding of the new capital and the rebirth of the Thai nation after the Burmese invasion. Successive kings have all left their mark here, and the palace complex now covers 2 acres, though very little apart from the wat is open to tourists.

The only **entrance** to the complex in 2km of crenellated walls is the Gate of Glorious Victory in the middle of the north side, on Thanon Na Phra Lan. This brings you onto a driveway with a tantalizing view of the temple's glittering spires on the left and the dowdy buildings of the Offices of the Royal Household on the right: this is the powerhouse of the kingdom's ceremonial life, providing everything down to chairs and catering, even lending an urn when someone of rank dies. Among these buildings, the hagiographic Queen Sirikit Museum of Textiles, which claims to show how she invented the Thai national dress in the 1960s, is included in the admission ticket but well worth missing, though you might want to check out the museum

A WORD OF WARNING

When you're heading for the Grand Palace or Wat Pho, you may well be approached by someone, possibly pretending to be a student or an official, who will tell you that the sight is closed when it's not, or some other lies to try to lead you away from the entrance, because they want to take you on a shopping trip for souvenirs, tailored clothes or, if you seem really gullible, gems (see box, p.190). The opening hours of the Grand Palace – but not Wat Pho – are indeed sometimes erratic because of state occasions, but you can check the details out on its website, ⓦ palaces.thai.net – and even if it's closed on the day you want to visit, that's no reason to throw yourself at the mercy of these shysters.

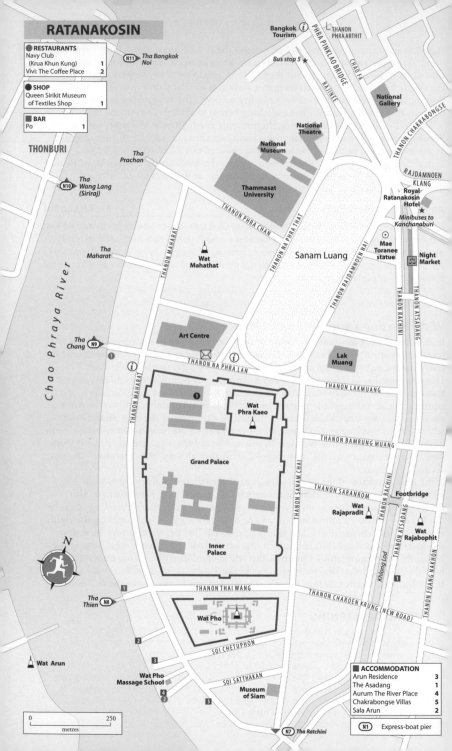

RATANAKOSIN

● RESTAURANTS
Navy Club
  (Krua Khun Kung)   1
Vivi: The Coffee Place   2

● SHOP
Queen Sirikit Museum
of Textiles Shop   1

■ BAR
Po   1

THONBURI

N11 *Tha Bangkok Noi*

Bangkok Tourism ⓘ

THANON PHRA ARTHIT

PHRA PINKLAO BRIDGE

CHAO FA

RAJINEE

Bus stop 5 ★

National Gallery

National Theatre

THANON CHAKRABONGSE

Tha Prachan

National Museum

RAJDAMNOEN KLANG

Royal Ratanakosin Hotel

Minibuses to Kanchanaburi

N10 *Tha Wang Lang (Siriraj)*

Thammasat University

THANON PHRA CHAN

THANON NA PHRA THAT

Mae Toranee statue ⊙

Night Market ♫

Tha Maharat

Wat Mahathat

Sanam Luang

THANON RAJDAMNOEN NAI

THANON RACHINI

THANON ATSADANG

Chao Phraya River

Art Centre

N9 *Tha Chang*

ⓘ

THANON NA PHRA LAN

ⓘ

Lak Muang

THANON LAKMUANG

THANON MAHARAT

❶

Wat Phra Kaeo

Grand Palace

THANON BAMRUNG MUANG

THANON SANAM CHAI

THANON SARANROM

Wat Rajapradit

Footbridge

THANON RACHINI

Wat Rajabophit

THANON ATSADANG

THANON FUANG NAKHON

Inner Palace

Khlong Lod

❶

THANON THAI WANG

N8 *Tha Thien*

THANON CHAROEN KRUNG (NEW ROAD)

❶

Wat Pho

❷

Wat Arun

SOI CHETUPHON

Wat Pho Massage School

❸

❹
❷

SOI SATTHAKAN

Museum of Siam

❺

N ↑

0   250
metres

■ ACCOMMODATION
Arun Residence   3
The Asadang   1
Aurum The River Place   4
Chakrabongse Villas   5
Sala Arun   2

N1 Express-boat pier

N7 ▼ *Tha Ratchini*

shop (see p.185). Turn left at the end of the driveway for the ticket office and entrance turnstiles.

As this is Thailand's most sacred site, you have to **dress in smart clothes**: no vests or see-through clothes; men must wear full-length trousers, women trousers or over-the-knee skirts. Suitable garments can be borrowed from the office to the right just inside the Gate of Glorious Victory (free, deposit of B200 per item).

Wat Phra Kaeo

It makes you laugh with delight to think that anything so fantastic could exist on this sombre earth.
                                             W. Somerset Maugham, The Gentlemen in the Parlour

Entering the temple is like stepping onto a lavishly detailed stage set, from the immaculate flagstones right up to the gaudy roofs. Reinforcing the sense of unreality, the whole compound is surrounded by arcaded walls, decorated with extraordinary murals of scenes from the *Ramayana*. Although it receives hundreds of foreign sightseers and at least as many Thai pilgrims every day, the temple, which has no monks in residence, maintains an unnervingly sanitized look, as if it were built only yesterday.

The approach to the bot

Inside the entrance turnstiles, you're confronted by 6m-tall **yaksha**, gaudy demons from the *Ramayana*, who watch over the Emerald Buddha from every gate of the temple and ward off evil spirits; the king of the demons, green, ten-faced Totsagan (labelled "Tosakanth"), stands to the left of the entrance by the southwest corner of the golden Phra Si Ratana Chedi. Less threatening is the toothless old codger, cast in bronze and sitting on a plinth immediately inside the turnstiles by the back wall of the bot, who represents a Hindu **hermit** credited with inventing yoga and herbal medicine. In front of him is a large grinding stone where previously herbal practitioners could come to grind their ingredients – with enhanced powers, of course. Skirting around the bot, you'll reach its **main entrance** on the eastern side, in front of which stands a cluster of grey **statues**, which have a strong Chinese feel: next to Kuan Im, the Chinese *bodhisattva* of mercy shown holding a bottle of *amritsa* (sacred elixir), are a sturdy pillar topped by a lotus flower, which Bangkok's Chinese community presented to Rama IV during his 27 years as a monk, and two handsome cows which commemorate Rama I's birth in the Year of the Cow. Worshippers make their offerings to the Emerald Buddha at two small, stand-in Buddhas here, where they can look at the main image through the open doors of the bot without messing up its pristine interior with gold leaf, candle wax and joss-stick ash.

The bot and the Emerald Buddha

The **bot**, the largest building of the temple, is one of the few original structures left at Wat Phra Kaeo, though it has been augmented so often it looks like the work of a wildly inspired child. Eight *sema* stones mark the boundary of the consecrated area around the bot, each sheltering in a psychedelic fairy castle, joined by a low wall decorated with Chinese porcelain tiles, which depict delicate landscapes. The walls of the bot itself, sparkling with gilt and coloured glass, are supported by 112 golden garudas (birdmen) holding nagas (serpents), representing the god Indra saving the world by slaying the serpent-cloud that had swallowed up all the water. The symbolism reflects the king's traditional role as a rainmaker.

Of the bot's three doorways, the largest, in the middle, is reserved for the king himself. Inside, a 9m-high pedestal supports the tiny **Emerald Buddha**, a figure whose mystique draws pilgrims from all over Thailand – as well as politicians accused of corruption, who traditionally come here to publicly swear their innocence. Here especially you must act with respect, sitting with your feet pointing away from the Buddha. The spiritual power of the 60cm jadeite image derives from its legendary

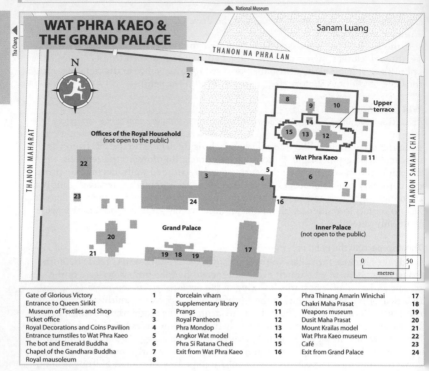

Gate of Glorious Victory	1	Porcelain viharn	9	Phra Thinang Amarin Winichai	17
Entrance to Queen Sirikit		Supplementary library	10	Chakri Maha Prasat	18
Museum of Textiles and Shop	2	Prangs	11	Weapons museum	19
Ticket office	3	Royal Pantheon	12	Dusit Maha Prasat	20
Royal Decorations and Coins Pavilion	4	Phra Mondop	13	Mount Krailas model	21
Entrance turnstiles to Wat Phra Kaeo	5	Angkor Wat model	14	Wat Phra Kaeo museum	22
The bot and Emerald Buddha	6	Phra Si Ratana Chedi	15	Café	23
Chapel of the Gandhara Buddha	7	Exit from Wat Phra Kaeo	16	Exit from Grand Palace	24
Royal mausoleum	8				

past. Reputed to have been created by the gods in India, it was discovered when lightning cracked open an ancient chedi in Chiang Rai in the early fifteenth century. The image was then moved around the north, dispensing miracles wherever it went, before being taken to Laos for two hundred years. As it was believed to bring great fortune to its possessor, the future Rama I snatched it back when he captured Vientiane in 1779, installing it at the heart of his new capital as a talisman for king and country.

Seated in the *Dhyana Mudra* (meditation), the Emerald Buddha has three **costumes**, one for each season: the crown and ornaments of an Ayutthayan king for the hot season; a gilt monastic robe for the rainy season, when the monks retreat into the temples; this is augmented with a full-length gold shawl in the cool season. To this day it's the job of the king himself to ceremonially change the Buddha's costumes – though in recent years, due to the present king's age, the Crown Prince has conducted proceedings. The Buddha was granted a new set of these three costumes in 1997: the old set is now in the Wat Phra Kaeo Museum (see p.56) while the two costumes of the new set that are not in use are on display among the blinding glitter of crowns and jewels in the Royal Decorations and Coins Pavilion, which lies between the ticket office and the entrance to Wat Phra Kaeo.

Among the paraphernalia in front of the pedestal sits the tiny, silver **Phra Chai Lang Chang** (Victory Buddha), which Rama I always carried into battle on the back of his elephant for luck and which still plays an important part in coronation ceremonies. Recently covered in gold, it occupies a prestigious spot dead centre, but is obscured by the umbrella of a larger gold Buddha in front. The tallest pair of a dozen standing Buddha images, all made of bronze but encased in gold and raising both hands to dispel fear, are at the front: Rama III dedicated the one on the Emerald Buddha's left to Rama I, the one on his right to Rama II, and Rama IV enshrined relics of the Buddha in their crowns.

The Chapel of the Gandhara Buddha

Near the entrance to the bot, in the southeastern corner of the temple precinct, look out for the exquisite scenes of rice sheaves, fish and turtles painted in gold on blue glass on the doors and windows of the **Chapel of the Gandhara Buddha** (labelled "Hor Phra Kanthara Rat"). The decorations allude to the fertility of the rice fields, as this building was crucial to the old royal rainmaking ritual and is still used during the Royal Ploughing Ceremony (see p.59). Adorning the roof are thousands of nagas, symbolizing water; inside the locked chapel, among the paraphernalia used in the ritual, is kept the Gandhara Buddha, a bronze image in the gesture of calling down the rain with its right hand, while cupping the left to catch it. In times of drought the king would order a week-long rainmaking ceremony to be conducted, during which he was bathed regularly and kept away from the opposite sex while Buddhist monks and Hindu Brahmins chanted continuously.

The Royal Pantheon and minor buildings

On the north side of the bot, the eastern end of the **upper terrace** is taken up with the **Prasat Phra Thep Bidorn**, known as the **Royal Pantheon**, a splendid hash of styles. The pantheon has its roots in the Khmer concept of *devaraja*, or the divinity of kings: inside are bronze and gold statues, precisely life-size, of all the kings since Bangkok became the Thai capital. Constructed by Rama IV, the building is open only on special occasions, such as Chakri Day (April 6), when the dynasty is commemorated, and Coronation Day (May 5).

From here you get the best view of the **royal mausoleum**, the **porcelain viharn** and the **supplementary library** to the north (all of which are closed to tourists, though you can sometimes glimpse Thai Buddhists worshipping in the library), and, running along the east side of the temple, a row of eight bullet-like **prangs**, each of which has a different nasty ceramic colour. Described as "monstrous vegetables" by Somerset Maugham, they represent, from north to south, the Buddha, Buddhist scripture, the monkhood, the nunhood, the Buddhas who attained enlightenment but did not preach, previous emperors, the Buddha in his previous lives and the future Buddha.

The Phra Mondop and Phra Si Ratana Chedi

In the middle of the terrace, dressed in deep-green glass mosaics, the **Phra Mondop** was built by Rama I to house the *Tripitaka*, or Buddhist scripture, which the king had rewritten at Wat Mahathat in 1788, the previous versions having all been lost in the sacking of Ayutthaya. It's famous for the mother-of-pearl cabinet and solid-silver mats inside, but is never open. Four tiny **memorials** at each corner of the mondop show the symbols of each of the nine Chakri kings, from the ancient crown representing Rama I to the present king's discus, while the bronze statues surrounding the memorials portray each king's lucky white elephants, labelled by name and pedigree. A contribution of Rama IV, on the north side of the mondop, is a **scale model of Angkor Wat**, the prodigious Cambodian temple, which during his reign (1851–68) was under Thai rule (apparently, the king had wanted to shift a whole Khmer temple to Bangkok but, fortunately, was dissuaded by his officials). At the western end of the terrace, you can't miss the golden dazzle of the **Phra Si Ratana Chedi**, which Rama IV erected, in imitation of the famous bell-shaped chedis at Ayutthaya's Wat Phra Si Sanphet (see p.119), to enshrine a piece of the Buddha's breastbone.

1

The murals

Extending for about a kilometre in the arcades that run inside the wat walls, the **murals of the Ramayana** depict every blow of this ancient story of the triumph of good over evil, using the vibrant buildings of the temple itself as backdrops, and setting them off against the subdued colours of richly detailed landscapes. Because of the damaging humidity, none of the original work of Rama I's time survives: maintenance is a never-ending process, so you'll always find an artist working on one of the scenes. The story is told in 178 panels, labelled and numbered in Thai only, starting in the middle of the northern side opposite the porcelain viharn: in the first episode, a hermit, while out ploughing, finds the baby Sita, the heroine, floating in a gold urn on a lotus leaf and brings her to the city. Panel 109 near the gate leading to the palace buildings shows the climax of the story, when Rama, the hero, kills the ten-headed demon Totsagan (Ravana), and the ladies of the enemy city weep at the demon's death. Panel 110 depicts his elaborate funeral procession, and in 113 you can see the funeral fair, with acrobats, sword-jugglers and tightrope-walkers. In between, Sita – Rama's wife – has to walk on fire to prove that she has been faithful during her fourteen years of imprisonment by Totsagan. If you haven't the stamina for the long walk round, you could sneak a look at the end of the story, to the left of the first panel, where Rama holds a victory parade and distributes thank-you gifts.

The palace buildings

The exit in the southwest corner of Wat Phra Kaeo brings you to the palace proper, a vast area of buildings and gardens, of which only the northern edge is on show to the public. Though the king now lives in the Chitrlada Palace in Dusit, the **Grand Palace** is still used for state receptions and official ceremonies, during which there is no public access to any part of the palace.

Phra Maha Monthien

Coming out of the temple compound, you'll first of all see to your right a beautiful Chinese gate covered in innumerable tiny porcelain tiles. Extending in a straight line behind the gate is the **Phra Maha Monthien**, which was the grand residential complex of earlier kings.

Only the **Phra Thinang Amarin Winichai**, the main audience hall at the front of the complex, is open to the public. The supreme court in the era of the absolute monarchy, it nowadays serves as the venue for ceremonies such as the king's birthday speech. Dominating the hall are two gleaming, intricately carved thrones that date from the reign of Rama I: a white umbrella with the full nine tiers owing to a king shelters the front seat, while the unusual *busbok* behind is topped with a spired roof and floats on a boat-shaped base. The rear buildings are still used for the most important part of the elaborate coronation ceremony, and each new king is supposed to spend a night there to show solidarity with his forefathers.

Chakri Maha Prasat

Next door you can admire the facade of the "farang with a Thai crown", as the **Chakri Maha Prasat** is nicknamed. Rama V, whose portrait you can see over its entrance, employed an English architect to design a purely Neoclassical residence, but other members of the royal family prevailed on the king to add the three Thai spires. This used to be the site of the elephant stables: the large red tethering posts are still there and the bronze elephants were installed as a reminder. The building displays the emblem of the Chakri dynasty on its gable, which has a trident (*ri*) coming out of a *chak* (a discus with a sharpened rim). The only part of the Chakri Maha Prasat open to the public is the ground-floor **weapons museum**, which houses a forgettable display of hooks, pikes and guns.

1

THE RAMAYANA/RAMAKIEN

The **Ramayana** is generally thought to have originated as an oral epic in India, where it appears in numerous dialects. The most famous version is that of the sage Valmiki, who is said to have drawn together the collection of stories as a tribute to his king over two thousand years ago. From India, the *Ramayana* spread to all the Hindu-influenced countries of Southeast Asia and was passed down through the Khmers to Thailand, where as the **Ramakien** it has become the national epic, acting as an affirmation of the Thai monarchy and its divine Hindu links. As a source of inspiration for literature, painting, sculpture and dance-drama, it has acquired the authority of holy writ, providing Thais with moral and practical lessons, while its appearance in the form of films and comic strips shows its huge popular appeal. The version current in Thailand was composed by a committee of poets sponsored by Rama I (all previous Thai texts were lost in the sacking of Ayutthaia in 1767), and runs to three thousand pages – available in an abridged English translation by M.L. Manich Jumsai (see p.219).

The central story of the *Ramayana* concerns **Rama** (in Thai, Phra Ram), son of the king of Ayodhya, and his beautiful wife **Sita**, whose hand he wins by lifting, stringing – and breaking – a magic bow. The couple's adventures begin when they are exiled to the forest, along with Rama's good brother, **Lakshaman** (Phra Lak), by the hero's father under the influence of his evil stepmother. Meanwhile, in the city of Lanka (Longka), the demon king **Ravana** (Totsagan) has conceived a passionate desire for Sita and, disguised as a hermit, sets out to kidnap her. By transforming one of his demon subjects into a beautiful deer, which Rama and Lakshaman go off to hunt, Ravana catches Sita alone and takes her back to Lanka. Rama then wages a long war against the demons of Lanka, into which are woven many battles, spy scenes and diversionary episodes, and eventually kills Ravana and rescues Sita.

The Thai version shows some characteristic differences from the Indian, emphasizing the typically Buddhist virtues of filial obedience and willing renunciation. In addition, Hanuman, the loyal monkey general, is given a much more playful role in the *Ramakien*, with the addition of many episodes which display his cunning and talent for mischief, not to mention his promiscuity. However, the major alteration comes at the end of the story, when Phra Ram doubts Sita's faithfulness after rescuing her from Totsagan. In the Indian story, this ends with Sita being swallowed up by the earth so that she doesn't have to suffer Rama's doubts any more; in the *Ramakien* the ending is a happy one, with Phra Ram and Sita living together happily ever after.

The Inner Palace

The **Inner Palace** (closed to the public), which used to be the king's harem, lies behind the gate on the left-hand side of the Chakri Maha Prasat. Vividly described in M.R. Kukrit Pramoj's *Si Phaendin* (see p.220), the harem was a town in itself, with shops, law courts and an all-female police force for the huge population: as well as the current queens, the minor wives and their children (including pre-pubescent boys) and servants, this was home to the daughters and consorts of former kings, and the daughters of the aristocracy who attended the harem's finishing school. Today, the Inner Palace houses a school of cooking, fruit-carving and other domestic sciences for well-bred young Thais.

Dusit Maha Prasat

On the western side of the courtyard, the delicately proportioned **Dusit Maha Prasat**, an audience hall built by Rama I, epitomizes traditional Thai architecture. Outside, the soaring tiers of its red, gold and green roof culminate in a gilded *mongkut*, a spire shaped like the king's crown, which symbolizes the 33 Buddhist levels of perfection. Each tier of the roof bears a typical *chofa*, a slender, stylized bird's-head finial, and several *hang hong* (swans' tails), which represent three-headed nagas. Inside, you can still see the original throne, the **Phra Ratcha Banlang Pradap Muk**, a masterpiece of mother-of-pearl inlaid work. When a senior member of the royal

1

family dies, the hall is used for the lying-in-state: the body, embalmed and seated in a huge sealed urn, is placed in the west transept, waiting up to two years for an auspicious day to be cremated.

The Wat Phra Kaeo Museum

In the nineteenth-century Royal Mint in front of the Dusit Maha Prasat – next to a small, basic **café** – the **Wat Phra Kaeo Museum** houses a mildly interesting collection of artefacts donated to the Emerald Buddha, along with architectural elements rescued from the Grand Palace grounds during restoration in the 1980s. Highlights include the bones of various kings' white elephants, and upstairs, the Emerald Buddha's original costumes and two useful scale models of the Grand Palace, one as it is now, the other as it was when first built. Also on the first floor stands the grey stone slab of the Manangasila Seat, where Ramkhamhaeng, the great thirteenth-century king of Sukhothai, is said to have sat and taught his subjects. It was discovered in 1833 by Rama IV during his monkhood and brought to Bangkok, where Rama VI used it as the throne for his coronation.

Wat Pho (Wat Phra Chetuphon)

Soi Chetuphon, to the south of the Grand Palace • Daily 8am–6.30pm • B200 • ⓦ watpho.com

Where Wat Phra Kaeo may seem too perfect and shrink-wrapped for some, **Wat Pho** is lively and shambolic, a complex arrangement of lavish structures which jostle with classrooms, basketball courts and a turtle pond. Busloads of tourists shuffle in and out of the **north entrance**, stopping only to gawp at the colossal Reclining Buddha, but you can avoid the worst of the crowds by using the **main entrance** on Soi Chetuphon to explore the huge compound.

Wat Pho is the oldest temple in Bangkok and is older than the city itself, having been founded in the seventeenth century under the name Wat Photaram. Foreigners have stuck to the contraction of this old name, even though Rama I, after enlarging the temple, changed the name in 1801 to **Wat Phra Chetuphon**, which is how it is generally known to Thais. The temple had another major overhaul in 1832, when Rama III built the chapel of the Reclining Buddha, and turned the temple into a public centre of learning by decorating the walls and pillars with inscriptions and diagrams on subjects such as history, literature, animal husbandry and astrology. Dubbed Thailand's first university, the wat is still an important centre for traditional

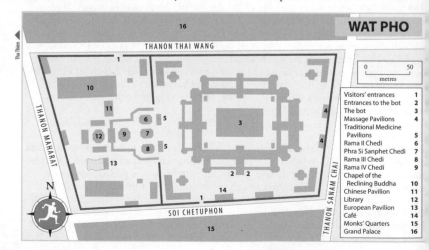

WAT PHO

THANON THAI WANG

Tha Tihen

THANON MAHARAT

SOI CHETUPHON

THANON SANAM CHAI

N

0   50
metres

Visitors' entrances	1
Entrances to the bot	2
The bot	3
Massage Pavilions	4
Traditional Medicine Pavilions	5
Rama II Chedi	6
Phra Si Sanphet Chedi	7
Rama III Chedi	8
Rama IV Chedi	9
Chapel of the Reclining Buddha	10
Chinese Pavilion	11
Library	12
European Pavilion	13
Café	14
Monks' Quarters	15
Grand Palace	16

THE ROYAL TONSURE CEREMONY

To the right and behind the Dusit Maha Prasat rises a strange model mountain, decorated with fabulous animals and topped by a castle and prang. It represents **Mount Krailas**, the Himalayan home of the Hindu god Shiva (Phra Isuan in Thai), and was built by Rama IV as the site of the **royal tonsure ceremony**, last held here in 1932, just three months before the end of the absolute monarchy. In former times, Thai children generally had shaved heads, except for a tuft or topknot on the crown, which, between the age of eleven and thirteen, was cut in a Hindu initiation rite to welcome adolescence. For the royal children, the rite was an elaborate ceremony that sometimes lasted seven days, culminating with the king's cutting of the hair knot, which was then floated away on the Chao Phraya River. The child was then bathed at the model Krailas, in water representing the original river of the universe flowing down the central mountain.

---

medicine, notably **Thai massage** (see p.182), which is used against all kinds of illnesses, from backaches to viruses.

The eastern courtyard

The main entrance on Soi Chetuphon is one of a series of sixteen monumental gates around the main compound, each guarded by stone **giants**, many of them comic Westerners in wide-brimmed hats – ships that exported rice to China would bring these statues back as ballast.

The entrance brings you into the eastern half of the main complex, where a courtyard of structures radiates from the bot in a disorientating symmetry. To get to the **bot**, the principal congregation and ordination hall, turn right and cut through the two surrounding cloisters, which are lined with hundreds of Buddha images. The elegant bot has beautiful teak doors decorated with mother-of-pearl, showing stories from the *Ramayana* (see p.55) in minute detail. Look out also for the stone bas-reliefs around the base of the bot, which narrate the story of the capture and rescue of Sita from the *Ramayana* in 152 action-packed panels. The plush interior has a well-proportioned altar on which ten statues of disciples frame a graceful, Ayutthayan Buddha image containing the remains of Rama I, the founder of Bangkok (Rama IV placed them there so that the public could worship him at the same time as the Buddha).

Back outside the entrance to the double cloister, keep your eyes open for a miniature mountain covered in statues of naked men in tall hats who appear to be gesturing rudely: they are *rishis* (hermits), demonstrating various positions of healing massage. Skirting the southwestern corner of the cloisters, you'll come to two pavilions between the eastern and western courtyards, which display plaques inscribed with the precepts of traditional medicine, as well as anatomical pictures showing the different pressure points and the illnesses that can be cured by massaging them.

The western courtyard

Among the 99 chedis strewn about the grounds, the four **great chedis** in the western courtyard stand out as much for their covering of garish tiles as for their size. The central chedi is the oldest, erected by Rama I to hold the remains of the most sacred Buddha image of Ayutthaya, the Phra Si Sanphet. Later, Rama III built the chedi to the north for the ashes of Rama II and the chedi to the south to hold his own remains; Rama IV built the fourth, with bright blue tiles, though its purpose is uncertain.

In the northwest corner of the courtyard stands the chapel of the **Reclining Buddha**, a 45m-long gilded statue of plaster-covered brick which depicts the Buddha entering Nirvana, a common motif in Buddhist iconography. The chapel is only slightly bigger than the statue – you can't get far enough away to take in anything but a surreal

1

close-up view of the beaming 5m smile. As for the feet, the vast black soles are beautifully inlaid with delicate mother-of-pearl showing the 108 *lakshanas*, or auspicious signs, which distinguish the true Buddha. Along one side of the statue are 108 bowls: putting a coin in each will bring you good luck and a long life.

Museum of Siam (National Discovery Museum)

Thanon Sanam Chai · Tues–Sun 10am–6pm · B300, free after 4pm · ☎ 02 225 2777, ⓦ museumsiam.com

The excellent **Museum of Siam** is a high-tech, mostly bilingual attraction that occupies the century-old, European-style, former Ministry of Commerce. It looks at what it is to be Thai, with lots of humorous short films and imaginative touches such as shadow-puppet cartoons and war video games. In addition, the museum stages playful temporary exhibitions, which in the past have let visitors have a go at rice-growing, and examine Thailand's enduring love affair with foreign commodities. Generally, it's great fun for adults and kids, and there's a nice little indoor-outdoor **café-restaurant** in the grounds run by the Black Canyon chain. The museum hosts **Noise Market** over three weekends a year (ⓦ facebook.com/noisemarketfest), a great little festival-cum-market of indie music, handicrafts and food.

The museum exhibition kicks off with the prehistory of Southeast Asia, or Suvarnabhumi (Land of Gold) as ancient Indian documents refer to it, and the legendary arrival of Buddhism via missionaries sent by the great Indian emperor, Ashoka (Asoke). Much space is devoted to Ayutthaya, where we learn that during that kingdom's four-hundred-year history, there were no fewer than twenty outbreaks of war with the Burmese states, before the final annihilation in 1767. Beyond this, look out for a fascinating map of Thonburi, King Taksin's new capital between 1768 and 1782, as drawn by a Burmese spy. In the Bangkok period, there's coverage of the Chinese in Thailand and of early twentieth-century racialism, but next to nothing on the country's Muslims. Towards the end, under the banner of westernization, visitors can wind up cartoon peep-shows and dress up in colonial-style uniform shirts.

Sanam Luang

Sprawling across 30 acres north of the Grand Palace, **Sanam Luang** is one of the last open spaces left in Bangkok, a bare field where residents of the capital gather in the

---

KITE FLYING

Flying intricate and colourful **kites** is now done mostly for fun in Thailand, but it has its roots in more serious activities. Filled with gunpowder and fitted with long fuses, kites were deployed in the first Thai kingdom at Sukhothai (1240–1438) as machines of war. In the same era, special *ngao* kites, with heads in the shape of bamboo bows, were used in Brahmin rituals: the string of the bow would vibrate in the wind and make a noise to frighten away evil spirits (nowadays noisy kites are still used, though only by farmers, to scare the birds). By the height of the Ayutthayan period (1351–1767) kites had become largely decorative: royal ceremonies were enhanced by fantastically shaped kites, adorned with jingling bells and ornamental lamps.

In the nineteenth century, Rama V, by his enthusiastic lead, popularized kite flying as a wholesome and fashionable recreation. **Contests** are now held all over the country between February and April, when winds are strong enough and farmers traditionally have free time after harvesting the rice. These contests fall into two broad categories: those involving manoeuvrable flat kites, often in the shapes of animals; and those in which the beauty of static display kites is judged. The most popular contest of all, which comes under the first category, matches two teams, one flying star-shaped *chulas*, 2m-high "male" kites, the other flying the smaller, more agile *pakpaos*, diamond-shaped "females". Each team uses its skill and teamwork to ensnare the other's kites and drag them back across a dividing line.

early evening to meet, eat and play. On its western side and spreading around Thammasat University and Wat Mahathat, especially on Sundays, scores of small-time hawkers sell amulets (see box, p.72), taking advantage of the spiritually auspicious location. In the early part of the year, especially in March, the sky is filled with **kite-fighting** contests (see box below).

The field is also the venue for national ceremonies, such as **royal cremations**, when huge, intricate, wooden *meru* or *phra mane* (funeral pyres) are constructed, representing Mount Meru, the Himalayan centre of the Hindu-Buddhist universe; and the **Ploughing Ceremony**, held in May at a time selected by astrologers to bring good fortune and rain to the coming rice harvest. Revived in 1960 to boost the status of the monarchy during the Cold War, the elaborate Brahmin ceremony is led by an official from the Ministry of Agriculture, who stands in for the king in case the royal power were to be reduced by any failure in the ritual. At the designated time, the official cuts a series of circular furrows with a plough drawn by two white oxen, and scatters rice from the king's experimental crop station at Chitrlada Palace, which has been sprinkled with lustral water by the Brahmin priests of the court. When the ritual is over, spectators rush in to grab handfuls of the rice, which they then plant in their own paddies for good luck.

The lak muang

Thanon Rajdamnoen Nai, southeast corner of Sanam Luang

At 6.54am on April 21, 1782 – the astrologically determined time for the auspicious founding of Bangkok – a pillar containing the city's horoscope was ceremonially driven into the ground opposite the northeast corner of the Grand Palace. This phallic pillar, the **lak muang** – all Thai cities have one, to provide a home for their guardian spirits – was made from a 4m tree trunk carved with a lotus-shaped crown. In the nineteenth century, Rama IV had a new, shorter *lak muang* made, and the two pillars now amicably cohabit in an elegant shrine surrounded by immaculate gardens.

Hundreds of worshippers come every day to pray and offer flowers, particularly childless couples seeking the gift of fertility. In one corner of the gardens you can often see short performances of **classical dancing**, paid for by well-off families when they have a piece of good fortune to celebrate.

Silpakorn University Art Centre

Thanon Na Phra Lan, directly across the road from the entrance to the Grand Palace • Mon–Fri 9am–7pm, Sat 9am–4pm • Free • ☎ 02 623 6115 ext 11418 or 11419, ⓦ www.art-centre.su.ac.th

Housed partly in the throne hall of a palace built during the reign of Rama I, the **Silpakorn University Art Centre** stages regular exhibitions by students, teachers, artists-in-residence and national artists. The country's first art school, Silpakorn was founded in 1935 by Professor Silpa Bhirasri, the much-revered, naturalized Italian sculptor; a charming, shady garden along the east wall of the art centre is dotted with his sculptures.

Wat Mahathat

Main entrance on Thanon Maharat, plus a back entrance on Thanon Na Phra That on Sanam Luang

Eighteenth-century **Wat Mahathat** provides a welcome respite from the surrounding tourist hype, and a chance to engage with the eager monks studying at **Mahachulalong-korn Buddhist University** here. The wat buzzes with purpose; it's the most important centre of Buddhist learning in Southeast Asia, the nation's centre for the Mahanikai monastic sect (where Rama IV spent many years as a monk before becoming king in 1851), and houses one of the two Buddhist universities in Bangkok. It's this activity,

1

and the chance of interaction and participation, rather than any special architectural features, that make a visit so rewarding. The many university-attending monks at the wat are friendly and keen to practise their English, and are more than likely to approach you: diverting topics might range from the poetry of Dylan Thomas to English football results.

Vipassana Meditation Centre

Section Five, Wat Mahathat • Practice daily 7–11am, 1–4pm & 6–8/9pm • Donations welcome • ☎ 02 222 6011 or ☎ 02 222 4981

At the wat's **Vipassana Meditation Centre**, where the monk teachers speak some English, sitting and walking meditation practice, with chanting and dhamma talks, is available (there's now a competing "Meditation Study and Retreat Center", nearby in Section One of the wat, but this is less geared towards foreign meditators). Participants generally stay in the simple surroundings of the meditation building itself, and must wear white clothes (available to rent at the centre) and observe the eight main Buddhist precepts (see p.208).

The National Museum

Thanon Na Phra That, northwest corner of Sanam Luang • Wed–Sun 9am–4pm, some rooms may close at lunchtime; free English guided tours Wed & Thurs 9.30am; usually some rooms are closed for restoration, as advertised at the ticket office • B200 • ☎ 02 224 1333

The **National Museum** houses a colossal hoard of Thailand's chief artistic riches, ranging from sculptural treasures in the north and south wings, through bizarre decorative objects in the older buildings, to outlandish funeral chariots and the exquisite Buddhaisawan chapel, as well as sometimes staging worthwhile temporary exhibitions. It's worth making time for the free guided tours in English run by the National Museum Volunteers (who also organize interesting lectures and excursions; ⓦwww.museumvolunteersbkk.net): they're generally entertaining and their explication of the choicest exhibits provides a good introduction to Thai religion and culture. There's also a restaurant inside the museum grounds, by the funeral chariots building, which dishes up decent, inexpensive Thai food.

History building

The first building you'll come to near the ticket office houses an overview of the authorized history of Thailand, including a small archeological gem: a black stone **inscription**, credited to King Ramkhamhaeng of Sukhothai, which became the first capital of the Thai nation (c.1278–99) under his rule. Discovered in 1833 by the future Rama IV, Mongkut, it's the oldest extant inscription using the Thai alphabet. This, combined with the description it records of prosperity and piety in Sukhothai's Golden Age, has made the stone a symbol of Thai nationhood. There's recently been much controversy over the stone's origins, arising from the suggestion that it was a fake made by Mongkut, but it seems most likely that it is indeed genuine, and was written partly as a kind of prospectus for Sukhothai, to attract traders and settlers to the underpopulated kingdom.

The main collection: southern building

At the back of the compound, two large modern buildings, flanking an old converted palace, house the museum's **main collection**, kicking off on the ground floor of the **southern building**. Look out here for some historic sculptures from the rest of Asia (S1), including one of the earliest representations of the Buddha, from Gandhara in modern-day Pakistan. Alexander the Great left a garrison at Gandhara, which explains why the image is in the style of Classical Greek sculpture: for example, the *ushnisha*, the supernatural bump on the top of the head, which symbolizes the Buddha's intellectual and spiritual power, is rationalized into a bun of thick, wavy hair.

Upstairs, the **prehistory** room (S6) displays axe heads and spear points from Ban Chiang in the northeast of Thailand, one of the earliest Bronze Age cultures ever discovered. Alongside are many roughly contemporaneous metal artefacts from Kanchanaburi province, as well as some excellent examples of the developments of Ban Chiang's famous pottery. In the adjacent **Dvaravati** room (S7; sixth to eleventh centuries), the pick of the stone and terracotta Buddhas is a small head in smooth, pink clay from Wat Phra Ngam, Nakhon Pathom, whose downcast eyes and faintly smiling full lips typify the serene look of this era. At the far end of the first floor, you can't miss a voluptuous Javanese statue of elephant-headed Ganesh, Hindu god of wisdom and the arts, which, being the symbol of the Fine Arts Department, is always freshly garlanded. As Ganesh is known as the clearer of obstacles, Hindus always worship him before other gods, so by tradition he has grown fat through getting first choice of the offerings – witness his trunk jammed into a bowl of food in this sculpture.

Room S9 next door contains the most famous piece of **Srivijaya** art (seventh to thirteenth centuries), a bronze Bodhisattva Padmapani found at Chaiya (according to Mahayana Buddhism, a *bodhisattva* is a saint who has postponed his passage into Nirvana to help ordinary believers gain enlightenment). With its pouting face and lithe torso, this image has become the ubiquitous emblem of southern Thailand. The rough chronological order of the collection continues back downstairs with an exhibition of **Khmer** and **Lopburi** sculpture (seventh to fourteenth centuries), most notably some dynamic bronze statuettes and stone lintels. Look out for an elaborate lintel from Ku Suan Tang, Buriram (S3), which depicts Vishnu reclining on the dragon Ananta in the sea of eternity, dreaming up a new universe after the old one has been annihilated in the Hindu cycle of creation and destruction. Out of his navel comes a lotus, and out of this emerges four-headed Brahma, who will put the dream into practice.

The main collection: northern building

The second half of the survey, in the northern building, begins upstairs with the **Sukhothai** collection (thirteenth to fifteenth centuries; N7–8), which features some typically elegant and sinuous Buddha images, as well as chunky bronzes of Hindu gods and a wide range of ceramics. The **Lanna** rooms (roughly thirteenth to sixteenth centuries; N5–6) include a miniature set of golden regalia, among them tiny umbrellas and a cute pair of filigree flip-flops, which would have been enshrined in a chedi. An ungainly but serene Buddha head, carved from grainy, pink sandstone, represents the **Ayutthaya** style of sculpture (fourteenth to eighteenth centuries; N9–10): the faintest incision of a moustache above the lips betrays the Khmer influences that came to Ayutthaya after its conquest of Angkor. A sumptuous scripture cabinet, showing a cityscape of old Ayutthaya, is a more unusual piece, one of a surviving handful of such carved and painted items of furniture.

Downstairs in the section on **Bangkok** or **Ratanakosin** art (eighteenth century onwards; N1), a stiffly realistic standing bronze brings you full circle. In his zeal for Western naturalism, Rama V had the statue made in the Gandhara style of the earliest Buddha image displayed in the first room of the museum.

The funeral chariots

To the east of the northern building, beyond the café on the left, stands a large garage where the fantastically elaborate **funeral chariots** of the royal family are stored. Pre-eminent among these is the Royal Chariot of Great Victory, built by Rama I in about 1789 for carrying the urn at his father's funeral. The 11m-high structure symbolizes heaven on Mount Meru, while the dragons and divinities around the sides – piled in five golden tiers to suggest the flames of the cremation – represent the mythological inhabitants of the mountain's forests. Each weighing

1

around forty tonnes and requiring the pulling power of three hundred men, the teak chariots last had an outing in 2012, for the funeral of the only child of Rama VI, Princess Bejaratana.

Wang Na (Palace of the Second King)

The sprawling central building of the compound was originally part of the **Wang Na**, a huge palace stretching across Sanam Luang to Khlong Lod, which housed the "second king", appointed by the reigning monarch as his heir and deputy. When Rama V did away with the office in 1887, he turned the palace into a museum, which now contains a fascinating array of Thai objets d'art. As you enter (room 5), the display of sumptuous rare gold pieces behind heavy iron bars includes a well-preserved armlet taken from the ruined prang of fifteenth-century Wat Ratburana in Ayutthaya. In adjacent room 6, an intricately carved ivory seat turns out, with gruesome irony, to be a *howdah*, for use on an elephant's back. Among the masks worn by *khon* actors next door (room 7), look out especially for a fierce Hanuman, the white monkey-warrior in the *Ramayana* epic, gleaming with mother-of-pearl.

The huge and varied ceramic collection in room 8 includes some sophisticated pieces from Sukhothai, while the room behind (9) holds a riot of mother-of-pearl items, whose flaming rainbow of colours comes from the shell of the turbo snail from the Gulf of Thailand. It's also worth seeking out the display of richly decorated musical instruments in room 15.

The Buddhaisawan chapel

The second-holiest image in Thailand, after the Emerald Buddha, is housed in the **Buddhaisawan chapel**, the vast hall in front of the eastern entrance to the Wang Na. Inside, the fine proportions of the hall, with its ornate coffered ceiling and lacquered window shutters, are enhanced by painted rows of divinities and converted demons, all turned to face the chubby, glowing **Phra Sihing Buddha**, which according to legend was magically created in Sri Lanka in the second century and sent to Sukhothai in the thirteenth century. Like the Emerald Buddha, the image was believed to bring good luck to its owner and was frequently snatched from one northern town to another, until Rama I brought it down from Chiang Mai in 1795 and installed it here in the second king's private chapel. Two other images (in Nakhon Si Thammarat and Chiang Mai) now claim to be the authentic Phra Sihing Buddha, but all three are in fact derived from a lost original – this one is in a fifteenth-century Sukhothai style. It's still much loved by ordinary people and at Thai New Year in April is carried out to the nearby City Hall, where it sits for three days while worshippers sprinkle it with water as a merit-making gesture.

The careful detail and rich, soothing colours of the surrounding two-hundred-year-old **murals** are surprisingly well preserved; the bottom row between the windows narrates the life of the Buddha, beginning in the far right-hand corner with his parents' wedding.

Tamnak Daeng

On the south side of the Buddhaisawan chapel, the gaudily restored **Tamnak Daeng** (Red House) stands out, a large, airy Ayutthaya-style house made of rare golden teak, surmounted by a multi-tiered roof decorated with swan's-tail finials. Originally part of the private quarters of Princess Sri Sudarak, elder sister of Rama I, it was moved from the Grand Palace to the old palace in Thonburi for Queen Sri Suriyen, wife of Rama II; when her son became second king to Rama IV, he dismantled the edifice again and shipped it here to the Wang Na compound. Inside, it's furnished in the style of the early Bangkok period, with some of the beautiful objects that once belonged to Sri Suriyen, a huge, ornately carved box-bed, and the uncommon luxury of an indoor bathroom.

The National Gallery

4 Thanon Chao Fa, across from the National Theatre on the north side of Sanam Luang • Wed–Sun 9am–4pm • B200 • ☎ 02 281 2224, ⓦ ngbangkok.wordpress.com

If wandering around Bangkok's National Museum doesn't finish you off, the **National Gallery** nearby probably will. In its upstairs gallery, it displays some rather beautiful early twentieth-century temple banners depicting Buddhist subjects, but the permanent collection of twentieth-century Thai art downstairs is largely uninspiring and derivative. Its temporary exhibitions can be pretty good, however. The fine old building that houses the gallery is also worth more than a cursory glance – it was constructed in typical early twentieth-century, Neoclassical style, by Carlo Allegri, Rama V's court architect, as the Royal Mint.

THANON KHAO SAN

Banglamphu and the Democracy Monument area

Best known as the site of the travellers' hub Thanon Khao San, the Banglamphu district, immediately north of Ratanakosin, has some noteworthy temples and still boasts a number of wooden shophouses and narrow alleyways alongside the purpose-built guesthouses, travel agents and jewellery shops. But the most interesting sights in this part of the city are found in the charmingly old-fashioned neighbourhoods to the south and east of the huge stone Democracy Monument, which forms the centrepiece of an enormous roundabout that siphons traffic from the Rajdamnoen Klang artery.

Most of these old neighbourhoods are within walking distance of the Khao San guesthouses and equally accessible from the Grand Palace; their proximity to the royal district means they retain a traditional flavour, unsullied by high-rise architecture. The string of temple-supply shops around Wat Suthat and Sao Ching Cha makes Thanon Bamrung Muang a rewarding area to explore, there are some great traditional food shops along Thanon Tanao, and the amulet market in the grounds of Wat Rajnadda is also worth seeking out.

ARRIVAL AND DEPARTURE   BANGLAMPHU AND THE DEMOCRACY MONUMENT AREA

2

By boat This is the fastest and least stressful way of getting here. There are Chao Phraya express-boat stops in the area: N13 (Phra Arthit), a few hundred metres west of Thanon Khao San; N14 (Rama VIII Bridge), at the western end of Samsen Soi 5; and N15 (Thewet), at the west end of Thanon Krung Kasem. Banglamphu is also served by public boats along Khlong Saen Saeb to and from their Phan Fah terminus near the Golden Mount; their Tha Saphan Hua Chang stop, which is a few minutes' walk from Siam Square and the Ratchathewi and Siam Skytrain stops, is especially useful.

By Skytrain In addition to connecting to the Skytrain via Khlong Saen Saeb boat, the other fast way to get on to the BTS system is to take a taxi from Banglamphu to BTS National Stadium.

By bus For access from anywhere else you can make use of the city bus network: Democracy Monument is served by buses from all parts of the city and is a landmark hard to miss; if you're coming from eastern or northern parts of the city (such as Hualamphong Station, Siam Square or Sukhumvit), get off the bus as soon as you see it rather than waiting for Rajdamnoen Klang's more westerly stop outside the *Royal Ratanakosin Hotel*, where it's almost impossible to cross the multiple lanes of traffic.

Banglamphu

Banglamphu's primary attraction is the legendary **Thanon Khao San**, a tiny sliver of a road no more than 400m long, which was built over a canal in 1892 and is now established as *the* backpackers' hub of Southeast Asia. Crammed with guest-houses and restaurants serving yoghurt shakes and muesli, its sidewalks lined with tattooists and hair-braiders, it's a lively, high-energy place that's fun to visit even if you're not staying here – the area is a cultural curiosity in its own right, a unique and continually evolving expression of global youth culture fuelled by Thai entrepreneurship. Cheap clothes, jewellery and handicrafts are all good buys here (little is top quality on Khao San, but vendors are quick to pick up on global trends)

BANGLAMPHU'S BUS STOPS AND ROUTES

The main bus stops serving Banglamphu are on Thanon Rajdamnoen Klang: with nearly thirty westbound and eastbound routes, you can get just about anywhere in the city from here. But there are some other useful pick-up points in Banglamphu for routes running out of the area. To make things simpler, we've assigned numbers to these **bus stops**, though they are not numbered on the ground. Where there are two stops served by the same buses they share a number. Bus stops are marked on the Banglamphu map (see p.66).

Bus Stop 1: Thanon Krung Kasem, north side
#53 (clockwise) to Hualamphong train station

Bus Stop 2: Thanon Phra Sumen, south side; and Thanon Phra Arthit, east side
#53 (anticlockwise) to the Grand Palace and Chinatown

Bus Stop 3: Thanon Phra Arthit, west side; and Thanon Phra Sumen, north side
#3 to Chatuchak Weekend Market and Northern Bus Terminal
#53 (clockwise) to Hualamphong train station (change at Bus Stop 1, but same ticket)

Bus Stop 4: Thanon Chakrabongse
#3 to Wat Pho, the Museum of Siam, Pak Khlong Talat and Wongwian Yai train station
#15 to Jim Thompson's House, Siam Square and Thanon Silom

Bus Stop 5: Thanon Rajinee (Rachini)
#124 to Southern Bus Terminal

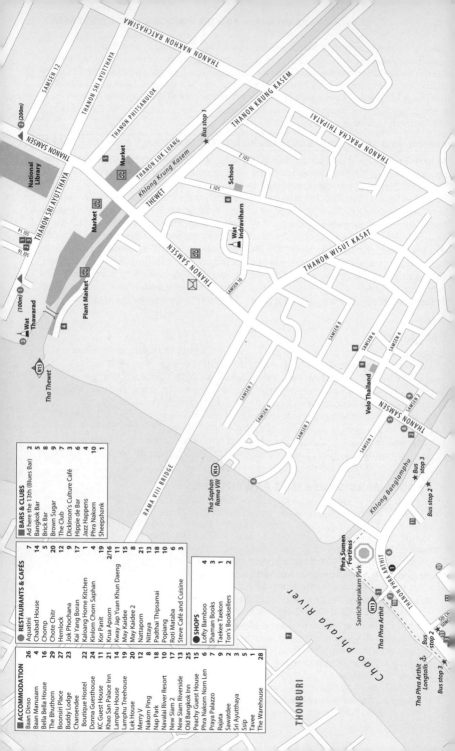

ACCOMMODATION
Baan Dinso	26
Baan Manusarn	4
Bella Bella House	16
The Bhuthorn	29
Boonsin Place	27
Buddy Lodge	23
Charoendee	
Boutique Hostel	22
Donna Guesthouse	24
KC Guest House	11
Khao San Palace Inn	21
Lamphu House	14
Lamphu Treehouse	19
Lek House	20
Merry V	12
Nakorn Ping	8
Nap Park	18
Navalai River Resort	10
New Siam 2	17
New Siam Riverside	13
Old Bangkok Inn	25
Peachy Guest House	15
Phra Nakorn Norn Len	6
Praya Palazzo	7
Rajata	9
Sawatdee	2
Sri Ayutthaya	3
Ssip	5
Tavee	1
The Warehouse	28

● RESTAURANTS & CAFÉS
Aquatini	7
Chabad House	14
Chomp	5
Chote Chitr	20
Hemlock	12
Jok Phochana	9
Kai Yang Boran	17
Kaloang Home Kitchen	1
Kinlom Chom Saphan	4
Kor Panit	19
Krua Apsorn	2/16
Kway Jap Yuan Khun Daeng	11
May Kaidee	15
May Kaidee 2	8
Nattaporn	21
Nittaya	13
Padthai Thipsamai	18
Poplang	10
Roti Mataba	6
Steve Café and Cuisine	3

■ BARS & CLUBS
Ad here the 13th (Blues Bar)	2
Bangkok Bar	5
Brick Bar	8
Brown Sugar	9
The Club	7
Dickinson's Culture Café	3
Hippie de Bar	6
Jazz Happens	4
Phra Nakorn	10
Sheepshank	1

● SHOPS
Lofty Bamboo	4
Shaman Books	3
Taekee Taekon	1
Ton's Booksellers	2

BANGLAMPHU AND THE DEMOCRACY MONUMENT AREA

0   200

metres

King Prajadhipok (Rama VII) Museum

LAN LUANG

DAMRONG RAK

Tha Phan Foh

Khlong Saen Saeb

Golden Mount & Wat Saket

THANON RATCHADAMNOEN NOK

NAKHORN SAWAN

THANON BORIPHAT

Khlong Ong Ang

Phra Mahakhan Fortress Community

THANON MAHACHAI

Queen's Gallery

THANON PHRA SUMEN

Loha Prasat

RAJDAMNOEN KLANG

Wat Rajnadda

THANON PRACHA TIPATAI

THANON DINSO

Democracy Monument

THANON DINSO

City Hall

Sao Ching Cha

THANON MAHANNOP

THANON BAMRUNG MUANG

Wat Suthat

THANON PHRA SUMEN

Wat Bowonives

THANON BOWONNIWET

THANON TANI

SOI SIBSAN

P.O.

Ratchadamnoen P.O.

DAMNOEN KLANG NEUA

Bus stop 7

Lomprayah

THANON TANAO

TROK SIN

Temple Supplies

TROK NAWA

THANON TANAO

Wat Rajbophit

THANON BAM BHU TRI

Pian's

ETC

THANON KHAO SAN

RAJDAMNOEN KLANG

DAMNOEN KLANG NEUA

SOI DAMNOEN KLANG TAI

THANON TANAO

BUNSRI

THANON PHRARONG PHUTON

THANON KANLAYANA MAITRI

TROK MATOM

DAMNOEN KLANG TAI

THANON BURANASIT

San Chao Poh Seua

Police Station

True

Bus stop 6

ATS

TROK SA-KE

THANON ATSADANG

THANON ATSADANG

Royal Rattanakosin Hotel

Minibuses to Kanchanaburi

Bus stop 6

Night Market

THANON CHAKRABONGSE

Sor Vorapin's Gym

Olavi Travel

National Gallery

CHAO FA

PHINKLAO BRIDGE

RAJINEE

Bus stop 5

National Theatre

National Museum

Thammasat University

Mae Toranee statue

THANON RAJDAMNOEN NAI

Lak Muang

THANON LAK MUANG

Sanam Luang

THANON NA PHRA THAT

Wat Mahathat

N

Express-boat pier

Khlong Saen Saeb boat stop

and it's also a good spot to organize onward travel – bearing in mind the innumerable Khao San scams (see p.37).

Though ultra budget-conscious world travellers are still Khao San's main customers, Banglamphu attracts higher-spending sophisticates to its growing number of **stylish restaurants** and **lively bars and clubs**. At night, young Thais from all over the city gather here to browse the fashion stalls and pavement displays set up by local art students, mingling with the crowds of foreigners and squashing into the trendy bars and clubs that have made Khao San one of the city's most happening places to party (see p.169). Banglamphu boasts a surprising range of eating places too, from bohemian Thai restaurants located on Thanon Phra Athit to famous traditional shophouses on Thanon Tanao (see p.159).

Wat Chana Songkhram
Thanon Chakrabongse

Sandwiched between Thanon Khao San and the Chao Phraya River, at the heart of the Banglamphu backpackers' ghetto, stands the lusciously renovated eighteenth-century **Wat Chana Songkhram**. As with temples throughout the country, the compound doubles as general-purpose neighbourhood yard; beside a knot of stalls selling secondhand books and travellers' clothes, a stream of tourists cuts through the wat en route between the river and Khao San. It's worth slowing down for a closer look, though: the bot's roof gables are beautifully ornate, embossed with a golden relief of Vishnu astride Garuda, enmeshed in an intricate design of red and blue glass mosaics, and the golden finials are shaped like nagas. Peeking over the compound walls onto the guesthouses and bars of Soi Ram Bhuttri is a row of *kuti*, or monks' quarters: simple, elegant wooden cabins on stilts with steeply pitched roofs.

Thanon Phra Athit

Thanon Phra Athit, the Banglamphu road that runs alongside the (mostly obscured) Chao Phraya River, is known for its arty atmosphere and numerous little bar-restaurants that draw crowds of students from nearby Thammasat University. Many of these places open only at night, but some serve passing tourists during the day. There are also a few shops selling unusual Thai crafts and art-photocards towards the northern end of the road.

This northern stretch of Thanon Phra Athit is dominated by the crenellated whitewashed tower of **Phra Sumen Fortress** (also known as Phra Sumeru), a renovated corner of the original eighteenth-century city walls that stands beside the river and its juncture with Khlong Banglamphu. The fortress was the northernmost of fourteen octagonal towers built by Rama I in 1783 to protect the royal island of Ratanakosin – the only other surviving tower, also renovated, is Phra Mahakhan Fortress, next to the Golden Mount (see p.71). The Phra Sumen Fortress originally contained 38 rooms for storing ammunition but now there's nothing to see inside the tower. However, it makes a striking landmark and the area around it has been turned into a pleasant grassy riverside recreation area, **Santichaiprakarn Park**, with English-language signs describing the history of the fortifications. A park sign also highlights one of the area's last remaining lamphu trees (*duabanga grandiflora*), which continues to grow in a muddy pool on the edge of the river to the left of the royal *sala*. Lamphu trees were once so common in this neighbourhood that they gave the area its name – Banglamphu means "the place with lamphu trees" – though they have all but disappeared now.

The riverside walkway

Phra Sumen Fortress marks the northernmost limit of a **riverside walkway** that runs down to Phra Pinklao Bridge. The walkway provides a good view of the boats and barges on the Chao Phraya and takes you past the front entrances of two very grand and beautifully restored buildings, both currently occupied by international organizations. The United Nations' Food and Agriculture Organization (FAO) uses the early twentieth-century mansion known as **Baan Maliwan** as its library (closed to casual visitors), while the nearby UNICEF office is housed in the late nineteenth-century palace of one of the wives of Rama IV, which also served as the headquarters of the clandestine Seri Thai resistance movement during World War II. Both mansions show their most elegant faces to the river as visitors would have arrived by boat. On the eastern side of Thanon Phra Arhit, there's another fine early twentieth-century mansion, **Baan Phra Athit**, at number 201/1.

2

Wat Indraviharn
Thanon Wisut Kasat, about 20min walk north of Khao San • 10min walk from Chao Phraya express-boat stops N14 and N15

Though it can't match the graceful serenity of Ratanakosin's enormous Reclining Buddha at Wat Pho, Banglamphu has its own super-sized Standing Buddha at **Wat Indraviharn** (also spelt Wat Intharawihan or Wat In), a glittering 32m-high mirror-plated statue of the Buddha bearing an alms bowl. Commissioned by Rama IV in the mid-nineteenth century to enshrine a Buddha relic from Sri Lanka (in the topknot), it's hardly the most elegant of images, but the 30cm-long toenails peep out beneath offertory garlands of fragrant jasmine, and you can get reasonable views of the neighbourhood by climbing the stairways of the supporting tower; when unlocked, the doorways in the upper tower give access to the statue's hollow interior, affording vistas from shoulder level. The rest of the temple compound features the usual amalgam of architectural and spiritual styles, including a Chinese shrine and statues of Ramas IV and V.

Unfortunately, Wat Indraviharn is an established hangout for **con-artists** offering tourists a tuk-tuk tour of Bangkok for a bargain B20, which invariably features a hard-sell visit to a jewellery shop (see p.190). Avoid all these hassles by hailing a passing metered taxi instead, or by catching one of the dozens of buses that run along Thanon Samsen.

Democracy Monument and around
The megalithic yellow-tinged wings of **Democracy Monument** (*Anu Sawari Pracha Tippatai*) loom provocatively over Thanon Rajdamnoen Klang, the avenue that connects the Grand Palace and the new royal district of Dusit, and have since their erection in 1939 acted as a focus for pro-democracy rallies. Conceived as a testimony to the ideals that fuelled the 1932 revolution and the changeover to a constitutional monarchy, the monument's positioning between the royal residences is significant, as are its dimensions, which allude to June 24, 2475 BE (1932 AD), the date the system was changed. In the decades since, Thailand's leaders have promulgated numerous interim charters and constitutions, the more repressive and regressive of which have been vigorously challenged in demonstrations on these very streets.

THE OCTOBER 14 MEMORIAL
One of the biggest and most notorious demonstrations around the Democracy Monument was the fateful student-led protest of October 14, 1973, when half a million people gathered on Rajdamnoen Klang to demand an end to the autocratic regime of the so-called "Three Tyrants". It was savagely quashed and turned into a bloody riot that culminated in the death of several hundred protesters at the hands of the police and the military; the Three Tyrants were forced into exile and a new coalition government was soon formed. After three decades of procrastination, the events of this catastrophic day were finally commemorated with the erection of the **October 14 Memorial**, a small granite amphitheatre encircling an elegant modern chedi bearing the names of some of the dead; photographs and a bilingual account of the ten-day protest fill the back wall. The memorial stands in front of the former headquarters of Colonel Narong Kittikachorn, one of the Three Tyrants, 200m west of Democracy Monument, at the corner of Rajdamnoen Klang and Thanon Tanao.

2

Thanon Tanao

A stroll down **Thanon Tanao** brings you into some engagingly old-fashioned neighbourhoods of nineteenth-century wooden shophouses, which are especially famous for their specialist **traditional Thai foods**. Many of these places have been making their specialities for generations, and there are all sorts of fun things to browse here, even if you're not inclined to taste, from beef noodles to pigs' brain soup, home-made ice cream to sticky rice with mango. If you are after some recommendations on what to eat, the *Good Eats Ratanakosin* map (published by Pan Siam Publishing and available in major bookshops) is an exhaustive survey, which is especially handy given that few of these places have English-language signs or shop numbers.

The area around the south end of Thanon Tanao is also sometimes referred to as **Sao Ching Cha** (see below), after the **Giant Swing**, which is easily reached either by following any of the eastbound lanes off Tanao to Thanon Dinso, or by browsing the Buddhist paraphernalia stalls that take you there via Thanon Bamrung Muang. Alternatively, if you continue to walk one block south along Tanao you'll reach the lovely little temple of Wat Rajabophit.

San Chao Poh Seua

Thanon Tanao • Daily 6am–5pm, till 9pm during the Vegetarian Festival (see p.158) • Free

Not far south of Thanon Rajdamnoen Klang sits **San Chao Poh Seua**, the **Tiger God Shrine**, an atmospheric, incense-filled Taoist shrine honouring the Chinese tiger guardian spirit and the God of the North Stars, whose image graces the centre of the main altar. It's a favourite with Chinese-Thais who come here to pray for power, prestige and successful pregnancy and offer in return pork rashers, fresh eggs, sticky rice, bottles of oil and sugar tigers.

Wat Rajabophit

Thanon Rajabophit, one block south of the Tanao/Bamrung Muang intersection, just to the east of Khlong Lod (see map, p.50)

One of Bangkok's prettiest temples, **Wat Rajabophit** is another example of the Chinese influence in this neighbourhood. It was built by Rama V in 1869–70 and, typical of him, is unusual in its design, particularly the circular cloister that encloses a chedi and links the rectangular bot and viharn. Every external wall in the compound is covered in the pastel shades of Chinese *bencharong* ceramic tiles, creating a stunning overall effect, while the bot interior looks like a tiny banqueting hall, with gilded Gothic vaults and intricate mother-of-pearl doors.

Thanon Bamrung Muang

Thanon Bamrung Muang, which runs east from Thanon Tanao to Sao Ching Cha and Wat Suthat, was an old elephant trail that, a hundred years ago, became one of the first paved streets in Bangkok. It's famous as the best place in Thailand to buy **Buddhist paraphernalia**, or *sanghapan*, and is well worth a browse. The road is lined with shops selling everything a good Buddhist might need, from household offertory tables to temple umbrellas and cellophane-wrapped Buddha images up to 2m high. They also sell special alms packs for donating to monks, which typically come in saffron-coloured plastic buckets (used by monks for washing their robes, or themselves), and include such necessities as soap, toothpaste, soap powder, toilet roll, candles and incense.

Sao Ching Cha

Midway along Thanon Bamrung Muang, just in front of Wat Suthat

You can't miss the towering, red-painted teak posts of **Sao Ching Cha**, otherwise known as the **Giant Swing**. This strange contraption was once the focal point of a Brahmin ceremony to honour the Hindu god Shiva's annual visit to Earth, in which teams of young men competed to swing up to a height of 25m and grab a suspended bag of gold with their teeth. The act of swinging probably symbolized the rising and setting of the sun, though legend also has it that Shiva and his consort Uma were banned from swinging in heaven because doing so caused cataclysmic floods on Earth – prompting Shiva to demand that the practice be continued on Earth to ensure moderate rains and bountiful harvests. Accidents were so common with the terrestrial version that it was outlawed in the 1930s.

Wat Suthat
Thanon Bamrung Muang • Daily 8.30am–4pm • B20

Wat Suthat is one of Thailand's six most important temples, built in the early nineteenth century to house the 8m-high statue of the meditating **Phra Sri Sakyamuni Buddha**, which is said to date from 1361 and was brought all the way down from Sukhothai by river. It now sits on a glittering mosaic dais, which contains some of the ashes of Rama VIII, the elder brother of the current king, surrounded with surreal murals that depict the last 24 lives of the Buddha rather than the more usual ten. The encircling galleries contain 156 serenely posed Buddha images, making a nice contrast to the **Chinese statues** dotted around the temple courtyards, most of which were brought over from China during Rama I's reign, as ballast in rice boats; there are some fun character studies among them, including gormless Western sailors and pompous Chinese scholars.

Wat Rajnadda
5min walk east of Democracy Monument, at the point where Rajdamnoen Klang meets Thanon Mahachai • **Loha Prasat** Daily 9am–5pm • Free

Among the assortment of religious buildings known collectively as **Wat Rajnadda**, the most striking is the multi-tiered, castle-like, early nineteenth-century **Loha Prasat**, or "Iron Monastery", whose 37 forbidding metal spires represent the 37 virtues necessary for attaining enlightenment. Modelled on a Sri Lankan monastery, its tiers are pierced by passageways running north–south and east–west (fifteen in each direction at ground level), with small meditation cells at each point of intersection.

Wat Rajnadda Buddha Centre
In the southeast (Thanon Mahachai) corner of the temple compound, Bangkok's biggest **amulet market**, the **Wat Rajnadda Buddha Centre**, comprises at least a hundred stalls selling tiny Buddha images of all designs. Alongside these miniature charms (see box, p.72) are statues of Hindu deities, dolls and carved wooden phalluses, also bought to placate or ward off disgruntled spirits, as well as love potions and CDs of sacred music.

Phra Mahakhan Fortress community
Thanon Mahachai

The **Phra Mahakhan Fortress community**, across the road from Wat Rajnadda, occupies the land between the whitewashed crenellations of the renovated eighteenth-century city walls and Khlong Ong Ang. It's a historic, working-class neighbourhood where some of the houses date from the early nineteenth century, and has been the object of a recent urban renovation programme. It now welcomes visitors with informative signboards describing some of its traditions, including massage therapy, fish bladder soup and *likay* popular theatre. In the block of shops on Thanon Mahachai, immediately south of the crenellations, are a famous traditional Thai perfume shop and several places specializing in Thai and Chinese antiques.

Wat Saket
Easiest access is along Thanon Boriphat (the specialist street for custom-carved wooden doors), 5min walk south from the khlong bridge and Phan Fah canal-boat stop at the eastern end of Rajdamnoen Klang

Beautifully illuminated at night, when it seems to float unsupported above the neighbourhood, the gleaming gold chedi of late eighteenth-century **Wat Saket** actually

2

AMULETS

To invite good fortune, ward off malevolent spirits and gain protection from physical harm, many Thais wear or carry at least one **amulet** at all times. The most popular images are copies of sacred statues from famous wats, while others show revered monks, kings (Rama V is a favourite) or healers. On the reverse side, a yantra is often inscribed, a combination of letters and figures also designed to deflect evil, sometimes of a very specific nature: protecting your durian orchards from gales, for example, or your tuk-tuk from oncoming traffic. Individually hand-crafted or mass-produced, amulets can be made from bronze, clay, plaster or gold, and some even have sacred ingredients added, such as special herbs, or the ashes of burnt holy texts. But what really determines an amulet's efficacy is its history: where and by whom it was made, who or what it represents and who consecrated it. Stories of miracle cures and lucky escapes also prompt a rush on whatever amulet the survivor was wearing. Monks are often involved in the making of the images and are always called upon to consecrate them – the more charismatic the monk, the more powerful the amulet. Religious authorities take a relaxed view of the amulet industry, despite its anomalous and commercial functions, and proceeds contribute to wat funds and good causes.

The **belief in amulets** is thought to have originated in India, where tiny images were sold to pilgrims who visited the four holy sites associated with the Buddha's life. But not all amulets are Buddhist-related; there's a whole range of other enchanted objects to wear for protection, including tigers' teeth, rose quartz, tamarind seeds, coloured threads and miniature phalluses. Worn around the waist rather than the neck, the phallus amulets provide protection for the genitals as well as being associated with fertility, and are of Hindu origin.

For some people, amulets are not only a vital form of spiritual protection, but valuable **collectors' items** as well. Amulet-collecting mania is something akin to stamp collecting and there are at least half a dozen Thai magazines for collectors, which give histories of certain types, tips on distinguishing between genuine items and fakes, and personal accounts of particularly powerful amulet experiences. The most rewarding places to watch the collectors and browse the wares yourself are at Wat Rajnadda Buddha Centre (see p.71), the biggest amulet market and probably the best place in Bangkok; along "Amulet Alley" on Trok Mahathat, between Wat Mahathat (see p.59) and the river, where streetside vendors will have cheaper examples; and at Chatuchak Weekend Market (see p.106). Prices start as low as B50 and rise into the thousands.

sits atop a structure known as the **Golden Mount**. Being outside the capital's city walls, the wat initially served as a crematorium and then a dumping ground for sixty thousand plague victims left to the vultures because they couldn't afford funeral pyres. There's no sign of this grim episode at modern-day Wat Saket of course, which these days is a smart, buzzing hive of religious activity at the base of the golden hilltop chedi. Wat Saket hosts an enormous annual **temple fair** in the first week of November, when the mount is illuminated with lanterns and the compound seethes with funfair rides and travelling theatre shows.

The Golden Mount
Daily 8am–5pm • B20

The **Golden Mount**, or **Phu Khao Tong**, dates back to the early nineteenth century, when Rama III commissioned a huge chedi to be constructed here, using building materials from the ruined fortresses and walls of the former capital, Ayutthaya. However, the ground proved too soft to support the chedi. The whole thing collapsed into a hill of rubble, but as Buddhist law states that a religious building can never be destroyed, however tumbledown, fifty years later Rama V simply crowned it with the more sensibly sized chedi we see today, in which he placed some relics of the Buddha's teeth from India, donated by the British government. These days the old rubbly base is picturesquely planted with shrubs and shady trees and dotted with gravestones and memorials. Winding stairways take you up to the chedi terrace and a fine view over

Banglamphu and Ratanakosin landmarks, including the golden spires of the Grand Palace, the finely proportioned prangs of Wat Arun across the river beyond and, further upriver, the striking superstructure of the Rama VIII Bridge.

King Prajadhipok (Rama VII) Museum

Thanon Lan Luang • Tues–Sun 9am–4pm • B40 • ⓦ kingprajadhipokmuseum.org

Appropriately located just 400m east of Democracy Monument, the **King Prajadhipok Museum** exists to "promote democracy", though its mission is tinged with irony: it charts the life of **Rama VII**, a weak king who was in thrall to the old guard of courtiers, but was forced by the coup of 1932 to accept the end of his absolute monarchy and a transition to democratic constitutional monarchy. Situated within the elegant European-style walls of an early twentieth-century former shop, the museum is hardly an unmissable attraction, though its displays are accessible and easy to digest, and offer expansive English-language captions. The section explaining the background to the 1932 revolution is the most important, featuring browsable copies of early drafts of the Constitution and some insight into the exchanges between the king and the committed group of intellectuals behind this radical political change. When this group finally seized power in 1932, Rama VII took the compromise option, later presiding at a ceremony in which the Constitution was officially conferred. It wasn't long, however, before relations between Rama VII and Thailand's new leaders soured, leading to his abdication in 1935. Rama VII was a keen amateur film-maker and he commissioned the building of Thailand's first cinema, the Sala Chalermkrung Theatre (see p.178), in 1933; the museum contains a miniature replica of this movie theatre, where old films from the Rama VII era are screened twice daily, at 10.30am and 2.30pm.

The Queen's Gallery

North across Rajdamnoen Klang from Wat Rajnadda, on the corner of Thanon Phra Sumen • Mon, Tues & Thurs–Sun 10am–7pm • B30 • ⓣ 02 281 5361, ⓦ queengallery.org

The privately funded, five-storey **Queen's Gallery** hosts temporary shows of contemporary Thai art, plus the occasional exhibition by foreign artists, and makes a more stimulating alternative to the rather staid National Gallery down the other end of Rajdamnoen Klang. Its bookshop sells hard-to-find Thai art books.

2

Chinatown and Pahurat

When the newly crowned Rama I decided to move his capital across to the east bank of the river in 1782, the Chinese community living on the proposed site of his palace was obliged to relocate downriver, to the Sampeng area. Two centuries on, Chinatown has grown into the country's largest Chinese district, a sprawl of narrow alleyways, temples and shophouses packed between Charoen Krung (New Road) and the river, separated from Ratanakosin by the Indian area of Pahurat – famous for its cloth and dressmakers' trimmings – and bordered to the east by Hualamphong train station.

The **Chinese influence** on Thai culture and commerce has been significant ever since the first Chinese merchants gained a toehold in Ayutthaya in the fourteenth century. Following centuries of immigration and intermarriage, there is now some Chinese blood in almost every Thai citizen, including the king, and Chinese-Thai business interests play an enormous role in the Thai economy. This is played out at its most frantic in Chinatown, whose real estate is said to be among the most valuable in the country; there are over a hundred gold and jewellery shops along Thanon Yaowarat alone.

For the tourist, Chinatown is chiefly interesting for its **markets**, shophouses, open-fronted warehouses and remnants of colonial-style architecture, though it also harbours a few noteworthy **temples**. A meander through its most interesting neighbourhoods could easily fill up a whole day, allowing for frequent breaks from the thundering traffic and choking fumes. For the most authentic Chinatown experience, it's best to come during the week, as some shops and stalls shut at weekends; on weekdays they begin closing around 5pm, after which time the neighbourhood's other big draw – its **food** – takes centre stage.

3

ARRIVAL AND GETTING AROUND CHINATOWN AND PAHURAT

Arrival The easiest way to reach Chinatown is either by subway to Hualamphong Station, or by Chao Phraya express boat to Tha Rachawongse (Rajawong; N5) at the southern end of Thanon Rajawong. A westward extension of the subway is being built (with a proposed opening in 2017), with new stations at Wat Mangkon Kamalawat and Pahurat. This part of the city is also well served by buses, with Hualamphong a useful and easily recognized place to disembark. Be warned that buses and taxis may take an unexpectedly circuitous route due to the many and complex one-way systems in Chinatown.

Getting around Orientation in Chinatown can be tricky: the alleys (often known as trok rather than the more usual soi) are extremely narrow, their turn-offs and other road signs often obscured by mounds of merchandise and thronging crowds, and the longer ones can change their names several times. For a detailed tour of the alleys and markets, use *Nancy Chandler's Map of Bangkok* (see p.32); alternatively, ask for help at the BMA tourist information booth (Mon–Sat 9am–5pm) just northwest of the Chinese Arch at the beginning of Thanon Yaowarat, beside Soi 5.

Wat Traimit

Thanon Mittaphap Thai-China, just west of Hualamphong train and subway stations (exit 1) • Daily 8am–5pm; exhibitions closed Mon • Golden Buddha only B40; Golden Buddha and exhibitions B100 • Ⓦ wattraimitr-withayaram.com

The obvious place to start a Chinatown tour is on its eastern perimeter, with **Wat Traimit** and its famous Golden Buddha. You can see the temple mondop's golden spire from quite a distance, a fitting beacon for the gleaming treasure housed on its third floor, the world's largest solid-gold Buddha. It's an apt attraction for a community so closely linked with the gold trade, even if the image has nothing to do with China's spiritual heritage. A recent attempt has been made to bridge this gap, with the installation of exhibitions of varying interest on the mondop's first and second floors, covering the history of Chinatown and of the iconic Buddha image.

The Golden Buddha

Over 3m tall and weighing five tonnes, the **Golden Buddha** gleams as if coated in liquid metal, seated on a white marble lotus-pad pedestal and surrounded with offerings of lotus flowers. It's a fine example of the curvaceous grace of Sukhothai art, slim-waisted and beautifully proportioned. Cast in the thirteenth century, the image was brought to Bangkok by Rama III, completely encased in stucco – a common ruse to conceal valuable statues from would-be thieves. The disguise was so good that no one guessed what was underneath until 1955 when the image was accidentally knocked in the process of being moved to Wat Traimit, and the stucco cracked to reveal a patch of gold. Just in time for Buddhism's 2500th anniversary, the discovery launched a country-wide craze for tapping away at plaster Buddhas in search of hidden precious metals, but Wat Traimit's is still the most valuable – it is valued, by weight alone, at over US$10 million.

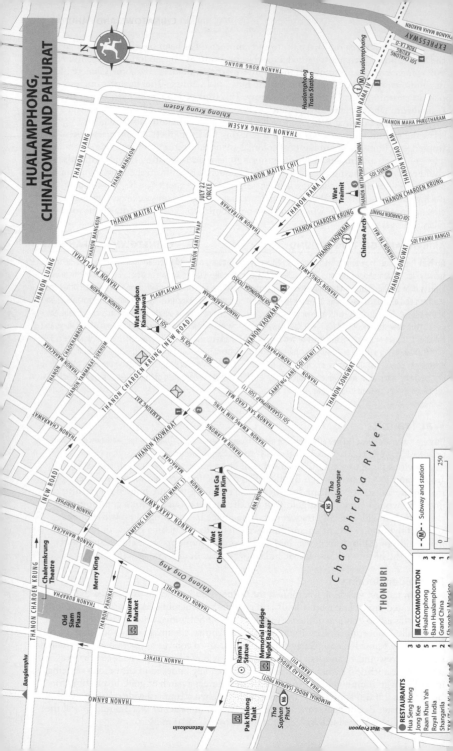

The exhibitions

The exhibition on the making and history of the Golden Buddha, on the second floor of the mondop, is fairly missable, but the **Yaowarat Chinatown Heritage Centre** on the floor below is rather more compelling. Interesting though sanitized, its display boards trace the rapid expansion of the Chinese presence in Bangkok from the late eighteenth century, first as junk traders, later as labourers and tax farmers. Enhancing the story are a diorama of life on board a junk, lots of interesting photos from the late nineteenth century onwards and a fascinating scale model of Thanon Yaowarat in its 1950s heyday, when it was Bangkok's business and entertainment hub.

Sampeng Lane

From Wat Traimit, walk northwest from the big China Gate roundabout along Thanon Yaowarat, and make a left turn onto Thanon Songsawat to reach Sampeng Lane

One of Chinatown's most enjoyable shopping alleys, **Sampeng Lane** (also signposted as Soi Wanit 1) is where the Chinese community first settled in the area, when they were moved from Ratanakosin in the late eighteenth century to make way for the Grand Palace. Stretching southeast–northwest for about 1km, it's a great place to browse, unfurling itself like a serpentine department store and selling everything from Chinese silk pyjama trousers to computer games at bargain rates. Similar goods are more or less gathered in sections, so at the eastern end you'll find mostly cheap jewellery and hair accessories, for example, before passing through stalls specializing in ceramics, Chinese lanterns, then shoes, clothes (west of Thanon Rajawong) and, as you near Pahurat, fabrics, haberdashery and irresistibly girlie accessories.

Soi Issaranuphap

Taking a right turn about halfway down Sampeng Lane will bring you into **Soi Issaranuphap** (also signed along its course as Yaowarat Soi 11, then Soi 6, and later Charoen Krung sois 16 and 21). Packed with people from dawn till dusk, this long, dark alleyway, which also traverses Charoen Krung, is where locals come in search of ginseng roots (essential for good health), quivering fish heads, cubes of cockroach-killer chalk and a gastronome's choice of dried mushrooms and brine-pickled vegetables. Alleys branch off to florid Chinese temples and tiny squares before Soi Issaranuphap finally ends at the Thanon Plaplachai intersection amid a flurry of shops specializing in paper **funeral art**. Believing that the deceased should be well provided for in their afterlife, Chinese people buy miniature paper replicas of necessities to be burned with the body: especially popular are houses, cars, suits of clothing and, of course, money.

Wat Mangkon Kamalawat

Best approached via its dramatic multi-tiered gateway 10m up Thanon Charoen Krung from the Soi Issaranuphap junction

If Soi Issaranuphap epitomizes age-old Chinatown commerce, then **Wat Mangkon Kamalawat** (also known as **Wat Leng Noei Yee** or, in English, "Dragon Flower Temple") stands as a fine example of the community's spiritual practices. Built in 1871, it receives a constant stream of devotees, who come to leave offerings at the altars inside this important Mahayana Buddhist temple. As with the Theravada Buddhism espoused by the Thais, Mahayana Buddhism fuses with other ancient religious beliefs, notably Confucianism and Taoism, and the statues and shrines within Wat Mangkon cover the spectrum. As you pass through the secondary gateway, under the glazed ceramic gables topped with undulating Chinese dragons, you're greeted by a set of four outsize statues of bearded and rather forbidding sages, each symbolically clasping either a parasol, a pagoda, a snake's head or a mandolin. Beyond them, a series of Buddha images swathed in saffron netting occupies the next chamber, a lovely open-sided room of gold

3

paintwork, red-lacquered wood, lattice lanterns and pictorial wall panels inlaid with mother-of-pearl. Elsewhere in the compound are booths selling devotional paraphernalia, a Chinese medicine stall and a fortune-teller.

Wat Ga Buang Kim

From Thanon Rajawong, take a right turn into Thanon Anawong and a further right turn into the narrow, two-pronged Soi Krai

The typical neighbourhood temple of **Wat Ga Buang Kim** is set around a tiny, enclosed courtyard. This particular wat is remarkable for its exquisitely ornamented "vegetarian hall", a one-room shrine with altar centrepiece framed by intricately carved wooden tableaux of gold-painted miniatures arranged as if in sequence, with recognizable characters reappearing in new positions and in different moods. The hall's outer wall is adorned with small tableaux, too, the area around the doorway at the top of the stairs peopled with finely crafted ceramic figurines drawn from Chinese opera stories. The other building in the wat compound is a stage used for Chinese opera performances.

Wat Chakrawat

Thanon Chakrawat

Wat Chakrawat is home to several long-suffering crocodiles, not to mention monkeys, dogs and chess-playing local residents. **Crocodiles** have lived in the tiny pond behind the bot for about fifty years, ever since one was brought here after being hauled out of the Chao Phraya River, where it had been endangering the limbs of bathers. The original crocodile – stuffed – sits in a glass case overlooking the current generation in the pond.

Across the other side of the wat compound is a grotto housing two unusual Buddhist artefacts. The first is a black silhouette on the wall, decorated with squares of gold leaf and believed to be the Buddha's shadow. Nearby, the statue of a fat monk looks on. The story goes that this monk was so good-looking that he was forever being tempted by the attentions of women; the only way he could deter them was to make himself ugly, which he did by gorging himself into obesity.

Nakhon Kasem

Further along Thanon Chakrawat from Wat Chakrawat, away from the river, is the site of the old **Nakhon Kasem** (literally "City of Happiness"), bordered by Thanon Charoen Krung and Thanon Yaowarat to the north and south and Chakrawat and Boriphat roads to the east and west. This grid of lanes was originally famous as the Thieves' Market and was latterly known for its musical instrument shops, but the traders have been forced to move out and it's now undergoing a major redevelopment as a shopping centre.

Pahurat

West of Khlong Ong Ang, in the small square south of the intersection of Chakraphet and Pahurat roads, is the area known as **Pahurat**, where Bangkok's sizeable Indian community congregates. Unless you're looking for *bidi* cigarettes, Punjabi sweets or Bollywood VCDs, curiosity-shopping is not as rewarding here as in Chinatown, but it's good for all sorts of **fabrics**, from shirting to curtain materials and sari lengths.

Also here, at the Charoen Krung/Thanon Triphet intersection, is **Old Siam Plaza**, a colonial-look shopping centre whose nostalgia theme continues in part inside, with its ground-floor concourse given over to stalls selling traditional, handmade Thai snacks, sweets and sticky desserts. The adjacent Sala Chalermkrung Theatre sometimes stages classical Thai drama for non-Thai speakers (see p.178).

Pak Khlong Talat and Memorial Bridge night bazaar

Pak Khlong Talat West of the north side of Memorial Bridge • Daily 24hr • **Memorial Bridge night bazaar** Tues–Sun roughly 6pm–midnight • Chao Phraya express boat to Tha Saphan Phut (N6)

A browse through the 24-hour flower and vegetable market, **Pak Khlong Talat**, is a fitting way to round off a day in Chinatown, though it's also a great place to come before dawn, when market gardeners from Thonburi and beyond boat and drive their freshly picked produce across the Chao Phraya ready for sale to shopkeepers, restaurateurs and hoteliers. The market has been operating from covered halls between the southern ends of Khlong Lod, Thanon Banmo, Thanon Chakraphet and the river bank since the nineteenth century and is the biggest wholesale market in the capital. The flower stalls, selling twenty different varieties of cut orchids and countless other tropical blooms, spill onto the streets along the riverfront, and though prices are lowest in the early morning, you can still get some good bargains in the afternoon. Most evenings, the riverside end of nearby Thanon Triphet and the area around the base of **Memorial Bridge** (Saphan Phut) hosts a huge **night bazaar** that's dominated by cheap and idiosyncratic fashions – and by throngs of teenage fashion victims.

For the most interesting **approach** to the flower market from the Old Siam Plaza, turn west across Thanon Triphet to reach Thanon Banmo, and then follow this road south down towards the Chao Phraya. As you near the river, notice the facing rows of traditional Chinese shophouses, still in use today, which retain their characteristic (peeling) pastel-painted facades, shutters and stucco curlicues. There's an entrance into the market on your right, and just after sundown this southernmost stretch of Thanon Banmo fills with handcarts and vans unloading the most amazing mountains of fresh blooms.

3

Thonburi

For fifteen years between the fall of Ayutthaya in 1767 and the founding of Bangkok in 1782, the west-bank town of Thonburi, across the Chao Phraya from modern-day Bangkok, stood in as the Thai capital, under the rule of General Phraya Taksin. Its time in the spotlight was too brief for the building of the fine monuments and grand temples like those that had graced the earlier capitals at Sukhothai and Ayutthaya, but some of its centuries-old canals (khlongs), which once transported everyone and everything, have endured. It is these ancient waterways and the fascinating ways of life that depend on them that still continue to constitute Thonburi's main attractions and draw visitors to the area.

EXPLORING THONBURI BY BOAT

The most popular way to explore the sights of Thonburi is by **boat**, taking in Wat Arun and the Royal Barge Museum, then continuing along Thonburi's network of small canals. We've detailed some interesting, fixed-price tours below, but generally it's just a question of turning up at a pier on the Bangkok side of the Chao Phraya and chartering a longtail. At Tha Phra Arthit express-boat pier or at the pier about 100m south of it in front of *Venice Vanich Restaurant*, a kiss-me-quick hour-long ride will cost B1000, while a two-hour trip, taking in an orchid farm deep among the Thonburi canals, costs B1800. You can also charter your own longtail from Tha Thien near Wat Pho, River City shopping centre, Tha Sathorn and other piers.

Many tours include visits to one of Thonburi's two main **floating markets**, both of which are heavily touristed and rather contrived. **Wat Sai** floating market is very small, very commercialized and worth avoiding; **Taling Chan** floating market is also fairly manufactured but more fun, though it only operates on Saturdays and Sundays (roughly 9am–4pm). Taling Chan market is held on Khlong Chak Phra, in front of Taling Chan District Office, a couple of kilometres west of Thonburi train station, and can also be reached by catching a/c bus #79 from Thanon Rajdamnoen Klang in Banglamphu. For a more authentic floating-market experience, consider heading out of Bangkok to Amphawa, in Samut Songkhram province (see p.131).

Arguably more photogenic, and certainly a lot more genuine than the floating markets, are the individual **floating vendors** who continue to paddle from house to house in Thonburi, touting anything from hot food to plastic buckets. You've a good chance of seeing some of them in action on almost any longtail boat tour on any day of the week, particularly in the morning.

Mitchaopaya Travel Service Tha Chang – on the left at the start of the pier, as you walk in from Thanon Na Phra Lan ☎ 02 623 6169. Licensed by TAT, offering fixed-price trips along the Thonburi canals of varying durations: in 1hr (B1000/boat, maximum 6 people, or B450/person if you can join in with other people), you'll pass Wat Arun and the Royal Barge Museum without stopping; in 90min (B1300), you'd have time to stop at either; while in 2hr (B1500) you'll have time to go right down the back canals on the Thonburi side and visit an orchid farm. On Saturday and Sunday, the 2hr trip takes in Taling Chan floating market, or you could head to the more authentic Lat

Mayom floating market in 3hr (B2500; best in the morning), far to the west in a leafy, more traditional part of Thonburi.
Pandan Tour 780/488 Thanon Charoen Krung ☎ 087 109 8873, ⓦ thaicanaltour.com. A selection of full-day tours of the Thonburi canals, the floating markets and beyond on an eco-friendly, natural-gas-powered teak boat, in small groups with a good English-speaking guide, starting from B2300/person, including lunch.
Real Asia 10/5–7 Soi Aree, Soi 26, Thanon Sukhumvit ☎ 02 665 6364, ⓦ realasia.net. Runs guided full-day walking and boat tours of the Thonburi canals for B2400/person, including lunch.

In some quarters, life on this side of the river still revolves around these **canals**: vendors of food and household goods paddle their boats along the waterways that crisscross the residential areas, and canalside factories use them to ferry their wares to the Chao Phraya River artery. Venture onto the backroads just three or four kilometres west of the river and you find yourself surrounded by market gardens and rural homes, with no hint of the throbbing metropolis across on the other bank. The most popular way to explore these old neighbourhoods is by **boat**, but joining a bicycle tour of the older neighbourhoods is also very rewarding (see p.28). Most boat trips also encompass Thonburi's imposing riverside Temple of the Dawn, **Wat Arun**, and often the **Royal Barge Museum** as well, though both are easily visited independently, as are the small but historic temple of **Wat Rakhang** and the surprisingly intriguing and child-friendly cemetery at **Wat Prayoon**.

ARRIVAL AND GETTING AROUND   THONBURI

Arrival Getting to Thonburi is generally just a matter of crossing the river. Use Phra Pinklao or Memorial/Phra Pokklao Bridge, take a cross-river ferry, or hop on one of the express boats, which make several stops on the Thonburi

bank. The planned subway extension from Hualamphong, due to open in 2017, will include a station near Wat Arun.
Getting around If you're not exploring Thonburi on a boat tour (see box above), getting around the district can

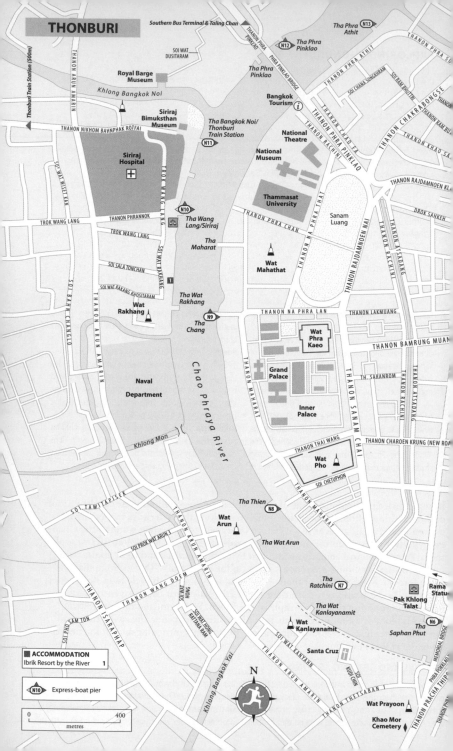

be complicated as the lack of footbridges over canals means that walking between sights often involves using the heavily trafficked Thanon Arun Amarin. A more convoluted alternative would be to leapfrog your way up or down the river by boat, using the various cross-river ferries that connect the Thonburi bank with the Chao Phraya express-boat stops on the other side.

Royal Barge Museum

Soi Wat Dusitaram, north bank of Khlong Bangkok Noi • Daily 9am–5pm • B100, plus B100 for a camera permit • Take the Chao Phraya express boat to Tha Phra Pinklao (N12), or cross-river ferry from under Pinklao Bridge in Banglamphu to Tha Phra Pinklao, then walk up the road 100m and take the first left down Soi Wat Dusitaram; if you are coming by bus from the Bangkok side (#507, #509 and #511 all cross the river here), get off at the first stop on the Thonburi side, which is at the mouth of Soi Wat Dusitaram – signs from Soi Wat Dusitaram lead you through a jumble of walkways and stilt-houses to the museum (10min)

Since the Ayutthaya era, kings of Thailand have been conveyed along their country's waterways in royal barges. For centuries, these slender, exquisitely elegant, black-and-gold wooden vessels were used on all important royal outings, and even up until 1967 the current king would process down the Chao Phraya to Wat Arun in a flotilla of royal barges at least once a year, on the occasion of Kathin, the annual donation of robes by the laity to the temple at the end of the rainy season. But the boats, some of which are a hundred years old, are becoming quite frail, so **royal barge processions** are now held only every few years to mark special anniversaries. However, if your trip happens to coincide with one of these magnificent events, you shouldn't miss it (see ⓦtourismthailand.org). Fifty or more barges fill the width of the river and stretch for almost 1km, drifting slowly to the measured beat of a drum and the hypnotic strains of ancient boating hymns, chanted by over two thousand oarsmen dressed in luscious brocades.

The eight beautifully crafted vessels at the heart of the ceremony are housed in the **Royal Barge Museum**. Up to 50m long and intricately lacquered and gilded all over, they taper at the prow into imposing mythical figures after a design first used by the kings of Ayutthaya. Rama I had the boats copied and, when those fell into disrepair, Rama VI commissioned exact reconstructions, some of which are still in use today. The most important is *Sri Suphanahongse*, which bears the king and queen and is graced by a glittering 5m-high prow representing the golden swan Hamsa, mount of the Hindu god Brahma; constructed from a single piece of timber, it's said to be the largest dugout boat in the world. In front of it floats *Anantanagaraj*, fronted by a magnificent seven-headed naga and bearing a Buddha image. The newest addition to the fleet is *Narai Song Suban*, which was commissioned by the current king for his golden jubilee in 1996; it is a copy of the mid-nineteenth century original and is crowned with a black Vishnu (Narai) astride a garuda figurehead. A display of miniaturized royal barges at the back of the museum re-creates the exact formation of a traditional procession.

The Siriraj museums

Siriraj Hospital • Mon & Wed–Sun 10am–5pm • B300 for admission to all museums, B200 for the Siriraj Bimuksthan Museum only • ⓦ si.mahidol.ac.th/museums • Take an orange-flag Chao Phraya express boat to Tha Thonburi Railway Station/Bangkok Noi (N11)

The enormous Siriraj teaching hospital – where the ailing 87-year-old King Bhumibol is currently residing, in the penthouse of one of the central buildings – is home to no fewer than six museums. Right in front of express-boat pier N11, the **Siriraj Bimuksthan Museum** shelters some engaging exhibits on the history of the neighbourhood. Scattered widely around the hospital compound, the other five museums are devoted mostly to medical curiosities, ranging from internal organs and liver flukes to the corpses of notorious murderers and foetuses of conjoined twins; poorly captioned and ghoulish, they're all rather forgettable.

The Siriraj Bimuksthan Museum

The **Siriraj Bimuksthan Museum** occupies the former Bangkok Noi Railway Station, a typical example of red-brick municipal architecture dating from 1950. It's given over largely to a history of medicine in Thailand, featuring a long roll call of members of the royal family – including Prince Siriraj, son of Rama V – taking credit for introducing Western medicine, and a room on traditional medicine. Probably more interesting, however, is the building that traces local history: at the mouth of the strategic Bangkok Noi canal, this area was around the turn of the nineteenth century the site of the Wang Lang (Rear Palace), home of the "third king", a deputy to the "second king" who lived across the river in the Wang Na (Front Palace; now part of the National Museum). The canal mouth was home to an important floating market and dockyards, over which, in 1890, a royal opium den was built. The dockyards, however, have yielded the museum's most impressive exhibit: a largely intact, 24m, nineteenth-century, wooden merchant ship that was excavated from the nearby mud in 2003.

ENG AND CHANG, THE SIAMESE TWINS

Eng (In) and Chang (Chan), the "original" **Siamese twins**, were born in Samut Songkhram in 1811, when Thailand was known as Siam. The boys' bodies were joined from breastbone to navel by a short fleshy ligament, but they shared no vital organs and eventually managed to stretch their connecting tissue so that they could stand almost side by side instead of permanently facing each other.

In 1824 the boys were spotted by entrepreneurial Scottish trader Robert Hunter, who returned five years later with an American sea merchant, Captain Abel Coffin, to convince the twins' mother to let them take her sons on a world tour. Hunter and Coffin anticipated a lucrative career as producer-managers of an exotic **freak show**, and were not disappointed. They launched the twins in Boston, advertising them as "the Monster" and charging the public 50 cents to watch the boys demonstrate how they walked and ran. Though shabbily treated and poorly paid, the twins soon developed a more theatrical show, enthralling their audiences with acrobatics and feats of strength, and earning the soubriquet "the eighth wonder of the world". At the age of 21, having split from their exploitative managers, the twins became self-employed, but continued to tour with other companies across the world. Wherever they went, they would always be given a thorough examination by local **medics**, partly to counter accusations of fakery, but also because this was the first time the world and its doctors had been introduced to conjoined twins. Such was the twins' international celebrity that the term "Siamese twins" has been used ever since. Chang and Eng also sought advice from these doctors on surgical separation – an issue they returned to repeatedly right until their deaths but never acted upon, despite plenty of gruesome suggestions.

By 1840 the twins had become quite wealthy and decided to settle down. They were granted American citizenship, assumed the family name Bunker, and became slave-owning **plantation farmers** in North Carolina. Three years later they married two local sisters, Addie and Sally Yates, and between them went on to father 21 children. The families lived in separate houses and the twins shuttled between the two, keeping to a strict timetable of three days in each household; for an intriguing imagined account of this bizarre state of affairs, read Darin Strauss's novel *Chang and Eng* (see p.220). Chang and Eng had quite different personalities, and relations between the two couples soured, leading to the division of their assets, with Chang's family getting most of the land, and Eng's most of the slaves. To support their dependants, the twins were obliged to take their show back on the road several times, on occasion working with the infamous showman P. T. Barnum. Their final tour was born out of financial desperation following the 1861–65 Civil War, which had wiped out most of the twins' riches and led to the liberation of all their slaves.

In 1874, Chang succumbed to bronchitis and died; Eng, who might have survived on his own if an operation had been performed immediately, died a few hours later, possibly of shock. They were 62. The twins are buried in White Plains in North Carolina, but there's a **statue** of them near their birthplace in Samut Songkhram, on an untended plot of land surrounded by local government buildings just south of Route 3092, aka Thanon Ekachai, about 4km northeast of town.

Wat Rakhang

Take a cross-river ferry from Tha Chang express-boat pier (near the Grand Palace) to Wat Rakhang's pier, or walk 5min from the Tha Wang Lang express-boat pier, south (left) through the Phrannok pierside market

The charming riverside temple of **Wat Rakhang** (Temple of the Bells) gets its name from the five large bells donated by King Rama I and is notable for the hundreds of smaller chimes that tinkle away under the eaves of the main bot and, more accessibly, in the temple courtyard, where devotees come to strike them and hope for a run of good luck. To be extra certain of having their wishes granted, visitors also buy loaves of bread from the temple stalls and feed the frenzy of fat fish in the Chao Phraya River below. Behind the bot stands an attractive eighteenth-century wooden *ho trai* (scripture library) that still boasts some original murals on the wooden panels inside, as well as exquisitely renovated gold-leaf paintwork on the window shutters and pillars.

Walking to Wat Rakhang from the Tha Wang Lang express-boat pier, you'll pass through the enjoyable **Phrannok pierside market**, which is good for cheap clothes and tempting home-made snacks, especially sweet ones.

Wat Arun

Daily 8.30am–6pm · B50 · ⓦ watarun.org · Take the cross-river ferry from the pier adjacent to the Chao Phraya express-boat pier at Tha Thien

Almost directly across the river from Wat Pho rises the enormous, five-spired prang of **Wat Arun**, the Temple of Dawn, probably Bangkok's most memorable landmark and familiar as the silhouette used in the TAT logo. It looks particularly impressive from the river as you head downstream from the Grand Palace towards the *Oriental Hotel*, but is ornate enough to be well worth stopping off for a closer look. However, the temple is currently in the middle of a B150 million restoration project, swathing the main prang in scaffolding: it's still possible to get into the temple, but not to climb the prang.

A wat has occupied this site since the Ayutthaya period, but only in 1768 did it become known as the Temple of Dawn – when General Phraya Taksin reputedly reached his new capital at the break of day. The temple served as his royal chapel and housed the recaptured Emerald Buddha for several years until the image was moved to Wat Phra Kaeo in 1785. Despite losing its special status after the relocation, Wat Arun continued to be revered, and its corncob prang was reconstructed and enlarged to its present height of 81m by Rama II and Rama III.

The prang that you see today is classic Ayutthayan style, built as a representation of Mount Meru, the home of the gods in Khmer cosmology. Both the **central prang** and the four minor ones that encircle it are studded all over with bits of broken porcelain, ceramic shards and tiny bowls that have been fashioned into an amazing array of polychromatic flowers. The statues of mythical *yaksha* demons and half-bird, half-human *kinnari* that support the different levels are similarly decorated. The crockery probably came from China, possibly from commercial shipments that were damaged at sea, and the overall effect is highly decorative and far more subtle than the dazzling glass mosaics that clad most wat buildings. On the first terrace, the mondops at each cardinal point contain statues of the Buddha at birth (north), in meditation (east), preaching his first sermon (south) and entering Nirvana (west). The second platform surrounds the base of the prang proper, whose closed entranceways are guarded by four statues of the Hindu god Indra on his three-headed elephant Erawan. In the niches of the smaller prangs stand statues of Phra Pai, the god of the wind, on horseback.

Wat Prayoon

Off Thanon Pracha Thipok, 3min walk from Memorial Bridge; though on the Thonburi bank, it's easiest to reach from the Bangkok side, by walking over Memorial Bridge from the express ferry stop at Tha Saphan Phut (N6)

Just west of the Thonburi approach to Memorial Bridge, the unusual **Khao Mor cemetery** makes an unexpectedly enjoyable place to take the kids, with its miniaturized shrines and resident turtles. Its dolls'-house-sized chedis and shrines are set on an artificial hillock, which was constructed by Rama III to replicate the pleasing shapes made by dripping candle wax; it's the most famous *khao mor* (miniature mountain) in Bangkok, an art form that's been practised in Thailand since the early eighteenth century. Wedged in among the grottoes, caverns and ledges of this uneven mass are numerous memorials to the departed, forming a not-at-all sombre gallery of different styles, from traditional Thai chedis, bots and prangs to more foreign designs like the tiny Wild West house complete with cacti at the front door. Turtles fill the pond surrounding the mound and you can feed them with the bags of banana and papaya sold nearby. The cemetery is part of **Wat Prayoon** (officially Wat Prayurawongsawat) but located in a separate compound to the southeast side of the wat.

Memorial Bridge

It wasn't until 1932 that Thonburi was linked to Bangkok proper by the **Memorial Bridge**, or **Saphan Phut**, constructed by Dorman Long who also built the Sydney Harbour Bridge. It commemorates the hundred and fiftieth anniversary of the foundation of the Chakri dynasty and of Bangkok, and is dedicated to Rama I (or Phra Buddha Yodfa, to give him his official title), whose bronze statue sits at the Bangkok approach. The bridge carries traffic across to Thonburi and has proved to be such a crucial river crossing it has since been supplemented by the adjacent twin-track **Saphan Phra Pokklao**.

4

VIMANMEK PALACE

Dusit

Connected to Ratanakosin via the boulevards of Rajdamnoen Klang and Rajdamnoen Nok, spacious, leafy Dusit has been a royal district since the reign of Rama V, King Chulalongkorn (1860–1910). The first Thai monarch to visit Europe, Rama V returned with plans for the modernization of his capital, the fruits of which are most visible in Dusit, notably at Vimanmek Palace and Wat Benjamabophit. Even now, Rama V still commands a loyal following, and his statue, which stands in Royal Plaza, is presented with offerings every week and is the focus of celebrations on Chulalongkorn Day (Oct 23). On December 2, Dusit is the venue for the spectacular annual Trooping the Colour, when hundreds of magnificently uniformed Royal Guards demonstrate their allegiance to the king by parading around Royal Plaza. Across from Chitrlada Palace, Dusit Zoo makes a pleasant enough place to take the kids.

5

Today, the Dusit area retains its European feel, and much of the country's decision-making goes on behind the high fences and impressive facades along its tree-lined avenues: the building that houses the National Parliament is here, as is Government House, and the king's official residence, Chitrlada Palace, occupies the eastern edge of the area. Normally a calm, stately district, in both 2008 and 2013 Dusit became the focus of **mass anti-government protests** by royalist yellow-shirts, who occupied Thanon Rajdamnoen Nok for several months on both occasions, creating a heavily defended temporary village in this most refined of neighbourhoods.

ARRIVAL AND DEPARTURE   DUSIT

By bus From Banglamphu, you can get to Dusit by taking the #70 (non-expressway) bus from Rajdamnoen Klang and getting off near the Rama V statue for Wat Benjamabophit, or outside the zoo and Elephant Museum on Thanon U-Thong Nai; or the #56 from Thanon Phra Sumen and alighting at the corner of Thanon Ratchasima and Thanon Rajwithi (known as the Kan Reuan

intersection), near the main entrance to Dusit Park. From downtown Bangkok, easiest access is by bus from the Skytrain stop at Victory Monument; there are many services from here, including #28 and #108.

By boat Take the express boat to Tha Thewet and then it's about a 30min walk to Dusit Park, the zoo or Wat Benjamabophit.

Dusit Park

Main entrance on Thanon Rajwithi, with another ticket gate opposite Dusit Zoo on Thanon U-Thong Nai • Tues–Sun 9.30am–4.30pm, last admission 3.15pm • B100, or free with a Grand Palace ticket, which remains valid for one week • ⓦ vimanmek.com

The outstanding feature of what's known as **Dusit Park** is the breezy, elegant **Vimanmek Palace**, which was originally built by Rama V as a summer retreat on Ko Si Chang; however, he realized that the palace was strategically too vulnerable, after the French briefly invaded the island in the 1890s, and had it transported here bit by bit in 1901. The ticket price also covers entry to a dozen other specialist collections in Dusit Park, which these days resembles a theme park, with piped muzak, cafés, souvenir shops, heavy security and lots of coach tours. Among these collections, which include antique textiles, photographs taken by the king, royal ceremonial paraphernalia and antique clocks, housed in handsome, pastel-painted, former royal residences, the most interesting are the Support Museum and Elephant Museum. Note that the same **dress rules** apply here as to the Grand Palace (see p.51), though T-shirts and sarongs are for sale for those who do not pass muster.

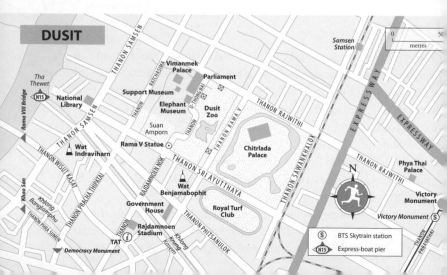

Vimanmek Palace

Dusit Park • Free guided tours in English at 11am & 2pm

Built almost entirely of golden teak without a single nail, the coffee-coloured, L-shaped **Vimanmek Palace** is encircled by delicate latticework verandas that look out onto well-kept lawns, flower gardens and lotus ponds. Not surprisingly, this "Celestial Residence" soon became Rama V's favourite palace, and he and his enormous retinue of officials, concubines and children stayed here for lengthy periods between 1902 and 1906. All of Vimanmek's 81 rooms were out of bounds to male visitors, except for the king's own apartments in the octagonal tower, which were entered by a separate staircase.

On display inside is Rama V's collection of **artefacts** from all over the world, including *bencharong* ceramics, European furniture and bejewelled Thai betel-nut sets. Considered progressive in his day, Rama V introduced many newfangled ideas to Thailand: the country's first indoor bathroom is here, as is the earliest typewriter with Thai characters, and some of the first portrait paintings – portraiture had until then been seen as a way of stealing part of the sitter's soul.

The Support Museum

Immediately behind (to the east of) Vimanmek Palace, Dusit Park

The **Support Museum** is housed in a very pretty hundred-year-old building, the Abhisek Dusit Throne Hall, which was formerly used for meetings and banquets. It showcases the exquisite handicrafts produced under Queen Sirikit's charity project, Support, which works to revitalize traditional Thai arts and crafts. Outstanding exhibits include a collection of handbags, baskets and pots woven from the *lipao* fern that grows wild in southern Thailand; jewellery and figurines inlaid with the iridescent wings of beetles; gold and silver nielloware; and lengths of intricately woven silk from the northeast.

Chang Ton Royal Elephant National Museum

Just behind (to the east of) the Support Museum, inside the Thanon U-Thong Nai entrance to Dusit Park

These buildings once served as the stables for the king's white elephants. Now that the sacred pachyderms have been relocated, the stables have been turned into the **Chang**

THE ROYAL WHITE ELEPHANTS

In Thailand, the most revered of all elephants are the so-called **white elephants** – actually tawny brown albinos – which are considered so sacred that they all, whether wild or captive, belong to the king by law. Their special status originates from Buddhist mythology, which tells how the previously barren Queen Maya became pregnant with the future Buddha after dreaming one night that a white elephant had entered her womb. The thirteenth-century King Ramkhamhaeng of Sukhothai adopted the beast as a symbol of the great and the divine, decreeing that a Thai king's greatness should be measured by the number of white elephants he owns. A white elephant appeared on the Thai national flag until 1917, and the present king, Rama IX, has ten white elephants, the largest royal collection to date.

Before an elephant can be granted official "white elephant" status, it has to pass a stringent assessment of its physical and behavioural **characteristics**. Key qualities include a paleness of seven crucial areas – eyes, nails, palate, hair, outer edges of the ears, tail and testicles – and an all-round genteel demeanour, manifested, for instance, in the way in which it cleans its food before eating, or in a tendency to sleep in a kneeling position. Tradition holds that an elaborate ceremony should take place every time a new white elephant is presented to the king: the animal is paraded with great pomp from its place of capture to Dusit, where it's anointed with holy water in front of an audience of priests and dignitaries, before being housed in the royal stables. Recently, though, the king has called time on this exorbitantly expensive ritual, and the royal white elephants now live in less luxurious, rural accommodation under the care of the Thai Elephant Conservation Centre.

The expression "white elephant" probably derives from the legend that the kings used to present certain troublesome noblemen with one of these exotic creatures. The animal required expensive attention but, being royal, could not be put to work in order to pay for its upkeep.

5

Ton Royal Elephant National Museum. Inside you'll find some interesting pieces of paraphernalia, including sacred ropes, mahouts' amulets, magic formulae, and photos of the ceremony in which a white elephant is granted royal status (see box, p.89).

Dusit Zoo (Khao Din)

Entrances on Thanon Rajwithi, on Thanon U-Thong Nai across from the Elephant Museum in Dusit Park, and on Thanon Rama V, within walking distance of Wat Benjamabophit • Daily 8am–6pm • B150, children B70 • ⓦ dusitzoo.org

Dusit Zoo, also known as **Khao Din**, was once part of the Chitrlada Palace gardens, but is now a public park. All the usual suspects are here in the zoo, including big cats, elephants, orang-utans, chimpanzees and a reptile house, but the enclosures are pretty basic. However, it's a reasonable place for kids to let off steam, with plenty of shade, a full complement of English-language signs, a lake with pedalos, tram rides and lots of food stalls and cafés.

Wat Benjamabophit

Corner of Thanon Sri Ayutthaya and Thanon Rama V: 200m south of the zoo's east entrance, or about 600m from Vimanmek's U-Thong Nai gate • Daily 7am–6pm • B20 • ⓦ facebook.com/watbencha

Wat Benjamabophit (aka Wat Ben) is a fascinating fusion of classical Thai and nineteenth-century European design, with the Carrara-marble walls of its bot – hence the tourist tag **"The Marble Temple"** – pierced by unusual stained-glass windows, neo-Gothic in style but depicting figures from Thai mythology. Rama V commissioned the temple in 1899, at a time when he was keen to show the major regional powers, Britain and France, that Thailand was *siwilai* (civilized), in order to baulk their usual excuse for colonizing. The temple's sema stones are a telling example of the compromises involved: they're usually prominent markers of the bot's sacred area, but here they're hard to spot, decorative and almost apologetic – look for the two small, stone lotus buds at the front of the bot on top of the white, Italianate balustrade. Inside the unusually cruciform bot, a fine replica of the highly revered Phra Buddha Chinnarat image of Phitsanulok presides over the small room containing some of Rama V's ashes. The courtyard behind the bot houses a gallery of Buddha images from all over Asia, set up by Rama V as an overview of different representations of the Buddha.

Wat Benjamabophit is one of the best temples in Bangkok to see religious **festivals** and rituals. Whereas monks elsewhere tend to go out on the streets every morning in search of alms, at the Marble Temple the ritual is reversed, and merit-makers come to them. Between about 5.30 and 7 or 7.30am, the monks line up on Thanon Nakhon Pathom, their bowls ready to receive donations of curry and rice, lotus buds, incense, even toilet paper and Coca-Cola; the demure row of saffron-robed monks is a sight that's well worth getting up early for. The evening candlelight processions around the bot during the Buddhist festivals of Maha Puja (in Feb) and Visakha Puja (in May) are among the most entrancing in the country.

Museum of Floral Culture

315 Yaek Soi Ongkarak 13 (continuation northwards of Thanon Nakhon Ratchasima), Soi 28, Thanon Samsen • Tues–Sun 10am–6pm • B150 includes guide • ☎ 02 669 3633–4, ⓦ floralmuseum.com • 20min walk (northeast), or a motorcycle-taxi ride, from Tha Payap (N18) express-boat pier, served by orange-flag boats

Said to be the only one of its kind in the world, the **Museum of Floral Culture** has been recently opened by the renowned floral artist, Sakul Intakul. The terms are deliberately generalized here, as this is about not only flower arranging, but so much more: floral designs and uses in Thailand and other Asian cultures. Guides will lead you around the beautiful garden and the century-old, colonial-style, teak mansion, where the diverse exhibits cover temple offerings of flowers, sketches of some of Khun Sakul's most famous designs and floral artefacts from his travels around Asia. There's a lovely tea shop on one of the verandas, and the museum holds occasional floral workshops for adults and children.

JIM THOMPSON'S HOUSE

Downtown Bangkok

Extending east from the main rail line and south to Thanon Sathorn and beyond, downtown Bangkok is central to the colossal expanse of Bangkok as a whole, but rather peripheral in a sightseer's perception of the city. In this modern high-rise area, you'll find the main shopping centres around Siam Square, though don't come looking for an elegant commercial piazza here: the "square" is in fact a grid of small streets, sheltering trendy fashion shops, cinemas and inexpensive restaurants. It lies to the southeast of Pathumwan intersection, the junction of Thanon Rama I (in Thai, "Thanon Phra Ram Neung") and Thanon Phrayathai, and the name is applied freely to the surrounding area. Further east, you'll find yet more shopping malls around the noisy and glittering Erawan Shrine.

6

The Erawan Shrine is located where Rama I becomes Thanon Ploenchit, an intersection known as Ratchaprasong. It was here that the opposition redshirts set up a fortified camp for several months in early 2010, before the Democrat Party government sent in the troops, leading to the deaths of 91 people. It's once more possible to stroll in peace above the cracked pavements, noise and fumes of Thanon Rama I, using the elevated **walkway** that runs beneath the Skytrain lines all the way from the Siam Paragon shopping centre to the Erawan Shrine (further progress is blocked by Central and Chitlom Skytrain stations). East of Ratchaprasong, you pass under the expressway flyover and enter the farang hotel, shopping and entertainment quarter of **Thanon Sukhumvit**.

The area south of Thanon Rama I is dominated by Thailand's most prestigious centre of higher learning, Chulalongkorn University, and the green expanse of **Lumphini Park**. Thanon Rama IV (in Thai "Thanon Phra Ram Sii") then marks another change of character: downtown proper, centring around the high-rise, American-style boulevard of **Thanon Silom**, the heart of the financial district, extends from here to the river. Alongside the smoked-glass banks and offices, and opposite Convent Road, site of Bangkok's Carmelite nunnery, lies the dark heart of Bangkok nightlife, **Patpong**.

Surprisingly, among downtown's vast expanse of skyscraping concrete, the main attractions for visitors are four attractive museums housed in historic teak houses: **Jim Thompson's House**, the **Ban Kamthieng**, the **Suan Pakkad Palace Museum** and **M.R. Kukrit's Heritage Home**. The area's other tourist highlight is **Siam Ocean World**, a high-tech aquarium that both kids and adults can enjoy. The accounts of the sights below are arranged roughly north–south.

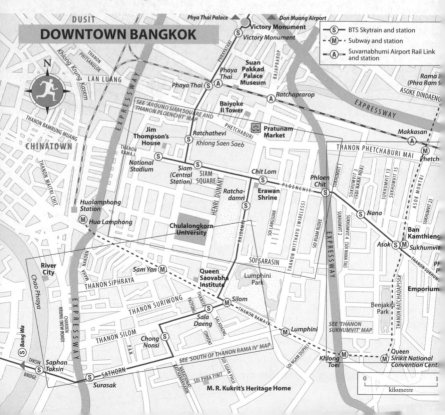

By Skytrain and subway All of the sights reviewed here are within walking range of a Skytrain station; some of the sights are also served by the subway.

By boat The fastest way to head downtown from Banglamphu is by public boat along Khlong Saen Saeb, beginning near Democracy Monument. A slower but much more scenic route (and during rush hours, possibly quicker than a bus from Banglamphu downtown) is to take an express boat downriver, then change onto the Skytrain at BTS Saphan Taksin.

Victory Monument

6

Northern downtown is cut through by several major thoroughfares, including the original road to the north, Thanon Phaholyothin, which runs past the weekend market and doesn't stop until it gets to the border with Myanmar at Mae Sai, 900km away – though it's now more commonly known as Highway 1, at least in between towns. The start of Phaholyothin is marked by the stone obelisk of **Victory Monument** (*Anu Sawari Chaisamoraphum*, or just *Anu Sawari*), which can be seen most spectacularly from Skytrains as they snake their way round it. It was erected after the Indo-Chinese War of 1940–41, when Thailand pinched back some territory in Laos and Cambodia while the French government was otherwise occupied in World War II, but nowadays it commemorates all of Thailand's past military glories.

Suan Pakkad Palace Museum

352–4 Thanon Sri Ayutthaya • Daily 9am–4pm • B100 • ☏ 02 246 1775–6 ext 229, ⓦ suanpakkad.com • 5min walk from BTS Phaya Thai

The **Suan Pakkad Palace Museum** stands on what was once a cabbage patch (*suan pakkad*) but is now one of the finest gardens in Bangkok. Most of this private collection of beautiful Thai objects from all periods is displayed in four groups of traditional wooden houses, which were transported to Bangkok from various parts of the country.

In House no. 8, as well as in the Ban Chiang Gallery in the modern Chumbhot-Pantip Center of Arts in the palace grounds, you'll find a very good collection of elegant, whorled pottery and bronze jewellery, which the former owner of Suan Pakkad Palace, Princess Chumbhot, excavated from tombs at Ban Chiang, the major Bronze Age settlement in the northeast. Scattered around the rest of the museum are some fine ceramics and attractive Thai and Khmer religious sculptures; an extensive collection of colourful papier-mâché *khon* masks; beautiful betel-nut sets; monks' elegant ceremonial fans; and some rich teak carvings, including a two-hundred-year-old temple door showing episodes from *Sang Thong*, a folk tale about a childless king and queen who discover a handsome son in a conch shell.

The Lacquer Pavilion

The highlight of Suan Pakkad is the renovated **Lacquer Pavilion**, across the reedy pond at the back of the grounds. Set on stilts, the pavilion is actually an amalgam of two eighteenth- or late seventeenth-century temple buildings, a *ho trai* (library) and a *ho khien* (writing room), one inside the other, which were found between Ayutthaya and Bang Pa-In. The interior walls are beautifully decorated with gilt on black lacquer: the upper panels depict the life of the Buddha while the lower ones show scenes from the *Ramayana*. Look out especially for the grisly details in the tableau on the back wall, showing the earth goddess drowning the evil forces of Mara. Underneath are depicted some European dandies on horseback, probably merchants, whose presence suggests that the work was executed before the fall of Ayutthaya in 1767. The carefully observed details of daily life and nature are skilful and lively, especially considering the restraints that the lacquering technique places on the artist, who has no opportunity for corrections or touching up.

Phya Thai Palace

Thanon Rajwithi · Guided tours Tues 1pm, Thurs 1pm, Sat 9.30am & 1.30pm · Free, donations towards the palace upkeep welcome ·
ⓣ 02 354 7987 or ⓣ 02 354 7732, ⓦ phyathaipalace.org · About 10min walk west of Victory Monument and its Skytrain station

A grandiose and eccentric relic of the early twentieth century, the **Phya Thai Palace** was built mostly by **Vajiravudh**, Rama VI, who lived here from 1919 for the last six years of his reign. After his death, the palace initially became the most luxurious hotel in Southeast Asia (an attempt by Rama VII to recoup some of the vast fortune squandered by his predecessor), incorporating Thailand's first radio station, then, after the 1932 coup, it was turned into a military hospital. Parts of the airy, rambling complex have been splendidly restored by the Palace Fan Club, while others show nearly a century's worth of wear and tear, and one building is still used as offices by Phra Mongkutklao Army Hospital; you're quite likely to come across a musical performance or rehearsal as you're being guided round the otherwise empty rooms. It's well worth buying the excellent guidebook, not only to help the palace restoration fund, but also to read the extraordinary story of **Dusit Thani**: this miniature utopian city was set up by King Vajiravudh on an acre of the palace grounds (now dismantled) as a political experiment complete with two daily newspapers, elections and a constitution – only a decade or so before a real constitution was forcibly imposed on the monarchy after the coup of 1932.

The palace buildings

Most of the central building, the **Phiman Chakri Hall**, is in a sumptuous, English, Art Nouveau style, featuring silk wallpaper, ornate murals, Italian marble – and an extravagant but unusable fireplace that reminded Vajiravudh of his schooling in England. The king's first bedroom, decorated in royal red and appointed with a huge, step-down, marble bath, later went for B120 a night as a hotel suite. Outside in the grounds, between a pond used for bathing and the canal which gave access to Khlong Samsen, Vajiravudh first constructed for himself a simple wooden house so that he could keep an eye on the builders, the **Mekhala Ruchi Pavilion**, which later became the king's barber's. In front of the Phiman Chakri Hall, the **Thewarat Sapharom Hall**, a neo-Byzantine teak audience hall built by Rama V, is still used for occasional **classical concerts**. Don't leave without sampling the lovely Art Nouveau **coffee shop**, a former waiting room covered in ornate teak carving.

Jim Thompson's House

Just off Siam Square at the north end of Soi Kasemsan 2, Thanon Rama I · Daily from 9am, viewing on frequent 30–40min guided tours, last tour 5pm; shop 9am–8pm · B100 · ⓣ 02 216 7368, ⓦ jimthompsonhouse.com · BTS National Stadium, or via a canalside path from the Khlong Saen Saeb pier at Saphan Hua Chang

Jim Thompson's House is a kind of Ideal Home in elegant Thai style, and a peaceful refuge from downtown chaos. The house was the residence of the legendary American adventurer, entrepreneur, art collector and all-round character whose mysterious disappearance in the jungles of Malaysia in 1967 has made him even more of a legend among Thailand's farang community (see box, p.96).

Apart from putting together this beautiful home, completed in 1959, Thompson's most concrete contribution was to turn traditional silk-weaving in Thailand from a dying art into the highly successful international industry it is today. The complex now includes a **shop**, part of the Jim Thompson Thai Silk Company chain (see p.186), and an excellent **bar-restaurant** (see p.163).

Above the shop, the **Jim Thompson Center for the Arts** is a fascinating gallery that hosts both traditional and modern temporary exhibitions on textiles and the arts, such as royal maps of Siam in the nineteenth century or *mor lam*, the folk music of the northeast. Ignore any con men at the entrance to the soi looking for gullible tourists to escort on rip-off shopping trips, who'll tell you that the house is closed when it isn't.

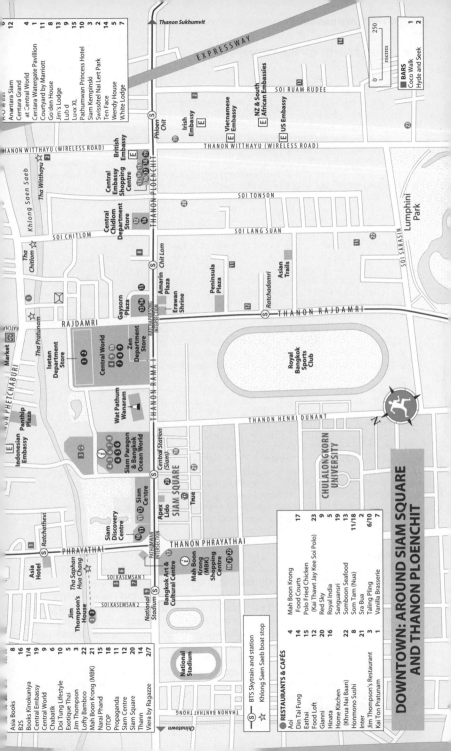

DOWNTOWN: AROUND SIAM SQUARE AND THANON PLOENCHIT

6

THE LEGEND OF JIM THOMPSON

Thai silk-weavers, art dealers and conspiracy theorists all owe a debt to **Jim Thompson**, who even now, nearly fifty years after his disappearance, remains Thailand's most famous farang. An architect by trade, Thompson left his New York practice in 1940 to join the Office of Strategic Services (later to become the CIA), a tour of duty that was to see him involved in clandestine operations in North Africa, Europe and, in 1945, the Far East, where he was detailed to a unit preparing for the invasion of Thailand. When the mission was pre-empted by the Japanese surrender, he served for a year as OSS station chief in Bangkok, forming links that were later to provide grist for endless speculation.

After an unhappy and short-lived stint as part-owner of the *Oriental Hotel*, Thompson found his calling with the struggling **silk-weavers** of the area near the present Jim Thompson House, whose traditional product was unknown in the West and had been all but abandoned by Thais in favour of less costly imported textiles. Encouragement from society friends and an enthusiastic write-up in *Vogue* convinced him there was a foreign market for Thai silk, and by 1948 he had founded the Thai Silk Company Ltd. Success was assured when, two years later, the company was commissioned to make the costumes for the Broadway run of *The King and I*. Thompson's celebrated eye for colour combinations and his tireless promotion – in the early days, he could often be seen in the lobby of the *Oriental* with bolts of silk slung over his shoulder, waiting to pounce on any remotely curious tourist – quickly made his name synonymous with Thai silk.

Like a character in a Somerset Maugham novel, Thompson played the role of Western exile to the hilt. Though he spoke no Thai, he made it his personal mission to preserve traditional arts and architecture (at a time when most Thais were more keen to emulate the West), assembling his famous Thai house and stuffing it with all manner of Oriental objets d'art. At the same time he held firmly to his farang roots and society connections: no foreign gathering in Bangkok was complete without Jim Thompson, and virtually every Western luminary passing through Bangkok – from Truman Capote to Ethel Merman – dined at his table (even though the food was notoriously bad).

If Thompson's life was the stuff of legend, his disappearance and presumed death only added to the mystique. On Easter Sunday, 1967, Thompson, while staying with friends in a cottage in Malaysia's Cameron Highlands, went out for a stroll and never came back. A massive search of the area, employing local guides, tracker dogs and even shamans, turned up no clues, provoking a rash of fascinating but entirely unsubstantiated theories. The grandfather of them all, advanced by a Dutch psychic, held that Thompson had been lured into an ambush by the disgraced former prime minister of Thailand, Pridi Panomyong, and spirited off to Cambodia for indeterminate purposes; later versions, supposing that Thompson had remained a covert CIA operative all his life, proposed that he was abducted by Vietnamese Communists and brainwashed to be displayed as a high-profile defector to Communism. More recently, an amateur sleuth claims to have found evidence that Thompson met a more mundane fate, having been killed by a careless truck driver and hastily buried.

The house

The grand, rambling **house** is in fact a combination of six teak houses, some from as far afield as Ayutthaya and most more than two hundred years old. Like all traditional houses, they were built in wall sections hung together without nails on a frame of wooden pillars, which made it easy to dismantle them, pile them onto a barge and float them to their new location. Although he had trained as an architect, Thompson had difficulty in putting them back together again; in the end, he had to go back to Ayutthaya to hunt down a group of carpenters who still practised the old house-building methods. Thompson added a few unconventional touches of his own, incorporating the elaborately carved front wall of a Chinese pawnshop between the drawing room and the bedroom, and reversing the other walls in the drawing room 0so that their carvings faced into the room.

The impeccably tasteful **interior** has been left as it was during Jim Thompson's life, even down to the place settings on the dining table – Thompson entertained guests most nights and to that end designed the house like a stage set. Complementing the fine artefacts from throughout Southeast Asia is a stunning array of Thai arts and crafts, including one of the best collections of traditional Thai paintings in the world. Thompson picked up plenty of bargains from the Thieves' Quarter (Nakhon Kasem) in Chinatown, before collecting Thai art became fashionable and expensive. Other pieces were liberated from decay and destruction in upcountry temples, while many of the Buddha images were turned over by ploughs, especially around Ayutthaya. Some of the exhibits are very rare, such as a headless but elegant seventh-century Dvaravati Buddha and a seventeenth-century Ayutthayan teak Buddha.

After the guided tour, you're free to look again, at your leisure, at the former rice barn and gardener's and maid's houses in the small, jungly **garden**, which display some gorgeous traditional Thai paintings and drawings, as well as small-scale statues and Chinese ceramics.

Bangkok Art and Cultural Centre

Junction of Rama I and Phrayathai roads • Tues–Sun 10am–9pm • Free • ☎ 02 214 6630–1, ⓦ bacc.or.th • BTS National Stadium

A striking, white hunk of modernity, the prestigious **Bangkok Art and Cultural Centre** houses several galleries on its upper floors, connected by spiralling ramps like New York's Guggenheim, as well as several performance spaces. It hosts temporary shows by contemporary artists from Thailand and abroad across all media, from the visual arts to music and design, and there's usually something interesting on here – coming in from BTS National Stadium, there's a blackboard inside the entrance where the day's events and shows are chalked up in English.

Sea Life Bangkok Ocean World

Basement of Siam Paragon shopping centre (east end), Thanon Rama I • Daily 10am–9pm, last admission 8pm; shark feeds 1pm & 4pm, as well as many other timed feedings (detailed on the website) • B990 (online, weekday early-bird and family discounts available); B2000 including "Ocean Walker"; behind-the-scenes tour B200; shark dive from B5300; 5D films B250 • ☎ 02 687 2000, ⓦ sealifebangkok.com • BTS Siam

Spread over two spacious floors, **Bangkok Ocean World** is an impressive, Australian-built aquarium. Despite the high admission price, it gets crowded at weekends and during holidays, and can be busy with school groups on weekday afternoons. Among outstanding features of this US$30-million development are an 8m-deep glass-walled tank, which displays the multicoloured variety of a coral reef drop-off to great effect, and a long, under-ocean tunnel where you can watch sharks and rays swimming over your head. In this global piscatorial display of around four hundred species, locals such as the Mekong giant catfish are not forgotten, while regularly spaced touch-screen terminals provide information in English about the creatures on view. It's even possible to walk in an underwater tunnel wearing a diving helmet (the "Ocean Walker"), or dive with the sharks, whether you're a licensed diver or not. You can also take a behind-the-scenes tour and watch – through 3D glasses – underwater cartoons in "5D Cinema Xtreme", where the chairs move and there are occasional sprays of water.

The Erawan Shrine

Corner of Thanon Ploenchit and Thanon Rajdamri • Daily 24hr • Free • BTS Chit Lom

For a glimpse of the variety and ubiquity of Thai religion, drop in on the **Erawan Shrine** (*Saan Phra Prom* in Thai). Remarkable as much for its setting as anything else, this shrine to Brahma, the ancient Hindu creation god, and Erawan, the many-headed elephant he created, squeezes in on one of the busiest and noisiest intersections in modern Bangkok. And it's not the only one: half a dozen other Hindu shrines are dotted around Ratchaphrasong intersection, most notably **Trimurti**, who combines the

6

three main gods, Brahma, Vishnu and Shiva, on Thanon Rajdamri outside Central World near the intersection's opposite corner. Modern Bangkokians see Trimurti as a sort of Cupid figure, and those looking for love bring red offerings.

The *Grand Hyatt Erawan Hotel*, towering over the Erawan Shrine, is the reason for its existence and its name. When a string of calamities held up the building of the original hotel in the 1950s, spirit doctors were called in, who instructed the owners to build a new home for the offended local spirits: the hotel was then finished without further mishap. Ill fortune struck the shrine itself, however, in early 2006, when a young Muslim man, who was suffering from mental illness, smashed the Brahma statue to pieces with a hammer – and was then brutally beaten to death by an angry mob. An exact replica of the statue was quickly installed, incorporating the remains of the old statue to preserve the spirit of the deity.

Be prepared for sensory overload here: the main structure shines with lurid glass of all colours and the overcrowded precinct around it is almost buried under scented garlands and incense candles. You might also catch a group of traditional dancers performing here to the strains of a small classical orchestra – worshippers hire them to give thanks for a stroke of good fortune. To increase their future chances of such good fortune, visitors buy a bird or two from the flocks incarcerated in cages here; the bird-seller transfers the requested number of captives to a tiny hand-held cage, from which the customer duly liberates the animals, thereby accruing merit. People set on less abstract rewards will invest in a lottery ticket from one of the physically disabled sellers: they're thought to be the luckiest you can buy.

Pratunam Market

Corner of Thanon Phetchaburi and Thanon Ratchaprarop • Daily, daylight hours

Ten minutes' walk north of the Erawan Shrine and extending northwest from the corner of Rajaprarop and Phetchaburi roads, **Pratunam Market** is famous for its low-cost, low-quality casual clothes. The vast, dark warren of stalls is becoming touristy near the hotels on its north side, but there are still bargains to be had elsewhere, especially along the market's western side.

Baiyoke II Tower

222 Thanon Ratchaprarop • Mon–Fri 10am–10.30pm, Sat & Sun 9.30am–10.30pm • B300 before 6pm, B400 after 6pm • ⓦ baiyokehotel.com

On the north side of the Pratunam Market stands **Baiyoke II Tower**, which at 304m is currently the tallest building in Bangkok. High-speed lifts whisk you to the revolving observation deck on the 84th floor, where you can enjoy the breathtaking views of the city that stretch as far as the Gulf of Thailand. In 2016, however, it's due to be outgrown by the 313m Maha Nakhon building, which is under construction on Thanon Narathiwat Ratchanakharin.

Ban Kamthieng (Kamthieng House)

131 Thanon Asok Montri (Soi 21 off Thanon Sukhumvit) • Tues–Sat 9am–5pm • B100 • ⓦ siam-society.org • BTS Asok or Sukhumvit subway

A traditional northern Thai residence, **Ban Kamthieng** was moved in the 1960s from Chiang Mai to just off Thanon Sukhumvit and set up as an ethnological museum by the Siam Society. The delightful complex of polished teak buildings makes a pleasing oasis beneath the towering glass skyscrapers that dominate the rest of Sukhumvit. It differs from Suan Pakkad, Jim Thompson's House and M.R. Kukrit's Heritage Home in being the home of a rural family, and the objects on display give a fair insight into country life for the well heeled in northern Thailand.

The house was built on the banks of the Ping River in the mid-nineteenth century, and the ground-level display of farming tools and fish traps evokes the upcountry practice of fishing in flooded rice paddies to supplement the supply from the rivers. Upstairs, the main display focuses on the ritual life of a typical Lanna household, explaining the role of the spirits, the practice of making offerings, and the belief in talismans, magic shirts and male tattoos. The rectangular lintel above the door is a *hum yon*, carved in floral patterns that represent testicles and are designed to ward off evil spirits. Walk along the open veranda to the authentically equipped kitchen to see a video lesson in making spicy frog soup, and to the granary to find an interesting exhibition on the ritual practices associated with rice farming.

Thailand Creative and Design Centre (TCDC)

6th floor of the Emporium Shopping Centre, Thanon Sukhumvit between sois 22 and 24 · Tues–Sun 10.30am–9pm · Free · ⓦ tcdc.or.th · BTS Phrom Pong

Appropriately located in Emporium, one of Bangkok's most fashion-conscious shopping plazas, the **Thailand Creative and Design Centre** seeks to celebrate, promote and inspire innovative design through exhibitions, talks, a resource centre and shop (see p.186). Alongside often fascinating temporary exhibitions, the concise but thought-provoking permanent bilingual display focuses on the cultural contexts of design classics from around the world, beginning with the Louis Vuitton trunk of 1854 and including Thai fabrics and playful household items.

The Queen Saovabha Memorial Institute (Snake Farm)

Corner of Thanon Rama IV and Thanon Henri Dunant · Live shows Mon–Fri 2.30pm, Sat, Sun & hols 11am · B200 · ⓦ saovabha.com · 10min walk from BTS Sala Daeng, or from Sam Yan or Si Lom subway stations

The **Queen Saovabha Memorial Institute** (*Sathan Saovabha*) is a bit of a circus act, but an entertaining, informative and worthy one at that. It's often simply known as the **Snake Farm**, but takes its formal name from one of Rama V's wives, who was a notable campaigner. Run by the Thai Red Cross, the institute has a double function: to produce snake-bite serums, and to educate the public on the dangers of Thai snakes. The latter mission involves putting on live demonstrations of snake handling and feeding. Well presented and safe, these displays gain a perverse fascination from the knowledge that the strongest venoms of the snakes on show can kill in only three minutes. If you're still not herpetologically sated, you can look round the attached exhibition space, where dozens of Thai snakes live in cages.

Lumphini Park

Thanon Rama IV · Daily roughly 5am–9pm · Free · BTS Saladaeng or Si Lom or Lumphini subway stations

If you're sick of cars and concrete, head for **Lumphini Park** (*Suan Lum*), where the air is almost fresh and the traffic noise dies down to a low murmur. Named after the town in Nepal where the Buddha was born, it was the country's first public park, donated by Rama VI, whose statue by Silpa Bhirasri (see p.215) stands at the main, southwest entrance. The park is arrayed around two lakes, where you can join the locals in feeding the turtles and fish with bread or take out a pedalo or rowing boat, and is landscaped with a wide variety of local trees and numerous pagodas and pavilions, usually occupied by chess-players. In the early morning and at dusk, people hit the outdoor gym on the southwest side of the park, or en masse do aerobics, balletic t'ai chi or jogging along the yellow-marked circuit, stopping for the twice-daily broadcast of the national anthem. On late Sunday afternoons in the cool season (usually Dec to mid-Feb), free classical concerts by the Bangkok Symphony Orchestra (ⓦbangkoksymphony.org) draw in scores of urban picnickers.

6

THAILAND'S SEX INDUSTRY

Bangkok owes its reputation as the carnal capital of the world to a **sex industry** adept at peddling fantasies of cheap thrills on tap. More than a thousand sex-related businesses operate in the city, but the gaudy neon fleshpots of Patpong and Sukhumvit's Soi Nana and Soi Cowboy give a misleading impression of an activity that is deeply rooted in Thai culture: the overwhelming majority of Thailand's prostitutes of both sexes (estimated at anywhere between 200,000 and 700,000) work with Thai men, not farangs.

Prostitution and polygamy have long been intrinsic to the Thai way of life. Until Rama VI broke with the custom in 1910, Thai kings had always kept concubines, only a few of whom would be elevated to royal mothers. The practice was aped by the nobility and, from the early nineteenth century, by newly rich merchants keen to have lots of sons. Though the monarch is now monogamous, many men of all classes still keep **mistresses**, known as *mia noi* (minor wives), or have casual girlfriends (*gig*); the common view is that an official wife (*mia luang*) should be treated like the temple's main Buddha image – respected and elevated upon the altar – whereas the minor wife is like an amulet, to be taken along wherever you go. For less wealthy men, prostitution is a far cheaper option: at least two-fifths of sexually active Thai men are thought to visit brothels twice a month.

The **farang sex industry** is a relatively new development, having started during the Vietnam War, when the American military set up seven bases around Thailand. The GIs' appetite for "entertainment" attracted women from surrounding rural areas to cash in on the boom, and Bangkok joined the fray in the late 1960s. By the mid-1970s, the GIs had left, but tourists replaced them, lured by advertising that diverted most of the traffic to Bangkok and Pattaya. Sex tourism has since grown to become an established part of the Thai economy and has spread to Phuket, Hat Yai, Ko Samui and Chiang Mai.

The majority of the women who work in the country's go-go bars and "bar-beers" (outdoor hostess bars) come from the poorest areas of north and northeast Thailand. **Economic refugees**, they're easily drawn into an industry in which they can make in a single night what would take a month to earn in the rice fields. Many women opt for a couple of years in the sex bars to help pay off family debts and improve the living conditions of parents stuck in the poverty trap.

Many bar girls, and male prostitutes too, are looking for longer-term **relationships** with their farang customers, bringing a temporary respite from bar work and perhaps even a ticket out. A surprising number of one-night transactions do develop into some sort of holiday romance, with the young woman accompanying her farang "boyfriend" (often twice her age) around the country and maintaining contact after he's returned home. It's a common joke that some bar girls field half a dozen mobile phones so they can juggle all their various "sponsors". An entire sub-genre of novels and confessional memoirs (among them the classic *Hello, My Big Big Honey!: Letters to Bangkok Bar Girls and Their Revealing Interviews*) testifies to the role money plays in all this, and highlights the delusions common to both parties, not to mention the cross-cultural incomprehension.

Despite its ubiquity, prostitution has been **illegal** in Thailand since 1960, but sex-industry bosses easily circumvent the law by registering their establishments as clubs, karaoke bars or massage parlours, and making payoffs to the police and politicians. Sex workers, on the other hand, often endure exploitation and violence from pimps and customers rather than face fines and long rehabilitation sentences. Hardly surprising that many prefer to go freelance, working the clubs and bars in non-red-light zones such as Thanon Khao San. Life is made even more difficult because abortion is illegal in Thailand. The **anti-prostitution law**, however, does attempt to treat sex workers as victims rather than criminals and penalizes parents who sell their children. A high-profile voice in the struggle to improve the **rights of sex workers** is the Empower Foundation (Ⓦempowerfoundation.org), which not only organizes campaigns and runs education centres for bar workers but also manages its own bar in Chiang Mai.

Inevitably, **child prostitution** is a significant issue in Thailand, but NGOs such as ECPAT (Ⓦecpat.net) say numbers have declined over the last decade, due to zero-tolerance and awareness campaigns. The government has also strengthened legislation against hiring a prostitute under the age of 18, and anyone caught having sex with an under-15 is now charged with rape. The disadvantaged are still targeted by traffickers however, who "buy" children from desperately poor hill-tribe and other minority families and keep them as bonded slaves until the debt has been repaid.

Patpong

Concentrated into two lanes running between the eastern ends of Thanon Silom and Thanon Suriwong, the neon-lit go-go bars of the **Patpong** district loom like rides in a tawdry sexual Disneyland. In front of each bar, girls cajole passers-by with a lifeless sensuality while insistent touts proffer printed menus and photographs detailing the degradations on show. Inside, bikini-clad women gyrate to Western music and play hostess to the (almost exclusively male) spectators; upstairs, live shows feature women who, to use Spalding Gray's phrase in *Swimming to Cambodia*, "do everything with their vaginas except have babies".

Patpong was no more than a sea of mud when the capital was founded on the marshy river bank to the west, but by the 1960s it had grown into a flash district of dance halls for rich Thais, owned by a Chinese millionaire godfather, educated at the London School of Economics and by the OSS (forerunner of the CIA), who gave his name to the area. In 1969, an American entrepreneur turned an existing teahouse into a luxurious nightclub to satisfy the tastes of soldiers on R&R trips from Vietnam, and so Patpong's transformation into a Western sex reservation began. At first, the area was rough and violent, but over the years it has wised up to the desires of the affluent farang, and now markets itself as a packaged concept of Oriental decadence.

The centre of the skin trade lies along the interconnected sois of **Patpong 1 and 2**, where lines of go-go bars share their patch with respectable restaurants, a 24-hour supermarket and an overabundance of pharmacies. Even the most demure tourists – of both sexes – turn out to do some shopping at the night market down the middle of Patpong 1, where hawkers sell fake watches, bags and designer T-shirts. By day, a relaxed hangover descends on the place. Farang men slump at the open-air bars on Patpong 2, drinking and watching videos, unable to find anything else to do in the whole of Bangkok. Running parallel to the east, **Soi Thaniya** is Patpong's Japanese counterpart, lined with hostess bars and some good restaurants, while the focus of Bangkok's gay scene, **Silom 2** (ie Soi 2, Thanon Silom) and the more mixed **Silom 4**, flank Thaniya.

The west end of Thanon Silom

Further west along **Thanon Silom** from Patpong, in a still-thriving South Indian enclave, lies the colourful landmark of the **Maha Uma Devi Temple**. Also known as **Sri Mahamariamman** or **Wat Khaek**, this vibrant, gaudy Hindu shrine was built in 1895 in honour of Shiva's consort, Uma. Carrying on to the river, the strip west of Charoen Krung (New Road) reveals some of the history of Bangkok's early dealings with foreigners in the fading grandeur of the old trading quarter. Here you'll find the only place in Bangkok where you might be able to eke out an architectural walk, though it's hardly compelling. Incongruous churches and "colonial" buildings – the best being the Authors' Wing of the *Oriental Hotel*, where nostalgic afternoon teas are served – are hemmed in by the spice shops and *halal* canteens of the growing Muslim area around Thanon Charoen Krung.

M.R. Kukrit's Heritage Home

19 Soi Phra Pinit (Soi 7, Thanon Narathiwat Ratchanakharin) • Daily 10am–4pm, though it's often closed for social engagements, so worth phoning ahead to check • B50 • ☎ 02 286 8185, ⓦ kukritshousefund.com • 10min walk south then east from Thanon Sathorn; 20min walk from BTS Chong Nonsi

M.R. Kukrit's Heritage Home (*Baan Mom Kukrit*) is the beautiful traditional house and gardens of one of Thailand's leading figures of the twentieth century. M.R. (*Mom Rajawongse*, a princely title) Kukrit Pramoj (1911–95) was a remarkable all-rounder, descended from Rama II on his father's side and, on his mother's side, from the influential ministerial family, the Bunnags. Kukrit graduated in Philosophy, Politics and Economics from Oxford University and went on to become a university lecturer back in Thailand, but his greatest claim to fame is probably as a writer: he founded, owned and penned a daily column for *Siam Rath*, the most influential Thai-language newspaper, and wrote short stories, novels, plays and poetry. He was also a respected performer in classical dance-drama (*khon*), and he starred as an Asian prime minister, opposite Marlon Brando, in the Hollywood film, *The Ugly American*. In 1974, during an especially turbulent period for Thailand, life imitated art, when Kukrit was called on to become Thailand's prime minister at the head of a coalition of seventeen parties. However, just four hundred days into his premiership, the Thai military leadership dismissed him for being too anti-American.

The **residence**, which has been left just as it was when Kukrit was alive, reflects his complex character. In the large, open-sided *sala* (pavilion) for public functions, near the entrance, is an attractive display of *khon* masks, including a gold one that Kukrit wore when he played the demon king, Totsagan (Ravana). In and around the adjoining Khmer-styled garden, keep your eyes peeled for the *mai dut*, sculpted miniature trees similar to bonsai, some of which Kukrit worked on for decades. The living quarters beyond are made up of five teak houses on stilts, assembled from various parts of central Thailand and joined by an open veranda. The bedroom, study and various sitting rooms are decked out with beautiful objets d'art; look out especially for the carved bed that belonged to Rama II and the very delicate, two-hundred-year-old nielloware (gold inlay) from Nakhon Si Thammarat in the formal reception room. In the small family prayer room, Kukrit Pramoj's ashes are enshrined in the base of a reproduction of the Emerald Buddha.

CERAMIC AT WAT CHALERM PHRA KIAT

Chatuchak Weekend Market and the outskirts

The amorphous clutter of Greater Bangkok doesn't harbour many attractions, but there are a handful of places on the outskirts of the city that make pleasant half-day outings. Nearly all the places described in this chapter can be reached fairly painlessly by some sort of city transport, either by ferry up the Chao Phraya River or by Skytrain, subway or city bus. If you're in Bangkok on a Saturday or Sunday, it's well worth making the effort to visit the enormous Chatuchak Weekend Market, where you could browse away an entire day among the thousands of stalls selling everything from handmade paper to bargain-priced sarongs.

The open-air Prasart Museum boasts many finely crafted replicas of traditional Thai buildings and is recommended for anyone who hasn't got the time to go upcountry and admire Thailand's temples and palaces *in situ*. Taking a boat ride up the Chao Phraya River makes a nice change to sitting in city-centre traffic, and the upstream town of Nonthaburi and the tranquil but less easily accessible island of Ko Kred provide the ideal excuse for doing just that.

Chatuchak Weekend Market (JJ)

Occupies a huge patch of ground extending northwest from the corner of Phaholyothin and Kamphaeng Phet roads • Sat & Sun roughly 9am–6/7pm, though many stalls open earlier and some close later • ⓦ chatuchak.org

With over eight thousand open-air stalls to peruse, and wares as diverse as Lao silk, Siamese kittens and designer lamps, the enormous **Chatuchak Weekend Market**, or **JJ** as it's usually abbreviated (from "Jatu Jak"), is undoubtedly Bangkok's most enjoyable – and exhausting – shopping experience.

The market also contains a controversial **wildlife** section that has long doubled as a clearing house for protected and endangered species such as gibbons, palm cockatoos and Indian pied hornbills, many of them smuggled in from Laos and Cambodia and sold to private animal collectors and foreign zoos. The illegal trade goes on beneath the counter, despite occasional crackdowns, but you're bound to come across fighting cocks around the back, miniature flying squirrels being fed milk through pipettes, and iridescent red-and-blue Siamese fighting fish, kept in individual jars and shielded from each other's aggressive stares by sheets of cardboard.

Where to shop

Chatuchak is divided into 27 numbered **sections**, plus a dozen unnumbered ones, each of them more or less dedicated to a particular genre, for example household items, plants and secondhand books, and if you have several hours to spare, it's fun just to browse at whim. The market's primary customers are Bangkok residents in search of idiosyncratic fashion clothing (try sections 5 and 6) and homewares (sections 2, 3, 4, 7 and 8), but Chatuchak also has plenty of collector- and tourist-oriented **stalls**; best buys include antique lacquerware, unusual sarongs, traditional cotton clothing and crafts from the north, silver jewellery, and ceramics, particularly the five-coloured *bencharong*. For handicrafts (including musical instruments) and traditional textiles, you should start with sections 22, 24, 25 (which features textiles from northern Thailand) and 26, which are all in a cluster at the southwest (Kamphaeng Phet subway) end of the market; sections A, B and C, behind the market's head office and information centre, are also full of interesting artefacts.

Foodies will want to check out **Talat Or Tor Khor** (the Agricultural Market Organization Market), a covered market that sells a fantastic array of fruit, vegetables and other produce from around the country, as well as prepared dishes to take away or to eat at the food court; it's on the south side of Thanon Kamphaeng Phet, next to Kamphaeng Phet subway station. The best place to get a drink in Chatuchak Weekend Market is *Viva 8* (see p.172).

ARRIVAL AND GETTING AROUND

CHATUCHAK WEEKEND MARKET (JJ)

Arrival Kamphaeng Phet subway station exits right into the most interesting, southwestern, corner of the market; on the northeast side of the market are Chatuchak Park subway and Mochit BTS stations. Coming from Banglamphu, either get a bus to BTS National Stadium or BTS Ratchathewi, or take the #503 (non-expressway version) or #509 bus all the way (about 1hr) from Rajdamnoen Klang; once the MRT extension has opened, it should be possible to catch an express boat to Tha Tien, then walk 5min to Sanam Chai station, for subway trains to Chatuchak Park or Kamphaeng Phet stations.

Getting around A few very small electric trams circulate around the market's main inner ring road, transporting weary shoppers for free, though they always seem to be full.

INFORMATION

Maps *Nancy Chandler's Map of Bangkok* has a fabulously detailed and informatively annotated map of all the sections in the market. Maps are also posted at various points around the market, including in the subway stations. For specific help you can ask at the market office, on the main inner ring road near Gate 1 off Thanon Kamphaeng Phet 2, which also has ATMs and currency exchange booths.

The Prasart Museum

9 Soi 4A, Soi Krungthep Kreetha, Thanon Krungthep Kreetha • Tues–Sun 9am–2pm • B1000 for 1 person; for 2 people or more, B500 per person • Call ☎ 02 379 3601 to book the compulsory tour

Located on the far eastern edge of the city, the **Prasart Museum** is an unusual open-air exhibition of traditional Asian buildings, put together by wealthy entrepreneur and art-lover Khun Prasart. The museum is rarely visited – partly because of the intentionally limited opening hours and inflated admission price, and partly because it takes a long time to get there by public transport – but it makes a pleasant day out and is worth the effort.

Set in a gorgeously lush tropical garden, the museum comprises about a dozen beautifully crafted replicas of **traditional buildings**, including a golden teak palace inspired by the Tamnak Daeng at the National Museum, a Chinese temple and water garden, a Khmer shrine and a Sukhothai-era teak library set over a lotus pond. Some have been pieced together from ruined originals, while others were constructed from scratch. Many are filled with antique **artefacts**, including Burmese woodcarvings, prehistoric pottery from Ban Chiang and Lopburi-era statuettes. There's also an exquisite collection of *bencharong* ceramics.

7

ARRIVAL AND DEPARTURE   THE PRASART MUSEUM

By bus Regular and a/c bus #93 runs almost to the door: pick it up near its starting point on Thanon Si Phraya near River City and the GPO, or anywhere along its route on Phetchaburi and Phetchaburi Mai roads (both the Khlong Saen Saeb canal boats and the subway have potentially useful stops at the Thanon Asok Montri/Sukhumvit Soi 21 junction with Thanon Phetchaburi Mai). The #93 terminates on Thanon Krungthep Kreetha, but you should get off a couple of stops before the terminus, at the first stop on Thanon Krungthep Kreetha, as soon as you see the sign for the Prasart Museum (about 1hr 15min by bus from Si Phraya). Follow the sign down Soi Krungthep Kreetha, go past the golf course and, after about a 15min walk, turn off down Soi 4A.

By boat To speed things up, instead of a bus ride, you could take the Khlong Saen Saeb canal boat all the way to Tha The Mall Bangkapi (about 40min from Phan Fah, seven stops after the confusingly similar Tha The Mall Ram stop). It is then a very short taxi ride to the museum.

By train Another time saver is to take the Suvarnabhumi Airport Rail Link from Phaya Thai to Hua Mark station, which leaves you within a very short taxi ride of The Prasart Museum.

Nonthaburi

Chao Phraya Express Boat to Nonthaburi, the last stop upriver for most (N30), under 1hr from Central Pier (Sathorn) on an orange-flag boat

A trip to **NONTHABURI**, the first town and province beyond the northern boundary of Bangkok, is the easiest excursion you can make from the centre of the city and affords a perfect opportunity to recharge your batteries. Nonthaburi is the last stop upriver for most express boats and the ride itself is most of the fun, weaving round huge, crawling sand barges and tiny canoes. The slow pace of the boat gives you plenty of time to take in the sights on the way. On the north side of Banglamphu, beyond the elegant, new **Rama VIII Bridge**, which shelters the Mekong whisky distillery on the west bank, you'll pass in turn, on the east bank: the Bangkhunprom Palace and the adjacent Devaves Palace, two gleamingly restored former princely residences in the Bank of Thailand compound; the royal boathouse at Tha Wasukri in front of the National Library, where you can glimpse the minor ceremonial boats that escort the grand royal barges; the city's first Catholic church, Holy Conception, founded in the seventeenth century during King Narai of Ayutthaya's reign and rebuilt in the early nineteenth; and, beyond Krungthon Bridge, the Singha brewery. Along the route are dazzling Buddhist temples and drably painted mosques, catering for Bangkok's growing Muslim population, as well as a few remaining communities who still live in houses on stilts or houseboats – around Krungthon Bridge, for example, you'll see people living on the huge teak vessels used to carry rice, sand and charcoal.

Disembarking at suburban Nonthaburi, on the east bank of the river, you won't find a great deal to do, in truth. There's a market that's famous for the quality of its fruit, while the attractive, old Provincial Office across the road is covered in wooden latticework. To break up your trip with a slow, scenic drink or lunch, you'll find a floating seafood restaurant, *Rim Fang*, to the right at the end of the prom.

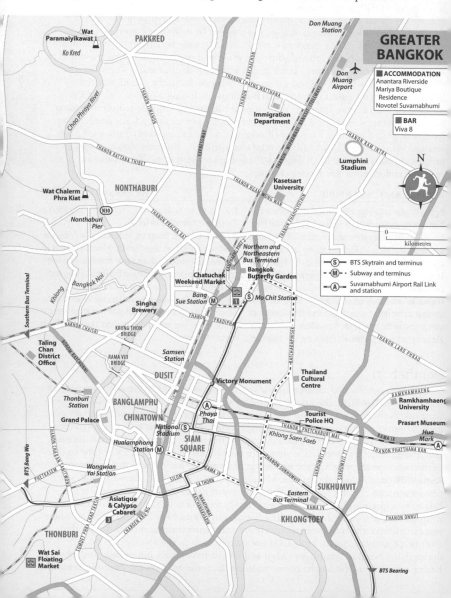

DURIANS

The naturalist Alfred Russel Wallace, eulogizing the taste of the **durian**, compared it to "rich butter-like custard highly flavoured with almonds, but intermingled with wafts of flavour that call to mind cream cheese, onion sauce, brown sherry and other incongruities". He neglected to discuss the smell of the fruit's skin, which is so bad – somewhere between detergent and dog excrement – that durians are barred from Thai hotels and aeroplanes. The different **varieties** bear strange names that do nothing to make them more appetizing: "frog", "golden pillow", "gibbon" and so on. However, the durian has fervent admirers, perhaps because it's such an acquired taste, and because it's considered a strong aphrodisiac. Aficionados discuss the varieties with as much subtlety as if they were vintage Champagnes, and treat the durian as a social fruit, to be shared around, despite a price tag of up to B3000 each. They also pour scorn on the Thai government scientists who have recently genetically developed an odourless variety, the Chanthaburi 1 durian.

The most famous durian orchards are around Nonthaburi, where the fruits are said to have an incomparably rich and nutty flavour due to the fine clay soil. To see these and other plantations such as mango, pomelo and jackfruit, your best bet is to hire a longtail from Nonthaburi pier to take you west along Khlong Om Non. If you don't smell them first, you can recognize durians by their sci-fi appearance: the shape and size of a rugby ball, but slightly deflated, they're covered in a thick, pale-green shell which is heavily armoured with short, sharp spikes (*duri* means "thorn" in Malay). By cutting along one of the faint seams with a good knife, you'll reveal a white pith in which are set a handful of yellow blobs with the texture of a wrinkled soufflé: this is what you eat. The taste is best when the smell is at its highest, about three days after the fruit has dropped. Be careful when out walking near the trees: because of its great weight and sharp spikes, a falling durian can lead to serious injury, or even an ignominious death.

Wat Chalerm Phra Kiat

1km north of Nonthaburi pier on the west bank of the river • From the express-boat pier take the ferry straight across the Chao Phraya and then catch a motorbike taxi or walk

Set in relaxing grounds on the west bank of the river, elegant **Wat Chalerm Phra Kiat** injects a splash of urban refinement among a grove of breadfruit trees. The beautifully proportioned temple, which has been lavishly restored, was built by Rama III in memory of his mother, whose family lived and presided over vast orchards in the area. Inside the walls of the temple compound, you feel as if you've come upon a stately folly in a secret garden, and a strong Chinese influence shows itself in the unusual ribbed roofs and elegantly curved gables, decorated with pastel ceramics. The restorers have done their best work inside: look out especially for the simple, delicate landscapes on the shutters.

Ko Kred

The tiny island of **KO KRED** lies in a particularly sharp bend in the Chao Phraya, about 7km north of Nonthaburi pier, cut off from the east bank by a waterway created in the eighteenth century to make the cargo route from Ayutthaya to the Gulf of Thailand just that little bit faster. Although it's been discovered by day-trippers from Bangkok, this artificial island remains something of a time capsule, a little oasis of village life completely at odds with the metropolitan chaos downriver. Roughly 10 square kilometres in all, Ko Kred has no roads, just a concrete track that follows its circumference, with a few arterial walkways branching off towards the interior. Villagers, the majority of whom are Mon, descendants of immigrants from Myanmar during the reigns of Taksin and Rama II, use a small fleet of motorbike taxis to cross their island, but as a sightseer you're much better off on a rental bicycle or just on foot: a round-island walk takes about an hour and a half.

There are few sights as such on Ko Kred, but its lushness and comparative emptiness make it a perfect place in which to wander. You'll no doubt come across one of the island's potteries and kilns, which churn out the regionally famous earthenware flowerpots and small water-storage jars and employ a large percentage of the village workforce. The island's clay is very rich in nutrients and therefore excellent for fruit-growing, and banana trees, coconut palms, pomelo, papaya, mango and durian trees all grow in abundance on Ko Kred, fed by an intricate network of irrigation channels that crisscrosses the interior. In among the orchards, the Mons have built their wooden houses, mostly in traditional style and raised high above the marshy ground on stilts.

Wat Paramaiyikawat

Ko Kred boasts a handful of attractive riverside wats, most notably **Wat Paramaiyikawat** (also called **Wat Poramai**), at the main pier at the northeast tip of the island. This engagingly ramshackle eighteenth-century temple was restored by Rama V in honour of his grandmother, with a Buddha relic placed in its leaning, white, riverside chedi, which is a replica of the Mutao Pagoda in Hanthawadi (now Bago), capital of the Mon kingdom in Myanmar. Among an open-air scattering of Burmese-style alabaster Buddha images, the tall bot shelters some fascinating nineteenth-century murals, depicting scenes from temple life at ground level and the life of the Buddha above, all set in delicate imaginary landscapes.

ARRIVAL AND DEPARTURE   KO KRED

The easiest but busiest time to visit Ko Kred is at the weekend, when you can take a boat tour from central Bangkok. At other times, getting there by public transport is a bit of a chore.

By boat tour The Mitchaopaya Travel Service (B300; ☏ 02 623 6169 or ☏ 02 225 6179) runs boat tours to Ko Kred on Saturdays, Sundays and public holidays, leaving Tha Chang in Ratanakosin at 9am, returning at about 4.30pm. On the way, you'll cruise along Khlong Bangkok Noi and Khlong Om, and call in at the Royal Barge Museum (see p.83), Wat Chalerm Phra Kiat in Nonthaburi (see p.109), and Wat Poramai and Ban Khanom Thai on Ko Kred, where you can buy traditional sweets and watch them being made.

By public transport Your best option is to take a Chao Phraya Express Boat to Nonthaburi, then bus #32 (ordinary and a/c, coming from Wat Pho via Banglamphu) or a taxi (about B100) to Pakkred or a chartered longtail boat direct to Ko Kred (about B300). There are also fast, ordinary and a/c #166 buses from the northwest side of Victory Monument (accessible by Skytrain) to Pakkred, which are your best option for getting back as the #32 stops a fair way from Nonthaburi pier on its inbound journey. From Pakkred, the easiest way of getting across to the island is to hire a longtail boat, although shuttle boats cross at the river's narrowest point to Wat Poramai from Wat Sanam Neua, about a 1km walk or motorbike-taxi ride south of the Pakkred pier (getting off the bus at Tesco Lotus in Pakkred will cut down the walk to Wat Sanam Neua).

AYUTTHAYA

Excursions from Bangkok

Regular bus and train services from Bangkok give access to a number of enjoyable excursions, all of which are perfectly feasible as day-trips, though some also merit an overnight stay. The fertile plain to the north of the capital is bisected by the country's main artery, the Chao Phraya River, which carries boat tours to supplement the area's trains and buses. The monumental kitsch of the nineteenth-century palace at Bang Pa-In provides a sharp contrast with the atmospheric ruins further upriver at the former capital of Ayutthaya, where ancient temples, some crumbling and overgrown, others still very much in use, are arrayed in a leafy setting. You could visit the two sites on a long day-trip from Bangkok, but separate outings or an overnight stay in Ayutthaya will let you make the most of the former capital's many attractions.

To the west of the capital, the enormous nineteenth-century stupa at **Nakhon Pathom** is undeniably impressive and well worth the short journey from Bangkok; it's often visited in conjunction with an early-morning outing to the floating markets of **Damnoen Saduak**, though these are so popular with tourists that they seem staged and contrived. Better to venture a few kilometres further south to the more authentic floating markets around **Amphawa**, near **Samut Songkhram**, whose quaint canalside neighbourhoods are complemented by some appealing riverside accommodation that makes this a perfect overnight break from Bangkok. Getting there – on a rural, single-track train line – is half the fun. Tradition is also central to the untouristed town of **Phetchaburi**, with its many charming temples and hilltop royal palace.

Northwest of the capital, **Kanchanaburi** has long attracted visitors to the notorious **Bridge over the River** Kwai, and the extraordinary, POW-built Death Railway that crosses it. But the town harbours many even more affecting World War II memorials and occupies a gloriously scenic riverside location, best savoured by spending a night in a raft house moored to the river bank. Finally, for a taste of Thailand's finest monuments and temples in just one rewarding bite, just beyond Bangkok's southeastern suburbs there's the well-designed open-air museum at **Muang Boran Ancient City**, which contains beautifully crafted replicas of the country's top buildings.

Muang Boran Ancient City

33km southeast of central Bangkok in Samut Prakan • Daily 9am–7pm • B700 9am–4pm, B350 4–7pm • ⓦ ancientcitygroup.net • A/c bus #511 from Bearing Skytrain station (or from Thanon Rama I or Banglamphu) to Samut Prakan, then songthaew #36 to Muang Boran; otherwise, Muang Boran operates free pick-ups three times a day from Bearing Skytrain station (see their website for times), via Erawan Museum, an overblown exercise in spiritual psychedelia under the same ownership

A day-trip out to the **Muang Boran Ancient City** open-air museum is a great way to enjoy the best of Thailand's architectural heritage in relative peace and without much effort. Occupying a huge park shaped like Thailand itself, the museum comprises more than a hundred traditional Thai buildings scattered around pleasantly landscaped grounds and is best toured by rented **bicycle** (B50), though doing it on foot is just about possible. Many of the buildings are copies of the country's most famous monuments, and are located in the appropriate "region" of the park, with everything from Bangkok's Grand Palace (central region) to the spectacularly sited hilltop Khmer Khao Phra Viharn sanctuary (northeast) represented here. There are also some original structures, including a rare scripture library rescued from Samut Songkhram (south), and some painstaking reconstructions from contemporary documents of long-vanished gems, of which the Ayutthaya-period Sanphet Prasat Palace (central) is a particularly fine example, as well as some purely imaginary designs. A sizeable team of restorers and skilled craftspeople maintains the buildings and helps keep some of the traditional techniques alive; if you come here during the week you can watch them at work.

Bang Pa-In

Little more than a roadside market, the village of **BANG PA-IN**, 60km north of Bangkok, has been put on the tourist map by its extravagant and rather surreal **Royal Palace**, even though most of the buildings can be seen only from the outside. King Prasat Thong of Ayutthaya first built a palace on this site, 20km downstream from his capital, in the middle of the seventeenth century, and it remained a popular country residence for the kings of Ayutthaya. The palace was abandoned a century later when the capital was moved to Bangkok, only to be revived in the middle of the nineteenth century when the advent of steamboats shortened the journey time upriver. Rama IV (1851–68) built a modest residence here, which his son Chulalongkorn (Rama V), in his passion for westernization, knocked down to make room for the eccentric melange of European, Thai and Chinese architectural styles visible today.

TRAVELLING OUT OF BANGKOK

BY TRAIN

Nearly all trains depart from **Hualamphong Station**. The 24-hour State Railways (SRT) information booth at Hualamphong Station keeps English-language **timetables**, detailing types of trains and ticket classes available on each route, as well as fares and supplementary charges; a third-class ticket in a non-air-conditioned carriage on a Rapid train from Hualamphong to Ayutthaya, for example, will set you back just B45. Otherwise you can try phoning the Train Information Hotline on ☎ 1690; the SRT's main website (ⓦ railway.co.th) carries English-language timetables, while the affiliated ⓦ www.thairailticket.com gives prices. For more comprehensive information and advice, go to ⓦ seat61.com/thailand.htm. There's a range of city transport to and from Hualamphong and left-luggage facilities at the station (see p.44).

The main non-Hualamphong service is the twice-daily service to Kanchanaburi and Nam Tok via Nakhon Pathom, which leaves from **Thonburi Station** (sometimes still referred to by its former name, **Bangkok Noi Station**), across the river from Banglamphu in Thonburi. The station is about an 850m walk west of the Thonburi Railway Station N11 express boat stop; frequent red songthaews (public pick-ups) run passengers between the N11 pier and the train station (5min). The other non-Hualamphong departure is the service to Samut Sakhon (aka Mahachai), for connections to Samut Songkhram, which leaves from **Wongwian Yai Station**, also in Thonburi. Access is by Skytrain to Wongwian Yai (S8) or by bus #3 from Thanon Chakrabongse in Banglamphu.

BY BUS

Destinations in this chapter are served by air-conditioned buses (*rot air*) from two major terminals in Bangkok, both on the outskirts of the city, as well as by air-conditioned minibuses (*rot tuu*) as detailed in the accounts. As regards fares, a one-way ticket to Ayutthaya, for example, typically costs B60.

The huge, airport-like **Southern Bus Terminal**, or **Sathaanii Sai Tai Mai**, is at the junction of Thanon Borom Ratchonni and Thanon Phutthamonthon Sai 1 in Taling Chan, an interminable 11km west of the Chao Phraya River and Banglamphu, so access to and from city accommodation can take an age, even in a taxi. It handles departures to destinations west of Bangkok, such as Nakhon Pathom, Damnoen Saduak, Samut Songkhran, Phetchaburi and Kanchanaburi, and to all points south of the capital. To reach the terminal, take city bus #124, #511 or #516 from Banglamphu, #516 from Thewet, or #511 from Thanon Sukhumvit.

The **Northern Bus Terminal**, or **Sathaanii Mo Chit**, is the departure point for buses to Bang Pa-In, Ayutthaya and all northern and northeastern towns. It's on Thanon Kamphaeng Phet 2, near Chatuchak Weekend Market in the far north of the city; Mo Chit Skytrain station and Chatuchak Park subway station are within a short motorbike taxi or tuk-tuk ride, or take a city bus direct to the bus terminal: ordinary and a/c #3 and a/c #509 run from Banglamphu.

The palace

Daily 8am–4pm, ticket office closes 3.30pm • B100 • Electric cart rental B400 first hour, B100 subsequent hours • ⓦ palaces.thai.net • Visitors are asked to dress respectfully, so no vests, shorts or sandals

Set in manicured grounds on an island in the Chao Phraya River, and based around an ornamental lake, the **palace** complex is flat and compact, and easy to see on foot. The best approach is to explore slowly, following walkways that crisscross the lake.

The lakeside and covered bridge

On the north side of the lake stand a two-storey, colonial-style residence for the royal relatives and the Italianate **Varobhas Bimarn** (**Warophat Phiman**, "Excellent and Shining Heavenly Abode"), which housed Chulalongkorn's throne hall and still contains private apartments where the present royal family sometimes stays, though the lavishly furnished rooms by the entrance are usually open to the public. A covered bridge links this outer part of the palace to the **Pratu Thewarat Khanlai** ("The King of the Gods Goes Forth Gate"), the main entrance to the inner palace, which was reserved for the king and his immediate family. The high fence that encloses half of the bridge allowed the women of the harem to cross without being seen by male courtiers.

Aisawan Thiphya-art

You can't miss the glittering **Aisawan Thiphya-art** ("Divine Seat of Personal Freedom") in the middle of the lake: named after King Prasat Thong's original palace, it's the only example of pure Thai architecture at Bang Pa-In. The elegant tiers of the pavilion's roof shelter a bronze statue of Chulalongkorn.

The inner palace

In the inner palace, the **Uthayan Phumisathian** ("Garden of the Secured Land"), recently rebuilt by Queen Sirikit in grand, neocolonial style, was Chulalongkorn's favourite house. After passing the candy-striped **Ho Withun Thasana** ("Sage's Lookout Tower"), built so that the king could survey the surrounding countryside, you'll come to the main attraction of Bang Pa-In, the **Phra Thinang Wehart Chamrun Residential Hall** ("Palace of Heavenly Light"). A masterpiece of Chinese design, the mansion and its contents were shipped from China and presented as a gift to Chulalongkorn in 1889 by the Chinese Chamber of Commerce in Bangkok. The sumptuous interior gleams with fantastically intricate lacquered and gilded wooden screens, hand-painted porcelain floor tiles and ebony furniture inlaid with mother-of-pearl.

The obelisk

The simple marble **obelisk** behind the Uthayan Phumisathian was erected by Chulalongkorn to hold the ashes of Queen Sunandakumariratana, his favourite wife. In 1881, Sunanda, who was then 21 and expecting a child, was taking a trip on the river here when her boat capsized. She could have been rescued quite easily, but the laws concerning the sanctity of the royal family left those around her no option: "If a

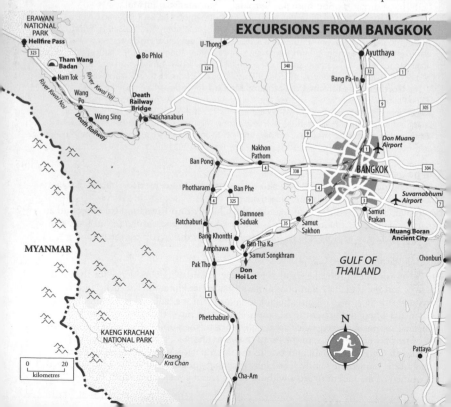

boat founders, the boatmen must swim away; if they remain near the boat [or] if they lay hold of him [the royal person] to rescue him, they are to be executed." Following the tragedy, King Chulalongkorn became a zealous reformer of Thai customs and strove to make the monarchy more accessible.

ARRIVAL AND EATING   BANG PA-IN

Bang Pa-In can easily be visited on a day-trip from Bangkok or Ayutthaya; many day-trips from both destinations feature a stop here (see p.118).

By train The best route from Bangkok is by train from Hualamphong Station, which takes just over an hour to reach Bang Pa-In (on arrival, note the separate station hall built by Chulalongkorn for the royal family). All trains continue to Ayutthaya, with half going on to Lopburi. Note that trains from Ayutthaya are more frequent than the English-language timetable implies (most Ayutthaya guesthouses keep the full Thai timetable). From Bang Pa-In's train station it's a 2km hike to the palace, or you can take a motorbike taxi for about B40. Returning to the station, catch a motorized samlor from the market, about 300m southwest of the palace entrance.
Destinations Ayutthaya (12 daily; 15min); Bangkok

Hualamphong (12 daily; 1hr 30min).
By bus Slow buses leave Bangkok's Northern Mo Chit terminal (roughly every 30min; 2hr) and stop at Bang Pa-In market, about 300m southwest of the palace entrance. This is also the easiest place to catch a bus back to Bangkok.
By songthaew From Ayutthaya, large songthaews leave Thanon Naresuan roughly every half hour for the 20min journey to Bang Pa-In market, returning from the same spot.
Eating There are food stalls just outside the palace gates, and at Bang Pa-In market, plus a couple of well-appointed riverside restaurants (no English signs) between the railway station and the palace, opposite Wat Chumpol Nikarayam.

Ayutthaya

In its heyday as the booming capital of the Thai kingdom, **AYUTTHAYA**, 80km north of Bangkok, was so well endowed with temples that sunlight reflecting off their gilt decoration was said to dazzle from 5km away. Wide, grassy spaces today occupy much of the atmospheric site, which now resembles a graveyard for temples: grand, brooding red-brick ruins rise out of the fields, satisfyingly evoking the city's bygone grandeur while providing a soothing contrast to more glitzy modern temple architecture. A few intact buildings help form an image of what the capital must have looked like, while three fine museums flesh out the picture.

The core of the ancient capital was a 4km-wide **island** at the confluence of the Lopburi, Pasak and Chao Phraya rivers, which was once encircled by a 12km-long wall, crumbling parts of which can be seen at the Phom Petch fortress in the southeast corner. A grid of broad roads now crosses the island, known as **Ko Muang**: the hub of the small modern town occupies its northeast corner, around the Thanon U Thong and Thanon Naresuan junction, but the rest is mostly uncongested and ideal for exploring by bicycle.

There is much pleasure to be had, also, from soaking up life on and along the encircling **rivers**, either by taking a boat tour or by dining at one of the waterside restaurants. It's very much a working waterway, busy with barges carrying cement, rice

8

VISITING AYUTTHAYA – ORIENTATION AND TEMPLE PASS

The majority of Ayutthaya's ancient remains are spread out across the western half of the island in a patchwork of parkland: **Wat Phra Mahathat** and **Wat Ratburana** stand near the modern centre, while a broad band runs down the middle of the parkland, containing the **Royal Palace** (Wang Luang) and temple, the most revered Buddha image, at **Viharn Phra Mongkol Bopit**, and the two main **museums**. To the north of the island you'll find the best-preserved temple, **Wat Na Phra Mane**, and **Wat Phu Khao Thong**, the "Golden Mount"; to the west stands the Khmer-style **Wat Chai Watthanaram**; while to the southeast lie the giant chedi of **Wat Yai Chai Mongkol** and **Wat Phanan Choeng**, still a vibrant place of worship. The city's main temples can be visited for a reduced rate when you buy the special six-in-one **pass** (B220; valid for 30 days), which is available from most temple ticket offices.

and other heavy loads to and from Bangkok and the Gulf and with cross-river ferry services that compensate for the lack of bridges. In addition, places like The Million Toy Museum are also worth a visit, providing a balance to the sombre mood of all the ancient culture.

Ayutthaya comes alive each year for a week in mid-December, with a **festival** that commemorates the town's listing as a **World Heritage Site** by UNESCO on December 13, 1991. The highlight is the nightly *son et lumière* show, featuring fireworks and elephant-back fights, staged around the ruins.

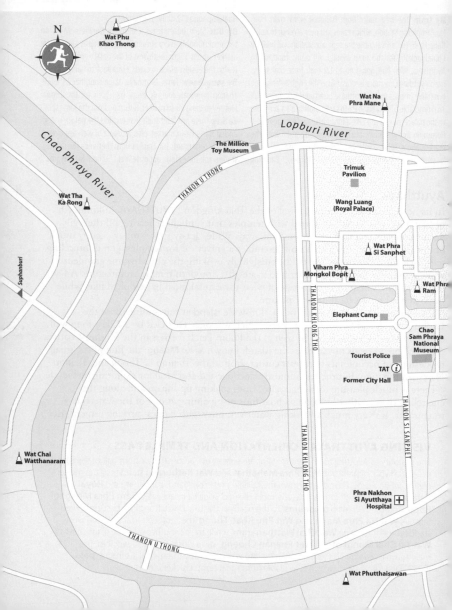

Brief history

Ayutthaya takes its name from the Indian city of Ayodhya (Sanskrit for "invincible"), the legendary birthplace of Rama, hero of the *Ramayana* epic. It was founded in 1351 by U Thong – later **Ramathibodi I** – after Lopburi was ravaged by smallpox, and it rose rapidly through exploiting the expanding trade routes between India and China. Stepping into the political vacuum left by the decline of the Khmer empire at Angkor and the first Thai kingdom at Sukhothai, by the mid-fifteenth century Ayutthaya controlled an empire covering most of the area of modern-day Thailand.

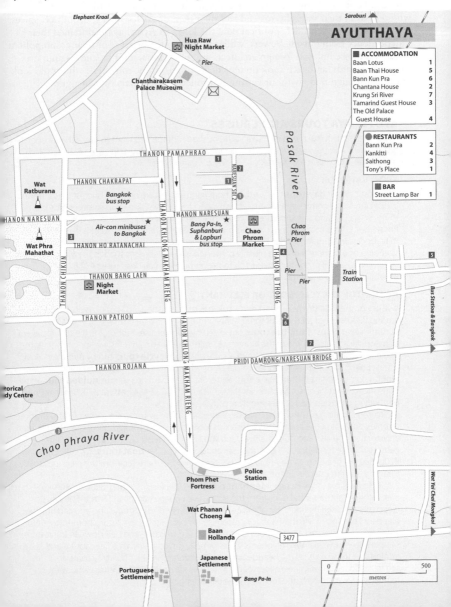

Built entirely on canals, few of which survive today, Ayutthaya grew into an enormous amphibious city, which by 1685 had one million people – roughly double the population of London at the same time – living largely on houseboats in a 140km network of waterways.

Ayutthaya's golden age

Ayutthaya's great wealth attracted a swarm of **foreign traders**, especially in the seventeenth century. At one stage around forty different nationalities, including Chinese, Persians, Portuguese, Dutch, English and French, were settled here, many of whom lived in their own ghettos and had their own docks for the export of rice, spices, timber and hides. With deft political skill, the kings of Ayutthaya maintained their independence from outside powers, while embracing the benefits of their cosmopolitan influence: they employed foreign architects and navigators, used Japanese samurai as royal bodyguards, and even took on outsiders as their prime ministers, who could look after their foreign trade without getting embroiled in the usual court intrigues.

AYUTTHAYA TOURS AND CRUISES

Ayutthaya is relatively spread out, so if you're pushed for time and want to make the most of its historic ruins and busy waterways, consider joining one of the **day-trips** from Bangkok. With more time, you can explore by tuk-tuk, bicycle or boat.

FROM BANGKOK

The most popular **day-trips** to Ayutthaya from Bangkok feature only the briefest whizz around the old city's two or three main temples, making a stop at the Bang Pa-In summer palace en route (see p.112) and rounding the day off with a three-hour river cruise back down the Chao Phraya from the northern Bangkok suburb of Nonthaburi; Grand Pearl Cruise is one of the main operators (W grandpearlcruise.com; B1900). You can also cruise the river in more style, spending one or more nights on plushly converted teak rice-barges such as the *Mekhala* (W asian-oasis.com) or the two owned by the *Anantara Riverside Hotel* (T 02 477 0770, W bangkok-cruises.anantara.com).

BY TUK-TUK, BICYCLE, BOAT OR ELEPHANT

If you're pushed for time you could hire a **tuk-tuk** for a whistle-stop tour of the old city for around B200 an hour (or B500 for three hours), either from the train station or from Chao Phrom market. **Sunset tuk-tuk tours** organized by guesthouses (about 2hr; B300/vehicle) are also popular, taking in some of the illuminated ruins (the five main ruins are lit nightly 7–9pm) and ending at the night market, or there are the guided **bicycle tours** run by Ayutthaya Boat & Travel (T 081 733 5687, W ayutthaya-boat.com), whose itineraries include the ruins by day or night, a combination cycle and boat tour and a dinner cruise. For a serious **guided tour** of the ruins, local expert Professor Monton at Classic Tour (T 081 832 4849; about B2000/person/day, depending on group size) comes highly recommended.

Circumnavigating Ayutthaya by boat is a very enjoyable way to take in some of the outlying temples, and possibly a few lesser-visited ones too; many of the temples were designed to be approached and admired from the river, and you also get a leisurely look at twenty-first-century riverine residences. All guesthouses and agencies offer **boat tours**, typically charging B200–300 per person for a two-hour trip; boats can also be chartered from the pier outside the Chantharakasem Palace museum.

It's also possible to take a brief **elephant ride** (B400/person for 20min, B500 for 30min) past a couple of the central ruins from the roadside elephant "camp" on Thanon Pathon. The elephants and their mahouts are photogenically clad in period costume and you can buy the elephants bananas while they wait for custom, or simply watch them return home after 6pm when they rumble across to the northeast side of town to bathe and bed down in the restored sixteenth-century kraal. Wild elephants were formerly driven to the kraal for capture and taming, but these days it's the headquarters of Elephantstay (W elephantstay.com), an organization that runs three- to fourteen-day residential packages for visitors who want to ride, feed, water and bathe the ninety resident elephants.

8

In decline

In 1767, this four-hundred-year-long age of stability and prosperity came to an end. After more than two centuries of recurring tensions, the Burmese captured and ravaged Ayutthaya, taking tens of thousands of prisoners. With even the wats in ruins, the city was abandoned to the jungle, but its memory endured: the architects of the new capital on Ratanakosin island perpetuated Ayutthaya's layout in every possible way.

On the island

Most of Ayutthaya's main sights, as well as most accommodation and restaurants, are located on the island, so it makes sense to begin your exploration here, then branch out to sights off the island if you have time.

Wat Phra Mahathat

1km west of the new town centre along Thanon Naresuan • Daily 8am–6pm • B50, or included with the B220 six-in-one pass

Heading west out of the new town centre brings you to the first set of ruins – a pair of temples on opposite sides of the road. The overgrown **Wat Phra Mahathat**, on the left, is the epitome of Ayutthaya's nostalgic atmosphere of faded majesty. The name "Mahathat" (Great Relic Chedi) indicates that the temple was built to house remains of the Buddha himself: according to the royal chronicles – never renowned for historical accuracy – King Ramesuan (1388–95) was looking out of his palace one morning when ashes of the Buddha materialized out of thin air here. A gold casket containing the ashes was duly enshrined in a grand 38m-high prang. The prang later collapsed, but the reliquary was unearthed in the 1950s, along with a hoard of other treasures, including a gorgeous marble fish, which opened to reveal gold, amber, crystal and porcelain ornaments – all now on show in the Chao Sam Phraya National Museum (see p.120).

8

You can climb what remains of the prang to get a view of the grassy complex, with dozens of brick spires tilting at impossible angles and headless Buddhas scattered around like spare parts in a scrapyard; look out for the serene (and much photographed) head of a stone Buddha that has become nestled in a bodhi tree's roots.

Wat Ratburana

Across the road from Wat Phra Mahathat • Daily 8am–6pm • B50, or included with the B220 six-in-one pass

The towering **Wat Ratburana** was built in 1424 by King Boromraja II to commemorate his elder brothers, Ay and Yi, who managed to kill each other in an elephant-back duel over the succession to the throne, thus leaving it vacant for Boromraja. Here, four elegant Sri Lankan-style chedis lean outwards as if in deference to the main prang, on which some of the original stuccowork can still be seen, some of which has been restored, including fine statues of garudas swooping down on nagas. It's possible to descend steep steps inside the prang to the crypt, where on two levels you can make out fragmentary murals of the early Ayutthaya period.

Wat Phra Ram

West of Wat Phra Mahathat • Daily 8am–6pm • B50, or included with the B220 six-in-one pass

West of Wat Phra Mahathat you'll see a lake, now surrounded by a popular park, and the slender prang of **Wat Phra Ram**, built in the late fourteenth century on the site of Ramathibodi's cremation by his son and successor as king, Ramesuan. Sadly, not much of the prang's original stuccowork remains, but you can still get an idea of how spectacular it would have looked when the city was at its zenith.

Wat Phra Si Sanphet and the Wang Luang (Royal Palace)

Both sites lie to the northwest of Thanon Si Sanphet from Wat Phra Ram • Both daily 7am–6pm • Both B50, or included with the B220 six-in-one pass

Wat Phra Si Sanphet was built in 1448 by King Boromatrailokanat as a private chapel, and was formerly the grandest of Ayutthaya's temples. Even now, it's one of the best preserved.

The wat took its name from one of the largest standing metal images of the Buddha ever known, the **Phra Si Sanphet**, erected here in 1503. Towering 16m high and covered in 173kg of gold, it did not survive the ravages of the Burmese, though Rama I rescued the pieces and placed them inside a chedi at Wat Pho in Bangkok. The three remaining grey chedis in the characteristic style of the old capital were built to house the ashes of three kings, and have now become the most familiar image of Ayutthaya.

The site of this royal wat was originally occupied by Ramathibodi I's wooden palace, which Boromatrailokanat replaced with the bigger **Wang Luang**, stretching to the Lopburi River on the north side. Successive kings turned the Wang Luang into a vast complex of pavilions and halls, with an elaborate system of walls designed to isolate the inner sanctum for the king and his consorts. The palace was destroyed by the Burmese in 1767 and plundered by Rama I for its bricks, which he needed to build the new capital at Bangkok. Now you can only trace the outlines of a few walls in the grass and inspect an unimpressive wooden replica of an open pavilion – better to consult the model of the whole complex in the Historical Study Centre (see below).

Viharn Phra Mongkol Bopit

On the south side of Wat Phra Si Sanphet • Daily 8am–5pm • Free

Viharn Phra Mongkol Bopit attracts tourists and Thai pilgrims in about equal measure. The pristine hall – a replica of a typical Ayutthayan viharn, with its characteristic chunky lotus-capped columns around the outside – was built in 1956, with help from the Burmese to atone for their flattening of the city two centuries earlier, in order to shelter the revered **Phra Mongkol Bopit**, which, at 12.45m high (excluding the base), is one of the largest bronze Buddhas in Thailand. The powerfully austere image, with its flashing mother-of-pearl eyes, was cast in the fifteenth century, then sat exposed to the elements from the time of the Burmese invasion until its new home was built. During restoration, the hollow image was found to contain hundreds of Buddha statuettes, some of which were later buried around the shrine to protect it.

The Million Toy Museum

In the northwest corner of the island, just west of the Royal Palace and the westernmost bridge over the Lopburi River • Tues–Sun 9am–4pm • B50 • ⓦ milliontoymuseum.com

After a few hours gazing at the ruins of ancient temples, it comes as a welcome relief to enter the quirky, private **Million Toy Museum**, where cabinets on two floors are packed not only with toys, but also with odd items like Queen Elizabeth II coronation mugs from 1953. Kids love it, and even adults will recognize a few favourites from childhood, such as Superman, Minnie Mouse, Donald Duck and Goofy. There's a café out front that is also full of toy characters, and seats in a shady garden where you can rest your legs.

Chao Sam Phraya National Museum

10min walk south of Viharn Phra Mongkol Bopit • Wed–Sun 8.30am–4pm, last admission 3.30pm • B150

The largest of the town's three museums is the **Chao Sam Phraya National Museum**, where most of the moveable remains of Ayutthaya's glory – those that weren't plundered by treasure-hunters or taken to the National Museum in Bangkok – are exhibited. Apart from numerous Buddhas and some fine woodcarving, the museum is bursting with **gold treasures**, including the original relic casket from Wat Mahathat, betel-nut sets and model chedis, and a gem-encrusted fifteenth-century crouching elephant found in the crypt at Wat Ratburana.

Historical Study Centre

Thanon Rotchana, a 5min walk from Chao Sam Phraya National Museum • Daily 8.30am–4.30pm • B100

It's worth paying a visit to the **Historical Study Centre**, if only to check out its scale model of the Royal Palace before you set off to wander around the real thing. The visitors' exhibition upstairs puts Ayutthaya's ruins in context, dramatically presenting a broad social history of the city through videos, sound effects and reconstructions of temple murals. Other exhibits include model ships and a peasant's wooden house.

Chantharakasem Palace Museum

In the northeast corner of the island • Wed–Sun 8.30am–4pm • B100

The **Chantharakasem Palace** was traditionally the home of the heir to the Ayutthayan throne. The Black Prince, Naresuan, built the first *wang na* (palace of the front) here in about 1577 so that he could guard the area of the city wall that was most vulnerable to enemy attack. Rama IV (1851–68) had the palace restored and it now houses a **museum** displaying many of his possessions, including a throne platform overhung by a white *chat*, a ceremonial nine-tiered parasol that is a vital part of a king's insignia. The rest of the museum features beautiful ceramics and Buddha images, and a small arsenal of cannon and muskctry.

Off the island

It's easy enough to visit places off the island via various bridges across the river, especially if you're travelling around on a bike. If you're pushed for time, the two main sights are Wat Chai Watthanaram to the west, and Wat Yai Chai Mongkol to the southeast of the island.

Wat Na Phra Mane

On the north bank of the Lopburi River, opposite the Wang Luang • Daily 8.30am–5pm • B20

Wat Na Phra Mane is in some respects Ayutthaya's most rewarding temple, being the only one from the town's golden age that survived Burmese attacks, though frequent refurbishments make it appear quite new.

The main **bot**, built in 1503, shows the distinctive features of Ayutthayan architecture – outside columns topped with lotus cups, and slits in the walls instead of windows to let the air circulate. Inside, underneath a rich red-and-gold coffered ceiling that represents the stars around the moon, sits a powerful 6m-high Buddha in the disdainful, over-decorated royal style characteristic of the later Ayutthaya period.

In sharp contrast is the dark-green **Phra Khan Thavaraj Buddha**, which dominates the tiny viharn behind to the right. Seated in the "European position", with its robe delicately pleated and its feet up on a large lotus leaf, the gentle figure conveys a reassuring serenity. It's advertised as being from Sri Lanka, the source of Thai Buddhism, but more likely is a seventh- to ninth-century Mon image from Wat Phra Mane at Nakhon Pathom.

Wat Phu Khao Thong

2km northwest of Wat Na Phra Mane • Daily dawn–dusk • Free

Head northwest of Wat Na Phra Mane and you're in open country, where the 50m-high chedi of **Wat Phu Khao Thong** rises steeply out of the fields. In 1569, after a temporary occupation of Ayutthaya, the Burmese erected a Mon-style chedi here to commemorate their victory. Forbidden by Buddhist law from pulling down a sacred monument, the Thais had to put up with this galling reminder of the enemy's success until it collapsed nearly two hundred years later, when King Borommakot promptly built a truly Ayutthayan chedi on the old Burmese base – just in time for the Burmese to return in 1767 and flatten the town. This "Golden Mount" has recently been restored, with a colossal equestrian statue of King Naresun, conqueror of the Burmese, to keep it company. You can climb 25m of steps up the side of the chedi to look out over the countryside and the town, with glimpses of Wat Phra Si Sanphet and Viharn Phra Mongkok Bopit in the distance.

Wat Tha Ka Rong

Opposite the northwest corner of the island, near the confluence of the Chao Phraya and Lopburi rivers • Daily dawn–dusk • Free

This modern temple is wild – think Buddha goes to Disneyland. Highlights include a room full of enormous statues of famous monks, motion-activated skeletons, robots and other mannequins that *wai* as you pass and ask for a donation, and the plushest

8

bathrooms you'll see in town. There's also a floating market on the riverside selling souvenirs, and an interesting display of Buddha images from neighbouring countries.

Wat Chai Watthanaram

Across the river, southwest of the island · Daily 8am–6pm · B50, or included with the B220 six-in-one pass

It's worth the bike or boat ride to reach the elegant brick-and-stucco latticework of Khmer-style stupas at **Wat Chai Watthanaram**. Late afternoon is a popular time to visit, as the sun sinks photogenically behind the main tower.

King Prasat Thong built Wat Chai Watthanaram in 1630, possibly to commemorate a victory over Cambodia, designing it as a sort of Angkorian homage, around a towering central Khmer corncob **prang** encircled by a constellation of four minor prangs and eight tiered and tapered chedis. Most of the stucco facing has weathered away to reveal the red-brick innards in pretty contrast, but a few tantalizing fragments of stucco relief remain on the outside of the chedis, depicting episodes from the Buddha's life. Around the gallery that connects them sits a solemn phalanx of 120 headless seated Buddhas, each on its own red-brick dais but showing no trace of their original skins, which may have been done in black lacquer and gold leaf. To the east a couple of larger seated Buddhas look out across the river from the foundations of the old bot.

Wat Yai Chai Mongkol

Southeast of the island, about 2km from the station · Daily 8am–5pm · B20 · If cycling here, avoid the multi-laned Pridi Damrong/Naresuan Bridge and Bangkok road by taking the river ferry across to the train station and then heading south 1.5km before turning east to the temple

Across the Pasak River southeast of the island, you pass through Ayutthaya's new business zone and some rustic suburbia before reaching the ancient but still functioning **Wat Yai Chai Mongkol**. Surrounded by formal lawns, flowerbeds and much-photographed saffron-draped Buddhas, the wat was established by Ramathibodi I in 1357 as a meditation site for monks returning from study in Sri Lanka. King Naresuan put up the beautifully curvaceous **chedi** to mark the decisive victory over the Burmese at Suphanburi in 1593, when he himself had sent the enemy packing by slaying the Burmese crown prince in an elephant-back duel. Built on a colossal scale to outshine the Burmese Golden Mount on the opposite side of Ayutthaya, the chedi has come to symbolize the prowess and devotion of Naresuan and, by implication, his descendants right down to the present king. By the entrance, the **reclining Buddha** was also constructed by Naresuan. A huge modern glass-walled shrine to the revered king dominates the back of the temple compound.

Wat Phanan Choeng

Near the confluence of the Chao Phraya and Pasak rivers, to the west of Wat Yai Chai Mongkol · Daily 8am–5pm · B20

In Ayutthaya's most prosperous period, the docks and main trading area were located near the confluence of the Chao Phraya and Pasak rivers, to the west of Wat Yai Chai Mongkol. This is where you'll find the oldest and liveliest working temple in town, **Wat Phanan Choeng**. The main viharn is often filled with the sights, sounds and smells of an incredible variety of merit-making activities, as devotees burn huge pink Chinese incense candles, offer food and rattle fortune sticks. It's even possible to buy tiny golden statues of the Buddha to be placed in one of the hundreds of niches that line the walls, a form of votive offering peculiar to this temple. If you can get here during a festival, especially Chinese New Year, you're in for an overpowering experience.

The 19m-high Buddha, which almost fills the hall, has survived since 1324, shortly before the founding of the capital, and tears are said to have flowed from its eyes when Ayutthaya was sacked by the Burmese. However, the reason for the temple's popularity with the Chinese is to be found in the early eighteenth-century shrine by the pier, with its image of a beautiful Chinese princess who drowned herself here because of a king's infidelity: his remorse led him to build the shrine at the place where she had walked into the river.

Baan Hollanda

Just south of Wat Phanan Choeng • Wed–Sun 9am–5pm • B50 • ⓦ baanhollanda.org

During Ayutthaya's heyday in the sixteenth and seventeenth centuries, foreign merchants were attracted here to trade with the Siamese, and were permitted to set up trading posts on either side of the Chao Phraya River to the southeast of the island. Three settlements have now been turned into museums recounting foreign relations with Siam, and of these, **Baan Hollanda** (the Dutch settlement) is the most interesting (the others are those of the Japanese and Portuguese). Established in 2013 in order to inform visitors about the history of the Dutch in Siam, the exhibition covers Siamese–Dutch relations from the first arrival of the Dutch East India Company in 1604. The Dutch bought rice, tin, deerskins and wood from Siam and in return sold Japanese silver and Indian printed textiles to the Siamese. The centre also demonstrates how the Dutch have mastered the art of flood protection in their own country so that a large percentage of its population lives below sea level without fear, and there's an opportunity for visitors to pick up a pair of ceramic clogs or a windmill at the museum shop.

ARRIVAL AND DEPARTURE

AYUTTHAYA

BY TRAIN
The best way of getting to Ayutthaya from Bangkok is by train (with departures mostly in the early morning and evening); trains continue on to Nong Khai and Ubon Ratchathani in the northeast, and to the north and Chiang Mai. The station is on the east bank of the Pasak; to get to the centre of town, take a ferry from the jetty 100m west of the station (last ferry around 8pm; B5) across and upriver to Chao Phrom pier; it's then a 5min walk to the junction of Thanon U Thong and Thanon Naresuan, near most guest-houses (if you're going to stay at *Bann Kun Pra*, however, take the ferry from the neighbouring jetty, which runs directly across the river and back). The station has a useful left-luggage service (24hr; B30 per piece per day).

Destinations Bangkok Hualamphong (around 35 daily; 1hr 30min–2hr); Chiang Mai (6 daily; 10hr 45min–13hr 10min); Lopburi (18 daily; 45min–1hr 30min); Nong Khai (5 daily; 9hr 30min); Phitsanulok (12 daily; 3hr 30min–6hr 20min); Ubon Ratchathani (7 daily; 7hr 20min–10hr 30min).

BY BUS OR MINIBUS
From/to Bangkok Frequent buses to Ayutthaya depart Bangkok's Northern Mo Chit terminal. Most pull in at the bus stop on Thanon Naresuan, near the main accommodation area, though some long-distance services only stop at Ayutthaya's bus terminal, 5km to the east of the centre on Highway 1, from where you'll need a tuk-tuk to get into town (B150–200). Private a/c minibuses from

Bangkok's Victory Monument and Southern Bus Terminal finish their routes opposite the Thanon Naresuan bus stop (both about every 20min during daylight hours). Services in the opposite direction, returning to Bangkok, leave from all the above-mentioned drop-off points. There are also tourist minibuses that connect Ayutthaya with Suvarnabhumi Airport and Thanon Khao San.

From/to Kanchanaburi Travelling from Kanchanaburi, it's possible to bypass the Bangkok gridlock, either by hooking up with an a/c tourist minibus (daily; 3hr) arranged through guesthouses in Kanchanaburi or, under your own steam, by taking a public bus to Suphanburi (every 20min; 1hr 30min), then changing to an Ayutthaya bus, which will drop you off on Thanon Naresuan. To travel from Ayutthaya to Kanchanaburi, the easiest option is to book a seat on a minibus through one of the guesthouses.

Other services Fast but cramped tourist minibuses serve Sukhothai, and there are also connecting minibuses for Ko Samet and Ko Chang, an overnight bus service to Chiang Mai and another to Siem Reap in Cambodia. These depart from the bus terminal to the east of the city centre.

Destinations Bangkok (every 20min; 1hr 30min–2hr); Chiang Mai (12 daily; 9hr); Chiang Rai (10 daily; 12hr); Kamphaeng Phet (6 daily; 5hr); Lampang (12 daily; 8hr); Lamphun (12 daily; 9hr); Lopburi (every 20min; 2hr); Phitsanulok (10 daily; 5hr); Sukhothai (12 daily; 4hr 30min–6hr); Suphanburi (every 30min; 1hr); Tak (6 daily; 6hr).

8

GETTING AROUND

Busloads of tourists descend on Ayutthaya's sights during the day, but the area covered by the old capital is large enough not to feel swamped. Distances are deceptive, so it's not a good idea to walk everywhere.

By bicycle or motorbike Bicycles can be rented at guesthouses, around the train station and from the tourist police. Watch out, though, as some places try to charge up to B100 per day – double the usual rate. Some guesthouses

and a few cheaper outlets in front of the station rent small motorbikes.

By tuk-tuk Tuk-tuks are easy enough to flag down on the street. Their set routes for sharing passengers are more useful

AYUTTHAYA EXHIBITIONS

While visiting the branch of the Tourist Information Centre on the site of the former city hall (see below), it's well worth heading upstairs to the smartly presented multi-media **exhibition** on Ayutthaya (daily 8.30am–4.30pm; free), which provides an engaging introduction to the city's history, an overview of all the sights, including a scale-model reconstruction of Wat Phra Si Sanphet, and insights into local traditional ways of life. Also on this floor, there's the **Ayutthaya National Art Museum** (Mon, Tues & Thurs–Sun 8.30am–4.30pm; free), which has depictions of animals, people and landscapes by Thai artists, including a drawing in black ink by former Prime Minister Chuan Leekpai.

for locals than for tourists, but a typical journey in town on your own should only cost B50. If you want to hire a tuk-tuk for the day, it's best to head for the ferry landing at Chao Phrom Pier or the area around Naresuan Soi 2.

By motorbike taxi Motorbikes charge around B40 for medium-range journeys.

INFORMATION

Tourist information TAT's helpful Ayutthaya Tourist Information Centre (daily 8.30am–4.30pm; ☏ 035 246076, ✉ tatyutya@tat.or.th) is split between a room on the ground floor of the former city hall (on the west side of Thanon Si Sanphet, opposite the Chao Sam Phraya National Museum), and an ornate wooden building a short walk further north on the same stretch of road.

ACCOMMODATION

8

Ayutthaya offers a good choice of accommodation, including a small ghetto of **budget guesthouses** on and around the soi that runs north from Chao Phrom market to Thanon Pamaphrao; it's sometimes known as Soi Farang but is actually signed as Naresuan Soi 2 at the southern end and Pamaphrao Soi 5 at the northern.

Baan Lotus 20 Thanon Pamaphrao ☏ 035 251988. Two large wooden buildings set in a huge overgrown compound with a pond and pavilion for relaxing out back. One building consists of fan rooms and the other with a/c; rooms are a good size but sparsely furnished. It's a wonderfully restful location just a few steps from the restaurants and bars on Soi Farang. Fan B450, a/c B600

Baan Thai House 199 Moo 4, Sri Krung Villa, 600m east of the train station ☏ 035 245555, ⓦ baanthaihouse .com. Twelve immaculate a/c villas with sloping pitched roofs, set around manicured tropical gardens and a huge artificial pond with its own wooden water wheel and rowing boats (free for guests to use). Rooms have flatscreen TVs, wooden floors and delicately carved furnishings, plus classy outdoor showers. Perks include personal service, a spa, an outdoor pool and an excellent restaurant. B2400

Bann Kun Pra 48/2 Thanon U Thong, just north of Pridi Damrong Bridge ☏ 035 241978, ⓦ bannkunpra.com. The best rooms in the rambling, hundred-year-old teak house here have shared bathrooms and gorgeous river-view balconies. There are also two newer and slightly noisier blocks near the road, where you can choose between cheap, single-sex dorm rooms with individual lockable tin trunks, or newly renovated en-suite doubles with a/c, attractive wooden floors and private terraces overlooking the waterway. They also offer river tours and a warm welcome. Dorms B250, fan doubles B600, a/c doubles B1100

Chantana House 12/22 Naresuan Soi 2 ☏ 035 323200, ✉ chantanahouse@yahoo.com. At the quieter end of the travellers' soi, this low-key guesthouse has simple, boxy but spotlessly clean en-suite fan and a/c rooms, though not all have outward-facing windows. Kind, friendly staff, but not much English spoken. Fan B400, a/c B600

Krung Sri River 27/2, Thanon Rojana ☏ 035 244333, ⓦ krungsririver.com. Ayutthaya's most prominent central hotel occupies nine storeys in a prime if noisy position beside the Pridi Damrong Bridge, with some standard rooms and all suites enjoying river views. Furnishings aren't exactly chic, but there's a/c and TVs throughout, an attractive third-floor pool and a car park. B2100

The Old Place Guest House 102 Thanon U Thong, just south of the Chao Phrom Pier ☏ 035 211161. Plain fan and a/c rooms with stark white walls and en-suite bathrooms, in a good location near the pier and markets. Fan B350, a/c B500

★ Tamarind Guest House On a lane off Thanon Chikul in front of the entrance to Wat Mahathat ☏ 081 6557937. Tucked away from the main road, this quirky guesthouse has bags of character and its seven rooms are all different in design, though all have attractive wooden floors and bright colour schemes. There's a great, multi-level family room and the owner can help with sightseeing plans. Free coffee, tea and cookies. B646

EATING AND DRINKING

Other than the restaurants listed below, the *roti* (Muslim pancake) stalls near the hospital around the southern end of Thanon Si Sanphet are good for daytime snacks and after dark there are a couple of **night markets**. There's an excellent one with a wide range of food beside the river at Hua Raw, about 10min walk north of Naresuan Soi 2, and another at the west end of Thanon Bang Laen, 150m south of Wat Phra Mahathat. Competing singers at the clutch of **bar-restaurants** can make Soi Farang a bit of a battle of the bands after 9pm, but it's fun and lively, and free with your beer.

Bann Kun Pra Thanon U Thong, just north of Pridi Damrong Bridge ☏ 035 241978, ⊛ bannkunpra.com. The riverside dining terrace here is just as atmospheric as the lovely guesthouse upstairs (see opposite), and enjoys fine views. It specializes in reasonably priced fish and seafood, notably prawns, and the red curry with beef and jackfruit (B140) is good too. Most mains around B150. Daily 7am–10.30pm.

Kankitti 7/1 Moo 2, Thanon U Thong, on the south side of town ☏ 035 241971. Congenial spot where, on a riverbank terrace or a moored boat with views of Wat Phutthaisawan's white prang, you can dine on Ayutthaya's most famous delicacy, river prawns (around B1600 per kilo), or on less expensive but nevertheless very tasty dishes such as green curry with fishballs (B120). Daily 9am–9.30pm.

★ **Saithong** 45 Moo 1 Thanon U Thong ☏ 035 241449. On the south side of the island, just east of Kankitti, this place has an attractive riverside terrace and a cosy a/c room, and its seafood is especially popular among Thais, so it's often full on weekend evenings. Try the seabass with spicy lemon sauce (B150) or the *yum Saithong* – a spicy salad with shrimp, chicken, squid and ham (B150). Live music from 6pm each evening. Daily 10am–10pm.

Street Lamp Bar Naresuan Soi 2. One of the most popular bars on the street, with regular live music, ranging from country to rock and blues, and cheap, ice-cold beer. Simple dishes like fried rice from B55. Daily 7am–midnight.

Tony's Place 12/18 Naresuan Soi 2 ☏ 035 252578, ⊛ tonyplace-ayutthaya.com. The size of this cavernous timbered restaurant on the ground floor of the guesthouse, plus its cushioned chill-out areas and blasting music, makes this a popular travellers' meeting place; the typical food (most dishes B80–120) and beer are cheap enough but nothing special, and staff are rather disinterested. Daily 7am–midnight.

DIRECTORY

Banks and ATMs There are plenty of banks with exchange services and ATMs around the junction of Thanon Naresuan and Naresuan Soi 2.

Hospital The government Phra Nakhon Si Ayutthaya hospital is at the southern end of Thanon Si Sanphet (☏ 035 241888).

Tourist police Based just to the north of the TAT office on Thanon Si Sanphet (☏ 035 242352 or ☏ 1155).

Nakhon Pathom

Even if you're just passing through, you can't miss the star attraction of **NAKHON PATHOM**: the enormous stupa **Phra Pathom Chedi** dominates the skyline of this otherwise unexceptional provincial capital, 56km west of Bangkok. Probably Thailand's oldest town, Nakhon Pathom (derived from the Pali for "First City") is thought to be the point at which **Buddhism** first entered the region now known as Thailand, more than two thousand years ago. Then the capital of a sizeable Mon kingdom, it was important enough to rate a visit from two missionaries dispatched by King Ashoka of India, one of Buddhism's great early evangelists. Even today, the province of Nakhon Pathom retains a high Buddhist profile – aside from housing the country's holiest chedi, it also contains **Phuttamonthon**, Thailand's most important Buddhist sanctuary and home of its supreme patriarch.

The **Phra Pathom Chedi** is easily visited while travelling from Bangkok to Kanchanaburi or vice versa; alternatively, since it's on train lines heading to Hua Hin, Surat Thani and Malaysia, the town works well as a stopover on the way south from Bangkok. Everything described below is within walking distance of the railway station.

Phra Pathom Chedi

400m south of the train station • Daily 7am–5pm • B60

Although the Buddha never actually came to Thailand, legend held that he rested in Nakhon Pathom after wandering the country, and the original **Phra Pathom Chedi** may have been erected to represent this. The first structure resembled Ashoka's great stupa at Sanchi in India, with its inverted bowl shape and spire that topped 39m. Local chronicles, however, tell how the chedi was built in the sixth century as an act of atonement by the foundling Phraya Pan who murdered the tyrant Mon king before realizing that he was his father. Statues of both father and son stand inside the viharns of the present chedi.

Whatever its true origins, the first chedi fell into disrepair and was later rebuilt with a prang during the Khmer period, between the eighth and twelfth centuries. Abandoned to the jungle once more, it was rediscovered by the future Rama IV in 1853 who, mindful that all Buddhist monuments are sacred however dilapidated, set about encasing the old prang in the enormous new 120m-high plunger-shaped chedi, making it one of the tallest stupas in the world. Its distinctive cladding of shimmering golden-brown tiles was completed several decades later.

The present-day chedi is much revered and holds its own week-long Phra Pathom Chedi **fair**, around the time of Loy Krathong (see p.36) in mid-November, which attracts musicians, fortune-tellers and of course plenty of food stalls.

Around the chedi

Approaching the chedi from the main (northern) staircase, you're greeted by the 8m-high Sukhothai-style Buddha image known as **Phra Ruang Rojanarit**, installed in front of the north viharn. There's a viharn at each of the cardinal points, and they all have an inner and an outer chamber containing tableaux of the life of the Buddha.

Proceeding clockwise around the chedi, as is the custom at all Buddhist monuments, you can weave between the outer promenade and the inner cloister via ornate doors that punctuate the dividing wall. The outer promenade is ringed by Buddha images employing a wide variety of mudras, or hand gestures, each of which has a specific meaning for Buddhists, and most of them are explained on plaques beside them. Throughout the rest of the country, most Buddha images portray one of just five or six common mudras, making this collection rather unique. The promenade is also dotted with **trees**, many of which have religious significance, such as the bodhi tree (*ficus religiosa*), under one of which the Buddha was meditating when he achieved enlightenment.

The wall of the **east viharn** features a diagrammatic cross section of the chedi showing the encased original at its core, while beside the **south viharn** staircase is a three-dimensional replica of the original chedi with its Khmer prang (east side) and a model of the venerated chedi at Nakhon Si Thammarat (west side). The **west viharn** houses two reclining Buddhas: a sturdy, 9m-long figure in the outer chamber and a more delicate portrayal in the inner one.

Phra Pathom Chedi National Museum

Just east from the bottom of the chedi's south staircase • Wed–Sun 9am–noon & 1–4pm • B100

Within the chedi compound are a couple of similarly named museums. The newer, more formal setup, the **Phra Pathom Chedi National Museum**, displays a good collection of Dvaravati-era (sixth to eleventh centuries) artefacts excavated nearby, including Wheels of Law – an emblem introduced by Theravada Buddhists before naturalistic images were permitted – and Buddha statuary with the U-shaped robe and thick facial features characteristic of Dvaravati sculpture. Together, the exhibits tell the story of how external influences, particularly those from India, shaped local beliefs.

Phra Pathom Chedi Museum

Halfway up the steps near the east viharn • Wed–Sun 9am–noon & 1–4pm • Free

The **Phra Pathom Chedi Museum** is a magpie's nest of a collection, offering a broader, more domestic introduction to Nakhon Pathom's history than the National Museum. More a curiosity shop than a museum, the small room and entranceway are filled with Buddhist amulets, seashells, gold and silver needles, Chinese ceramics, Thai musical instruments and ancient statues – enough for a short but satisfying browse.

CLOCKWISE FROM TOP LEFT BRIDGE OVER THE RIVER KWAI (P.140); MUANG BORAN ANCIENT CITY (P.112); FLOATING VENDOR, DAMNOEN SADUAK (P.129); PHRA PATHOM CHEDI (P.125) >

Sanam Chandra Palace

A 10min walk west of the chedi along Thanon Rajdamnoen (or a B30 ride on a motorbike taxi) • Daily 9am–4pm (ticket office closes at 3.30pm) • B50 or free with ticket for Bangkok's Grand Palace • Electric cart rental: B400 first hour, B100 for subsequent hours • Ⓦ palaces.thai.net

Before ascending the throne in 1910, Rama VI made several pilgrimages to the Phra Pathom Chedi, eventually choosing this 335-acre plot west of the pagoda as the location for a convenient new country retreat. The resulting complex of elegant wooden buildings, known as **Sanam Chandra Palace**, was designed to blend Western and Eastern styles, and a handful of its main buildings are now open to the public. Its principal structure, the **Jalimangalasana Residence**, evokes a miniature Bavarian castle, complete with turrets and red-tiled roof; the **Marirajrattabalang Residence** is a more oriental-style pavilion, built of teak and painted a deep rose colour inside and out; and the **Thub Kwan Residence** is an unadorned traditional Thai-style house of polished, unpainted golden teak. They each contain royal artefacts and memorabilia and, as such, visitors should take care to dress appropriately. All three buildings are within walking distance of the two main entrances to the palace grounds, so it's only worth hiring an electric cart if you want to explore the outer reaches of the extensive grounds.

Contemporary Thai Art Centre

Just outside Sanam Chandra's southern perimeter, behind the Thub Kwan Residence on Thanon Rajamanka Nai • Tues–Sun 9am–4pm • Free • Ⓦ su.ac.th • If coming from the chedi, expect to pay around B30 for a motorbike taxi

If you're interested in modern Thai art it's well worth seeing what's on at the **Contemporary Thai Art Centre**. A purpose-built art centre set among outlying Sanam Chandra villas, it's the exhibition space for Bangkok's premier art school, Silpakorn University, whose satellite campus is just across the road. Their annual student show, held here every September and October, is usually very interesting.

8

ARRIVAL AND SERVICES   NAKHON PATHOM

By train To get to the chedi compound's northern gate from the train station, walk south for 200m down Thanon Rotfai, across the khlong and past the covered market.

Destinations Bangkok Hualamphong (12 daily; 1hr 35min); Bangkok Thonburi (2 daily; 1hr 10min); Butterworth (Malaysia; 2 daily; 19hr); Chumphon (11 daily; 5hr 40min–8hr 30min); Hat Yai (6 daily; 12hr 15min–16hr); Hua Hin (12 daily; 2hr 15min–3hr 15min); Kanchanaburi (2 daily; 1hr 25min); Nakhon Si Thammarat (2 daily; 14–15hr); Nam Tok (2 daily; 3hr 30min); Phetchaburi (10 daily; 1hr 20min–2hr 20min); Surat Thani (11 daily; 8hr–11hr 30min); Trang (2 daily; 13hr 30min–14hr 30min).

By bus Bus connections to Nakhon Pathom are good, especially from Bangkok's Southern Bus Terminal, Damnoen Saduak and Kanchanaburi. On arrival, buses drop passengers either in front of the police station across from the chedi's southern entrance, or beside the khlong, 100m from the northern gate. Buses heading for Kanchanaburi, Damnoen Saduak and Phetchaburi collect passengers outside the police station across from Thanon Kwaa Phra from the chedi's southern gate. Buses bound for Bangkok pick up from Thanon Phaya Pan on the north bank of the khlong, across from the *Mitpaisal Hotel*.

Destinations Bangkok (every 10min; 40min–1hr 20min); Damnoen Saduak (every 20min; 1hr); Kanchanaburi (every 20min; 1hr 45min–2hr).

Services You can change money at the exchange booth on Thanon Rotfai, beside the bridge over the khlong, one block south of the train station; several nearby banks also have ATMs.

ACCOMMODATION AND EATING

Fairy Tale 307 Thanon Rotfai, just south of the train station ☎ 081 913 8033. Almost hidden behind the food stalls that line the street, this cosy a/c café serves yummy crêpes, waffles and even French fries. It's an ideal spot to while away time waiting for a train. Mon–Sat 10.30am–7pm.

Hot-food stalls Just outside the chedi compound's southern wall, near the museum. The obvious place to eat during the day. There are lots of options here, from noodle soup to grilled chicken and rice dishes (mostly B30–60). Daily early morning till dusk.

Market In front of the station. Serves the usual takeaway or sit-down-and-eat goodies, including *khao kha moo*, stewed pork leg on rice served with pickled cabbage and a boiled egg (B30). The market really hits its stride after sunset. Hours vary, but usually at least mid-morning until around 9pm.

Mitpaisal Hotel 120/30 Thanon Phaya Pan ☎ 034 242422. This Chinese-Thai hotel is long overdue a make-over, but its dimly lit, a/c rooms are just passable, and it enjoys a convenient location, close to the train station and less than 200m from the chedi's north gateway. Wi-fi doesn't reach upper floors. Fan <u>B300</u>, a/c <u>B450</u>

Damnoen Saduak

To get an idea of what shopping in Bangkok used to be like before all the canals were tarmacked over, many people take an early-morning trip to the **floating market** (*talat khlong*) at **DAMNOEN SADUAK**. Sixty kilometres south of Nakhon Pathom and just over 100km from Bangkok, it's just about accessible on a day-trip from the capital with a very early start. Vineyards and orchards here back onto a labyrinth of narrow canals, and every morning between 6am and 11am local market gardeners ply these waterways in paddleboats full of fresh fruit, vegetables and tourist-tempting soft drinks and souvenirs. Most dress in the blue denim jacket and high-topped straw hat traditionally favoured by Thai farmers, so it all looks very picturesque; however, the setup is clearly geared to tourists rather than locals, so the place lacks an authentic aura. For a more engaging experience, consider going instead to the floating markets at Amphawa, 10km south of Damnoen Saduak (see p.131), or at Tha Ka, 10km to the east of Damnoen Saduak (see p.133).

The market

Daily 6–11am

The target for most tour groups is **Talat Khlong Ton Kem**, 2km west of Damnoen Saduak's tiny town centre at the intersection of Khlong Damnoen Saduak and Khlong Thong Lang. Many of the wooden houses here have been converted into warehouse-style souvenir shops and tourist restaurants, diverting trade away from the khlong vendors and into the hands of large commercial enterprises. Nonetheless, a semblance of traditional water trade continues, and the two bridges between Ton Kem and **Talat Khlong Hia Kui** (a little further south down Khlong Thong Lang) make decent vantage points.

Touts invariably congregate at the Ton Kem pier to hassle you into taking a **rowing boat trip** around the khlong network; this is worth considering and far preferable to being propelled between markets at top speed in one of the noisy longtail boats, which

8

VISITING THE FLOATING MARKETS

For many visitors to Thailand, an essential item on their itinerary is a trip to a **floating market**, to witness scenes of vendors selling fruit, flowers, vegetables and noodle dishes from **sampans** on the canals that were once the principal means of travelling around the country. Unfortunately, such bucolic scenes are from a bygone era, and while it's still possible to visit a floating market, many visitors regret the experience, feeling they've been led into a tourist trap, which is often exactly the case.

Most day tours from Bangkok head for **Damnoen Saduak** (see above), where visitors are whisked around in noisy longtail boats, which pause for souvenir hawkers to make their pitch in between staged photos of smiling vendors dressed in traditional outfits with neatly arranged boatloads of produce. Such day-trips also include visits to dubious animal shows or handicraft workshops in an attempt to extract more tourist dollars.

In recent years, Thais have started heading for **Amphawa** (see p.131) at weekends, which has a more authentic atmosphere than Damnoen Saduak, though the least commercialized floating market is at **Tha Ka** (see p.133) on weekends and certain dates in the lunar calendar. While most boat trips in these places focus on the markets, it's also possible to venture out onto the canals after dark to **watch the fireflies** twinkling romantically in their favourite lamphu trees like delicate strings of fairylights.

One problem of visits to this area is that most markets, with the exception of Amphawa, are at their best at the crack of dawn, but since they are around 100km from Bangkok, it takes at least a couple of hours for tour groups to get there. If you're keen to see them in the early hours, it's worth staying overnight in Damnoen Saduak, Amphawa or even Samut Songkhram (see p.130) and making arrangements for an early start; Tha Ka market is about 10km from each of these places. While they cover less distance than the longtail boats, rowing boats make for a more relaxing experience, and generally offer a ninety-minute ride for around B400; they are available for hire from Ton Kem pier in Damnoen Saduak, the main jetty in Amphawa or any of the resorts in Samut Songkhram. Don't forget to take a hat or umbrella and sunscreen.

cost far more to charter. For a less hectic and more sensitive look at the markets, explore via the walkways beside the canals.

ARRIVAL AND ACCOMMODATION   DAMNOEN SADUAK

BY BUS

From/to Bangkok Damnoen Saduak is 109km from Bangkok, so to reach the market in good time you have to catch one of the earliest a/c buses from the capital's Southern Bus Terminal (#78; every 40min from 6am; 2hr). Alternatively, you can join one of the day-trips from Bangkok, which generally give you two hours at the market, then stop at a handicraft village and/or animal show before dropping you back in the capital.

From Kanchanaburi Take a Ratchaburi-bound bus as far as Bang Phe (#461; every 15min from 5.10am; 1hr 15min), then change to bus #78 for the 30min journey to Damnoen Saduak.

From Phetchaburi and beyond To get to Damnoen Saduak from Phetchaburi or points further south, catch any

Bangkok-bound bus and change at Samut Songkhram.

Getting into town Damnoen Saduak's bus terminal is just north of Thanarat Bridge and Khlong Damnoen Saduak, on the main Nakhon Pathom–Samut Songkhram road, Highway 325. Frequent yellow songthaews cover the 2km to Ton Kem.

ACCOMMODATION

Maikaew Damnoen Resort 333 Moo 9 ☏ 032 254120–1, ⓦ maikaew.com. Just a few steps east of the floating market, this relaxing resort has a variety of luxurious rooms, some of which look out over the pool. They also offer a range of boat trips in the area (see website for details), so it makes a good springboard for exploration of the nearby canals. **B1500**

Samut Songkhram

Rarely visited by foreign tourists and yet within easy reach of Bangkok, the tiny estuarine province of **Samut Songkhram** is nourished by the Mae Khlong River as it meanders through on the last leg of its route to the Gulf. Fishing is an important industry round here, and big wooden boats are still built in riverside yards near the estuary; further inland, fruit is the main source of income, particularly pomelos, lychees, guavas and coconuts. But for visitors it is the network of three hundred **canals** woven around the river, and the traditional way of life the waterways still support, that makes a stay of a few days or more appealing. As well as some of the most interesting **floating markets** in Thailand – notably at **Amphawa** and **Tha Ka** – there are chances to witness traditional cottage industries such as palm-sugar production and *bencharong* ceramic-painting, plus more than a hundred historic temples to admire, a number of them dating back to the reign of Rama II, who was born in the province. The other famous sons of the region are Eng and Chang, the "original" Siamese twins, who grew up in the province (see box, p.84).

Samut Songkhram town

The provincial capital – officially called **SAMUT SONGKHRAM** but often referred to by locals as **Mae Khlong**, after the river that cuts through it – is a useful jumping-off point for trips to the floating markets at Amphawa and Tha Ka. It's a pleasant enough market town, which, despite its proximity to Bangkok, remains relatively unaffected by Western influences. However, there's little reason to linger here as all the local sights are out of town, mainly in **Amphawa** district a few kilometres upriver.

To savour a real Thai seaside atmosphere, make the 10km trip to Don Hoi Lot (regular songthaews run there from the bus station), from where you can gaze out across the murky waters of the Gulf of Thailand from the shade of casuarina trees. Thais flock here in droves to gobble up *hoi lot*, or worm shells, which are harvested in their sackloads at low tide. You can order them in any restaurant here, or buy them from street stalls, rent a mat and enjoy a picnic Thai-style.

ARRIVAL AND SERVICES   SAMUT SONGKHRAM TOWN

BY TRAIN

Samut Songkhram's train station is in the middle of town, on the eastern side of the Mae Klong River, with four trains

a day making the 1hr trip from and to Ban Laem, where you can connect with trains from/to Bangkok. It's a slow and convoluted journey, but more fun than the bus.

BY BUS OR MINIBUS

The journey to Samut Songkhram from Bangkok's Southern Bus Terminal (every 20min in both directions; 1hr 30min) is fast, but the views are mostly dominated by urban sprawl. Samut Songkhram's bus station is south of the market, across from the Siam Commercial Bank off Thanon Ratchayadruksa. When returning to Bangkok, there's also a minibus service to Victory Monument (approximately hourly; about 1hr 30min), which departs from Thanon Si Jumpa, about 100m east of the *Maeklong Hotel*.

CONNECTIONS TO AMPHAWA AND DAMNOEN SADUAK

By songthaew or bus Songthaews to Amphawa (approximately every 30min; 15min) and local buses to

Amphawa and Damnoen Saduak, via Highway 325, leave from the bus station.

By taxi-boat Taxi-boats operate from the Mae Khlong River pier, 50m west of the train station and market in the town centre. The journey upstream to Amphawa should take 20–30min.

By motorbike taxi At the Mae Khlong River pier, ferries (B2) take passengers across to the other side of the river, where motorbike taxis are available for the short ride to Amphawa (B40).

SERVICES

Banks and ATMs Currency exchange and ATMs are available at the branches of the main banks around the edge of Samut Songkhram market.

ACCOMMODATION AND EATING

Few people choose to stay in the town itself; however, there is a growing number of well-equipped resorts tucked away in the countryside around town. The **food stalls** near the pier, in the centre of town, make a pleasant spot for a cheap seafood lunch – for dessert, head to the **market**, near the train station, where you can buy fresh bananas, rambutans and watermelon slices. In the evening, food stalls along Thanon Si Jumpa just north of the railway station offer a wide variety of options.

Asita Eco Resort Beside a small canal about 1km west of town and just north of Highway 35 (Thanon Rama II) ☏034 767333, ⊛asitaresort.com. Choose between a Thai house and thatched villa at this small resort, which is crafted from eco-friendly materials. There's a good-sized pool, a spa and rowing boats on the adjacent canal for guests' use, plus a variety of tours on offer. Considerable discounts for weekday stays. B5000

The Legend Maeklong 1285 Thanon Pathummalai ☏034 701121 ⊛thelegendmaeklong.com. Located 100m north of the ferry landing on the western edge of the river, this place offers rooms in three beautiful wooden

houses, including a shuttered colonial building by the waterfront that dates back to the early 1900s. There are wooden furnishings throughout, plus a riverside restaurant with excellent river views. B2000

Maeklong Hotel 526/10–13 Thanon Si Jumpa ☏034 711150. This recently refurbished, small hotel in the town centre (150m north of the train station) is good value, with spacious and clean a/c rooms, though service is a bit hit and miss. Ask for a room out front, as these are much brighter than those out back. It's ideally located for browsing the many food stalls that set up along the street in the evening. B600

Amphawa

The district town of **AMPHAWA** is smaller and more atmospheric than Samut Songkhram, retaining original charm alongside modern development. Its old neighbourhoods hug the banks of the Mae Khlong River and the Khlong Amphawa tributary, the wooden homes and shops facing the water and accessed either by boat or on foot along one of the waterfront walkways. The tradition of holding a **floating market** on the canal near Wat Amphawan has been revived for tourists, with traders setting up at around noon and staying out until after sunset every Friday, Saturday and Sunday.

King Rama II Memorial Park

5min walk west of Amphawa market and khlong · **Park and Museum** daily 8.30am–5pm · Adults B30, children B10 · Accessible by both boat and road

King Rama II was born in Amphawa (his mother's home town) in 1767 and is honoured with a memorial park and temple erected on the site of his probable birthplace, beside the Mae Khlong River on the western edge of Amphawa town.

Rama II, or Phra Buddhalertla Naphalai, was a famously cultured king and a respected poet and playwright, and the **museum** at the heart of the **King Rama II Memorial Park** displays lots of rather esoteric Rama II memorabilia, including a collection of nineteenth-century musical instruments and a gallery of *khon* masks used in traditional theatre.

On the edge of the park, **Wat Amphawan** is graced with a statue of the king and decorated with murals that depict scenes from his life, including a behind-the-altar panorama of nineteenth-century Bangkok, with Ratanakosin Island's Grand Palace, Wat Pho and Sanam Luang still recognizable to modern eyes.

Amphawa Chaipattananurak

Located beside Khlong Amphawa, a 5min walk west of Amphawa market • ⓦ amphawanurak.com • Mon–Fri 9am–5pm; Sat–Sun 9am–9pm • Free

The **Amphawa Chaipattananurak** centre was established to conserve the cultural heritage of the town, and is divided into five areas, each of which provides interesting information about the traditional lifestyle of the region. The Community Exhibition Room reflects the way of life of local communities, the Agricultural Demonstration Farm features many of the local fruit trees, and the Nakhawarang Cultural Ground is used for performances of traditional music and puppet shows. There are also community shops selling local products and souvenirs, and an atmospheric coffee shop and tea house beside the canal with a retro interior.

Wat Chulamani

Beside Khlong Amphawa, a 20min walk east of Amphawa market, or a 5min boat ride

The canalside **Wat Chulamani** was until the late 1980s the domain of the locally famous abbot Luang Pho Nuang, a man believed by many to possess special powers, and followers still come to the temple to pay respects to his body, which is preserved in a glass-sided coffin in the main viharn. The breathtakingly detailed decor inside the viharn is testament to the devotion he inspired: the intricate black-and-gold lacquered artwork that covers every surface took years and cost millions of baht to complete. Across the temple compound, the bot's modern, pastel-toned murals tell the story of the Buddha's life, beginning inside the door on the right with a scene showing the young Buddha emerging from a tent (his birth) and being able to walk on lilypads straight away. The death of the Buddha and his entry into Nirvana are depicted on the wall behind the altar.

Pinsuwan bencharong showroom and workshop

A few hundred metres down the road from Wat Chulamani, just west of H325 (look for the P Ben sign in front of a compound of traditional houses) • Showroom daily 8am–noon & 1–5pm, workshop Mon–Sat 8am–noon & 1–5pm • Free • Accessible on foot, by bus or by canal

The Pinsuwan **bencharong workshop** specializes in reproductions of famous antique *bencharong* ceramics, the exquisite five-coloured pottery that used to be the tableware of choice for the Thai aristocracy and is now a prized collectors' item. Here you can watch the manufacturing process in action (though the workshop is closed on Sundays), and then buy items off the shelf or even order your own glittering, custom-made bowls, which can then be delivered to your hotel or shipped back home.

ARRIVAL AND DEPARTURE   AMPHAWA

From/to Bangkok Direct buses connect Amphawa with Bangkok's Southern Bus Terminal (every 20min; 2hr). Returning to Bangkok, hourly buses head for the Southern Bus Terminal, while several buses a day make the journey to the Northern Mo Chit terminal. There's no bus station in tiny Amphawa, but buses pull up by the market in the town centre.

From/to Samut Songkhram Frequent songthaews and local buses (both approximately every 30min; 15min) connect Amphawa market, which sets up beside the khlong, just back from its confluence with the river, with the market in Samut Songkhram.

GETTING AROUND

By boat The most appealing way to explore the area is by boat (see box, p.129).

By bicycle Some resorts, such as Baan Amphawa Resort & Spa, offer free use of bicycles for guests, or you can rent one from *Amphawa Na Non* (see opposite). Alternatively, you could join a one-day cycling tour of the area from Bangkok with Bangkok Bike Rides (see p.28) for B3200/person.

ACCOMMODATION AND EATING

Amphawa Na Non 36 Thanon Prachaset ☏ 034 752111 ⱳ amphawananon.com. This stylish new place sits on Amphawa's main street just a minute's walk from the floating market. It caters mostly to Thais but staff speak good English and the big, bright rooms offer every comfort. There's a ten percent discount on weekdays. B2500

Baan Amphawa Resort & Spa 22 Thanon Bangkapom Kaewfah ☏ 034 752222, ⱳ baanamphawa.com. A large, business-friendly resort hotel with attractive rooms in a series of traditional-style wooden buildings. There's a pool, a spa, and a reasonable restaurant, but prices are high. B3800

Baanrak Amphawa Beside Amphawa canal, just 300m from the market ☏ 089 1283838, ⱳ baanrak -amphawa.com. A clean, convenient and cosy homestay where rates on a weekday start from B1000, though weekend rates are considerably higher. Rooms are sparsely decorated but the owners are very helpful. B1600

Saban-Nga Baan Amphawa Resort & Spa, 22 Thanon Bangkapom Kaewfah ☏ 034 752222, ⱳ baanamphawa .com. The fresh fish dishes (try the stewed mackerel in sugar-cane juice and garlic; B150) at this spa hotel's upmarket restaurant are tasty enough, and the riverfront terrace is a great spot for an evening drink. However, the service sometimes struggles to match up to the surroundings. Daily 7am–10pm.

Tha Ka floating market

On Khlong Phanla in Ban Tha Ka • Sat & Sun roughly 7am–noon, plus the second, seventh and twelfth mornings of every fifteen-day lunar cycle (contact any TAT office for exact dates) • By boat, it can be reached in about half an hour from Amphawa or Damnoen Saduak; by car, it's signposted to the east of H325 between Damnoen Saduak and Amphawa

Unlike at the over-touristed market at nearby Damnoen Saduak, the **floating market** in the village of **Tha Ka** is still largely the province of local residents. It's possible to get here by boat from Amphawa or Damnoen Saduak, though most visitors come by road and begin their boat tour here. Market gardeners paddle up here in their small wooden sampans, or motor along in their noisy longtails, the boats piled high either with whatever's in season, be it pomelos or betel nuts, rambutans or okra, or with perennially popular snacks like hot noodle soup and freshly cooked satay. Their main customers are canalside residents and other traders, so the atmosphere is still pleasingly, but not artificially, traditional. As with the other markets in the area, boatmen also offer evening rides to watch the fireflies. The Tha Ka market attracts Thai tourist groups and occasional adventurous foreigners. It's best to pre-arrange a trip the day before through your accommodation in the area; expect to pay around B1000 for a half-day tour.

Phetchaburi

Straddling the Phet River about 120km south of Bangkok, the provincial capital of **PHETCHABURI** (sometimes "Phetburi") has been settled ever since the eleventh century, when the Khmers ruled the region. It was an important producer of salt, gathered from the nearby coastal salt pans, and rose to greater prominence in the seventeenth century as a trading post between the Andaman Sea ports and Ayutthaya. Despite periodic incursions from the Burmese, the town gained a reputation as a cultural centre – as the ornamentation of its older temples testifies – and after the new capital was established in Bangkok it became a favourite country retreat of Rama IV, who had a hilltop palace, **Phra Nakhon Khiri**, built here in the 1850s. Modern Phetchaburi is known for its limes and rose apples, but its main claim to fame is as one of Thailand's finest sweet-making centres, the essential ingredient for its assortment of *khanom* being the sugar extracted from the sweet-sapped palms that cover the province. This being very much a cottage industry, today's downtown Phetchaburi has lost relatively little of the ambience that so attracted Rama IV: the central riverside area is hemmed in by historic wats in varying states of disrepair, along with plenty of traditional wooden shophouses. The town's top three temples, described below, can be seen on a leisurely two-hour circular walk beginning from Chomrut Bridge, while Phetchaburi's other significant sight, the palace-museum at Phra Nakhon Khiri, is on a hill about 1km west of the bridge.

Despite the attractions of its old quarter, Phetchaburi gets few overnight visitors as most people see it on a day-trip from Bangkok, Hua Hin or Cha-am. The town sees

8

more overnighters during the **Phra Nakhon Khiri Fair**, spread over at least a week in March or April, which features parades in historic costumes, cooking demonstrations and traditional entertainments such as *likay* and *lakhon*.

Wat Yai Suwannaram
Thanon Phongsuriya, about 700m east of Chomrut Bridge

Of all Phetchaburi's temples, the most attractive is the still-functioning seventeenth-century **Wat Yai Suwannaram**. The temple's fine old teak **sala** has elaborately carved doors, bearing a gash reputedly inflicted by the Burmese in 1760 as they plundered their way towards Ayutthaya. Across from the *sala* and hidden behind high, whitewashed walls stands the windowless Ayutthaya-style bot. The bot compound overlooks a pond, in the middle of which stands a small but well-preserved scripture library, or **ho trai**: such structures were built on stilts over water to prevent ants and other insects destroying the precious documents. Enter the walled compound from the south and make a clockwise tour of the cloisters filled with Buddha statues before entering the bot itself via the eastern doorway (if the door is locked, one of the monks will get the key for you). The **bot** is supported by intricately patterned red and gold pillars and contains a remarkable, if rather faded, set of murals, depicting Indra, Brahma and other lower-ranking divinities ranged in five rows of ascending importance. Once you've admired the interior, walk to the back of the bot, passing behind the central cluster of Buddha images, to find another Buddha image seated against the back wall: climb the steps in front of this statue to get a close-up of the left foot, which for some reason was cast with six toes.

Wat Kamphaeng Laeng
Thanon Phra Song, a 15min walk east and then south of Wat Yai

The five tumbledown prangs of **Wat Kamphaeng Laeng** mark out Phetchaburi as the likely southernmost outpost of the Khmer empire. Built probably in the thirteenth

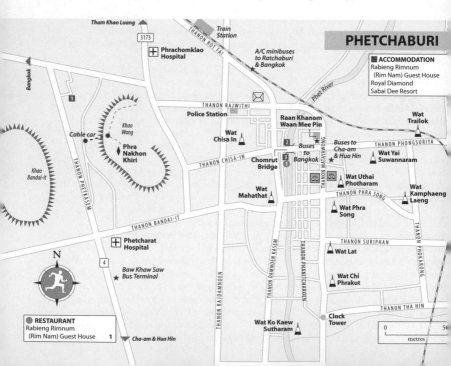

century to honour the Hindu deity Shiva and set out in a cruciform arrangement facing east, the laterite corncob-style prangs were later adapted for Buddhist use, as can be seen from the two that now house Buddha images. There has been some attempt to restore a few of the carvings and false balustraded windows, but these days worshippers congregate in the modern whitewashed wat behind these shrines, leaving the atmospheric and appealingly quaint collection of decaying prangs and casuarina topiary to chickens, stray dogs and the occasional tourist.

Wat Mahathat
Thanon Damnoen Kasem

Heading west along Thanon Phra Song from Wat Kamphaeng Laeng, across the river you can see the prangs of Phetchaburi's most fully restored and important temple, **Wat Mahathat**, long before you reach them. Boasting the "Mahathat" title only since 1954 – when the requisite Buddha relics were donated by the king – it was probably founded in the fourteenth century, but suffered badly at the hands of the Burmese. The five landmark prangs at its heart are adorned with stucco figures of mythical creatures, though these are nothing compared with those on the roofs of the main viharn and the bot. Instead of tapering off into the usual serpentine *chofa*, the gables are studded with miniature *thep* and *deva* figures (angels and gods), which add an almost mischievous vitality to the place. In a similar vein, a couple of gold-embossed crocodiles snarl above the entrance to the bot, and a caricature carving of a bespectacled man rubs shoulders with mythical giants in a relief around the base of the gold Buddha, housed in a separate mondop nearby.

Khao Wang

Dominating Phetchaburi's western outskirts stands Rama IV's palace, a stew of mid-nineteenth-century Thai and European styles scattered over the crest of the hill known as **Khao Wang** ("Palace Hill"). During his day, the royal entourage would struggle its way up the steep brick path to the summit, but now there's a **cable car** (daily 8.30am–4.30pm; B200 including admission to the palace) which starts from the western flank of the hill off Highway 4; there's also a path up the eastern flank, starting near Thanon Rajwithi. If you do walk up the hill, be warned that hundreds of quite aggressive monkeys hang out at its base and on the path to the top.

Up top, the wooded hill is littered with wats, prangs, chedis, whitewashed gazebos and lots more, in an ill-assorted combination of architectural idioms – the prang-topped viharn, washed all over in burnt sienna, is particularly ungainly. Whenever the king came on an excursion here, he stayed in the airy summer house, **Phra Nakhon Khiri** (daily 8.30am–4pm; B150), with its Mediterranean-style shutters and verandas. Now a museum, it houses a moderately interesting collection of ceramics, furniture and other artefacts given to the royal family by foreign friends. Besides being cool and breezy, Khao Wang also proved to be a good stargazing spot, so Rama IV, a keen astronomer, had an open-sided, glass-domed observatory built close to his sleeping quarters.

8

ARRIVAL AND DEPARTURE

PHETCHABURI

BY TRAIN

Phetchaburi station is on the north side of the town centre. Destinations Bangkok (Hualamphong Station 11 daily, Thonburi Station 2 daily; 2hr 45min–3hr 45min); Chumphon (12 daily; 4hr–6hr 30min); Hua Hin (14 daily; 1hr); Nakhon Pathom (13 daily; 1hr 30min–2hr); Nakhon Si Thammarat (2 daily; 12–13hr); Prachuap Khiri Khan (10 daily; 2–3hr); Ratchaburi (13 daily; 40min–1hr); Surat Thani (9 daily; 6hr 45min–9hr); Trang (2 daily; 13hr).

BY BUS

Phetchaburi is served mostly by through-buses on their way to or from Bangkok – all services between the capital and southern Thailand have to pass through the town on Highway 4.

Through-buses There's a small Baw Khaw Saw terminal on the east side of Highway 4 (Thanon Phetkasem), which is where southbound through-buses will set you down or pick you up. Northbound through-buses on their way to

Bangkok stop on the opposite side of the highway: ask to get off at "Sii Yaek Phetcharat", the crossroads of Highway 4 and Thanon Bandai-It by Phetcharat Hospital – otherwise you might be put off at the Big C Department Store about 5km south of town. Songthaews and motorbike taxis run between Highway 4 and the town centre.

From/to Cha-am and Hua Hin Non-a/c buses from and to Cha-am and Hua Hin use the small terminal in the town centre, less than a 10min walk from Chomrut Bridge.

From/to Bangkok The terminal for the one dedicated Phetchaburi–Bangkok a/c bus per day is about a 10min walk from Chomrut Bridge, on Thanon Matayawong. Note that if you're coming here from Kanchanaburi, you can avoid Bangkok by heading for Ratchaburi, where you can catch a bus, a/c minibus or train to Phetchaburi.

Destinations Bangkok (1 daily; 2hr 15min); Cha-am (roughly every 30min; 1hr 20min); Hua Hin (roughly every 30min; 1hr 50min).

BY MINIBUS

Several companies offer licensed a/c minibuses to the Southern Bus Terminal and Victory Monument in Bangkok, including one southeast of the train station (marked on our map) that also covers Ratchaburi.

GETTING AROUND

By samlor or songthaew Shared songthaews circulate round the town, but to see the major temples in a day and have sufficient energy left for climbing Khao Wang, you might want to hire a samlor or a songthaew for a couple of hours, at about B100–200/hr, depending on distance.

By bicycle or motorbike You can rent bicycles (B100/ day) and motorbikes (B250–350/day) from *Rabieng Rimnum Guest House* (see below).

INFORMATION AND TOURS

Tourist information There's no TAT office in town, but *Rabieng Rimnum Guest House* (see below) is a good source of local information. It also organizes day-trips and multi-day visits to Kaeng Krachan National Park for bird-watching and hiking (two or three nights are good for trekking into the jungle), roughly from November to June or July.

ACCOMMODATION

Rabieng Rimnum (Rim Nam) Guest House 1 Thanon Chisa-in, on the southwest corner of Chomrut Bridge ☎032 425707 or ☎089 919 7446, ⊛rabiengrimnum .com. Occupying a century-old house next to the Phet River and, less appealingly, a noisy main road, this popular, central guesthouse offers very simple rooms with shared, cold-water bathrooms, lots of local information and the best restaurant in town. Excellent rates for singles; en-suite bathrooms planned in some rooms. B240

Royal Diamond Soi Sam Chao Phet, in a grid of small streets just off the Phetkasem Highway ☎032 411061–70, ⊛royaldiamondhotel.com. On the northwest side of Khao Wang, this welcoming place is Phetchaburi's best upmarket option. The large, comfortable a/c rooms with hot water, TVs and fridges are fairly well insulated from the noise of the highway (though not necessarily from the live bands in the hotel's own beer garden). Very modest breakfast included. B800

Sabai Dee Resort 65 Thanon Khong Kacheng ☎086 344 4418. Centrally placed and friendly budget option opposite *Rabieng Rimnum Guest House*. All sharing cold-water bathrooms, accommodation is either in very simple bamboo bungalows with mosquito nets in a small garden by the river, or in more expensive but better-value, large, white rooms (fan or a/c) with polished wooden floors in the bright, airy, mostly wooden main building, which has a ground-floor café. Fan B250, a/c B500

EATING

As well as for *khanom*, Phetchaburi is famous for savoury **khao chae**: originally a Mon dish designed to cool you down in the hot season, it consists of rice in chilled, flower-scented water served with delicate, fried side dishes, such as shredded Chinese radish and balls of shrimp paste, dried fish and palm sugar. It's available at the day market until it sells out, usually around 3pm. There's a nice little **night market** on the small road parallel to and immediately west of Thanon Matayawong.

Rabieng Rimnum (Rim Nam) Guest House 1 Thanon Chisa-in, on the southwest corner of Chomrut Bridge ☎032 425707 or ☎089 919 7446, ⊛rabiengrimnum .com. The town's best restaurant, an airy, wooden house with riverside tables attached to the guesthouse of the same name. It offers a long and interesting menu of inexpensive Thai dishes, from banana-blossom salad (B80) to the tasty Phetchaburi speciality, sugar-palm fruit curry with prawns (B80), and is deservedly popular with local diners. Daily 8am–midnight.

PHETCHABURI'S KHANOM

Almost half the shops in Phetchaburi stock the town's famous **khanom** (sweet snacks), as do many of the souvenir stalls crowding the base of Khao Wang and vendors at the day market on Thanon Matayawong. The most well-known local speciality is *maw kaeng* (best sampled from Raan Khanom Waan Mee Pin on the west side of Thanon Matayawong, just north of Phongsuriya), a baked sweet egg custard made with mung beans and coconut and sometimes flavoured with lotus seeds, durian or taro. Other Phetchaburi classics to look out for include *khanom taan*, small, steamed, saffron-coloured cakes made with local palm sugar, coconut and rice flour, and wrapped in banana-leaf cases; and *thong yot*, orange balls of palm sugar and baked egg yolk.

Kanchanaburi

Set at the confluence of two rivers, the Kwai Noi and the Kwai Yai, the provincial capital of **KANCHANABURI** makes the perfect getaway from Bangkok, a two- to three-hour bus ride away. With its rich wartime history, plentiful supply of traveller-oriented accommodation and countless possibilities for easy forays into the surrounding countryside, there are plenty of reasons to linger here, and many visitors end up staying longer than planned. The big appeal is the river: that it's the famous River Kwai (pronounced "kwae" as in "quaint" rather than "kwai" as in "quite") is a bonus, but the more immediate attractions are the guesthouses and restaurants that overlook the waterway, many of them offering fine views of the jagged limestone peaks beyond. The other main attraction is the drama of a ride on the **Death Railway** (see box, p.140).

The heart of Kanchanaburi's ever-expanding travellers' scene dominates the southern end of **Thanon Maenam Kwai** (also spelt Kwae) and is within easy reach of the train station, but the real town centre is some distance away, running north from the bus station up the town's main drag, **Thanon Saeng Chuto**. Between this road and the river you'll find most of the town's **war sights**, with the infamous **Bridge over the River Kwai** marking the northern limit. Every day, tour groups and day-trippers descend on the Bridge, a symbol of Japanese atrocities in the region, though the town's main **war museum** and **cemeteries** are actually much more moving. Many veterans returning to visit the graves of their wartime comrades are understandably resentful that others have in some cases insensitively exploited the POW experience – the commercial buzz around the Bridge is a case in point. On the other hand, the **Thailand–Burma Railway Centre** provides shockingly instructive accounts of a period not publicly documented outside this region.

The **Chungkai war cemetery** and a handful of moderately interesting temples – including the intriguing temples at **Wat Tham Khao Poon** and **Wat Ban Tham** – provide the focus for pleasurable trips west of the town centre.

Kanchanaburi gets packed during its annual *son et lumière* **River Kwai Bridge Festival**, held over ten nights from the end of November to commemorate the first Allied bombing of the Bridge on November 28, 1944, so book accommodation well ahead at this time.

Thailand–Burma Railway Centre

Opposite the train station, next to the Don Rak Kanchanaburi War Cemetery on Thanon Jaokannun • Daily 9am–5pm • B160 • ⓦ tbrconline.com

The modern **Thailand–Burma Railway Centre** is by far the best place to start any tour of Kanchanaburi's World War II memorials. It was founded to provide an informed context and research centre for the thousands who visit the POW graves every week. The result is a comprehensive and sophisticated history of the entire Thailand–Burma Railway line, with plenty of original artefacts, illustrations and scale models, and particularly strong sections on the planning and construction of the railway, and on the subsequent operation, destruction and decommissioning of the line. There is more of a focus on the line itself here than at the more emotive Hellfire Pass Memorial Museum (see p.139), but the human stories are well documented too, notably via some extraordinary original photographs and video footage shot by Japanese engineers, as well as through unique interviews with surviving Asian labourers on the railway.

8

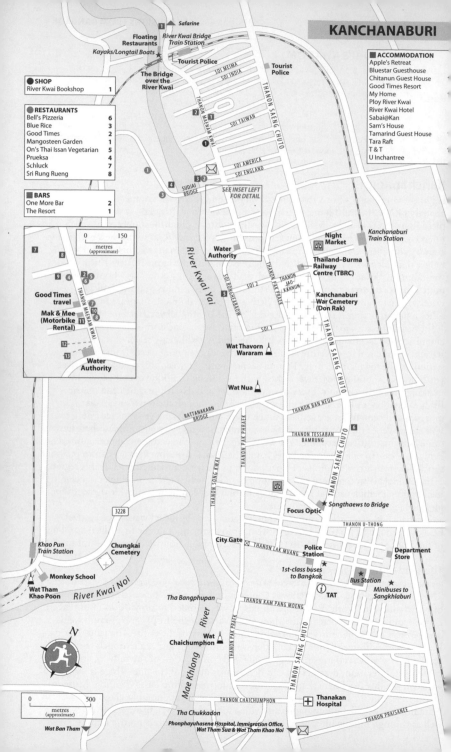

KANCHANABURI

SHOP
River Kwai Bookshop — 1

RESTAURANTS
Bell's Pizzeria — 6
Blue Rice — 3
Good Times — 2
Mangosteen Garden — 1
On's Thai Issan Vegetarian — 5
Prueksa — 4
Schluck — 7
Sri Rung Rueng — 8

BARS
One More Bar — 2
The Resort — 1

ACCOMMODATION
Apple's Retreat
Bluestar Guesthouse
Chitanun Guest House
Good Times Resort
My Home
Ploy River Kwai
River Kwai Hotel
Sabai@Kan
Sam's House
Tamarind Guest House
Tara Raft
T & T
U Inchantree

Safarine
Floating Restaurants
River Kwai Bridge Train Station
Kayaks/Longtail Boats
The Bridge over the River Kwai
Tourist Police
Tourist Police
SOI MEIMA
SOI INDIA
THANON SAENG CHUTO
THANON MAENAM KWAI
SOI TAIWAN
SOI AMERICA
SOI ENGLAND
SUDJAI BRIDGE
SEE INSET LEFT FOR DETAIL
Water Authority
Night Market
Kanchanaburi Train Station
Thailand–Burma Railway Centre (TBRC)
Kanchanaburi War Cemetery (Don Rak)
River Kwai Yai
SOI RONGHEBRON
SOI 2
THANON PAK PRAEK
THANON JAO-KANNUN
SOI 1
Wat Thavorn Wararam
Wat Nua
THANON BAN NEUA
RATTANAKARN BRIDGE
THANON TESSABAN BAMRUNG
6
THANON PAK PHRAEK
THANON SONG KWAI
Songthaews to Bridge
Focus Optic
THANON U-THONG
City Gate
THANON LAK MUANG
Police Station
Department Store
1st-class buses to Bangkok
Bus Station
Minibuses to Sangkhlaburi
TAT
THANON KAM PANG MOENG
3228
Khao Pun Train Station
Chungkai Cemetery
Monkey School
Wat Tham Khao Poon
River Kwai Noi
Tha Bangphupan
Wat Chaichumphon
THANON PAK PRAEK
Mae Khlong River
N
Wat Ban Tham
THANON CHAICHUMPHON
Thanakan Hospital
THANON SAENG CHUTO
THANON PRAISANEE
Tha Chukkadon
Phonphayuhasena Hospital, Immigration Office, Wat Tham Sua & Wat Tham Khao Noi

INSET:
0 — 150 metres (approximate)
7
8
9
6
2
5
Good Times travel
Mak & Mee (Motorbike Rental)
THANON MAENAM KWAI
7
10
11
8
12
13
Water Authority

0 — 500 metres (approximate)

The shop inside the entrance stocks some interesting books on the railway and also sells products made by the Weaving for Women project in Sangkhlaburi. Admission includes a free tea or coffee in the upstairs café.

Kanchanaburi War Cemetery (Don Rak)

Opposite the train station on Thanon Saeng Chuto • Free

One Allied POW died for each railway sleeper laid on the Thailand–Burma Railway (see box below), or so the story goes, and many of them are buried in Kanchanaburi's two war cemeteries, **Don Rak Kanchanaburi War Cemetery** and Chungkai Cemetery (see p.141). Of all the region's war sights, the cemeteries are the only places to have remained untouched by commercial enterprise. Don Rak is the bigger of the two, with 6982 POW graves laid out in straight lines amid immaculate lawns and flowering shrubs, maintained by the Commonwealth War Graves Commission. It was established after the war, on a plot adjacent to the town's Chinese cemetery, as the final resting place for the remains that had been hurriedly interred at dozens of makeshift POW-camp gravesites all the way up the line. Many of the identical stone memorial slabs in Don Rak state simply, "A man who died for his country"; others, inscribed with names, dates and regiments, indicate that the overwhelming majority of the dead were under 25 years old. A commemorative service is held here, and at Hellfire Pass, every year on April 25, Anzac Day.

THE DEATH RAILWAY

8

Shortly after entering World War II in December 1941, Japan, fearing an Allied blockade of the Bay of Bengal, began looking for an alternative supply route to connect its newly acquired territories that stretched from Singapore to the Myanmar–India border. In spite of the almost impenetrable terrain, the River Kwai basin was chosen as the route for a new **Thailand–Burma Railway**, the aim being to join the existing terminals of Nong Pladuk in Thailand (51km southeast of Kanchanaburi) and Thanbuyazat in Myanmar – a total distance of 415km.

About sixty thousand Allied POWs were shipped up from captured Southeast Asian territories to work on the link, their numbers later augmented by as many as two hundred thousand conscripted Asian labourers. Work began at both ends in June 1942. Three million cubic metres of rock were shifted and 14km of bridges built with little else but picks and shovels, dynamite and pulleys. By the time the line was completed, fifteen months later, it had more than earned its nickname, the **Death Railway**: an estimated sixteen thousand POWs and a hundred thousand Asian labourers died while working on it.

The appalling conditions and Japanese brutality were the consequences of the **samurai code**: Japanese soldiers abhorred the disgrace of imprisonment – to them, ritual suicide was the only honourable option open to a prisoner – and therefore considered that Allied POWs had forfeited any rights as human beings. Food rations were meagre for men forced into backbreaking eighteen-hour shifts, often followed by night-long marches to the next camp. Many suffered from beriberi, many more died of dysentery-induced starvation, but the biggest killers were cholera and malaria, particularly during the monsoon. It is said that one man died for every sleeper laid on the track.

The two lines finally met at Konkuita, just south of present-day Sangkhlaburi. But as if to underscore its tragic futility, the Thailand–Myanmar link saw less than two years of active service: after the Japanese surrender on August 15, 1945, the railway came under the jurisdiction of the British who, thinking it would be used to supply Karen separatists in Myanmar, tore up 4km of track at Three Pagodas Pass, thereby cutting the Thailand–Myanmar link forever. When the Thais finally gained control of the rest of the railway, they destroyed the track all the way down to Nam Tok, apparently because it was uneconomic. Recently, however, an Australian–Thai group of volunteers and former POWs has salvaged sections of track near the fearsome stretch of line known as **Hellfire Pass**, creating a memorial walk at the pass and founding an excellent museum at the site. There have been a number of books written about the Death Railway, including *The Railway Man* by Eric Lomax, which was made into a successful film (2013). The Thailand–Burma Railway Centre stocks a selection of such books, as do the town's bookshops.

RIDING THE DEATH RAILWAY

The two-hour journey along the notorious Thailand–Burma **Death Railway** from Kanchanaburi to Nam Tok is one of Thailand's most scenic and most popular train rides. Though the views are lovely, it's its history that makes the ride so special, so it's worth visiting the Thailand–Burma Railway Centre in Kanchanaburi before making the trip, as this provides a context for the enormous loss of human life and the extraordinary feat of engineering behind the line's construction (see p.137). Alternatively, take a bus from Kanchanaburi to the **Hellfire Pass Memorial Museum and Walk**, 18km from the line's current Nam Tok terminus, which provides an equally illuminating introduction to the railway's history, then take a bus back to Nam Tok and return to Kanchanaburi by train. A good tip, to get the best views, is to make sure you sit (or stand) on the right-hand side of the train on the journey back to Kanchanaburi, and on the left-hand side when travelling towards Nam Tok.

Leaving Kanchanaburi via the Bridge over the River Kwai, the train chugs through the Kwai Noi valley, stopping frequently at country stations decked with frangipani and jasmine. The first stop of note is Tha Kilen (1hr 15min), where you can alight for Prasat Muang Singh. About twenty minutes later the most hair-raising section of track begins: at **Wang Sing**, also known as Arrow Hill, the train squeezes through 30m-deep solid rock cuttings, dug at the cost of numerous POW lives; 6km further, it slows to a crawl at the approach to the **Wang Po viaduct**, where a 300m-long trestle bridge clings to the cliff face as it curves with the Kwai Noi – almost every man who worked on this part of the railway died. The station at the northern end of the trestle bridge is called **Tham Krasae**, after the cave that's hollowed out of the rock face beside the bridge; you can see the cave's resident Buddha image from the train. North of Tham Krasae, the train pulls in at **Wang Po Station** before continuing alongside a particularly lovely stretch of the Kwai Noi, its banks thick with jungle and not a raft house in sight, the whole vista framed by distant tree-clad peaks. Thirty minutes later, the train reaches **Nam Tok**, a small town that thrives chiefly on its position at the end of the line.

Three trains operate daily along the Death Railway in both directions, but they don't always run on time. Currently they're scheduled to leave Kanchanaburi at 6.07am, 10.35am and 4.26pm and to return from Nam Tok at 5.20am, 12.55pm and 3.30pm; Kanchanaburi TAT keeps up-to-date timetables (see p.143). If you're up at the Bridge, you can join the train five minutes later.

The Bridge over the River Kwai

Just west of the River Kwai Bridge Train Station • A 15–20min walk north of the main Thanon Maenam Kwai guesthouse area; alternatively, cycle or take a tuk-tuk (about B30–40)

For most people, the plain steel arches of the **Bridge over the River Kwai** come as a disappointment: as a war memorial it lacks both the emotive punch of the museums and the perceptible drama of spots further up the line, and as a bridge it looks nothing out of the ordinary – certainly not as awesomely hard to construct as it appears in David Lean's famous 1957 film, *Bridge on the River Kwai* (which was in fact shot in Sri Lanka). But it is the link with the multi-Oscar-winning film, of course, that draws tour buses by the dozen, and makes the Bridge approach seethe with trinket-sellers and touts. For all the commercialization of the place, however, you can't really come to the Kwai and not see it.

The fording of the Kwai Yai at the point just north of Kanchanaburi known as Tha Makkham was one of the first major obstacles in the construction of the Thailand–Burma Railway. Sections of a steel bridge were brought up from Java and reassembled by POWs using only pulleys and derricks. A temporary **wooden bridge** was built alongside it, taking its first train in February 1943; three months later the steel bridge was finished. Both bridges were severely damaged by Allied bombers (rather than commando-saboteurs as in the film) in 1944 and 1945, but the steel bridge was repaired after the war and is still in use today. The best way to see the bridge is by walking gingerly across it, or taking the **train** right over it: the Kanchanaburi–Nam Tok service crosses it three times a day in each direction, stopping briefly at the River Kwai Bridge station on the east bank of the river.

8

Thanon Pak Phraek

Between Rattanakarn Bridge and City Gate

Running north from Kanchanaburi's only remaining city gate, the historical significance of **Thanon Pak Phraek** has led the TAT to place information boards outside many of the old buildings, explaining their origin and use over the years. Most of these houses were built just outside the city walls in the late nineteenth or early twentieth century by Chinese and Vietnamese immigrants and reflect a variety of architectural styles. While some of the properties along the street are nothing more than run-down shophouses, others have been carefully restored and boast elaborate balconies with balustrades. Sadly, the tangle of electric cables along the street makes them less photogenic than they would otherwise be.

It's worth dropping by the TAT office (see p.143) before coming here to pick up an informative brochure and map of the street, so you can find out more about the buildings as you stroll along the street. The more interesting buildings include the former *Sumitrakarn Hotel*, the first hotel in Kanchanaburi, which was built in 1937 and finally closed its doors to the public in 1979; it now functions as a shop selling household goods. Others worth a close look are Sitthisang house, built in 1920 and renovated in 2009; and Boonyiam Jiaranai house, which has some elaborate stucco arches on the upstairs balcony.

Chungkai Cemetery

On the west bank of the Kwai Noi, 2km from Rattanakarn Bridge, along Route 3228 • 5–10min by tuk-tuk from the main Thanon Maenam Kwai guesthouse area

Scrupulously well-trimmed **Chungkai Cemetery** occupies a fairly tranquil roadside spot on the west bank of the Kwai Noi, at the site of a former POW camp. Some 1750 POWs are buried here; most of the gravestone inscriptions include a name and regimental insignia, and some with epitaphs such as "One corner of the world which is forever England". However, a number of the graves remain unnamed – at the upcountry camps, bodies were thrown onto mass funeral pyres, making identification impossible. The cemetery makes a pleasant cycle ride from Rattanakarn Bridge – much of the land in this area is sugar-cane country, for which Kanchanaburi has earned the title "sugar capital of Thailand".

Wat Tham Khao Poon

On the west bank of the Kwai Noi, 2km west along Route 3228 from Chungkai Cemetery and then Route 3305 (turn left at the railway line), or 4km from Rattanakarn Bridge • Daily dawn–dusk • B30 • Often included in boat trips from the bridge

At the top of Route 3305's only hill sits the cave temple **Wat Tham Khao Poon**. The attraction here is a nine-chambered cave connected by a labyrinth of dank stalactite-filled passages, where almost every ledge and knob of rock is filled with religious icons, the most important being the Reclining Buddha in the main chamber. Once out of the cave system, you can walk through a bamboo "museum" with some blurry pictures from World War II. If you arrived by road, follow the sealed road through the temple compound for 150m to reach a good vantage point over the Kwai Noi, just above the train tracks, presided over by an outsized, pot-bellied golden Buddha statue; if arriving by boat, you enter the wat compound via the cliff-side steps here.

Wat Ban Tham

12km south of town • Cross the Mae Khlong River at Thanon Mae Khlong, then turn left for the 6km ride south; alternatively, it can be reached by boat in around 30min from the centre

Because of the limestone landscape, caves are found right around Kanchanaburi and many of them have been sanctified as shrines. **Wat Ban Tham** is one such place, and is intriguing enough to make the 12km trip from the town centre worthwhile. Travelling south down the Mae Khlong to get to the temple is especially pleasant by longtail or kayak, but can also be done by road.

8

Wat Ban Tham was founded around six hundred years ago but its fame rests on the seventeenth-century love story that was supposedly played out in a cave on this site. A young woman called Nang Bua Klee was forced to choose between duty to her criminal father and love for the local hero by whom she had fallen pregnant; her father eventually persuaded Bua Klee to poison her sweetheart's food, but the soldier learned of the plot and killed both Bua Klee and their unborn son, whose souls are now said to be trapped in the cave at Wat Ban Tham. The cave is approached via an ostentatious Chinese-style dragon's mouth staircase, whose upper levels relate the legend in a gallery of brightly painted modern murals on the right-hand walls. Inside the cave, a woman-shaped stone has been painted in the image of the dead mother and is a popular object of worship for women trying to conceive: hopeful devotees bring pretty dresses and shoes for the image, which are hung in wardrobes to the side of the shrine, as well as toys for her son.

ARRIVAL AND DEPARTURE

BY TRAIN

The main Kanchanaburi train station (☎ 034 511285), not to be confused with the River Kwai Bridge station, is on Thanon Saeng Chuto, about 2km north of the town centre, but within walking distance of some of the Thanon Maenam Kwai accommodation. A samlor or tuk-tuk ride from here to Thanon Maenam Kwai accommodation will cost around B50.

Services to Kanchanaburi Trains are the most scenic way to get to Kanchanaburi, but there are only two daily from Bangkok's Thonburi station via Nakhon Pathom (7.45am and 1.55pm). If you're coming from Hua Hin, Chumphon and points further south, take the train to Ban Pong and then change to a Kanchanaburi-bound train (or bus – the bus stop is at the clocktower, about 1km from Ban Pong train station).

Reservations and tickets Reservations for any rail journey can be made at Kanchanaburi train station, or through Good Times tour agency (see p.145) for an extra B50. Tickets for the train ride to Bangkok or along the Death Railway to Nam Tok (see p.140) don't need advance booking.

Destinations Bangkok (Thonburi; 2 daily; 3hr); Nakhon Pathom (2 daily; 1hr 40min–2hr); Nam Tok (3 daily; 2hr 20min).

BY BUS

Kanchanaburi's bus station (☎ 034 515907) is at the southern edge of the town centre, a good 2km from most accommodation. Tuk-tuks and samlors wait here and will run you into the main Thanon Maenam Kwai accommodation area for around B60.

Services to Kanchanaburi The buses from Bangkok's Southern Bus Terminal and Northern Mo Chit terminal are faster than the train. From Lopburi, Ayutthaya (connecting with trains from Chiang Mai), or points further north, you'll

have to return to Bangkok, use a minibus service (see below) or change buses (onto #411) at Suphanburi, about 90km north of Kanchanaburi. Coming from Phetchaburi and Hua Hin, you need to change buses (onto #461) at Ratchaburi.

Moving on Government buses run from the bus station to Bangkok's Northern Mo Chit bus terminal, the Southern Bus Terminal, and to all destinations listed below. The first-class ticket office and departure point is beside the main road on the edge of the bus station, while the office for all other services is in the middle of the depot.

Destinations Bangkok (Northern Mo Chit terminal; 8 daily; 3hr); Bangkok (Southern Bus terminal; every 20min; 2hr 30min); Chiang Mai (2 daily; 11hr); Erawan (every 50min; 1hr 30min); Hua Hin (hourly; 3hr 30min); Nam Tok (every 30min; 1hr 30min); Nong Khai (2 daily; 11hr); Phu Nam Ron (4 daily; 1hr 30min); Ratchaburi (every 20min; 2hr); Rayong (2 daily; 7hr 30min); Sai Yok (every 30min; 2hr 30min); Sangkhlaburi (4 daily; 3hr); Suphanburi (every 20min; 2hr); Thong Pha Phum (every 30min; 3hr 30min); Three Pagodas Pass (3 daily; 4hr).

BY MINIBUS

Minibuses for Bangkok, Ayutthaya, Sangkhlaburi and Suvarnabhumi Airport arrive at and depart from the main bus station. Coming from Bangkok, a/c minibuses leave regularly from Thanon Khao San and Victory Monument; they are faster but more cramped than regular buses. Returning to Bangkok, if you book through your guesthouse they will pick you up at a designated time.

Destinations Ayutthaya (daily; 3hr, timed to connect with the night trains to Chiang Mai); Bangkok (Victory Monument; hourly; 2hr); Sangkhlaburi (every 20min; 3hr; tickets available from a booth at the back of the bus station); Suvarnabhumi Airport (6 daily; 2hr 30min–3hr).

GETTING AROUND

With tuk-tuks plying the main route between the bus station and the Bridge, and boatmen waiting to ferry you along the waterways, it's easy to get to and from Kanchanaburi's main sights.

By tuk-tuk A tuk-tuk from the guesthouses to the Bridge will cost around B30–40.

By songthaew Orange public songthaews run along Thanon Saeng Chuto, originating from outside the Focus

Optic optician's, three blocks north of the bus station, and travelling north via the Kanchanaburi War Cemetery (Don Rak), Thai–Burma Railway Centre, train station and access road to the Bridge (#2; every 15min until 6pm; 15min to the Bridge turn-off; B10).

By motorbike Many outlets, such as Mek and Mee (☎081 7571194) on Thanon Maenam Kwai, rent out motorbikes for around B200 per day.

By longtail boat Boats wait beside the Bridge for trips to riverside sights such as Wat Tham Khao Poon. Most of them ask around B900 for a 90min trip that includes about three stops.

By bicycle Guesthouses and tour agencies rent out bicycles for B50 a day – ideal for exploring the main town sights and the quiet rural backroads.

By kayak A green and sedate way of exploring the area is by kayak; you can rent one on the east side of the river just north of the Bridge or from tour agencies on Thanon Maenam Kwai. Alternatively, try French-run canoeing specialists Safarine, at 117 Soi Tha Makham, Moo 2 (☎086 049 1662, ⊛safarine .com), who charge B350 for 1hr 30min.

INFORMATION

Tourist information The helpful TAT office (daily 8.30am–4.30pm; ☎034 511200, ✉tatkan@tat.or.th) is just south of the bus station on Thanon Saeng Chuto and keeps up-to-date bus and train timetables. They can also provide a good map of the town and province, plus a booklet on Thanon Pak Phraek (see p.141).

ACCOMMODATION

Many people choose to make the most of the scenery by staying on or near the river, in either a **raft house** or a **guesthouse**, and the options are increasing as the town's building boom continues. The most popular area is around **Thanon Maenam Kwai**, which stretches 2km from Soi Rongheabaow to the Bridge, and is *the* backpackers' hub, crammed with bars, restaurants and tour agents; most guesthouses are at the riverside end of the small sois running off this thoroughfare, though few rooms actually have river views. For those that have views (which naturally have higher rates), the idyll can be plagued by longtail engines during the day and floating karaoke rafts at night, so you might want to book in for just one night until you've experienced the decibel levels for yourself. Bring mosquito repellent too, as many huts float among lotus swamps.

8

KANCHANABURI

Apple's Retreat On the west side of the river, 600m from Thanon Maenam Kwai ☎034 512017, ⊛applenoi -kanchanaburi.com. *Apple's Retreat* sits in a green and tranquil spot, with a lovely Kwai-side restaurant and terrace on the opposite side of the road by the river. The rather plain rooms with platform beds are in a two-storey building, enjoying views across farmland to the hills beyond, and there's a peaceful garden. Breakfast costs B200 extra. B790

Bluestar Guesthouse 241 Thanon Maenam Kwai ☎034 512161, ⊛bluestar-guesthouse.com. Popular, clued-up guesthouse with a wide range of good-value accommodation including very cheap, basic fan rooms and attractive, well-priced a/c bungalows set over a lotus swamp; and cabins raised on elevated piles with downstairs bathrooms and high-level bedrooms or private upper-level terraces. Fan doubles B200, a/c doubles B350, bungalows B650

Chitanun Guest House 47/3 Thanon Maenam Kwai, on the opposite side of the road from the river ☎034 624785, ⊛chitanungroup.com. A range of en-suite rooms – from basic white-walled crash pads with cold-water bathrooms to quite luxurious affairs with a/c and TV – set in a private compound full of tropical plants. It's a friendly place but beginning to look a bit worn. Fan B250, a/c B600

★Good Times Resort 265/5–7 Thanon Maenam Kwai ☎034 514241, ⊛good-times-resort.com. This is one of the newest and most attractive resorts in town, with a prime location by the river just north of the Sudjai Bridge. Just about all of the 36 spacious rooms have a balcony, some with pool view, but only one with river view. It's a good base for families as some rooms are connecting. The owner/manager Chalee is helpful and knowledgeable, and rates include a filling breakfast. B1050

My Home 1/16–18 Thanon Maenam Kwai, signposted down an unnamed soi just north of the Water Authority building ☎034 625555, ⊛myhomekan.com. This clean and smart place, on a quiet soi between Thanon Maenam Kwai and the river, is far enough away from all of the noisy bars to ensure a restful sleep, but still relatively central. The great-value en-suite, a/c rooms occupy a modern single-storey block, which backs onto a courtyard, and have brightly painted walls, while fan rooms are sparsely furnished and share bathrooms. Fan B350, a/c B600

Ploy River Kwai 79/2 Thanon Maenam Kwai ☎082 4753443, ⊛ploygh.com. Strikingly different in style from other guesthouses on this road, this is a smart little enclave set back off the road but with distant river views only from the restaurant. The chic, sleek, contemporary-look rooms have platform beds and a/c, with extra charged for those with open-air bathrooms or TVs. Good discounts if you book online. B1000

River Kwai Hotel 284/15–16 Thanon Saeng Chuto ☎034 510111, ⊛riverkwai.co.th. Despite the name, the town centre's top hotel is nowhere near the river, but it's very good value even if it lacks the atmosphere of its riverside competitors. Rooms are of a high standard, and all have a/c and cable TV. Facilities include a pool, spa and nightclub. B1800

★**Sabai@Kan** 317/4 Thanon Maenam Kwai ☎034 625544, ⓦsabaiatkan.com. This relaxing boutique hotel is located towards the northern end of Thanon Maenam Kwai, and while there are no river views, all rooms have wall-to-wall windows that overlook a pleasant prospect of a pool and shady garden. Rooms are spacious and well equipped, with thick mattresses on the beds. A decent buffet breakfast is included in the rate and staff are very efficient and helpful. B1400

Sam's House 14/2 Thanon Maenam Kwai ☎034 515956, ⓦsamsguesthouse.com. A huge variety of rooms, ranging from stone bungalows to raft houses on the river, some with great views though they're squeezed closely together. Staff are very helpful and can arrange boat pick-ups from the jetty. Fan B500, a/c B600

Tamarind Guest House 29/1 Thanon Maenam Kwai ☎034 518790, ⓔtamarind_guesthouse@yahoo.co.th. Smaller rooms than in some of the other riverside guest-houses, but the place is very clean and managed by friendly staff. Sleep in the house, or down by the waterfront in one of the raft-house rooms, which have river views and share a breezy terrace. Fan B400, a/c B600

Tara Raft 15/1 Soi Rongheabaow ☎086 3967349, ⓦtararoom.com. In a pretty location on a quiet stretch of the river just south of the Maenam Kwai hub, this place offers stylish raft-house rooms with great views for B900: they're large, en suite, and come with king-size beds and big TVs; the best have lovely outlooks from tiny terraces, and there's a large sundeck on top of the raft. The cheapest rooms have no view, and breakfast is not included. They also run *Tara Bed and Breakfast* (fan B250, a/c B350) at 99–101 Thanon Maenam Kwai. B600

T&T 1/14 Thanon Maenam Kwai, just north of My Home, on a soi leading down towards the river ☎034 514846, ⓦtandt-kanchanaburiguesthouse.com. A friendly and relaxing budget choice, with a small but attractive terrace overlooking the Kwai Yai. Sleeping options include small, fan-cooled singles with clean shared bathrooms, doubles in a floating raft house which have mattresses on the floor (also with shared bathrooms), and more luxurious rooms with a/c and private bathrooms. Fan B250, a/c B500

U Inchantree 443 Thanon Maenam Kwai ☎034 521584, ⓦukanchanaburi.com. Spectacularly located on a bend in the Kwai Yai River, a 5min walk north of the Bridge

(get off at the River Kwai Bridge train station if arriving by train), this luxurious, 26-room retreat has charming staff and what must be Kanchanaburi's most style-conscious rooms. They're not huge, but the powerful rain showers, snuggly white duvets and in-room iPod docks more than compensate. Outside, facilities include a riverside pool, a peaceful glass-fronted library and a restaurant serving superb buffet breakfasts. Best of all, you can keep your room for a full 24 hours, regardless of when you check in. B2700

OUT OF TOWN

Oriental Kwai 194/5 Moo 1, Ladya (off Route 3199) ☎034 588168, ⓦorientalkwai.com. In a quiet spot beside the Kwai Yai, 15km north of town, this Dutch–Thai-run little hotel offers just twelve thoughtfully designed cottages in a lush tropical garden with a pool. Cottages are a/c, have DVD players (with a big library of films to choose from) and are tastefully decorated in modern Asian accents; some are wheelchair accessible. There's nothing to see in the immediate area but the owners will give you plenty of ideas for exploring nearby, including boat rides to the Bridge. B2800

Royal River Kwai Resort 88 Moo 2, Kanchanaburi-Saiyok Road (about 7km northwest of town to the north of H323) ☎034 653342, ⓦroyalriverkwairesort .com. It's worth making the short trip out of town to this riverside resort with beautiful gardens, an excellent pool and well-maintained rooms, if only for its relaxing atmosphere. If you want river views, opt for the mini suite. There's also a very good restaurant and probably the best spa in the area. B1800

★**Xanadu 2008** 19/5 Moo 1, Tambon Nong Bua ☎080 021 3346, ⓦxanaduresort2008.com. With just ten en-suite bungalows in a sloping, tropical garden that leads down towards a peaceful section of the river, this welcoming place is ideal for families or couples in search of peace and quiet. There's a well-maintained pool, and English–Thai owners Dennis and Nee do everything they can to fill guests in on local happenings. Nee is an excellent cook, and the generous portions have to be seen to be believed, while Dennis has extensive local knowledge. It's a 9km drive from the Bridge, on the northern bank of the River Kwai Yai; join Route 3199 as you head north out of town, then turn left towards Nong Bua. B1200

EATING

Most of Kanchanaburi's guesthouses and raft houses have **restaurants**, and there's a cluster of floating restaurants beside the Bridge, serving good if rather pricey seafood to accompany the river views. A cheaper place to enjoy genuine local food is at the ever-reliable **night market**, which sets up alongside Thanon Saeng Chuto on the edge of the bus station. There are also a few food stalls at the **night bazaar**, which operates in front of the train station (Mon, Tues & Thurs–Sun 6–10pm).

Bell's Pizzeria 24/5 Thanon Maenam Kwai ☎081 010 6614, ⓦbellspizzeria.com. This popular Italian place has tables inside and out, and the menu, which runs from

carbonara right through to *phanaeng* curries, is extremely diverse. Pizzas from B170. Daily 5–11pm.

Blue Rice 153/4 Moo 4, Tamakam (cross the Sudjai Bridge

to the west side then turn north) ☎034 512017, ⓦapplenoi-kanchanaburi.com. Reliably tasty food prepared to traditional Thai recipes by Kanchanaburi's most famous cooking school. The short menu (B90–250) includes coconut- and cashew-laced *matsaman* curries – both meat and vegetarian varieties – as well as outstanding yellow curries. Every dish is prepared to order, so service can be slow. Also offers cookery classes (see below). Daily noon–2pm & 6–10pm.

Good Times 265/5–7 Thanon Maenam Kwai ☎034 514241, ⓦgood-times-resort.com. Located on the riverside just north of the Sudjai Bridge (walk through the resort to get there), this open-sided place offers a broad selection of well-prepared Thai and Western dishes. A fillet steak with all the trimmings will set you back B260, while fish and chips and meat pies (both B150) are other options. Most Thai dishes are priced at around B100, and it's a good choice for a filling breakfast if it's not included with your accommodation. Daily 7am–10pm.

★**Mangosteen Garden** 74/12 Moo 4, Tamakam (about 300m northwest of Sudjai Bridge, beyond Apple's Resort) ☎034 511814, ⓦmangosteencafe.net. This stand-out restaurant recently moved from its tiny shophouse on Thanon Maenam Kwai to a two-storey house and garden on the west side of the river, and now offers dining on a downstairs or upstairs terrace or in an a/c room, plus a play area for kids. The menu features tempting dishes such as red curry with duck (B130) and salmon steak on crushed potatoes with prawns and vegetables (B230), as well as smoothies, cocktails and wine. Daily 11.30am–10pm.

On's Thai Issan Vegetarian 36 Thanon Maenam Kwai ☎087 3642264, ⓦonthaiissan.com. There's a lively buzz around this simple streetside place, which only serves vegetarian dishes such as seaweed soup and *phat thai* (around B50 a dish). The buzz comes from On's students who learn how to make their favourite dishes on the street out front (see below). Daily 10am–9pm.

Prueksa 89 Thanon Maenam Kwai ☎094 4069921. This simple thatched hut turns out classic Thai dishes such as green curry (B60) at very reasonable prices, and cheap beers too. Daily 11am–11pm.

Schluck 20/1 Thanon Maenam Kwai ☎081 3559477. Cosy a/c restaurant that entices a regular crowd of expats with its menu of pizzas, salads and steaks (from B150), plus its decent selection of authentically spicy fish and yam dishes (B70–90) and French pastries too. Also has a few tables outside. Daily 4–10pm.

Sri Rung Rueng 10/1 Thanon Maenam Kwai ☎092 7981828. Well-priced restaurant with a huge menu of *tom kha*, *tom yam* and curries (yellow, red, green, *phanaeng* and *matsaman*), lots of which are available in veggie and non-veggie versions (from B70), plus steaks, seafood and cocktails. Daily 10am–10pm.

DRINKING AND NIGHTLIFE

Nightlife in Kanchanaburi is relatively low-key, though there's a string of hostess **bars** at the southern end of Thanon Maenam Kwai, offering loud music and cheapish beer, with sports on TV as an added attraction. Further north up the strip are several simple bars without hostesses, and some classy venues that attract a mostly Thai crowd.

One More Bar 44/3 Thanon Maenam Kwai ☎084 801 3933. A lively, sociable place to head to after dark, not least because it has a refreshing no-bar-girls policy. Staff are friendly, there's a mix of Thai and Western food and a range of beers, spirits and cocktails. Daily 8am–2am.

The Resort 318/2 Thanon Maenam Kwai ☎034 624606. For a taste of Thai nightlife, head up towards the north end of Thanon Maenam Kwai to this slick restaurant and bar, with fairy lights twinkling in the trees outside and various cosy corners in the a/c interior. There's live music every night from 8pm, and a wide range of draught and imported beers. Daily 5.30pm–1am.

DIRECTORY

Airline tickets Domestic and international tickets can be bought from Good Times Travel, 63/1 Thanon Maenam Kwai (☎034 624441, ⓦgood-times-travel.com).

Books There are several secondhand bookshops on Thanon Maenam Kwai, but the best stocked is the River Kwai Bookshop at 293 Thanon Maenam Kwai (☎034 511676; Mon, Tues & Thurs–Sun 10am–10pm).

Cookery classes Most famously at *Blue Rice*, run by *Khun Apple*: shop at the morning market and learn how to cook the basic Thai dishes at professional cooking stations (daily 9.30am–3pm; B1550). Vegetarians should sign up for classes with Khun On at *On's Thai Issan Vegetarian* (see above); she'll teach you how to make three dishes in two hours for B600, any time between 10am and 6pm.

Hospitals The private Thanakan Hospital (☎034 622366–75) is at 20/20 Thanon Saeng Chuto, at the southern end of town, near the junction with Thanon Chukkadon; the government-run Phahon Phonphayula-sena Hospital (☎034 511233 or ☎034 622999) is further south at 572/1 Thanon Saeng Chuto, near the junction with Thanon Mae Khlong.

Immigration office The office is located at 100/22 Thanon Mae Khlong ☎034 564279.

Tourist police For all emergencies, call the tourist police on the free 24hr phone line (☎1155), or contact them at their booth on Thanon Saeng Chuto (daily 9am–6pm; ☎034 512795), a short way east of the Bridge.

8

THE GARDEN SUITE, *HOTEL SUKHOTHAI*

Accommodation

Bangkok has appalling traffic jams, so think carefully about what you want to see and do before deciding which part of town to stay in: easy access to relevant train networks and river transport can be crucial. Advance reservations are recommended where possible during high season (Nov–Feb), though some guesthouses will only take cash deposits. In the reviews that follow, accommodation is air-conditioned, unless specified.

For ultra-cheap double rooms under B500, your widest choice lies with the guesthouses on and around **Banglamphu**'s Thanon Khao San. The most inexpensive rooms here are no-frills crash-pads – small and often windowless, with fans, thin walls and shared bathrooms – but Banglamphu also offers plenty of well-appointed mid-priced options with air-conditioning and swimming pools. Other, far smaller and less interesting travellers' ghettoes that might be worth considering are the generally dingy **Soi Ngam Duphli**, off the south side of Thanon Rama IV, which nevertheless harbours a couple of decent shoestring options; and **Soi Kasemsan I**, which is very handily placed next to Siam Square and firmly occupies the moderate range, though with a few rooms for around B600. The majority of the city's moderate and expensive rooms are scattered widely across the **downtown areas**, around Siam Square and Thanon Ploenchit, to the south of Thanon Rama IV and along **Thanon Sukhumvit**, and to a lesser extent in **Chinatown**. As well as easy access to transport links and shops, the downtown views from accommodation in these areas are a real plus.

Bangkok boasts an increasing number of exceptionally stylish **super-deluxe** hotels, with chic decor and excellent facilities that often include a **spa**. The cream of this accommodation, with rates starting from around B5000, is scenically sited along the banks of the Chao Phraya River, though there are a few top-notch hotels in the downtown area, which is also where you'll find the best business hotels.

ESSENTIALS

Family accommodation Many of the expensive hotels listed offer special deals for families, usually allowing one or two under-12s to share their parents' room for free, so long as no extra bedding is required. It's also often possible to cram two adults and two children into the twin rooms in inexpensive and mid-priced hotels (as opposed to guesthouses), as beds in these places are usually big enough for two. A number of guesthouses offer three-person rooms.

Long-stay accommodation If you plan on staying in

Bangkok longer, the most economical option is usually a room with a bathroom in an apartment building, which is likely to cost at least B6000 a month. Many foreigners end up living in apartments off Thanon Sukhumvit, around Victory Monument and Pratunam, or on Soi Boonprarop, off Thanon Rajaprarop just north of Pratunam. Visit the website for teachers of English in Thailand, ⓦ ajarn.com, for tips on living in Bangkok and finding an apartment, and try ⓦ sabaai.com for a wide choice of serviced apartments.

RATANAKOSIN AND AROUND

Several small, **upmarket hotels** have recently opened on the west side of Ratanakosin, which put you in a peerless location, in a quiet, traditional, heavily Chinese neighbourhood of low-rise shophouses, overlooking the river and on the doorsteps of Wat Pho and the Grand Palace. The restaurants and nightlife of Banglamphu are within walking distance if you fancy a bit more of a buzz, while the sights of Thonburi and Chinatown, and Saphan Taksin Skytrain station are just a public boat ride away. It's also well worth considering *Ibrik Resort by the River*, a small, appealing hotel directly opposite Ratanakosin on the Thonburi bank of the Chao Phraya, whose main link with the rest of the city is by cross-river boat.

Arun Residence 36 Soi Pratu Nokyung, Thanon Maharat ☏ 02 221 9158, ⓦ arunresidence.com; map p.50. Stunning views of Wat Arun and charming,

wooden-floored rooms and suites that mix traditional and contemporary Thai styles. Occupying an eccentrically converted shophouse (plumbing can sometimes be a

ACCOMMODATION PRICES

Throughout this Guide, the prices given for guesthouses and hotels represent the **minimum** you can expect to pay in each establishment in the **high season** (roughly July, Aug and Nov–Feb) for a typical **double room**, booked via the hotel website where available; there may however be an extra "peak" supplement for the Christmas–New Year period. If travelling on your own, expect to pay between sixty and one hundred percent of the rates quoted for a double room. Where a hostel or guesthouse also offers **dormitory beds**, the minimum price per bed is also given; where a place has both fan-cooled and air-conditioned rooms, we've given the minimum price for a double in each category. Top-end hotels will add **seven percent tax** – though this is due to increase to ten percent – and **ten percent service charge** to your bill; the prices given in the Guide are net rates after these taxes (usually referred to as "plus plus") have been added.

9

problem), the hotel also has an attractive lounge, a rooftop bar and a good European and Thai restaurant, *The Deck*, where breakfast (included in the price) is served. **B4000**

The Asadang Thanon Atsadang, corner of Thanon Phraya Si ☎085 180 7100, ⊛theasadang.com; map p.50. In an early twentieth-century Neoclassical mansion on Ratanakosin's doorstep, this very upscale B&B is perhaps a little truer to Thai roots than its sister, *The Bhuthorn* (see p.151), showcasing antique Thai furniture, carved lintels and attractive local fabrics; it's certainly airier and more spacious, with white wooden walls throughout. If you can manage the narrow, steep spiral staircase (and the higher rate, B4800), plump for the cute rooftop "Ratchabopit" overlooking the eponymous temple, which boasts a rocking chair, full-length windows and a private terrace overlooking Wat Rajabophit. Breakfast included. **B3300**

Aurum The River Place 394/27–29 Soi Pansook, Thanon Maharat ☎02 622 2248, ⊛aurum-bangkok .com; map p.50. Modelled on a French townhouse, with wooden shutters and wrought-iron balconies, this spruce four-storey hotel is set back very slightly from the river and four of the rooms are "City View" only, but the other eight offer at least partial views of the water. Splashed with colourful Thai fabrics and sporting heavily varnished wooden floors, the well-equipped rooms are a little on the small side, apart from those on the top floor. There's a daytime riverside café, *Vivi: The Coffee Place* (see p.159), where complimentary breakfast is served. **B3500**

Chakrabongse Villas 396 Thanon Maharat ☎02 222 1290, ⊛thaivillas.com; map p.50. Upmarket riverside accommodation with a difference: nine tranquil rooms, suites and villas beautifully furnished in a choice of Thai, Chinese and Moroccan styles, set in the luxurious gardens of hundred-year-old Chakrabongse House overlooking Wat

TOP FIVE RIVERSIDE STAYS

Anantara Riverside See p.154
Chakrabongse Villas See below
Ibrik Resort by the River See below
Peninsula Bangkok See p.155
Praya Palazzo See opposite

Arun. All have a/c and cable TV, and there's a small, attractive swimming pool and a riverfront pavilion for relaxing or dining (if ordered in advance). There are canoes and bicycles available for guests to use. **B5620**

★**Ibrik Resort by the River** 256 Soi Wat Rakhang ☎02 848 9220, ⊛ibrikresort.com; map p.82. With just three rooms, this is the most bijou of boutique resorts. Each room is beautifully appointed in boho-chic style, with traditional wood floors, modernist white walls and sparkling silk accessories – and two of them have balconies right over the Chao Phraya River. It's just like staying at a trendy friend's home, in a neighbourhood that sees hardly any other tourists. Located next door to *Supatra River House* restaurant and 5min walk from either express-boat stop Tha Wang Lang or the cross-river pier at Wat Rakhang (for Tha Chang and the Grand Palace). Breakfast included. **B4000**

Sala Arun 47 Soi Tha Thien, Thanon Maharat ☎02 622 2932–3, ⊛salaarun.com; map p.50. Sister property to *Arun Residence*, also on the river, two blocks up. The six teak-floored rooms (and one suite) feature objets d'art from the owners' worldwide travels, DVDs, iPod docks and balconies, while complimentary breakfast is served in the boldly coloured ground-floor café, which has a small terrace with armchairs facing Wat Arun (to get a view of the river and temple from your room, you'll have to pay B4200). **B3500**

BANGLAMPHU AND DEMOCRACY MONUMENT AREA

Nearly all backpackers head straight for Banglamphu, Bangkok's long-established travellers' ghetto just north of the Grand Palace, location of the **cheapest accommodation**, the best traveller-oriented facilities and some of the most enjoyable bars and restaurants in the city. A growing number of Khao San guesthouses are reinventing themselves as good-value **mini-hotels** boasting chic decor, swimming pools, and even views from the windows, but the cheap sleeps are still there, particularly immediately west of Khao San, around the neighbourhood temple Wat Chana Songkhram, and along riverside Thanon Phra Arthit – where you'll also find some **upscale places** offering prime views over the Chao Phraya. About a 10min walk north from Thanon Khao San, the handful of **guesthouses** scattered among the shophouses of the Thanon Samsen sois enjoy a more authentically Thai environment, while the Thewet area, a further 15min walk in the same direction or a 7min walk from the Thewet express-boat stop, is more local still. Heading south from Khao San, across multi-laned Rajdamnoen Klang, to the upscale guesthouses in the area immediately south of Democracy also puts you plumb in the middle of an interesting old neighbourhood, famous for its traditional shophouse restaurants. Theft is a problem in Banglamphu, particularly at the cheaper guesthouses, so don't leave anything valuable in your room and heed the guesthouses' notices about padlocks and safety lockers.

THANON KHAO SAN AND AROUND

Buddy Lodge 265 Thanon Khao San ☎02 629 4477, ⊛buddylodge.com; map pp.66–67. Stylish hotel right in the thick of the action, whose charming, colonial-style rooms are done out in cream, with louvred shutters,

balconies, marble bathrooms, a/c and polished dark-wood floors. There's a beautiful rooftop pool, a spa, a gym and several bars downstairs in the *Buddy Village* complex. Specify an upper-floor location away from Khao San to ensure a quieter night's sleep. **B1300**

Charoendee Boutique Hostel 189 Thanon Khao San ☎ 02 629 1980, ✉ charoendeehotel@gmail.com; map pp.66–67. Pleasantly surprising compound of pretty, colonial-style edifices with wooden shutters and lattice-work around a small, plant-strewn courtyard, hemmed in by a mess of surrounding buildings. Fan rooms share hot-water bathrooms, but it's well worth paying the extra for an a/c, en-suite room in the airy original building; good rates for singles. Free coffee and toast for breakfast. It's located at the bottom of a narrow alley, so is quieter than many nearby places. Fan B450, a/c B650

Donna Guesthouse 75 Thanon Ratchadamnoen Klang ☎ 02 281 9374; map pp.66–67. Down a tiny alley and hemmed in by other buildings, this friendly, bright, and very clean establishment occupies a cute, white, clapboard house opposite the west wall of Ratchadamnoen post office. Downstairs, the tile-floored, a/c rooms with en-suite cold showers are small but manageable, while upstairs, the seven wood-floored, fan rooms share three cold-water bathrooms. Fan B270, a/c B380

Khao San Palace Inn 139 Thanon Khao San ☎ 02 282 0578, ✆ khaosanpalace.com; map pp.66–67. Clean and well-appointed hotel, hung with appealing black-and-white photos of Bangkok, with a rooftop pool. Even the cheapest rooms have bathrooms, windows, a/c and satellite TV and are nicely tiled, making them good value, while some have panoramic views. B750

Lek House 125 Thanon Khao San ☎ 02 281 8441; map pp.66–67. Classic old-style Khao San guesthouse, in a stand-alone, multi-storey, yellow building, so most of the twenty rooms have windows; go for one on the front with a balcony, if you want the full Khao San blast. Bedrooms are small and basic, with fans and thin partition walls, and bathrooms are shared and cold-water. Less shabby than many others in the same price bracket and friendlier than most. Can get noisy at night as it's right next to popular *The Club* (see p.170). B240

Nap Park 5 Thanon Tani ☎ 02 282 2324, ✆ nappark .com; map pp.66–67. On a surprisingly untouristed street just north of Thanon Khao San, this lively new hostel shelters smart dorm beds with personal TVs, lockers and hot showers, as well as plenty of space for lounging, either inside in front of the TV or outside in the tamarind-shaded front yard. Women-only dorm and laundry available. B399

AROUND WAT CHANA SONGKHRAM AND PHRA ARTHIT

Bella Bella House Soi Ram Bhuttri ☎ 02 629 3090; map pp.66–67. Above an attractive, plant-strewn café, the pastel-coloured rooms here are no frills but well priced, and a few boast lovely views over Wat Chana Songkhram. The cheapest share cold-water bathrooms, a notch up gets you an en-suite hot shower, while the most expensive have a/c. Fan B350, a/c B530

KC Guest House 64 Trok Kai Chae, corner of Thanon Phra Sumen ☎ 02 282 0618, ✆ kc64guesthouse.com; map pp.66–67. Friendly, family-run guesthouse offering exceptionally clean, colourful rooms, either en suite (with hot water) or with shared, cold-water bathrooms. There's also a rooftop terrace and a decked eating area on the soi in front of 7-Eleven. Fan B450, a/c B750

Lamphu House 75 Soi Ram Bhuttri ☎ 02 629 5861–2, ✆ lamphuhouse.com; map pp.66–67. With smart bamboo beds, coconut-wood furniture and elegant rattan lamps in all the rooms, this travellers' hotel set round a quiet courtyard has a calm, modern feel. Cheapest fan rooms share facilities and have no outside view, while the more expensive options have balconies overlooking the courtyard and the triples and four-bed rooms are popular with families. Fan B460, a/c B690

Merry V Soi Ram Bhuttri ☎ 02 282 9267; map pp.66–67. Large, efficiently run guesthouse offering some of the cheapest accommodation in Banglamphu. Bottom-end rooms are basic and small, many share bathrooms and it's pot luck whether you get a window or not. Better en-suites with hot showers and a/c versions are also available. Decent rates for singles. Fan B240, a/c B550

Navalai River Resort 45/1 Thanon Phra Arthit ☎ 02 280 9955, ✆ navalai.com; map pp.66–67. Style-conscious riverfront hotel, with an elegant rooftop pool, modishly furnished rooms, and river views from the most desirable rooms. There's a/c, DVDs, bathtubs and private balconies, and the excellent riverside *Aquatini* restaurant is at ground level (see p.159). B2900

★New Siam 2 50 Trok Rong Mai ☎ 02 282 2795, ✆ newsiam.net; map pp.66–67. Very pleasant and well-run small hotel whose en-suite rooms with fan and cold shower or a/c and hot shower stand out for their thoughtfully designed extras such as in-room safes, cable TV and drying rails on the balconies. Occupies a quiet but convenient location and has a small streetside pool. Popular with families, and a/c triple rooms are also available. Fan B740, a/c B840

New Siam Riverside 21 Thanon Phra Arthit ☎ 02 629 3535, ✆ newsiam.net; map pp.66–67. Occupying a prime riverside spot, the latest in the *New Siam* empire offers well-designed, good-value rooms. Even the cheapest have a/c and full amenities, while the best of them boast fabulous river views from windows or private balconies. Also has a large riverside swimming pool and terrace restaurant. Breakfast included. B1490

Peachy Guest House 10 Thanon Phra Arthit ☎ 02 281 6471; map pp.66–67. Popular, good-value, long-running Bangkok institution set round a small, late-night courtyard bar. Offers lots of clean, simple, wooden-floored rooms, most with shared bathrooms but some with a/c. Fan B160, a/c B250

★Praya Palazzo 757/1 Soi 2, Thanon Somdet Phra Pinklao ☎ 02 883 2998, ✆ prayapalazzo.com; map pp.66–67. A peaceful riverside sanctuary right opposite

9

Banglamphu, this large, graceful, Italianate mansion has been lovingly restored by an architecture professor, with great attention to detail – right down to the wallpaper and lampshades – to give the feel of its 1920s origins. Twenty-first-century luxuries have been overlaid, of course, such as DVDs and, in the bathrooms, big-head showers to go alongside the brass taps and swathes of coloured marble. There's a lovely pool in the garden and an excellent restaurant too, serving royal Thai cuisine as well as afternoon tea. Access is by the free hotel boat, which shuttles across to Phra Arthit express-boat pier and up to Wat Rajathiwat (for Dusit) on demand. Breakfast included. **B5370**

SAMSEN SOIS AND THEWET

Baan Manusarn 8/11 Thanon Krung Kasem, Thewet ☎ 02 281 2976, ⓦ baanmanusarn.com; map pp.66–67. A genuine B&B, friendly and helpful, in a pleasant white building near the pier, offering large a/c rooms with lovely polished wooden floors, some sharing hot showers, and access to a kitchen and washing machine. Breakfast included. **B1400**

Lamphu Treehouse 155 Saphan Wanchat, Thanon Phracha Thipatai ☎ 02 282 0991–2, ⓦ lamphutreehotel .com; map pp.66–67. Named after the *lamphu* trees that line the adjacent canal, after which Banglamphu ("the riverside village with mangrove apple trees") is named, this attractively turned-out guesthouse offers a pool and smart, a/c rooms, all with balconies and plenty of polished wood fittings made of recycled golden teak, among other traditional Thai decorative elements. It's in a quiet neighbourhood but just a few minutes' walk from Democracy. Breakfast included. **B1650**

Nakorn Ping 9/1 Soi 6, Thanon Samsen ☎ 02 281 6574, ⓦ nakornpinghotel.com; map pp.66–67. In a low-rise, orange building dotted with plants on a fairly quiet soi, this place sports some classic elements of a Thai-Chinese hotel: spittoons for waste baskets, gnarly wooden furniture and little natural light. However, it's very clean, efficiently run and good value, offering fridges, cable TV and bathrooms in all rooms, and hot showers in the a/c options. Fan **B460**, a/c **B560**

★**Old Bangkok Inn** 609 Thanon Phra Sumen ☎ 02 629 1787, ⓦ oldbangkokinn.com; map pp.66–67. This chic little boutique guesthouse with an eco-friendly philosophy has just ten a/c rooms, each of them individually styled in dark wood, with antique northern Thai partitions, Burmese doors, beds and ironwork lamps, plus elegant contemporary-accented bathrooms. All rooms have a DVD player, some also have a tiny private garden. The guesthouse is located a 10min walk from Khao San. Long-stay discounts available. Breakfast included. **B3200**

★**Phra Nakorn Norn Len** 46 Thewet Soi 1, Thewet ☎ 02 628 8188–9, ⓦ phranakorn-nornlen.com; map pp.66–67. What was once a seedy short-time motel has been transformed into a bohemian haven with genuine eco-conscious and socially engaged sensibilities and a tangible fair-trade philosophy. Every one of the

> **TOP FIVE CHEAP SLEEPS**
> **Lub d** See p.152
> **New Road Guest House** See p.155
> **New Siam 2** See p.149
> **Sala Thai Daily Mansion** See p.155
> **Tavee** See below

comfortable, though not luxurious, rooms has been hand-painted to a different retro Thai design, and each has a cute bathroom, balcony and a/c. The rooftop bar enjoys unrivalled views of Wat Indraviharn's huge standing Buddha, and all kinds of free workshops, such as soap-making and cooking, are laid on for guests. Mostly organic vegetarian breakfast included. **B2200**

★**Rajata** Soi 6, Thanon Samsen ☎ 02 281 8977–8, ⓦ rajatahotel.com; map pp.66–67. This traditional motel of large bedrooms and bathrooms around a quiet courtyard has been subtly transformed with retro furniture, hundreds of plants and a friendly welcome. All of the shining white, spotlessly clean accommodation has a/c, satellite TV, hot showers, mini-bars and a complimentary breakfast in the courtyard café. **B1000**

Sawatdee 71 Thanon Sri Ayutthaya (at Soi 16), Thewet ☎ 02 281 0757; map pp.66–67. Cheap and basic, but friendlier than many in the Thewet area, this long-running old-style guesthouse offers no-frills fan rooms with partition walls, some with en-suite bathrooms. **B250**

Sri Ayutthaya 23/11 Thanon Sri Ayutthaya (at Soi 14), Thewet ☎ 02 282 5942, ⓦ facebook.com/sriayuttaya; map pp.66–67. The most attractive guesthouse in Thewet, where most of the good-sized rooms (choose between fan rooms without private bathroom and en suites with a/c) are elegantly done out with wood-panelled walls and beautiful polished-wood floors; these have been augmented by a few modern "Superior" rooms (B1200) done out in bright, fetching colours. Hot showers throughout. Fan **B500**, a/c **B700**

Ssip 42 Thanon Phitsanulok, Thewet ☎ 02 282 1899, ⓦ ssiphotelthailand.com; map pp.66–67. Genteel and helpful upmarket B&B where guests are served delicious and beautifully presented breakfasts. It's in a new building on busy Thanon Phitsanulok, but fitted with antique furniture and fixtures and polished-wood floors, as well as a/c, hot showers, TVs and fridges. **B3500**

★**Tavee** 83 Soi 14, Thanon Sri Ayutthaya, Thewet ☎ 02 280 1447, ⓦ facebook.com/taveeguesthouse; map pp.66–67. *Tavee* is located down a pedestrian alley behind *Sri Ayutthaya* and is owned by the same family, but is the quieter and friendlier of the two options. Behind the stylish little café, the fan rooms sport attractive wood floors and share chic hot-water bathrooms, while the en-suite a/c options are larger and enjoy a few more decorative touches. Fan **B450**, a/c **B750**

9

SOUTH OF DEMOCRACY

Baan Dinso 113 Trok Sin, Thanon Dinso ☎ 02 622 0560, ⓦ baandinso.com; map pp.66–67. This tasteful, upmarket little guesthouse occupies an elegant, carefully restored 1920s Thai house all done out in cool buttermilk paintwork and polished teak floors. Prices are a little steep, considering that all but the deluxe rooms have to use shared ground-floor, hot-water bathrooms, but they all have a/c, mini-bars and DVD players. Hostelling International members get a ten percent discount. Breakfast is included. Very good single rates. B2000

★**The Bhuthorn** 96 Thanon Phraeng Phuthon, just off Thanon Kanlayana Maitri ☎ 02 622 2270, ⓦ thebhuthorn .com; map pp.66–67. The architect-owners have beautifully converted this hundred-year-old shophouse into a B&B. Behind the small lobby lie just three elegant rooms (including a junior suite with a mezzanine for B5200), fitted with Chinese, Thai and Western dark-wood antique furniture, chandeliers, *khon* masks and other objets d'art, as well as modern comforts. Breakfast is included. B4200

Boonsiri Place 55 Thanon Buranasart ☎ 02 622 2189–91, ⓦ boonsiriplace.com; map pp.66–67. Run by two charming sisters, this mid-sized hotel is notable for its good value, environmentally conscious policies and location in a lively, seedy old neighbourhood, just a 10min walk from the Grand Palace. Each of its 48 large a/c rooms with hot showers (an extra B300 buys you considerably more space in a "Deluxe" room) is painted in vibrant colours and hung with a different artwork commissioned from the late Thai traditional temple artist Chanok Chunchob. Buffet breakfast included. B1400

The Warehouse 120 Thanon Bunsri ☎ 02 622 2935, ⓦ thewarehousebangkok.com; map pp.66–67. Just down the road from *Boonsiri Place*, this new low-rise hotel offers an appealing version of industrial chic, reinforced by its punningly named *Forklift Café*. Emblazoned with playful health and safety slogans, the a/c, en-suite rooms sport polished concrete floors, exposed wiring, blonde-wood furniture and crisp white linens. B1480

HUALAMPHONG, CHINATOWN AND PAHURAT

Set between the Ratanakosin sights and downtown, Chinatown is among the most frantic and fume-choked parts of Bangkok – and there's quite some competition. If you're in the mood, however, it's got plenty of interest, sees barely any Western overnighters, and is also very handy for Hualamphong Station, which is on the subway system.

@Hualamphong 326/1 Thanon Rama IV ☎ 02 639 1925, ⓦ at-hualamphong.com; map p.76. Directly opposite Hualamphong train station on busy Thanon Rama IV, a modern a/c hostel with bright, appealing private rooms and four- and six-bed mixed dorms, plenty of common areas and a left-luggage service. Dorms B400, doubles B1050

Baan Hualamphong 336/20 Soi Chalong Krung ☎ 02 639 8054, ⓦ baanhualampong.com; map p.76. Just 5min from Hualamphong, this stylish wooden guesthouse is the most welcoming of several similar places in the soi, with a traveller-friendly vibe. There are big, bright, twin rooms plus five-person dorms, but most bedrooms share bathrooms. It also has kitchen and laundry facilities, inviting lounging areas and a left-luggage service, and is open 24hr. Very good single rates. Dorms B250, fan doubles B590, a/c doubles B700

Grand China 215 Thanon Yaowarat ☎ 02 224 9977, ⓦ grandchina.com; map p.76. The poshest hotel in Chinatown boasts fairly luxurious accommodation in a richly coloured, contemporary style, in its 25-storey tower close to the heart of the bustle, with stunning views over all the city landmarks (the best take in the river) and a revolving panoramic restaurant. B2600

★**Shanghai Mansion** 479 Thanon Yaowarat, next to Scala shark's fin restaurant ☎ 02 221 2121, ⓦ shanghaimansion.com; map p.76. The most design-conscious accommodation in Chinatown has embraced the modern Chinoiserie look with gusto. It's not actually an historic mansion, but has been purpose-built on the site of a former Beijing opera house, with most bedrooms (and their windows and private terraces) facing onto an appealing, four-storey atrium, and thus cosily isolated from the Chinatown frenzy. Rooms are prettily done out in silks, lacquer-look furniture and lanterns, featuring a lot of sumptuous reds and purples, as well as a/c, hot showers and complimentary mini-bars. B3020

DOWNTOWN: AROUND SIAM SQUARE AND THANON PLOENCHIT

Siam Square and nearby Thanon Ploenchit are as **central** as Bangkok gets: all the accommodation listed here is within walking distance of a Skytrain or subway station. On hand are the city's best shopping possibilities – notably the phalanx of malls along Thanon Rama I – and a wide choice of Thai and international restaurants and food courts. There's no ultra-cheap accommodation around here, but a few scaled-up **guesthouses** complement the **expensive hotels**. Concentrated in their own small "ghetto" on Soi Kasemsan 1, which runs north off Thanon Rama I, between the Bangkok Art and Cultural Centre and Jim Thompson's House, these offer typical travellers' facilities and basic hotel comforts – a/c and en-suite hot-water bathrooms – at moderate prices; the Khlong Saen Saeb canal-boat pier, Tha Saphan Hua Chang (easily accessed via Thanon Phrayathai), is especially handy for heading west to the Golden Mount and beyond, to Ratanakosin.

9

A-One Inn 25/13 Soi Kasemsan 1, Thanon Rama I ☎02 215 3029 or ☎02 216 4770, ⓦwww.aoneinn.com; map p.95. The original upmarket guesthouse on this soi, and still justifiably popular, with plenty of facilities including a reliable left-luggage room. All bedrooms have fridges and satellite TV and come in a variety of sizes, including triples; breakfast included. B1400

Anantara Siam 155 Thanon Rajdamri ☎02 126 8866, ⓦanantara.com; map p.95. The stately home of Bangkok's top hotels, formerly *The Four Seasons*. Afternoon tea is still served in the monumental lobby, which is adorned with magnificent, vibrant eighteenth-century-style murals depicting the Thai cosmology, and flanked by acclaimed Thai, Italian and Japanese restaurants, a steakhouse and an opulent spa. The large and luxurious rooms are decorated in warm Thai colours and dark wood, and there's an excellent concierge service. B7885

Centara Grand at Central World 999/99 Thanon Rama 1 ☎02 100 1234, ⓦcentarahotelsresorts.com; map p.95. Occupying floors 23 to 55 atop the north end of the huge, glossy Central World mall with its fifty restaurants and fifteen cinema screens, this is a luxurious cocoon high above the hot, noisy city. Views from the brightly coloured, contemporary rooms and the restaurants – particularly *Red Sky* (see p.164) – are panoramic, and shared by the invitingly large swimming pool. A spa, gym and floodlit tennis courts flesh out the picture. B4450

Centara Watergate Pavillion 567 Thanon Ratchaprarop ☎02 625 1234, ⓦcentarahotelsresorts.com; map p.95. Bright and vibrant four-star hotel opposite Pratunam Market, 10min walk from the Airport Rail Link at Ratchaprop. There's no pool but there is a jacuzzi-cum-water feature where you can take a dip, and there's a spa and rooftop restaurant and bar; rooms have big-head showers but no bathtubs. B2280

Courtyard by Marriott 155/1 Soi Mahadlekluang 1, Thanon Rajdamri ☎02 690 1888, ⓦmarriott.com; map p.95. On a quiet but very handy soi, this hotel offers most of the facilities of a five-star, but at more manageable prices. The modern design is seductive, gleaming white outside, candy colours and plenty of natural light inside, and there's a long, narrow, infinity pool, a fitness centre and a spa. B3810

Golden House 1025/5–9 Thanon Ploenchit ☎02 252 9535–7, ⓦgoldenhousebangkok.com; map p.95. A very clean and welcoming small hotel in a peerless location, situated down a short soi by Chit Lom BTS. The plain but attractive parquet-floored bedrooms are equipped with a/c, hot water, cable TV and mini-bar – ask for one of the larger front rooms with bay windows, which leave just enough space for an armchair or two. Breakfast is included. B1610

Jim's Lodge 125/7 Soi Ruam Rudee, Thanon Ploenchit ☎02 255 3100, ⓦjimslodge.com; map p.95. In a relatively peaceful residential area, with friendly and helpful staff, offering international-standard facilities,

including a/c, hot showers, satellite TV and mini-bars, at bargain prices. B1100

Lub d 925/9 Thanon Rama I ☎02 612 4999, ⓦlubd.com; map p.95. Branch of the hip, well-run *Silom* hostel (see p.154), with similar style and facilities (including women-only dorms). It's right on Thanon Rama I, under BTS National Stadium, so handy for just about everything but rather noisy. Dorms B430, doubles B1560

Luxx XL 82/8 Soi Lang Suan ☎02 684 1111, ⓦstaywithluxx.com; map p.95. Quietly set back behind *Thang Long* restaurant, this hip boutique hotel is the younger, but bigger, brother of the original *Silom Luxx*. It shelters large, balconied "Studio" rooms in a seductive contemporary style, all red wood and grey stone, with DVD players (and a movie library), as well as a 13m, infinity-edge, slate pool. Discounts for longer stays. B1660

Pathumwan Princess Hotel 444 Thanon Phrayathai ☎02 216 3700, ⓦpprincess.com; map p.95. Central luxury hotel, at the southern end of MBK Shopping Centre, that's been refurbished in a crisp, modern style. Service is of a high standard, and the facilities include a very good Italian restaurant, overlooking a large, saltwater swimming pool on the eighth floor, a spa and a huge, popular fitness club, The Olympic, that encompasses squash and tennis courts and a 400m jogging track. B4200

Siam Kempinski 991/9 Thanon Rama I ☎02 162 9000, ⓦkempinski.com/bangkok; map p.95. Though it's in downtown's throbbing heart, right behind Paragon shopping centre, this top-of-the-range offering from Europe's oldest luxury hotel group styles itself as a resort: all rooms turn in on an artfully landscaped triangular garden with three pools (some ground-floor rooms even have direct access to one of the pools). As the site used to be part of the "lotus-pond palace", *Wang Sra Pathum*, the interior designers have made subtle but striking use of lotus motifs, complemented by over two hundred specially commissioned paintings and sculptures by Thai artists, amid the Art Deco-inspired architecture. There's also a beautiful spa and an excellent contemporary Thai restaurant, *Sra Bua* (see p.164). B10,240

★ **Swissôtel Nai Lert Park** 2 Thanon Witthayu ☎02 253 0123, ⓦswissotel.com; map p.95. This welcoming, low-rise hotel is distinguished by its lushly beautiful gardens, overlooked by many of the chic and spacious, balconied bedrooms; set into the grounds are a landscaped swimming pool, tennis courts, squash court and popular spa and health club. Good deli-café, cool bar and fine Japanese and Chinese restaurants. B4025

Ten Face 81 Soi 2, Soi Ruam Rudee ☎02 695 4242, ⓦtenfacebangkok.com; map p.95. The name comes from Totsagan, the ten-faced demon of the *Ramakien* (see box, p.55), and this place ingeniously combines sleek, contemporary design with striking artworks inspired by the national myth, without being gimmicky. All the rooms are spacious suites with espresso machines, free SIM cards and iPods, some with small kitchens; ask for a room at the back if you're worried about noise from the nearby expressway. There's a fusion restaurant, fitness centre, long, narrow "dipping" pool and shuttle service to Ploen Chit Skytrain, plus a special concierge, who DJs in the ultra-hip *Sita Bar* and dispenses the lowdown on Bangkok parties and happenings. B2900

Wendy House 36/2 Soi Kasemsan 1, Thanon Rama I ☎02 214 1149, ⓦwendyguesthouse.com; map p.95. Friendly and well-run guesthouse, with smart, clean and comfortable rooms, all with fridge and cable TV, most with queen-size double beds. Breakfast (included in the price) is available in the ground-floor café, and there's reliable luggage storage among a host of useful facilities. Long-stay discounts available. B1380

White Lodge 36/8 Soi Kasemsan 1, Thanon Rama I ☎02 216 8867 or ☎02 215 3041; map p.95. The cheapest guesthouse on the soi, and not always the cleanest, with plain white cubicles and a lively, welcoming atmosphere – the best rooms, bright and quiet, are on the upper floors. B600

THANON SUKHUMVIT

Thanon Sukhumvit is Bangkok's longest road – it keeps going east all the way to Cambodia – but for such an important artery it's far too narrow for the volume of traffic that needs to use it, and is further hemmed in by the Skytrain line that runs above it. Packed with **high-rise hotels** and office blocks, an impressive array of specialist restaurants (from Lebanese to Lao), and stall after stall selling cheap souvenirs and T-shirts, it's a lively place that attracts a high proportion of single male tourists to its enclaves of girlie bars on Soi Nana Tai and Soi Cowboy. But for the most part it's not a seedy area, and is home to many expats and middle-class Thais. The majority of overnighters are business travellers, though Sukhumvit also has several very good **mid-priced guesthouses**. Even at the west end of Sukhumvit, many of the sois are refreshingly quiet, even leafy; transport down the longer sois is provided by motorbike-taxi (*mohtoesai*) drivers who wait at the soi's mouth, clad in numbered waistcoats. Hotels further east are quite convenient for Suvarnabhumi Airport but far from the main shopping and eating hubs. Odd-numbered sois run off the north side of Thanon Sukhumvit, even-numbered off the south side; some of the sois have become important enough to earn their own names, which are often used in preference to their numbers; many sois are long enough to have sub-sois running off them, which usually have their own numbers (or names).

Amari Boulevard Soi 5 ☎02 255 2930, ⓦamari.com; map p.99. At this long-running but modernized four-star tourist hotel, it's worth paying a little extra for a deluxe room to enjoy fine views of the Bangkok skyline and have a bit more space and a DVD player. The attractive sixth-floor rooftop swimming pool and garden terrace becomes the Thai-food restaurant *Season* in the evenings. B3700

The Atlanta At the far southern end of Soi 2 ☎02 252 1650, ⓦtheatlantahotelbangkok.com; map p.99. A Bangkok institution, this classic, five-storey budget hotel was built in 1952 around a famously photogenic Art Deco-style lobby and continues to emphasize an old-fashioned hospitality. It offers some of the cheapest accommodation on Sukhumvit: rooms are plain and simple, though they are all en suite and some have a/c and hot water; many have small balconies. There's a swimming pool and kids' pool in the garden, a good restaurant and a free left-luggage facility. Fan B940, a/c B1050

Hilton Sukhumvit 11 Soi 24 ☎02 259 9017, ⓦhilton .com; map p.99. This new high-rise luxury hotel cleverly links the skyscraper cities of New York and Bangkok, with an Art Deco-influenced contemporary design that's intended to suggest 1920s Manhattan. The design continues in the excellent Italian restaurant, *Scalini*, and in the capacious bedrooms and their opulent bathrooms; on the rooftop are an infinity pool and a gym. B4760

Imm Fusion 1594/50 Thanon Sukhumvit, 30m walk west along Thanon Sukhumvit from BTS On Nut, exit 2, beyond Soi 50 ☎02 331 5555, ⓦimmhotel.com; map p.99. Step through the entrance of this attractively themed hotel and you could be in Morocco, with its rich earthy colours, wrought ironwork, pretty tiles and plenty of Moorish arches. The rooms are comfortable and equally tasteful, and come with a/c, hot showers, TV and breakfast. There's a gorgeous indoor pool, and the staff are charming. B1140

Napa Place 11/3 Soi Naphasap 2, off Soi 36 ☎02 661 5525, ⓦnapaplace.com; map p.99. Down a quiet sub-soi (second right off Soi 36), a 10min walk from BTS Thong Lo, this welcoming, family-friendly guesthouse offers plenty of cosy public spaces and large bedrooms, all with their own sitting areas. Teak floors and furniture are set off by cream furnishings and other natural colours in the very clean rooms, which feature a/c, hot water, mini-bars and cable TV. Breakfast included. B3040

Park Plaza 9 Soi 18 ☎02 658 7000, ⓦparkplaza.com; map p.99. The quieter and newer of two nearby Park Plazas, this small hotel is topped by an appealing, open-air 20m pool, gym and bar-restaurant on the eighth floor. Fitted with DVD players, the rooms sport a perky contemporary look, with bright colours set against businessman's black. B2600

Seven 3/15 Soi Sawasdee 1, off Soi 31 ☎02 662 0951, ⓦsleepatseven.com; map p.99. A personable welcome and plenty of local advice awaits once you head down the quiet alley to this super-stylish B&B. Bold, cartoon-like

9

murals, as well as DVDs, iPod docks, big-head showers and balconies, enhance the six rooms, which are priced according to size. All include a good continental breakfast, local calls and the loan of a local mobile phone. **B3000**

Suk 11 Behind the 7-Eleven store at 1/33 Soi 11 ☎ 02 253 5927–8, ⊕ suk11.com; map p.99. One of the most unusual little hotels in Bangkok, this is also the most backpacker-orientated guesthouse in the area, well run

and thoughtfully appointed. The interior of the apparently ordinary apartment-style building has been transformed to resemble a village of traditional wooden houses, accessed by a dimly lit plankway that winds past a variety of guest rooms, terraces and lounging areas. The rooms themselves are simple but comfortable, all with a/c, and some are en suite; all showers are hot. Good rates for singles; triples and family rooms also available. **B749**

DOWNTOWN: SOUTH OF THANON RAMA IV

South of Thanon Rama IV, the area sometimes known as Bangrak contains a full cross section of accommodation. Tucked away at its eastern edge, there are a few **cheap places** that are worth recommending in the small travellers' haunt of Soi Ngam Duphli and adjacent Soi Sri Bamphen and Soi Saphan Khu. The neighbourhood is often traffic-clogged and occasionally seedy, but is close to Lumphini Park and subway station and fairly handy for Suvarnabhumi Airport. As well as a fair scattering of **medium-range places**, the arc between Thanon Rama IV and the river also lays claim to the capital's biggest selection of **top hotels**, which are among the most opulent in the world. Traversed by the Skytrain, this area is especially good for eating and for gay and straight nightlife, mostly near the east end of Thanon Silom (around which several gay-friendly hotels are scattered). Staying by the river itself in the atmospheric area around Thanon Charoen Krung, also known as New Road, has the added advantage of easy access to express boats.

★ **Anantara Riverside** 257 Thanon Charoennakorn ☎ 02 476 0022, ⊕ anantara.com; map p.108. A luxury retreat from the frenetic city centre, well to the south on the Thonburi bank, but connected to Taksin Bridge (for the Skytrain and Chao Phraya express boats), 15min away, and to Asiatique, just across the river, by hotel ferries every 30min. Arrayed around a highly appealing, landscaped swimming pool, the tranquil, riverside gardens are filled with birdsong, while the stylish and spacious bedrooms come with varnished hardwood floors and balconies. There's a fitness centre, tennis courts, kids' club, a spa, and, among a wide choice of places to eat, a good Japanese teppanyaki house. **B4700**

Anantara Sathorn 36 Thanon Narathiwat Ratchanakharin ☎ 02 210 9000, ⊕ anantara.com; map pp.6–7. With its enclosed, 32m outdoor pool at the centre of activity, toddlers' pool and wide choice of suites, this high-rise hotel is very popular with families. There's also a gym, a tennis court, a very good spa and a fortieth-floor rooftop bar-restaurant, while the spacious, balconied rooms show restrained contemporary decor. Hotel mini-buses run to BTS Chong Nonsi hourly during the day, which is otherwise a 15min walk away. **B2880**

Baan Saladaeng 69/2 Soi 3, Thanon Saladaeng ☎ 02 636 3038, ⊕ baansaladaeng.com; map p.101. On a tiny, central alley, this chic, gay-friendly designer guesthouse offers eleven individually styled and priced rooms, such as the Pop Art Mania Room and the Mediterranean Suite, some with bathtubs and balconies and one with its bath on the balcony. A/c, rain showers, mini-bars, cable TV and comfy beds throughout. No children. Breakfast included. **B1300**

ETZ Hostel 5/3 Soi Ngam Duphli ☎ 02 286 9424, ⊕ etzhostel.com; map pp.6–7. Owned by the recommended ETC travel agent, and very handy for Lumphini

subway and Thanon Rama IV, though consequently a little noisy. Helpful and very clean, the hostel sports playful contemporary decor in primary colours, a popular roof terrace and a large, attractive lounge. The a/c dorms share hot showers and fit four to twelve people (one is women-only), or you could upgrade to a bright white double with large, en-suite, hot-water bathroom. Breakfast and luggage storage are available. Dorms **B200**, doubles **B950**

La Residence 173/8–9 Thanon Suriwong ☎ 02 266 5400–1, ⊕ laresidencebangkok.com; map p.101. A small, intimate boutique hotel where the tasteful, individually decorated bedrooms – including proper single rooms at proper single rates – stretch to mini-bars, safes and cable TV. Continental breakfast included. **B1930**

Lub d 4 Thanon Decho ☎ 02 634 7999, ⊕ lubd.com; map p.101. Meaning "sleep well" (*lap dii*), this buzzing, upmarket hostel has a/c and hot water throughout and an industrial feel to its stylishly lit decor. This crisp modernity extends to the bedrooms, among which the dorms (some women-only) and the bunk-bedded "Railway" private rooms ("Railway" twin B1150) share large bathroom areas, while the top-of-the-range en-suite doubles boast TVs. The hostel lays on some interesting activities and tours, and there's a popular bar and café, a movie lounge, washing machines and free storage facilities, but no kitchen. Dorms **B350**, doubles **B1720**

Luxx 6/11 Thanon Decho ☎ 02 635 8800, ⊕ staywithluxx .com; map p.101. Welcoming boutique hotel offering a good dose of contemporary style at reasonable prices. Decorated in white, grey and natural teak, the rooms feature DVD players and cute wooden baths surmounted by rain showers. There are discounts for longer stays. **B1170**

Malaysia 54 Soi Ngam Duphli ☎ 02 679 7127–36, ⊕ malaysiahotelbkk.com; map pp.6–7. Once a travellers' legend famous for its compendious noticeboard, now better known for its seedy 24hr coffee shop and massage parlour. The accommodation itself is reasonable value though: the rooms are large and have a/c, mini-bars and hot-water bathrooms; some have cable TV. There's also a swimming pool. Gay-friendly. B828

★**New Road Guest House** 1216/1 Thanon Charoen Krung, between sois 34 and 36 ☎ 02 630 9371, ⓦnewroadguesthouse.com; map p.101. Thai headquarters of Danish backpacker tour operator, Visit Beyond, offering a wide choice of accommodation around a courtyard off New Road, as well as a helpful service centre and travel agent, and interesting Thailand tours. There are mixed and women-only a/c dorms, as well as "Backpacker" fan rooms with mini-bars and well-equipped, hot-water bathrooms; a/c rooms sport attractive wooden floors, Thai decorative touches and cable TV. Guests can hang out in the restaurant, the sociable bar with pool table or the DVD room; free baggage storage available. Dorms B250, fan doubles B550, a/c doubles B1000

★**Peninsula Bangkok** 333 Thanon Charoennakorn ☎ 02 861 2888, ⓦpeninsula.com; map p.101. Located on the Thonburi bank, with shuttle boats down to Taksin Bridge and its BTS station, this is a superb top-class hotel: service is flawless, the ultra-luxurious decor stylishly blends traditional Western and Asian design, and every room has a panoramic view of the Chao Phraya. The lovely riverside gardens shelter a three-tiered pool, a beautiful spa, a fitness centre and a tennis court, while restaurants include the classy *Mei Jiang* Cantonese restaurant (see p.167). B11,000

Rose 118 Thanon Suriwong ☎ 02 266 8268–72, ⓦrosehotelbkk.com; map p.101. Set back from the main road but very handy for the city's nightlife, this hotel has been recently refurbished: the compact rooms (all with bathtubs) now boast a simple but stylish modernist look, enhanced by paintings and silk cushions. The ground-floor public rooms are more elegant again, and there's a beautiful swimming pool and a good Thai restaurant, *Ruen Urai* (see p.167), at the back. B1800

★**Sala Thai Daily Mansion** 15 Soi Saphan Khu ☎ 02 287 1436, ⓔsalathai.guesthouse@hotmail.com; map pp.6–7. The last and best of several budget guesthouses

on this quiet, narrow alleyway off Soi Saphan Khu, near Soi Sri Bamphen. A clean and efficiently run place, with bright, cheerful rooms with wall fans, sharing hot-water bathrooms, and a large, leafy roof garden. Decent rates for single rooms. Fan B400, a/c B600

★**Sukhothai** 13/3 Thanon Sathorn Tai ☎ 02 344 8888, ⓦsukhothai.com; map p.101. The most elegant of Bangkok's top hotels, its decor inspired by the walled city of Sukhothai, offers low-rise accommodation, as well as a beautiful garden spa, all coolly furnished in silks, teak and granite. Service is of the highest standard and the architecture makes the most of the views of the surrounding six acres of gardens, lotus ponds and pools dotted with statuary. There's also a health club, 25m infinity pool, squash and tennis courts, and excellent restaurants including *Celadon* (see p.166). B12,800

Swan 31 Soi 36, Thanon Charoen Krung ☎ 02 235 9271–3, ⓦswanhotelbkk.com; map p.101. Next to the stately residence of the French ambassador, this good-value, well-run and welcoming Chinese hotel has successfully upgraded, with regular renovations, to keep up with the times. Arrayed around a 15m pool, the rooms are bright, clean and spacious (though bathrooms in the standard rooms are small), with a/c, hot water, cable TV, mini-bars and safes; some have balconies with armchairs. Breakfast included. B1500

Swiss Lodge 3 Thanon Convent ☎ 02 233 5345, ⓦswisslodge.com; map p.101. Swish, friendly, good-value and eco-friendly boutique hotel, with high standards of service, just off Thanon Silom and ideally placed for business and nightlife. The tiny terrace swimming pool confirms the national stereotypes of neatness and clever design, while the restaurant offers a range of savoury and sweet fondues. Buffet breakfast included. B1940

Tarntawan Place 119/5–10 Thanon Suriwong ☎ 02 238 2620, ⓦtarntawan.com; map p.101. Set back from the main road, a pretty, flower-strewn lobby announces this welcoming and well-run, gay-friendly hotel. The decent-sized, well-equipped rooms are gracefully furnished in natural colours, and all have bathtubs. Guests also receive reduced-price entry to a gym and swimming pool on Soi Thaniya. Discounts for longer stays. B2080

SUVARNABHUMI AIRPORT

Mariya Boutique Residence 1627/2 Thanon Latkrabang ☎ 02 326 7854–5, ⓦmariyahotel.com; map p.108. Five minutes' drive from the airport to the northwest (with pick-ups available 24hr), this well-organized hotel offers hot water, a/c, fridge, cable TV, microwave, kettle and DVD players (on request) in all of the bedrooms, which feature some traditional Thai touches in the appealing decor. B1280

Novotel Suvarnabhumi ☎ 02 131 1111, ⓦnovotel .com; map p.108. The official airport hotel, set within

the complex and a 10min walk from Arrivals via a walkway in the basement (or catch the shuttle bus from outside Arrivals Gate 4). Offering smart, contemporary rooms with marble bathrooms, Thai, Japanese, Cantonese and international restaurants, a swimming pool and fitness centre, the *Novotel* operates on a 24hr basis – you can check in at any time, and check out 24hr later. B6015

Eating

Bangkok boasts an astonishing fifty thousand places to eat, ranging from makeshift streetside noodle shops to the most elegant of restaurants. Despite this glut, an awful lot of visitors venture no further than the front doorstep of their guesthouse, preferring the dining room's ersatz Thai or Western dishes to the more adventurous food to be found in even the most touristy accommodation areas.

Thai restaurants of all types are found all over the city. The best **gourmet Thai** restaurants operate from the downtown districts, proffering wonderful royal, traditional and regional cuisines that definitely merit a visit – though even here, you're unlikely to spend more than B600 per person. Over in Banglamphu, Thanon Phra Arthit is known for its idiosyncratic little restaurant-bars angled at young Thai diners. At the other end of the scale, as well as the **food courts** of shopping centres and department stores listed below, there are the **night markets** and **street stalls**, where you can generally get a lip-smacking feast for around B150 or less. These are so numerous in Bangkok that we can only flag a few promising areas – but wherever you're staying, you'll hardly have to walk a block in any direction before encountering something appealing.

10

ESSENTIALS

THAI CUISINE

Thai food is now hugely popular in the West, but nothing, of course, beats coming to Thailand to experience the full range of subtle and fiery flavours, constructed from the freshest ingredients. Four fundamental tastes are identified in Thai cuisine – spiciness, sourness, saltiness and sweetness. Lemon grass, basil, coriander, galangal, chilli, garlic, lime juice, coconut milk and fermented fish sauce (used instead of salt) are just some of the distinctive components that bring these tastes to life.

Curries (kaeng) Thai curries have as their foundation a variety of curry pastes, elaborate blends of herbs, spices, garlic, shallots and chilli peppers traditionally ground together with a pestle and mortar. The use of some of these spices, as well as of coconut cream, was imported from India long ago; curries without coconut cream are naturally less sweet and thinner, with the consistency of soups. While some curries, such as *kaeng karii* (mild and yellow) and *kaeng matsaman* (literally "Muslim curry", with potatoes, peanuts and usually beef), still show their roots, others have been adapted into quintessentially Thai dishes, notably *kueng khiuw wan* (sweet and green), *kaeng phet* (red and hot) and *kaeng phanaeng* (thick and savoury, with peanuts). *Kaeng som* generally contains vegetables and fish and takes its distinctive sourness from the addition of tamarind or, in the northeast, okra leaves. Traditionally eaten during the cool season, *kaeng liang* uses up gourds or other bland vegetables, but is made aromatic by the heat of peppercorns and shallots and the fragrance of basil leaves.

Soups (tom) An essential component of most shared meals, thai soups are eaten simultaneously with other dishes, not as a starter. They are often flavoured with the distinctive tang of lemon grass, kaffir lime leaves and galangal, and garnished with fresh coriander – and can be extremely hot, if the cook adds liberal handfuls of chillies to the pot. Two favourites are *tom kha kai*, a creamy coconut chicken soup; and *tom yam kung*, a hot and sour prawn soup without coconut milk. *Khao tom*, a starchy rice soup often eaten for breakfast, meets the approval of few Westerners, except as a traditional hangover cure.

Salads (yam) One of the lesser-known delights of Thai cuisine is salad, which can often impart all four of the fundamental flavours in an unusual and refreshing harmony. *Yam* can be made in many permutations – with noodles, meat, seafood or vegetables – but at the heart of every variety is fresh lime juice and a fiery sprinkling of chopped chillies. As well as *som tam*, *laap* and northeastern Thailand's *nam tok* (see box below), salads to look out for include *yam som oh* (pomelo), *yam hua plee* (banana flowers) and *yam plaa duk foo* (deep-fried catfish).

Noodle dishes Thais eat noodles when Westerners would dig into a sandwich – for lunch or as a late-night snack. Sold on street stalls everywhere, they come in assorted varieties – including *kway tiaw* (made with rice flour) and *ba mii* (egg noodles), *sen yai* (wide) and *sen lek* (thin) – and get boiled up as soups (*nam*), doused in gravy (*rat na*) or stir-fried (*haeng*, "dry", or *phat*, "fried"). Most famous of noodle dishes is *kway*

NORTHEASTERN FOOD

In Bangkok, northeastern food is the most prevalent of Thailand's several regional cuisines, partly due to the large numbers of migrants from the northeast (or Isaan) who work in the capital. Their staple food is **sticky rice** (*khao niaw*), which is more suited to the infertile lands of Isaan than the standard grain. Served in its own special rattan basket, it's usually eaten with the fingers – rolled up into small balls and dipped into chilli sauces. A classic combination is sticky rice with **som tam**, a spicy green-papaya salad with garlic, raw chillies, green beans, tomatoes, peanuts and dried shrimps (or fresh crab), and **kai yaang**, basted and barbecued chicken on a stick. Raw minced pork, beef or chicken is the basis of another popular Isaan dish, *laap*, a salad that's subtly flavoured with mint and lime. A similar northeastern salad is **nam tok**, featuring grilled beef or pork and roasted rice powder, which takes its name, "waterfall", from its refreshing blend of complex tastes.

10

tiaw phat thai – usually abbreviated to phat thai, meaning "Thai fry-up" – a delicious mix of fried noodles, bean sprouts, egg, tofu and spring onions, sprinkled with ground peanuts and lime juice, and often spiked with tiny dried shrimps.

Rice dishes Fried rice (khao phat) is the other faithful standby that features on menus right across the country. Also popular are cheap, one-dish meals served on a bed of steamed rice, notably khao kaeng (with curry), khao na pet (with roast duck) and khao muu daeng (with red-roasted pork).

Desserts (khanom) Desserts don't really figure on most restaurant menus, though a few places offer bowls of luk taan cheum, a jellied concoction of lotus or palm seeds floating in a syrup scented with jasmine or other aromatic flowers. Coconut milk is a feature of most other desserts, notably delicious coconut ice cream; khao niaw mamuang/ thurian (sticky rice with mango or durian); khao niaw daeng (sticky red rice mixed with coconut cream); takoh, which consists of squares of transparent jelly (jello) topped with coconut cream; and a royal Thai cuisine special of coconut custard (sangkhayaa) cooked inside a small pumpkin, whose flesh you can also eat.

INTERNATIONAL CUISINES

For the non-Thai cuisines, Chinatown naturally rates as the most authentic district for pure Chinese food; likewise neighbouring Pahurat, the capital's Indian enclave, is best for unadulterated Indian dishes, while there's a sprinkling of Indian and (mostly southern Thai) Muslim restaurants around Silom's Maha Uma Devi Temple and nearby Thanon Charoen Krung. Sukhumvit's Soi 3 is a hub for Middle Eastern cafés, complete with hookah pipes at the outdoor tables; good, comparatively cheap Japanese restaurants are concentrated, for example, on Soi Thaniya, at the east end of

Thanon Silom; and there's a Korean enclave in Sukhumvit Plaza, at the corner of Soi 12. The place to head for inexpensive, Western, travellers' food – from herbal teas and hamburgers to muesli – as well as a hearty range of veggie options, is Thanon Khao San; standards vary, but there are some definite gems among the blander establishments.

VEGETARIANS

Few Thais are vegetarian, but in the capital it's fairly easy to find specially concocted Thai and Western veggie dishes, usually at tourist-oriented restaurants. Even at the plainest street stall, it's usually possible to persuade the cook to rustle up a vegetable-only fried rice or noodle dish. If you're vegan you'll need to make clear you don't want egg when you order, as eggs get used a lot; cheese and other dairy produce don't feature at all in Thai cuisine.

PRACTICALITIES

Tipping In the more expensive restaurants listed below you may have to pay a ten percent service charge and seven percent VAT (at the time of writing this was due to rise to ten percent).

Health Hygiene is a consideration when eating anywhere in Bangkok, but being too cautious means you'll end up spending a lot of money and missing out on some real treats – you can be pretty sure any noodle stall or curry shop that's permanently packed with customers is a safe bet. Foods that are generally considered high risk include salads, shellfish, raw or undercooked meat, fish or eggs, ice and ice cream. Thais don't drink water straight from the tap, and neither should you: plastic bottles of drinking water (nam plao) are sold everywhere for around B10, as well as the usual multinational panoply of soft drinks.

RATANAKOSIN

The places reviewed below are especially handy for sightseers, but there are also plenty of street stalls around Tha Chang and a load of simple, studenty restaurants off the north end of Thanon Maharat near Thammasat University, as well as a decent restaurant at Arun Residence (see p.147).

YELLOW-FLAG HEAVEN FOR VEGGIES

Every year, for nine days during the ninth lunar month (between late Sept and Nov), Thailand's Chinese community goes on a **meat-free** diet to mark the onset of the **Vegetarian Festival** (Ngan Kin Jeh), a sort of Taoist version of Lent. Though the Chinese citizens of Bangkok don't go in for skewering themselves like their compatriots in Phuket, they do celebrate the Vegetarian Festival with gusto: some people choose to wear only white for the duration, all the temples throng with activity, and nearly every restaurant and food stall in Chinatown turns vegetarian for the period, flying small yellow flags to show that they are upholding the tradition and participating in what's essentially a nightly veggie food jamboree. For vegetarian tourists this is a great time to be in town – just look for the yellow flag and you can be sure all dishes will be one hundred percent vegetarian. Soya substitutes are a popular feature on the vegetarian Chinese menu, so don't be surprised to find pink prawn-shaped objects floating in your noodle soup or unappetizingly realistic slices of fake duck. Many hotel restaurants also get in on the act during the Vegetarian Festival, running special veggie promotions for a week or two.

DINNER CRUISES

The **Chao Phraya River** looks fabulous at night, when most of the noisy longtails have stopped terrorizing the ferries, and the riverside temples, other fine monuments such as the Grand Palace and an increasing number of historic houses are elegantly illuminated. Joining one of the nightly **dinner cruises** along the river is a great way to appreciate it all, especially on one of the converted, wooden rice-barges listed below, which are far preferable to the big, modern party boats. Call ahead to reserve a table and check departure details – some cruises may not run during the rainy season (May–Oct).

Loy Nava ☏ 02 437 4932, ⊚ loynava.com. The original, 40-year-old converted rice-barge service still departs Si Phraya pier twice nightly, at 6pm (to catch the sunset) and 8.10pm, with pick-ups also at Tha Sathorn. During the cruise you can enjoy a Thai, seafood or vegetarian meal, accompanied by live traditional music and dancing. B1400, including hotel pick-up in central Bangkok.

Manohra ☏ 02 476 0022, ⊚ manohracruises.com. Beautiful converted rice-barge operated by the *Anantara Riverside Resort* (see p.154), south of Taksin Bridge in Thonburi, serving Thai set dinners. Departs hotel at 7.30pm, returning 9.30pm, with pick-ups at Tha Sathorn possible. From B1750.

Navy Club (Krua Khun Kung) Tha Chang ☏ 02 222 0081; map p.50. Walk on by the prominent but overpriced *Navy Club 77 Café*, on the corner of Na Phra Lan and Maharat roads, to find this place immediately on the south side of the express-boat pier, announced by an English sign and a navy guard (don't be put off – anyone can eat here, even farangs). The decor's deeply institutionalized but the real draw is the shaded terrace built over the river, where you can enjoy excellent dried prawn and lemon-grass salad (B120), *haw*

mok thalay (seafood curry soufflé; B150) and other marine delights. Mon–Fri 11am–2pm & 4–10pm, Sat & Sun 11am–10pm.

Vivi: The Coffee Place Opposite Aurum on Soi Pansook, Thanon Maharat ☏ 02 226 4672; map p.50. Handy for Wat Pho, this cute café with a riverside terrace and an a/c room serves coffee and a wide range of drinks, plus cakes, sandwiches and snack portions of lasagne (B70). Daily 10am–8pm.

BANGLAMPHU AND THE DEMOCRACY MONUMENT AREA

Copycat entrepreneurship means that Khao San is stacked full of backpacker restaurants serving near-identical Western and (mostly) watered-down Thai food; there's even a lane, one block east, parallel to Thanon Tanao (behind *Burger King*), that's dominated by **vegetarian** cafés, following a trend started by *May Kaidee*. Hot-food stalls selling very cheap **night-market snacks** operate until the early hours. Things are more varied down on Thanon Phra Arthit, with its arty little **café-restaurants** favoured by Thammasat University students, while the riverside places, on Phra Arthit and further north off Thanon Samsen and in Thewet, tend to be best for **seafood** with a view. For the real old-fashioned Thai taste, though, browse southern Thanon Tanao, where traditional shophouses have been selling specialist sweets and savouries for generations.

AROUND THANON KHAO SAN

Chabad House 96 Thanon Ram Bhuttri ⊚ kosherthailand.com; map pp.66–67. A little piece of Israel, run by the Bangkok branch of the Jewish outreach Chabad-Lubavitch movement. Serves a well-priced, tasty kosher menu of schnitzels (B160), baba ganoush, falafels, hummus, salads and Jewish breads in a/c calm, on the ground floor of a long-established community centre and guesthouse; the best deal is five taster plates for B60. Mon–Thurs & Sun 10am–10pm, Fri 10am–3pm.

★**May Kaidee** East off Thanon Tanao ⊚ maykaidee .com; map pp.66–67. Simple, neighbourhood Thai vegetarian restaurant that still serves some of the best veggie food in Banglamphu despite having spawned several competitors on the same alley. Come for Western breakfasts or try the tasty green curry, the Vietnamese-style veggie spring rolls or the sticky black-rice pudding

with mango or banana. Most dishes B70–90. Also runs a variety of cookery courses (see p.160). Daily 9am–10pm.

Nittaya 136 Thanon Chakrabongse; map pp.66–67. This shop is nationally famous for its *nam phrik* (chilli dips) and curry pastes (which are available vacuum-packed), but it serves all kinds of food to take away – perhaps to eat in nearby Santichaiprakarn Park (see p.68) – including snacks and desserts. Mon–Sat 9am–6.30pm.

Popiang 43 Soi Ram Bhuttri; map pp.66–67. Very popular, friendly place for cheap seafood: BBQ mussels cost just B80, squid B140. Eat in the low-rent restaurant area or on the street beneath the temple wall. Claims to open daily 24hr.

PHRA ARTHIT AREA

Aquatini Navalai River Resort, 45/1 Thanon Phra Arthit ☏ 02 280 9955; map pp.66–67. Occupying a nice

10

wooden deck in a perfect breezy riverfront spot beside the express-boat pier (even better after sunset when the boats stop running), this hotel restaurant does exceptionally good mid-priced Thai food. Seafood's a speciality: the deep-fried ruby fish served with cashew nuts and bell peppers is very good, and their tangy coconut-milk *tom kha kai* soup is especially delicious. Most seafood mains B200–300. Daily 6.30am–11.45pm.

★**Hemlock** 56 Thanon Phra Arthit ☎02 282 7507; map pp.66–67. Small, stylish, a/c restaurant that's very popular with students and young Thai couples. Offers a long and interesting menu of unusual Thai dishes, including delicious green curry (B100) and several kinds of *laap* (spicy ground meat salad). The traditional *miang* starters (shiny green wild tea leaves filled with chopped vegetables, fish, prawn or meat) are also very tasty, and there's a good vegetarian selection. Worth reserving a table on Fri and Sat nights. Mon–Sat 4–11pm.

Kway Jap Yuan Khun Daeng Thanon Phra Arthit ☎085 246 0111; map pp.66–67. This basic, bustling canteen does a roaring trade with Thammasat University students, who come for the delicious *kway jap yuan*, noodle soup similar to Vietnamese *pho* but a little starchier – go for the version with egg (B57) and you're set up for the day. Find it in an historic shophouse, unmistakably painted white and green – colours which the flamboyant owner often sports himself. Mon–Sat 11am–9.30pm.

Roti Mataba 136 Thanon Phra Arthit ☎02 282 2119; map pp.66–67. Famous 70-year-old outlet for the ever-popular fried Indian breads, or *rotis*, served here in lots of sweet and savoury varieties, including with vegetable and meat curries (from B51), stuffed with meat and veg (*mataba*), and with bananas and condensed milk (B35); biryanis (*khao mok*) are also on offer. Choose between pavement tables and a basic upstairs a/c room. Tues–Thurs 10am–9pm, Fri–Sun 9.30am–9.30pm.

THANON SAMSEN AND THEWET

Chomp Corner of Soi 1, Thanon Samsen, ⓦfacebook.com/chompcafe; map pp.66–67. Cool café and social hub where polished-concrete floors and walls add to the rough-hewn look, offering tasty comfort food such as Western breakfasts and pasta mushroom alfredo (B160), and activities such as yoga and art exhibitions. Very child-friendly, with playgroups and babies' and kids' menus. Mon & Wed–Sun 8am–11pm.

Jok Phochana Soi 2, Thanon Samsen; map pp.66–67. This bare-basics, 40-year-old restaurant, which has featured on national TV, is about as real as you're going to get near Thanon Khao San; a green curry costs B70. The day's ingredients are colourfully displayed at the front of the shop, and the quiet pavement tables get more crowded as the night wears on. Daily 5pm–2am.

Kaloang Home Kitchen Beside the river (follow the bend round) at the far western end of Thanon Sri Ayutthaya ☎02 281 9228; map pp.66–67. Flamboyant service and excellent seafood attracts an almost exclusively Thai clientele to this open-air, no-frills, bare-wood restaurant that perches on stilts over the river. Dishes well worth sampling include the fried rolled shrimps served with a sweet dip and any of the host of Thai salads. Most mains are B100–150; expect to pay more for crab, shrimp and some fish dishes. Daily 11am–10pm.

Kinlom Chom Saphan Riverside end of Thanon Samsen Soi 3 ☎02 628 8382–3, ⓦkhinlomchomsaphan.com; map pp.66–67. This sprawling, waterside restaurant boasts close-up views of the lyre-like Rama VIII Bridge and is always busy with a youngish Thai crowd. The predominantly seafood menu (mostly B150–300) features everything from crab to grouper cooked in multiple ways, including with curry, garlic or sweet basil sauces, but never with MSG. Daily 11am–2am.

THAI COOKERY CLASSES IN BANGKOK

Baipai 8/91 Soi 54, Thanon Ngam Wongwan ☎02 561 1404, ⓦbaipai.com. Thorough, 4hr classes in a quiet, suburban house in northern Bangkok. The classes cost B2200, including transfers from central hotels. Closed Sun.

Helping Hands Klong Toey ⓦcookingwithpoo.com. Set up with the help of a Christian charity, a chance to experience the slums of Klong Toey and spend a morning with the ebullient Khun Poo learning to cook. The price of B1500 includes a market tour and free transfers from next to Phrom Pong BTS station. Closed Sun.

May Kaidee East of Thanon Khao San, off Thanon Tanao ☎089 137 3173, ⓦmaykaidee.com.

Banglamphu's famous vegetarian restaurant (see p.159) offers a huge variety of courses lasting anything from 2hr (B1000) to ten days (B15,000), including raw food and fruit-carving classes.

Thai House 22km from central Bangkok in Bangmuang ☎02 903 9611 or ☎02 997 5161, ⓦthaihouse.co.th. Set in a rural part of Nonthaburi province, here you can do one- (B3800) to three-day (B16,650) cooking courses, all including transfers from downtown. The three-day course includes vegetable and fruit carving, a market visit, all meals and homestay accommodation in a traditional wooden house.

10

Krua Apsorn Thanon Samsen, opposite Thanon Uthong Nok on the southwestern edge of Dusit ☎ 02 668 8788; map pp.66–67; Thanon Dinso ☎ 02 685 4531; map pp.66–67; ⓦ kruaapsorn.com. Very good, spicy and authentic food and a genteel welcome make this unpretentious, a/c restaurant popular with the area's civil servants – as well as the royalty whom they serve. Try the green fish-ball curry (B100) or the yellow curry with river prawns and lotus shoots (B120), both recommended by the leading Thai restaurant guide, MacDang, and then put out the fire in your mouth with home-made coconut sorbet. Thanon Samsen Mon–Sat 10.30am–7.30pm (generally closes early on Sat); Thanon Dinso Mon–Sat 10.30am–8pm.

May Kaidee 2 33 Thanon Samsen, between the khlong and Soi 1 ⓦ maykaidee.com; map pp.66–67. This a/c branch of Banglamphu's best-loved Thai veggie restaurant (see p.159) specializes in salads, raw food and juices. Daily 9am–10pm.

Steve Café and Cuisine Wat Thawarad ☎ 02 281 0915, ⓦ stevecafeandcuisine.com; map pp.66–67. In a lovely riverside setting with views of Rama VIII Bridge, come here for great service and a huge menu that encompasses southern Thai specialities, traditional central Thai and fusion dishes, including a very tasty and spicy salmon *laap* (B200). It's easy to see, right across the mouth of Khlong Krung Kasem from Tha Thewet express-boat pier, though harder to get there, walking round and right through the grounds of the temple. Mon–Fri 11.30am–2.30pm & 4.30–11pm, Sat & Sun 11.30am–11pm.

SOUTH OF DEMOCRACY

Chote Chitr 146 Thanon Phraeng Phuton ☎ 02 221 4082, ⓦ www.chotechitr.ch; map pp.66–67. The word's out about this unreconstructed, 80-year-old, shop-house restaurant of just half a dozen tables – it's been featured in the *New York Times* and the *FT*. However, the wide-ranging menu of Thai dishes (most about B100) in large, homely portions is still excellent. The formidable owner will explain what's good today, perhaps *nam phrik pla thu* (chilli dip with mackerel). Not everyone will be a fan of the pet dogs running around the tables. Mon–Sat noon–9pm.

Kai Yang Boran 474–476 Thanon Tanao, immediately to the south of the Chao Poh Seua Chinese shrine ☎ 02 622 2349; map pp.66–67. Locally famous grilled chicken (B200 for a small bird) and *som tam* (green papaya salad; B60) restaurant (with a/c), wallpapered with photos of celebrities who have eaten here. *Nam tok* salad with roast pork and several kinds of *laap* round out the northeastern menu. Daily 8.30am–9pm.

Kor Panit 431–433 Thanon Tanao, on the east side, directly opposite Thanon Phraeng Phuton; map pp.66–67. Outstanding takeaway coconut-laced sticky rice (currently B180/kg) has been sold here since 1932. No English sign, but look for the mango vendors outside, where you choose your variety to accompany the delicious *khao niaw* (sticky rice with coconut milk). Daily 7am–6pm.

Nattaporn 94 Thanon Phraeng Phuton, just off Thanon Kanlayana Maitri ☎ 02 221 3954; map pp.66–67. This family has been specializing in its famous home-made fresh coconut ice cream for over sixty years, topping it with classic Thai condiments like sweetcorn, red beans and taro balls. They also do mango, chocolate, coffee and tea flavours. No English sign, but it's a basic shophouse, right next door to *The Bhuthorn* guesthouse. Mon–Sat 8am–4pm.

Padthai Thipsamai 313 Thanon Mahachai (no English sign), near Wat Rajnadda ☎ 02 221 6280; map pp.66–67. The most famous *phat thai* in Bangkok, flash-fried by the same husband-and-wife team since 1966. The "special" option is huge, comes with especially juicy prawns, and is wrapped in a translucent, paper-thin omelette. Best washed down with fresh coconut juice. Daily, except alternate Wed, 5.30pm–1am.

HUALAMPHONG, CHINATOWN AND PAHURAT

Much of the fun of Chinatown dining is in the browsing of the **night-time hot-food stalls** that open up all along Thanon Yaowarat, around the mouth of Soi Issaranuphap (Yaowarat Soi 11) and along Soi Phadungdao (Soi Texas); wherever there's a crowd you'll be sure of good food. Pan Siam's *Good Eats: Chinatown* map, available from major bookshops, is also a great resource for the weirder local specialities.

Hua Seng Hong 371 Thanon Yaowarat ☎ 02 222 7053, ⓦ huasenghong.com; map p.76. Vibrant, ever-popular, few-frills restaurant, with an open kitchen out front alongside a stall that does a brisk, all-day trade in dim sum. Dishes from around B100, less for noodle soup, more for delicacies such as braised geese's feet. Daily 9am–1am.

Jong Kee 84 Soi Sukon 1, near Wat Traimit; map p.76. Famous, basic café serving nothing but delicious pork satay (B70 for 10 sticks) and sweet toast. No English sign, but look for the Shell sign (proof of a "Shell Chuan Chim" recommendation, a respected accolade for restaurants in Thailand). Mon 9.30am–2pm, Tues–Sun 9.30am–6pm.

Raan Khun Yah Wat Traimit; map p.76. Just to the right inside the temple's Thanon Mittaphap entrance, this basic, very traditional restaurant, now in its third generation of operation, is especially famous for its delicious and cheap *kaeng khiaw wan neua* (green beef curry; B35), on a menu that otherwise changes daily – look out for *lon*, a chilli dip with coconut milk, and *khanom jiin nam yaa*, rice noodles topped with spicy fish sauce. Mon–Fri 6.30am–1pm (some things will sell out earlier than that).

Royal India Just off Thanon Chakraphet at 392/1 ☏ 02 221 6565; map p.76; basement, Siam Paragon ☏ 02 610 7667; map p.95; Floor 5, Emporium shopping centre ☏ 086 973 8266; map p.99; ⊚ royalindiathailand .com. Great dhal, perfect parathas and famously good North Indian curries (from around B130), served in a dark, basic little a/c café in the heart of Bangkok's most Punjabi of neighbourhoods to an almost exclusively South Asian clientele. Daily 10am–10pm.

Shangarila 306 Thanon Yaowarat (corner of Thanon Rajawong) ☏ 02 224 5933; map p.76. Cavernous,

upmarket banquet hall serving Cantonese classics, including lots of seafood (mostly sold by weight), and lunchtime dim sum. Very popular, especially for family gatherings. Try the huge, very tasty, seared scallops with XO sauce (chillies, dried shrimps and brandy) for B500. Daily 10am–10pm.

T&K (Toi & Kid's Seafood) 49 Soi Phadungdao, corner of Thanon Yaowarat; map p.76. Hectic, rough-hewn street restaurant known for its barbecued seafood, with everything from prawns (from B150 a serving) to whole fish and clams on offer. Eat at crowded pavement tables by the busy road or inside in the basic a/c rooms. Tues–Sun 4.30pm–1am.

10

DOWNTOWN: AROUND SIAM SQUARE AND THANON PLOENCHIT

In this part of Downtown Bangkok, there are also branches of *Taling Pling* (see p.167), *Royal India* (see above), *Aoi* (see p.166) and *Somboon Seafood* (see p.167).

Din Tai Fung Floor 5, Central Embassy ⊚ dintaifung .com.sg; map p.95. This attractive and efficient all-day dim sum place is a branch of a Hong Kong restaurant that has a Michelin star. Its superb speciality is steamed pork dumplings with clear broth inside each one (B160), but other dishes such as spring rolls with duck and spring onion (B170) are also very tasty. Mon–Fri 11am–9.30pm, Sat & Sun 10.30am–9.30pm.

Eathai Basement, Central Embassy ⊚ centralembassy .com/eathai; map p.95. This upmarket food court – a branch of Chiang Mai's *Khun Churn* – is a great place to learn about the huge variety of Thai food, with kitchens from the various regions rustling up their local dishes, plus seafood, *nam phrik* and vegetarian specialities, traditional drinks and dessert stalls and a section devoted to street food. Daily 10am–9.30pm.

Food Loft Floor 7, Central Chidlom, Thanon Ploenchit ⊚ centralfoodloft.com; map p.95. Bangkok's top department store lays on a suitably upscale food court of all hues – Thai, Vietnamese, Chinese, Japanese, Korean, Indian, and Italian by *Gianni* (see below). Choose your own ingredients and watch them cooked in front of you, eat by the huge windows in the stylish, minimalist seating areas and then ponder whether you have room for a Thai or Western dessert. Daily 10am–10pm.

Gianni 34/1 Soi Tonson, Thanon Ploenchit ☏ 02 252 1619, ⊚ giannibkk.com; map p.95. Probably Bangkok's best independent Italian restaurant, offering a sophisticated blend of traditional and modern in both its decor and food. Twice-weekly shipments of artisan ingredients from the old country are used in dishes such as lobster and artichoke risotto and squid-ink spaghetti with clams, prawns and asparagus. Best to come for lunch Mon–Fri when there's a good-value set menu for B550. Daily 11.30am–2pm & 6–10pm.

★**Hinata** Central Embassy, Thanon Ploenchit ☏ 02 160 5935, ⊚ shin-hinata.com; map p.95. This

branch of a famous Nagoya restaurant offers exquisite sushi and great views over the leafy British Embassy grounds – or you can pay extra to sit at the counter and watch the master at work. Sets from B1200 for six pieces of nigiri sushi and six *maki* rolls (with a few extras thrown in if you come for lunch). Daily 11am–9.30pm.

★ **Home Kitchen (Khrua Nai Baan)** 94 Soi Lang Suan ☏ 02 253 1888, ⊚ khruanaibaan.com; map p.95. This congenial, unpretentious spot in an attractive a/c villa is like an upcountry restaurant in the heart of the city. On the reasonably priced Thai and Chinese picture menu, you're bound to find something delicious, including dozens of soups – try the *kaeng som*, with shrimp and acacia shoot omelette, for B150 – six kinds of *laap* and a huge array of seafood. Daily 8am–midnight.

Honmono Sushi Siam Paragon, Thanon Rama I ☏ 02 610 9240; map p.95. Owned by the Japanese expert on Thailand's version of Iron Chef, this place imports its seafood from Tokyo's Tsukiji Market five times a week and offers a very good-value sushi set for B380, including salad, miso soup, pickles and fruit. Daily 11am–10pm.

Inter 432/1–2 Soi 9, Siam Square ☏ 02 251 4689; map p.95. Honest, efficient Thai restaurant that's popular with students and shoppers, serving good one-dish meals from B68, as well as curries, soups, salads and fish, in a no-frills, fluorescent-lit canteen atmosphere. Daily 11am–10pm.

Jim Thompson's Restaurant Jim Thompson's House, 6 Soi Kasemsan 2, Thanon Rama I ☏ 02 612 3601, ⊚ jimthompson.com; map p.95. A civilized, moderately priced haven in the must-see house museum (see p.94), with delicious Thai dishes (around B200) such as grilled mushroom salad as well as desserts, cakes and other Western food. Daily 11am–5pm & 7–11pm.

Kai Ton Pratunam Thanon Phetchaburi, on the corner of Soi 30; map p.95. Famous anti-hangover refuge that serves just one dish: delicious *khao man kai*, boiled chicken

10

breast with broth, dipping sauces and rice that's been cooked in chicken stock. It'll set you back just B40, more if you ask for liver and other innards (*khreuang nai*, literally "the inner workings"). More choice is offered by the string of other popular food stalls on the same strip near the corner of Phetchaburi and Rajdamri roads. Daily 5.30am–2pm & 5pm–2am.

Mah Boon Krong Food Courts Corner of Rama I and Phrayathai rds ⓦmbk-center.co.th; map p.95. Two decent food courts at the north end of MBK: the long-running area on Floor 6 is a good introduction to Thai food, with English names and pictures of a huge variety of tasty, cheap one-dish meals from all over the country displayed at the various stalls (including vegetarian options), as well as fresh juices and a wide range of desserts; the upmarket version on Floor 5 is an international affair, spanning India, Italy, Vietnam, China, Indonesia, Mexico and Japan, plus good moussaka at *Olive*. Floor 6 daily 10am–roughly 8.30pm; Floor 5 daily 10am–10pm.

Polo Fried Chicken (Kai Thawt Jay Kee Soi Polo) Soi Polo, Thanon Witthayu ⓣ02 655 8489; map p.95. On the access road to the polo club, this simple restaurant is Bangkok's most famous purveyor of the ultimate Thai peasant dish, fried chicken. All manner of northeastern dishes, including fish, sausages and loads of salads, fill out the menu, but it would be a bit perverse to come here and not have the classic combo of finger-licking chicken (B100 for a half), *som tam* and sticky rice. Daily 7am–10pm.

Red Sky Centara Grand, 999/99 Thanon Rama 1 ⓣ02 100 1234, ⓦcentarahotelsresorts.com; map p.95. Opulent, blow-out restaurant, named for the great sunset views from its indoor-outdoor, 55th-floor perch. It purveys "the best of the land, sky and water" – be that Maine lobster, Dutch veal or Kobe beef – beautifully presented in complex, meticulous preparations, with a signature splash of red in each dish (B1000 upwards). Daily 5.30pm–1am.

Sanguansri 59/1 Thanon Witthayu ⓣ02 251 9378; map p.95. The rest of the street may be a multi-storey building site but this low-rise, canteen-like old-timer, run by a friendly bunch of middle-aged women, clings on. And

> **TOP FIVE RESTAURANTS WITH A VIEW**
> **Navy Club** See p.159
> **Manohra** See p.159
> **Hinata** See p.163
> **Red Sky** See below
> **Kaloang Home Kitchen** See p.160

where else around here can you lunch on a sweet, thick and toothsome *kaeng matsaman* for B70? It goes well with *kung pla*, a tasty, fresh prawn and lemon-grass salad that can be spiced to order. Mon–Sat 10am–3pm.

Som Tam (Nua) 392/14 Soi 5, Siam Square ⓣ02 251 4880; map p.95; Floor 4, Siam Centre ⓣ02 658 1000; map p.95. This basic but lively modern restaurant on a pedestrian alley is a great place to get to know the full range of Thai spicy salads. The *som tam* with pork crackling and sausage goes well with the very tasty deep-fried chicken (B115), or there's northeastern *laap* and *nam tok*, and central Thai salads (*yam*) by the dozen. Soi 5, Siam Square daily 10.45am–9.30pm; Siam Centre daily 10.45am–9pm.

Sra Bua Siam Kempinski Hotel (see p.152); map p.95. Molecular gastronomy comes to Bangkok, with great success. Operated by Copenhagen's Thai Michelin one-star, *Kiin Kiin*, this place applies some serious creativity and theatricality to Thai cuisine, in dishes such as frozen red curry with lobster salad, which perfectly distils the taste of the *kaeng daeng*. The grand decor, which encompasses two lotus ponds (*sra bua*), is matched by the prices, with the full works costing B2200–2700 for a multi-course set dinner. Daily noon–2pm (last orders) & 6–10pm.

Vanilla Brasserie Ground floor, Siam Paragon shopping centre ⓣ02 610 9383, ⓦvanillaindustry .com; map p.95. A sophisticated shrine to Western gourmet delights that combines restaurant, patisserie, crêperie and chocolatier. On offer are delicious parma ham and mascarpone crêpes (B390), salads and other main courses, spot-on desserts, and excellent teas and coffees. Daily 10am–10pm.

THANON SUKHUMVIT

In this area, there are also branches of *Aoi* (see p.166), *Royal India* (see p.163), *Ramentei* (see p.167) and *Himali Cha-Cha* (see p.166). For street food, check out the big, bustling **night market** at the mouth of Soi 38 (BTS Thong Lo), which includes popular stalls for *phat thai* and *khao man kai* (chicken served with marinated rice and chicken broth) and stays open till the early hours.

Baan Khanitha 36/1 Soi 23 ⓣ02 258 4128; map p.99; 69 Thanon Sathorn Tai, at the corner of Soi Suan Phlu ⓣ02 675 4200–1; map p.101; ⓦbaan-khanitha .com. The big attraction at this long-running favourite haunt of Sukhumvit expats is the setting in a traditional Thai house and leafy garden. The food is upmarket Thai and

fairly pricey, and includes lots of fiery salads (*yam*), and a good range of *tom yam* soups, green curries and seafood curries. Most mains cost B200–500. Daily 11am–11pm.

Barcelona Gaudí Ground floor, Le Premier 1 Condo, Soi 23 ⓣ02 661 7410, ⓦfacebook.com/barcelonagaudi thailand; map p.99. This appealing Catalan café offers lovely outdoor tables under a broad, shady tree and a short menu of very good Spanish dishes, including salads, paellas and tapas, as well as tasty *crema catàlana* (a bit like a crème brûlée) and on-the-money espressos. It's great value at lunchtime, when set menus start at B150, and is also popular at weekends for watching Spanish football games, when the house wine at B60/glass goes down a storm. Daily 11am–11pm; sometimes closed Mon.

★**Beirut** Basement, Ploenchit Centre, at the mouth of Soi 2 ☎02 656 7377; map p.99; 64 Silom building, set back off Thanon Silom behind Sabushi, opposite the Silom Complex ☎02 632 7448; map p.101 ⓦbeirut -restaurant.com. It's worth crossing the road from Bangkok's main Middle Eastern ghetto (Soi 3 and Soi 3/1) for the top-notch Lebanese food in this comfortable, a/c restaurant. Among dozens of salads and stuffed breads, the superb *motabel* (baba ganoush; B100) is fluffy and smoky, while the falafels are suitably moist inside and crunchy out. Good baklava, too. Ploenchit Centre daily 10am–10pm; 64 Silom building daily 11.30am–midnight.

★**Bolan** 24 Soi 53 (5min walk from BTS Thong Lo) ☎02 260 2961–2, ⓦbolan.co.th; map p.99. Meticulous and hugely successful attempt to produce authentic traditional food in all its complexity, while upholding the "Slow Food" philosophy. It'll give you a lipsmacking education in Thai cuisine, best enjoyed on the "Bolan Balance" set dinner menu (B2280). For lunch you might be offered *khanom jiin* and a dessert for B380. Tues & Wed 6–10.30pm (last orders), Thurs–Sun noon–2.30pm & 6–10.30pm.

Cabbages and Condoms 6–8 Soi 12 ☎02 229 4610, ⓦpda.or.th/restaurant; map p.99. The Population and Community Development Association of Thailand (PDA) runs this relaxing restaurant, decorated with condoms from around the world and the slogan "our food is guaranteed not to cause pregnancy". Try the chicken in pandanus leaves (B220) or the seafood green curry (B250); there's also a varied vegetarian menu. Daily 11am–10pm.

Dosa King Soi 11/1, with a back entrance on Soi 11 ☎02 651 1700, ⓦdosaking.net; map p.99. Usually busy with expat Indian diners, this vegetarian Indian restaurant serves good food from both north and south, including over a dozen different dosa (southern pancake) dishes, tandooris and the like. It's an alcohol-free zone so you'll have to make do with sweet lassi instead. Most dishes B100–200. Daily 11am–11pm.

Imoya Floor 3, Terminal Shop Cabin, 2/17–19 Soi 24 ☎02 663 5185–6; map p.99. The setting, in a block of shops beside Emporium where staircases seem to have been an afterthought, is unpromising, but this retro-style restaurant, decorated with old film posters, battered wood and corrugated iron, serves up consistently good Japanese food of all kinds, including sushi (from B60). Daily 5pm–midnight.

Le Dalat 57 Soi 23 (Soi Prasanmit) ☎02 259 9593, ⓦledalatbkk.com; map p.99. There's Indochinese

---

TOP FIVE TRADITIONAL THAI RESTAURANTS
Krua Apsorn See p.162
Raan Khun Yaah See p.162
Bolan See below
Sanguansri See opposite
Krua Aroy Aroy See p.166

---

romance aplenty at this delightful, re-created Vietnamese brick mansion decked out with pot plants, plenty of photos and eclectic curiosities. The extensive, high-class Vietnamese menu features favourites such as a *goi ca* salad of aromatic herbs and raw fish (B250) and *chao tom* shrimp sticks on sugar cane (B360). Good-value lunchtime sets (B360). Daily 11.30am–2.30pm & 5.30–10.30pm.

The Myth of MahaNaga 2 Soi 29 ☎02 662 3060, ⓦthemythbangkok.com; map p.99. The dining experience at this tranquil enclave is best appreciated after dark, when the fountain-courtyard tables are romantically lit. Cuisine is Thai fine dining, updated with contemporary techniques and some Western ingredients, featuring such tasty delights as *kaeng matsaman* with slow-cooked chicken breast and crispy sweet lotus (B300). Daily 5.30–11pm.

Soul Food Mahanakorn 56/10 Soi 55 (Soi Thong Lo; Exit 3 from BTS Thong Lo, then it's 100m up the soi on the right) ☎02 714 7708, ⓦsoulfoodmahanakorn.com; map p.99. If you already have your favourite stall for *som tam* or *laap*, this is not for you, but if not, this trim, welcoming, American–Thai bistro makes a great introduction to street food from around Thailand, using top-quality ingredients. The beef *khao soi* (curried noodle soup; B220) is thick and creamy, and the *som tam* (B150) is served with crispy chicken skin. Daily blackboard specials, and a huge selection of creative cocktails. Daily 5.30pm–midnight.

Suk 11 Soi 11 ☎02 253 5468; map p.99. Part of the idiosyncratic *Suk 11* guesthouse (see p.154), with which it shares a traffic-free sub-soi, this restaurant also re-creates an atmosphere of old-fashioned village Thailand, with its wooden building, fairy lights and plentiful foliage. The food is good, authentic Thai (mostly B150–300), with plenty of spicy *yam* salads, delicious mushroom *laap*, tasty *phanaeng* curry plus cocktails and imported wines served by the glass. Daily 4–10.45pm.

Supanniga Eating Room About 1km up Soi 55 (Soi Thong Lo) on the right from Thong Lo BTS ☎02 714 7508, ⓦsupannigaeatingroom.com; map p.99. This three-storey rustic-chic restaurant, decorated with lots of brass and gnarly wood, is a great place to try the distinctive cuisine of Chanthaburi, famous for its herbs and spices – the delicious *moo cha muang* (B170), a mild red pork curry, is a great place to start. The restaurant's other specialities are crab dishes and food from Isaan, where the family have

10

10

a boutique hotel in Khon Kaen. Daily 11.30am–2.30pm & 5.30–11.30pm.

★ **Vientiane Kitchen (Khrua Vientiane)** 8 Soi 36, about 50m south off Thanon Sukhumvit ✆02 258 6171, ⊛facebook.com/vientianekitchen; map p.99. Just a 3min walk west then south from BTS Thong Lo (Exit 2) and you're transported into a little piece of Isaan, where the menu's stocked full of northeastern delicacies, a live band sets the mood with heart-felt, sometimes over-amplified, *pong lang* folk songs, and

there are even performances by a troupe of traditional dancers (daily from 7.30pm). The Isaan-accented menu (mostly B100–300) includes vegetable soup with ants' eggs, spicy-fried frog, jackfruit curry and freshwater fish (from around B400), plus there's a decent range of veggie options such as *som tam* and sweet-and-sour dishes, and Thai desserts. With its airy, barn-like interior and mixed clientele of Thais and expats, it's a very enjoyable dining experience. Daily noon–midnight (last food orders 10.30pm).

DOWNTOWN: SOUTH OF THANON RAMA IV

Several popular groupings of **street stalls** are worth noting here: the top end of Thanon Convent, just off Thanon Silom; away to the west opposite the Maha Uma Devi Temple, Silom Soi 20; and the late-night noodle soup stalls on the east end of Thanon Suriwong. In this area, there are also branches of *Baan Khanitha* (see p.164) and *Beirut* (see p.165).

★ **Aoi** 132/10–11 Soi 6, Thanon Silom ✆02 235 2321–2; map p.101; ground floor, Siam Paragon ✆02 129 4348–50; map p.95; Floor 4, Emporium shopping centre; ✆02 664 8590–2; map p.99; ⊛aoi-bkk.com. One of the best places in town for a Japanese blowout, justifiably popular with the expat community. Excellent authentic food and elegant decor, with a superb sushi bar (around B1000 for a set). Thanon Silom daily 11.30am–2.30pm & 5.30/6pm–10.30/11pm; Siam Paragon Mon–Fri 11.30am–2.30pm & 5.30–10.30pm, Sat & Sun 11am–10.30pm; Emporium shopping centre daily 11/11.30am–2.30/3.30pm & 5/5.30–10.30pm.

★ **Celadon** Sukhothai Hotel, 13/3 Thanon Sathorn Tai ✆02 344 8888; map p.101. Consistently rated as one of the best hotel restaurants in Bangkok and a favourite with locals, serving outstanding traditional and contemporary Thai food from all over the country – try the delicious southern dipping sauce of spicy dried shrimps and the northern-style pork belly curry – in an elegant setting surrounded by lotus ponds. Daily noon–2.30pm (last orders) & 6.30–10.30pm.

Eat Me 1/6 Soi Phiphat 2, Thanon Convent ✆02 238 0931, ⊛eatmerestaurant.com; map p.101. Justly fashionable art gallery and restaurant in a striking, white modernist building, with changing exhibitions on the walls and a temptingly relaxing balcony. The eclectic, far-reaching menu features such mains as Japanese black cod with spicy coconut cream (B575), and the lemon grass crème brûlée is not to be missed. Daily 3pm–1am.

Harmonique 22 Soi 34, Thanon Charoen Krung, on the lane leading to Wat Muang Kae express-boat pier ✆02 237 8175; map p.101. A relaxing, welcoming, moderately priced restaurant (most mains B100–200) that's well worth a trip: tables are scattered throughout several converted shophouses, decorated with antiques and bric-a-brac, and a quiet, leafy courtyard, and the Thai food is varied and excellent, notably the house speciality crab curry. Mon–Sat 11am–10pm.

Himali Cha-Cha 1229/11 Soi 47/1, Thanon Charoen Krung ✆02 235 1569; map p.101; down a short alley off the north end of Thanon Convent ✆02 238 1478; map p.101; Sukhumvit Soi 31 ✆02 259 6677; map p.99; ⊛himalichacha.com. Fine, moderately priced North Indian restaurant, founded by a character who was chef to numerous Indian ambassadors, and now run by his son. Tasty chicken tikka masala (B195) and a good vegetarian selection, with a homely atmosphere and attentive service. Daily 11am–3.30pm & 6–10.30pm.

Home Cuisine Islamic Restaurant 186 Soi 36, Thanon Charoen Krung ✆02 234 7911, ⊛facebook.com /homecuisineislamic; map p.101. The short, cheap menu of Indian and southern Thai dishes here has proved popular enough to warrant a refurbishment in green and white, with comfy booths, pot plants, a/c inside and a few outdoor tables overlooking the colonial-style French embassy. The *khao mok kai* signature dish (B85), a typical hybrid version of a chicken biryani, served with aubergine curry, is delicious. Mon–Sat 11am–9.30pm, Sun 6–9.30pm.

Indian Hut 418 Thanon Suriwong ✆02 237 8812, ⊛indianhut-bangkok.com; map p.101. Bright, white-tablecloth, North Indian restaurant – look out for the Pizza Hut-style sign – that's reasonably priced (most mains B200–300) and justly popular with local Indians. For carnivores, tandoori's the thing, but there's also a wide selection of mostly vegetarian pakoras and other appetizers, as well as plenty of veggie main courses and breads, and a hard-to-resist house dhal. Daily 11am–11pm.

★ **Krua Aroy Aroy** 3/1 Thanon Pan (opposite the Maha Uma Devi Temple) ✆02 635 2365, ⊛facebook.com /kruaaroyaroy; map p.101. Aptly named "Delicious, Delicious Kitchen", this simple shophouse restaurant stands out for its choice of cheap, tasty, well-prepared dishes from all around the kingdom, notably *khao soi* (a curried soup with egg noodles from northern Thailand), *kaeng matsaman* and *khanom jiin* (rice noodles topped with curry). Daily 7am–about 8pm, or earlier if the food runs out.

Le Bouchon 37/17 Patpong 2, near Thanon Suriwong ☎02 234 9109; map p.101. Cosy Lyonnais bar-bistro that's much frequented by the city's French expats, offering home cooking such as salmon in white wine sauce (B540) and a good-value lunch set menu (B450); booking is strongly recommended. Mon–Sat noon–3pm & 6.30–11pm.

Mei Jiang Peninsula Hotel, 333 Thanon Charoennakorn ☎02 861 2888, ⓦpeninsula.com; map p.101. Probably Bangkok's best Chinese restaurant, with beautiful views of the hotel's riverside gardens, and very attentive and graceful staff. Cantonese specialities include excellent lunchtime dim sum, lobster rolls, cold marinated chicken with Szechuan chilli sauce (B460) and delicious teas. Daily 11.30am–2.30pm & 6–10.30pm.

★**Ramentei** 23/8–9 Soi Thaniya ☎02 234 8082; map p.101; Sukhumvit Soi 33/1 ☎02 662 0050; map p.99. Excellent Japanese noodle café, bright, clean and welcoming, under the same ownership as *Aoi* (see opposite). The open kitchen turns out especially good, huge bowls of miso ramen, which goes very well with the gyoza dumplings. Most dishes B150–200. 23/8–9 Soi Thaniya daily 11am–2am; Soi 33/1 daily 11am–midnight.

Ruen Urai Rose Hotel, 118 Thanon Suriwong ☎02 266 8268–72, ⓦruen-urai.com; map p.101. Set back behind the hotel, this peaceful, hundred-year-old, traditional house, with fine balcony tables overlooking the beautiful hotel pool, comes as a welcome surprise in this full-on downtown area. The varied Thai food is of a high quality: try the *tom khlong talay* (B300), a delicious, refined, spicy and sour soup from the northeast, with tamarind juice and herbs. Daily noon–11pm.

Sara Jane's 55/21 Thanon Narathiwat Ratchanakharin, between sois 4 & 6 ☎02 676 3338–9; map p.101. Long-standing, basic, a/c restaurant, popular with Bangkok's Isaan population, serving good, simple northeastern dishes, including a huge array of *nam tok*, *laap* and *som tam*, as well as Italian food – and a very tasty fusion of the two, spaghetti with *sai krok*, spicy Isaan sausage (B240). Daily 11am–2.30pm & 5.30–10pm.

Somboon Seafood Thanon Suriwong, corner of Thanon Narathiwat Ratchanakharin ☎02 233 3104; map p.101; Floor 5, Central Embassy ☎02 160 5965–6; map p.95; ⓦsomboonseafood.com. Highly favoured, bustling seafood restaurant, known especially for its crab curry (from about B300, depending on weight), with functional, modern decor and an array of marine life lined up in tanks awaiting its gastronomic fate. Thanon Suriwong daily 4–11.30pm; Central Embassy daily 11am–10pm.

★**Taling Pling** 653 Building 7, Ban Silom Arcade, Thanon Silom ☎02 236 4829–30; map p.101; Ground floor of Siam Paragon ☎02 129 4353–4; map p.95; Floor 3, Central World ☎02 613 1360–1; map p.95. One of the best Thai restaurants in the city outside of the big hotels, specializing in classic dishes from the four corners of the kingdom. The house deep-fried fish salad (B145) is delicious and refreshing, while the deeply flavoured green beef curry (B145) with roti is recommended by the leading Thai restaurant guides. The atmosphere's convivial and relaxing, too. Ban Silom Arcade and Siam Paragon branches daily 11am–10pm; Central World daily 11am–9.30pm.

10

THE SKY BAR

Drinking and nightlife

For many male visitors, nightfall is the signal to hit Bangkok's sex bars, most notoriously in the area off Thanon Silom known as Patpong (see p.103). Fortunately, Bangkok's nightlife has grown up in the past ten years to leave these neon sumps behind, and now offers everything from microbreweries and vertiginous, rooftop cocktail bars to chic clubs and dance bars, hosting top-class DJs. The high-concept bars of Sukhumvit and the lively venues of Banglamphu, in particular, pull in style-conscious Thai youth and are tempting an increasing number of travellers to stuff their party gear into their rucksacks. During the cool season, an evening at one of the pop-up beer gardens (usually Dec) is a pleasant way of soaking up the urban atmosphere (and the traffic fumes); you'll find them in hotel forecourts or sprawled in front of shopping centres all over the city, most notably Central World.

Among the city's club nights, look out for the interesting regular events organized by Zudrangma Record Store (ⓦzudrangmarecords.com), especially at their own bar Studio Lam (see p.171), which mix up dance music from all around Thailand and from all over the world.

Getting back to your lodgings should be no problem in the small hours: many bus routes run a (reduced) service throughout the night, and tuk-tuks and taxis are always at hand – though it's probably best for unaccompanied women to avoid using tuk-tuks late at night.

RATANAKOSIN

Po 203/1 Tha Thien, Thanon Maharat ⓣ02 622 3081; map p.50. When the Chao Phraya express boats start to wind down, this bar takes over the rustic wooden pier and the balcony above with their great sunset views across the river to Wat Arun. It's popular with local students and office workers, hence the loud Thai pop music; avoid the food in favour of beer and Thai whisky. Daily 6–11pm.

BANGLAMPHU AND THE DEMOCRACY MONUMENT AREA

11

The travellers' enclave of Banglamphu takes on a new personality after dark, when its hub, **Thanon Khao San**, becomes a "walking street", closed to all traffic but open to almost any kind of makeshift stall, selling everything from fried bananas and buckets of "very strong" cocktails to share, to bargain fashions and one-off artworks. Young Thais crowd the area to browse and snack before piling in to Banglamphu's more stylish **bars** and indie **live-music clubs**, most of which are free to enter (though some ask you to show ID first).

Ad Here the 13th (Blues Bar) 13 Thanon Samsen, opposite Soi 2, right by the start of the bridge over Khlong Banglamphu ⓣ089 7694613, ⓦon .fb.me/1FMLhg5; map pp.66–67. Relaxed little neighbourhood live-music joint with sociable seats out on the pavement, where musos congregate nightly to listen to Thai and expat blues and jazz bands (from about 9.30pm onwards). Well-priced beer and plenty of cocktails. Daily 6pm–midnight.

Bangkok Bar 100 Thanon Ram Bhuttri ⓣ02 281 2899; map pp.66–67. By far the most ambitious and best of several live-music places on this street, whose Thai indie-rock bands and DJs – including occasional big-name appearances – are popular with young locals. In a multi-tiered bar-restaurant around a fountain courtyard, the stage is on the first floor but can also be viewed from the second-floor balconies. Daily 6pm–late.

Brick Bar Buddy Village complex, 265 Thanon Khao San ⓦbrickbarkhaosan.com; map pp.66–67. Massive red-brick vault of a live-music bar whose regular roster of reggae, ska, rock'n'roll and Thai pop bands, and occasional one-off appearances, is hugely popular with Thai twenty-somethings and teens. Big, sociable tables are set right under the stage and there's food too. The biggest nights are Fri and Sat when there's sometimes an entry charge, depending on who's on. Daily 7pm–1.30am.

Brown Sugar 469 Thanon Phra Sumen ⓦbrown sugarbangkok.com; map pp.66–67. Bangkok's best jazz club is settling nicely into its smart, atmospherically lit new premises, which are hung with colourful modernist gig posters and include a leafy canalside terrace. It still has its famous Sun jam session, but is now allowing in a few early-evening acoustic sessions each week. The prices of drinks are pumped up to pay for the talent, though they include

---

OPENING HOURS, ID CHECKS AND ADMISSION CHARGES

Most bars and clubs in Bangkok are meant to **close** at 1am, while those at the east end of Silom and on Royal City Avenue can stay open until 2am. In previous years, there have been regular "social order" clampdowns by the police, strictly enforcing these closing times, conducting occasional urine tests for drugs on bar customers, and setting up widespread ID checks to curb under-age drinking (you have to be 20 or over to drink in bars and clubs). However, at the time of writing, things were much more chilled, with many bars and clubs staying open into the wee hours on busy nights and ID checks in only a few places. It's hard to predict how the situation might develop, but you'll soon get an idea of how the wind is blowing when you arrive in Bangkok – and there's little harm in taking a copy of your passport out with you, just in case. Nearly all bars and clubs in Bangkok are free, but the most popular of them will sometimes levy an admission charge of a couple of hundred baht on their busiest nights (which will usually include a drink or two), though this can vary from week to week.

imported beers on draught and in bottles. Café Tues–Sun roughly noon–10/11pm; bar-restaurant Tues–Thurs & Sun 5pm–midnight/1am, Fri & Sat 5pm–2am.

The Club 123 Thanon Khao San ☎02 629 1010, ⓦtheclubkhaosan.com; map pp.66–67. Thumping house tunes from an elevated, central DJ station with state-of-the-art lighting draw a sophisticated young Thai and international crowd. Daily 9pm–late.

Dickinson's Culture Café 64 Thanon Phra Athit ☎089 497 8422, ⓦon.fb.me/1aG0Rzk; map pp.66–67. Grungy shophouse café decorated with a mess of empty picture frames and traffic cones, which hosts some great DJs throughout the week – check out their Facebook page for line-ups. Sip on cocktails (including dozens of martinis) or buckets. Ask about the same owners' *Café Democ* and *Club Culture*, which are currently looking for new venues. Daily 9am–2pm.

★**Hippie de Bar** 46 Thanon Khao San ☎02 629 3508; map pp.66–67. Inviting courtyard bar set away from the main fray, surrounded by graffitied walls, TV screens and its own-brand fashion boutique. Attracts a mixed studenty/arty/high-society, mostly Thai crowd, to drink cheapish beer at its wrought-iron tables and park benches. Indoors is totally given over to kitsch, with plastic armchairs, Donny Osmond posters and ancient TVs. Daily 4pm–2am.

Jazz Happens Thanon Phra Arthit ☎02 282 9934, ⓦfacebook.com/jazzhappens; map pp.66–67. Typical Phra Arthit bar, full of students, with just one small room and a few sociable pavement tables, but what sets this place apart is that some of the students are from Silpakorn University's Faculty of Jazz, playing jazz here every night. Tuck into a decent selection of well-priced cocktails and a narrower choice of food while you're listening. Daily 7pm–1am.

Phra Nakorn 58/2 Soi Damnoen Klang Tai ☎02 622 0282; map pp.66–67. Styles itself as "a hangout place for art lovers", and it successfully pulls in the capital's artists and art students, who can admire the floodlit view of the Golden Mount from the candlelit rooftop terrace, tuck into good food and reasonably priced drinks and browse one of the regular exhibitions on the first floor. Daily 6pm–1am.

Sheepshank Tha Phra Arthit express-boat pier ⓦsheepshankpublichouse.com; map pp.66–67. Banglamphu's coolest new bar, set in a former boat-repair yard overlooking the Chao Phraya and the riverside walkway and sporting an industrial look that features black leather, silver studs, pulleys and girders. There's a wide selection of bottled craft beers from the US and Japan, as well as imaginative bar snacks and a long menu of more substantial gastropub dishes. Tues–Thurs 5.30pm–midnight, Fri–Sun 5.30pm–1am.

DOWNTOWN: AROUND SIAM SQUARE AND THANON PLOENCHIT

Siam Square has much less to offer after dark than Thanon Silom, further south. Out to the northeast, running south off Thanon Rama IX, lies RCA (Royal City Avenue). An officially sanctioned "nightlife zone" that's allowed to stay open until 2am, it's lined mostly with warehouse-like clubs that have a reputation as meat markets.

Coco Walk Thanon Phrayathai; map p.95. It would be hard not to enjoy yourself at this covered parade of loosely interchangeable but buzzing good-time bars, right beside Ratchathevi BTS. Popular with local students, they variously offer pool tables, live musicians, DJs and cover bands, but all have reasonably priced beer and food. Daily roughly 6pm–1am.

Hyde and Seek Ground floor, Athenée Residence, 65/1 Soi Ruam Rudee ☎02 168 5152–3, ⓦhydeandseek .com; map p.95. Classy but buzzy gastrobar, with nightly DJs and lots of attractive garden seating. Amid a huge range of drinks, there's a good selection of wines by the glass and imported beers on draught; the food menu features bar bites, pastas, salads and familiar dishes such as bangers and mash. Daily 11am–1am.

Raintree 116/63–4 Soi Ruamjit, Thanon Rangnam

☎02 245 7230, ⓦraintreepub.com; map pp.6–7. Near Victory Monument, two ordinary shophouses have been converted into this friendly, typical "good ol' boys" bar, with lots of rough timber furniture and the biggest water-buffalo skulls you've ever seen. Live, nightly music is mostly Songs for Life, mixed in with some *luk thung*, starting out low-key and soothing, and getting more raucous and danceworthy as the night hots up. Daily 5pm–1.30am.

Saxophone 3/8 Victory Monument (southeast corner), just off Thanon Phrayathai ☎02 246 5472, ⓦsaxophonepub.com; map pp.6–7. Lively, easy-going, spacious venue with decent Thai and Western food and a diverse collection of bands – mostly jazz and blues, plus acoustic guitar, funk, rock and reggae (details on their website) – which attracts a good mix of Thais and foreigners. Daily 6pm–2am.

THANON SUKHUMVIT

A night out on Thanon Sukhumvit could be subsumed by the girlie bars and hostess-run bar-beers (open-sided drinking halls with huge circular bars) on sois Nana and Cowboy, but there's plenty of style on Sukhumvit too, especially in the **rooftop bars** and enjoyably trendy **clubs**. The scene has been gravitating eastwards over the last few years: the fashionable bars and clubs on and around Soi Thong Lo (Soi 55) attract a "hi-so" (high-society) crowd, while those over on Soi Ekamai (Soi 63) are perhaps a little more studenty.

Apoteka Soi 11 ⓦapotekabangkok.com; map p.99. Attractive new bar, with exposed brick walls, a tempting snug off to one side and terrace tables facing *Q Bar*. Live nightly blues bands add to the appeal, though drinks are pricey. Daily 11am–1pm.

Cheap Charlie's Soi 11; map p.99. Idiosyncratic, long-running, low-tech, open-air bar that's famous for its cheap beer and customers' hall-of-fame gallery. It now offers the luxury of plastic tables and chairs, on a quiet, pedestrianized side-alley. Mon–Sat roughly 4.30pm–12.30am.

Clouds Ground floor, Seen Space, Soi 13, Soi Thong Lo (Soi 55) ☎02 185 2365, ⓦfacebook.com/cloudsbar; map p.99. On a sub-soi of Thong Lo, a couple of minutes' walk (west) from the co-owned *Iron Fairies*, this stylish open-fronted DJ bar is decorated with bouncing baubles and revolving clocks and plays mostly hip-hop and R&B. It gives onto a raucous shared courtyard, where you can tuck into raw oysters, fish'n'chips and draught and bottled imported beers. Mon–Thurs & Sun 5pm–1.30am, Fri & Sat 5pm–2am.

Finnegan's 23/1 Soi 4 (Nana Tai) ☎02 656 8160; map p.99. Probably the most authentically Irish of Bangkok's many "Oirish" bars, friendly Finnegan's offers draught Guinness, homely wood and leather decor, popular food and a wide array of TV sports, including rugby and Gaelic games. Daily 9am–1am.

Glow 96/4–5 Soi 23 ⓦfacebook.com/glowbkk; map p.99. This small, three-storey venue is one of the clubs of the moment, attracting an interesting roster of Thai and international DJs, such as Goldie and Fabio, to play house, techno and drum'n'bass. Daily 10pm–roughly 3am.

The Iron Fairies Just over 1km up Soi Thong Lo (Soi 55) from BTS Thong Lo ☎099 918 1600, ⓦtheironfairies .com; map p.99. High-concept bar that's designed to evoke a magical fairytale, with low lighting, jars of glitter (fairy dust) lining the walls and windows, gargoyles and lots of wooden structures including higgledy-piggledy staircases. Nightly live jazz including an open-mike night on Monday. Daily 6pm–2am.

Long Table Column Tower, 48 Soi 16 ☎02 302 2557–9, ⓦlongtablebangkok.com; map p.99. This achingly fashionable 25th-floor restaurant is named for its 25m-long communal centrepiece table, which seats seventy and serves contemporary Thai cuisine. But the real attraction is the sleek, Shanghai-style open-sided balcony bar whose "long-tail" cocktails give you ample time to lounge glamorously on the leather sofas and soak up the wraparound panoramas across downtown skyscrapers. Daily 5pm–2am.

Mikkeller 26 Yaek 2, Soi 10, Soi Ekamai (Soi 63) ☎02 381 9891, ⓦmikkellerbangkok.com; map p.99. This branch of the famous Danish microbrewery offers thirty craft beers on tap in a handsome suburban house furnished in blonde wood, with bean bags out on the lawn. Located (and signposted) down a sub-soi of a sub-soi of Ekamai and with the beer working out at about B500/pint, it's one for the beer geeks. Daily 5pm–midnight.

Nest 9th Floor, Le Fenix hotel, Soi 11 ☎02 255 0638, ⓦthenestbangkok.com; map p.99. Whether you unfurl on a daybed, curl up in a basket chair or recline under a hooded chaise longue at this aptly named, leafy, rooftop eyrie, you'll get an airy view of the condo-spiked skyline (there are covers for wet days) and a good choice of cocktails, Thai, Western and fusion main courses and tapas. There's music every night, be it DJs, singer-songwriters, Latin nights or occasional parties. Not as slick or spectacular as the more famous downtown sky bars but very pleasant. Daily 6pm–2am.

Q Bar (Q Up) 34 Soi 11 ☎082 308 3246, ⓦqbarbangkok .com; map p.99. Very dark, very trendy, New York-style bar-club occupying two floors and a terrace. Famous for its music from local and international DJs, *Q Bar* appeals to a mixed crowd of fashionable people, particularly on Fri and Sat nights. Its weekly roster currently features a live band on Wed, R&B all night on Fri and "Soulful Sundays". Don't turn up in shorts, singlets or sandals if you're male; ID required. Daily 10pm–2am.

Studio Lam About 100m up Soi 51 on the left, on the corner of the first sub-soi, about 5min walk west of BTS Thong Lo ☎02 261 6661, ⓦfacebook.com /studiolambangkok; map p.99. This friendly, cosy neighbourhood bar is the latest project of Zudrangma Records, whose record shop is just up the sub-soi to the left. The soundproofing and massive, purpose-built sound system give the game away: the music's the thing here, with DJs and live musicians playing driving *mor lam* and an eclectic choice of world sounds nightly. Tues–Sun 5/6pm–1/2am.

WTF 7 Soi 51 ☎02 662 6246, ⓦwtfbangkok.com; map p.99. Small, hip, Spanish-influenced bar-café and art gallery, which hosts occasional movie nights, left-field DJs and gigs. Adorned with luridly coloured Thai film posters and a great soundtrack, it offers global tapas, pâtés and a tempting variety of cocktails and wines. It's 5min walk west of BTS Thong Lo, 100m up Soi 51, near the mouth of a small sub-soi on the left. Tues–Sun 6pm–1am.

DOWNTOWN: SOUTH OF THANON RAMA IV

Most of the action here happens around the east end of Thanon Silom, though a few bars further west lay on great views of the river or the vast cityscape. If, among all the choice of nightlife around Silom, you do end up at one of Patpong's sex shows, watch out for hyper-inflated bar bills and other cons – plenty of customers get ripped off in some way, and stories of menacing bouncers are legion.

ALCOHOLIC DRINKS

The two most famous **local beers** (bia) are Singha (ask for "bia sing") and Chang, though many travellers find Singha's weaker brew, Leo, more palatable than either. In shops you can expect to pay around B35–40 for a 330ml bottle of these beers, B70 for a 660ml bottle. All manner of slightly pricier foreign beers are now brewed in Thailand, including Heineken and Asahi, and in Bangkok you'll find imported bottles from all over the world.

   Wine is now found on plenty of upmarket and tourist-oriented restaurant menus, but expect to be disappointed both by the quality and by the price, which is jacked up by heavy taxation. At about B100 for a hip-flask-sized 375ml bottle, the local **whisky** is a lot better value, and Thais think nothing of consuming a bottle a night, heavily diluted with ice and soda or Coke. The most palatable and widely available of these is Mekong, which is very pleasant once you've stopped expecting it to taste like Scotch; distilled from rice, Mekong is 35 percent proof, deep gold in colour and tastes slightly sweet. If that's not to your taste, a pricier Thai **rum** is also available, Sang Som, made from sugar cane, and even stronger than the whisky at forty percent proof. Check the menu carefully when ordering a bottle of Mekong from a bar in a tourist area, as they sometimes ask up to five times more than you'd pay in a guesthouse or shop.

11

Flann O'Brien's Corner of Silom and Thaniya roads ☎ 02 632 7515; map p.101. Welcoming Irish bar that's especially good for watching TV sport. A wide range of beers on draught including Guinness and Kilkenny bitter, popular food and varied live music Wed & Fri evenings. Daily 8am–1am.

★**The Sky Bar & Distil** Floor 63, State Tower, 1055 Thanon Silom, corner of Thanon Charoen Krung ☎ 02 624 9555, ⓦ lebua.com; map p.101. Thrill-seekers and view addicts shouldn't miss forking out for an alfresco drink here, 275m above the city's pavements – come around 6pm to enjoy the stunning panoramas in both the light and the dark. It's standing-only at *The Sky Bar*, a circular restaurant-bar built over the edge of the building with almost 360-degree views, but for the sunset itself, you're better off on the outside terrace of *Distil* on the other side of the building (where bookings are accepted), which has a wider choice of drinks, charming service and huge couches to recline on. The bars have become very popular since featuring in *The Hangover II* movie and have introduced a strict, smart-casual dress code. Daily 5/6pm–1am.

Tapas Room Club Soi 4, Thanon Silom ☎ 02 234 4737, ⓦ facebook.com/tapas.room; map p.101. Vaguely Spanish-oriented, pricey bar (but no tapas) with Moorish-style decor, whose outside tables are probably the best spot for checking out the comings and goings on this pedestrianized, partly gay soi. In the multi-roomed interior, which stretches up to a third-floor roof terrace, the music is mostly house, with added percussionists at the weekend. Daily 6/7pm–2am.

★**Tawandang German Brewery** 462/61 Thanon Rama III ☎ 02 678 1114–6, ⓦ tawandang.com; map p.101. A taxi ride south of Chong Nonsi BTS down Thanon Narathiwat Ratchanakharin – and best to book a table in advance – this vast all-rounder is well worth the effort. Under a huge dome, up to 1600 revellers enjoy good food, great micro-brewed German beer and a mercurial, hugely entertaining cabaret, featuring Fong Nam, who blend Thai classical and popular with Western styles of music, as well as magic shows, ballet and hip-hop dancing. Daily 5pm–1am.

Viva Aviv: The River Ground floor, River City shopping centre ☎ 02 639 6305, ⓦ vivaaviv.com; map p.101. With a lovely terrace on the river and a gnarly interior decor of hide-bound chairs and ships' winches, this bar offers cool sounds, some serious cocktails, good coffees and smoothies, as well as comfort food such as gourmet hot dogs, pizzas and salads. Daily 11am–midnight.

CHATUCHAK WEEKEND MARKET

Viva 8 Section 8 ☎ 02 618 7425; map p.108. Classy, relaxing bar that serves great cocktails, juices and coffees, where you can rest your feet while listening to DJs (from about 4pm) or tuck into paella that's theatrically prepared in a huge pan by a Spanish chef. Sat & Sun 7am–10pm.

Gay and lesbian Bangkok

Buddhist tolerance and a national abhorrence of confrontation and victimization combine to make Thai society relatively tolerant of homosexuality, if not exactly positive about same-sex relationships. Most Thais are extremely private and discreet about being gay, generally pursuing a "don't ask, don't tell" understanding with their family. Hardly any public figures are out, yet the predilections of several respected social, political and entertainment figures are widely known and accepted. There is no mention of homosexuality at all in Thai law, which means that the age of consent for gay sex is fifteen, the same as for heterosexuals.

THE GAY SCENE

Bangkok's **gay scene** is mainly focused on mainstream venues like karaoke bars, restaurants, massage parlours, gyms, saunas and escort agencies. Much of the action happens on Silom 4 (Thanon Silom, Soi 4; near Patpong) and on the more exclusive Silom 2 (towards Thanon Rama IV).

The farang-oriented gay **sex industry** is a tiny but highly visible part of Bangkok's gay scene and, with its tawdry floor shows and host services, it bears a dispiriting resemblance to the straight sex trade. Like their female counterparts in the heterosexual fleshpots, many of the boys working in the gay sex bars that dominate these districts are underage (anyone caught having sex with a prostitute below the age of 18 faces imprisonment). A significant number of gay prostitutes are gay by economic necessity rather than by inclination. As with the straight sex scene, we do not list the commercial gay sex bars.

The gay scene is heavily male, and there are hardly any **lesbian**-only venues, though quite a few gay bars are mixed. Thai lesbians generally eschew the word lesbian, which in Thailand is associated with male fantasies, instead referring to themselves as either *tom* (for tomboy) or *dee* (for lady).

This also means that gay rights are not protected under Thai law. However, most Thais are horrified by the idea of gay-bashing and generally regard it as unthinkable to spurn a child or relative for being gay. Although excessively physical displays of affection are frowned upon for both heterosexuals and homosexuals, Western gay couples should get no hassle about being seen together in public – it's more common, in fact, for friends of the same sex (gay or not) to walk hand-in-hand, than for heterosexual couples to do so.

Katoey (which can refer both to transgender women and to effeminate gay men, so often translated as "ladyboys") are also a lot more visible in Thailand than in the West. You'll find transgender women doing ordinary jobs and there are a number of *katoey* in the public eye too – including national volleyball stars and champion *muay thai* boxers. The government tourist office vigorously promotes the transgender cabarets in Bangkok (see p.178), all of which are advertised as family entertainment. *Katoey* also regularly appear as characters in soap operas, TV comedies and films, where they are depicted as harmless figures of fun. Richard Totman's *The Third Sex* (see p.218) offers an interesting insight into Thai *katoey*, their experiences in society and public attitudes towards them.

LISTINGS AND RESOURCES

Bangkok Lesbian ⓦ bangkoklesbian.com. Organized by foreign lesbians living in Thailand, Bangkok Lesbian posts general info and listings of the capital's lesbian-friendly hangouts on its website.

Dreaded Ned's ⓦ dreadedned.com. Guide to the scene in Thailand, with extensive listings.

Gay People in Thailand ⓦ thaivisa.com/forum/forum/ 27-gay-people-in-thailand. Popular forum for gay expats.

Travel Gay Asia ⓦ travelgayasia.com/destination /gay-thailand. Active, frequently updated site that covers listings and events all over the country.

Utopia ⓦ utopia-asia.com and ⓦ utopia-asia.com /womthai.htm. Lists clubs, bars, accommodation, tour operators, organizations and resources for gays and lesbians.

RESTAURANTS, BARS AND CLUBS

The bars, clubs and café-restaurants listed here, located around the east end of Thanon Silom and especially in the narrow alleys of Soi 2 and Soi 4, are the most notable of Bangkok's **gay nightlife** venues. Another strip of mostly gay bars can be found on the west end of Soi Sarasin at the top of Lumphini Park, but there are plans to redevelop the whole block. Advice on opening hours, admission charges and ID is given in Drinking and Nightlife (see box, p.169) – Soi 2, for example, operates a strict ID policy.

The Balcony Soi 4, Thanon Silom ☎02 235 5891, ⓦ balconypub.com; map p.101. Unpretentious, fun place with plenty of outdoor seats for people-watching, welcoming staff, reasonably priced drinks, upstairs karaoke and decent Thai and Western food. Happy hour till 8pm. Daily 5.30pm–late.

Dick's Café Duangthawee Plaza, 894/7–8 Soi Pratuchai, Thanon Suriwong ☎02 637 0078, ⓦ dickscafe.com; map p.101. Elegant day-and-night café-bar-restaurant, with a *Casablanca* theme to the decor (styling itself on *Rick's Café Americain*) and occasional art hibitions. On a traffic-free soi of go-go bars off the north de of Suriwong, it's ideal for drinking, eating decent Thai and Western food or just chilling out. Daily 11am–2am.

Disco Disco Soi 2, Thanon Silom; map p.101. Small, pared-down DJ bar with a minimalist, retro feel, playing good dance music to a fun young crowd. Daily 10pm–2am.

DJ Station Soi 2, Thanon Silom ☎ 02 266 4029, ⓦ dj-station.com; map p.101. Bangkok's most famous club, a highly fashionable but unpretentious three-storey venue, packed at weekends, attracting a mix of Thais and farangs, with a cabaret show nightly at around 11pm. Daily 10pm–2am.

GOD (Guys on Display) 60/18–21 Soi 2/1, Thanon Silom, in a small pedestrianized alley between Soi Thaniya and Soi 2 ☎ 02 632 8033; map p.101. Large, busy, three-level club with go-go dancers, somewhat more Thai-oriented than *DJ Station*. It tends not to fill up until *DJ Station* has closed; however, at the time of writing, since the military coup, GOD has been opening only on weekends, until 2/3am, though this is likely to be a temporary thing. Usually daily roughly 11pm–6am.

JJ Park 8/3 Soi 2, Thanon Silom ☎ 02 235 1227; map p.101. Classy, Thai-oriented bar, for relaxed socializing among an older set rather than raving, with karaoke and live music, and a Moroccan-themed chill-out annexe, *Club Café*, next door. Daily 10pm–2am.

Sphinx 98–104 Soi 4, Thanon Silom ☎ 02 234 7249; map p.101. Plush decor with a vaguely Egyptian theme, terrace seating and very good Thai and Western food attract a sophisticated crowd to this ground-floor bar and restaurant; karaoke upstairs at *Pharaoh's* on Fri & Sat. Daily 5pm–2am.

Telephone Pub 114/11–13 Soi 4, Thanon Silom ☎ 02 234 3279, ⓦ telephonepub.com; map p.101. Bangkok's first Western-style gay bar when it opened in 1987, this cruisy, dimly lit eating and drinking venue has a terrace on the alley, telephones on the tables inside for making new friends and karaoke upstairs. Daily 6pm–late.

12

Entertainment

The most accessible of the capital's performing arts is Thai dancing, particularly when served up in bite-size portions in tourist shows. Thai boxing is also well worth watching: the raucous live experience at either of Bangkok's two main national stadia far outshines the TV coverage. Two main companies put on spectacular ladyboy cabaret shows, while central Bangkok has more than forty cinemas, many of them on the top floors of shopping centres.

THAI DANCING

Thai dancing is performed for its original ritual purpose, usually several times a day, at the Lak Muang Shrine (see p.59) behind the Grand Palace and the Erawan Shrine (see p.97) on the corner of Thanon Ploenchit. Both shrines have resident troupes of dancers who are hired by worshippers to perform *lakhon chatri*, a sort of *khon* **dance-drama**, to thank benevolent spirits for answered prayers. The dancers are always dressed up in full gear and accompanied by musicians, but the length and complexity of the dance and the number of dancers depend on the amount of money paid by the supplicant: a price list is posted near the dance area. The musicians at the Erawan Shrine are particularly highly rated, though the almost comic apathy of the dancers there doesn't do them justice.

CULTURE SHOWS

The best way to experience the traditional performing arts is usually at a show designed for tourists, where background knowledge and stoic concentration are not essential; the spectacular Siam Niramit cultural extravaganza is a good introduction. Several tourist restaurants offer low-tech versions of the Siam Niramit experience, in the form of nightly **culture shows** that usually feature a medley of Thai dancing and classical music, perhaps with a martial-arts demonstration thrown in. In some cases there's a set fee for dinner and show, in others the performance is free but the à la carte prices are slightly inflated; it's always worth calling ahead to reserve, especially if you want a vegetarian version of the set menu.

Siam Niramit 19 Thanon Tiam Ruammit, 5min walk (or a free shuttle ride from Exit 1) from Thailand Cultural Centre subway, following signs for the South Korean embassy ☏ 02 649 9222, ⓦ siamniramit.com. Unashamedly tourist-oriented but the easiest place to get a glimpse of the variety and spectacle intrinsic to traditional Thai theatre. The 1hr 20min show presents a history of regional Thailand's culture and beliefs in a high-tech spectacular of fantastic costumes and huge chorus numbers,

enlivened by acrobatics and flashy special effects. The complex also includes crafts outlets and a buffet restaurant (dinner plus show from B1850). Tickets (from B1500) can be bought on the spot, online or through most travel agents. Daily 8pm.
Silom Village Thanon Silom ☏ 02 234 4581, ⓦ silomvillage.co.th. This complex of tourist shops stages a nightly 45min show at its Ruen Thep theatre (B700) to accompany a set menu of Thai food (available from 7.30pm). Daily 8.15pm.

TRADITIONAL DANCE-DRAMA

Drama pretty much equals dance in classical Thai theatre, and many of **the traditional dance-dramas** are based on the Hindu epic the *Ramayana* (in Thai, *Ramakien*), a classic adventure tale of good versus evil, which is taught in all the schools (see box, p.55). Not understanding the plots can be a major disadvantage, so try reading an abridged version beforehand such as *Thai Ramayana* (see p.219) and check out the wonderfully imaginative murals at Wat Phra Kaeo (see p.54), after which you'll certainly be able to sort the goodies from the baddies, if little else.

The most spectacular form of traditional Thai theatre is **khon**, a stylized drama performed in masks and elaborate costumes by a troupe of highly trained classical dancers. There's little room for individual interpretation in these dances, as all the movements follow a strict choreography that's been passed down through generations: each graceful, angular gesture depicts a precise event, action or emotion which will be familiar to educated *khon* audiences. The dancers don't speak, and the story is chanted and sung by a chorus who stand at the side of the stage, accompanied by a classical *phipat* orchestra.

A typical *khon* performance features several of the best-known **Ramakien** episodes, in which the main characters are recognized by their masks, headdresses and heavily brocaded costumes. Gods and humans don't wear masks, but the hero Rama and heroine Sita always wear tall gilded headdresses and often appear as a trio with Rama's brother Lakshaman. Monkey **masks** are wide-mouthed: monkey army chief Hanuman always wears white, and his two right-hand men – Nilanol, the god of fire, and Nilapat, the god of death – wear red and black respectively. In contrast, the demons have grim mouths, clamped shut or snarling; Totsagan, king of the demons, wears a green face in battle and a gold one during peace, but always sports a two-tier headdress carved with two rows of faces.

Even if you don't see a show, you're bound to come across finely crafted real and replica *khon* masks both in museums and in souvenir shops all over the country.

13

OTHER VENUES

Non-Thai-speaking audiences are likely to struggle with much of the **contemporary Thai theatre** performed in the city, though all the venues listed below occasionally stage shows that will appeal to visitors, be that experimental drama, **classical concerts** or performances by visiting international dance and theatre companies.

Chalermkrung Theatre (Sala Chalermkrung) 66 Thanon Charoen Krung, on the intersection with Thanon Triphet in Pahurat, next to Old Siam Plaza ☎02 222 0434, ⓦsalachalermkrung.com or ⓦthaiticketmajor .com. This Art Deco former cinema, dating from 1933, hosts mainstream traditional and contemporary theatre, plus regular *khon* performances with English subtitles. Performances cost from B800. Thurs & Fri 7.30pm.

National Theatre Sanam Luang, Ratanakosin ☎02 224 1342. Closed for renovation at the time of writing, but usually hosts roughly weekly shows of traditional performing arts such as *khon*, plus twice-monthly medley shows of music, dancing and *lakhon* (classical dance-drama) for tourists and other beginners (usually the first and last Fri of the month at 5pm). However, it's difficult to get information about what's on in English – try the nearby Bangkok Tourism Division (see p.32).

Thailand Cultural Centre Thanon Ratchadapisek ☎02 247 0028, ⓦthaiticketmajor.com; Thailand Cultural Centre subway. All-purpose venue, under the control of the Ministry of Culture, that hosts mainstream classical concerts, traditional and contemporary theatre, and visiting international dance and theatre shows.

CABARET

Glitzy and occasionally ribald entertainment is the order of the day at the capital's **ladyboy cabaret shows**, where luscious transvestites don glamorous outfits and perform over-the-top song and dance routines.

Calypso Cabaret Asiatique shopping centre (see p.184), Thanon Charoen Krung, 2km south of Saphan Taksin BTS ☎02 688 1415–7, ⓦcalypsocabaret.com. Shows twice nightly. B1200, or B900 if booked online, including one drink.

Playhouse Theatre Cabaret Asia Hotel, 296 Thanon Phrayathai, 1km north of Siam Square ☎02 215 0571, ⓦplayhousethailand.com; Ratchathevi Skytrain. Shows twice nightly. B1200.

THAI BOXING

The violence of the average **Thai boxing** (*muay thai*) match may be offputting to some, but spending a couple of hours at one of Bangkok's two main stadia, Rajdamnoen and Lumphini (which has recently moved out of the centre), can be immensely entertaining, not least for the enthusiasm of the spectators and the ritualistic aspects of the fights. Seats for foreigners cost B1000–2000 (cheaper, standing tickets are reserved for Thais). Sessions usually feature ten bouts, each

---

RITUALS OF THE RING

Thai boxing (*muay thai*) enjoys a following similar to football or baseball in the West: every province has a stadium, and whenever the sport is shown on TV you can be sure that large, noisy crowds will gather round the sets in streetside restaurants. The best place to see Thai boxing is at one of Bangkok's two main stadia, which between them hold bouts every night of the week (see opposite).

There's a strong spiritual and **ritualistic** dimension to *muay thai*, adding grace to an otherwise brutal sport. Each boxer enters the ring to the wailing music of a three-piece *phipat* orchestra, wearing the statutory red or blue shorts and, on his head, a sacred rope headband or *mongkhon*. Tied around his biceps are *phra jiat*, pieces of cloth that are often decorated with cabalistic symbols and may contain Buddhist tablets. The fighter then bows, first in the direction of his birthplace and then to the north, south, east and west, honouring both his teachers and the spirit of the ring. Next he performs a slow dance, claiming the audience's attention and demonstrating his prowess as a performer.

Any part of the body except the head may be used as an **offensive weapon** in *muay thai*, and all parts except the groin are fair targets. Kicks to the head are the blows that cause most knockouts. As the action hots up, so the orchestra speeds up its tempo and the betting in the audience becomes more frenetic. It can be a gruesome business, but it was far bloodier before modern boxing gloves were introduced in the 1930s, when the Queensbury Rules were adapted for *muay* – combatants used to wrap their fists with hemp impregnated with a face-lacerating dosage of ground glass.

13

consisting of five 3min rounds with 2min rests in between each round, so if you're not a big fan it may be worth turning up an hour late, as the better fights tend to happen later in the billing. To engage in a little *muay thai* yourself, visit one of several gyms around Bangkok that offer classes to foreigners.

Chacrit Muay Thai School 15/2 Soi 39, Thanon Sukhumvit ☎089 499 2052, ⓦ chacritmuaythaischool .com. Drop-in sessions cost B800/hr; longer courses are also available.

Lumphini Stadium Thanon Ram Intra ⓦ muaythailumpinee.net. This sixty-year-old stadium moved way out into the northern suburbs near Don Muang Airport in 2014. The schedule of upcoming fights is posted on its website. Usually Tues & Fri 6/6.30pm, Sat 4pm & 9pm.

Rajdamnoen Stadium Thanon Rajdamnoen Nok ⓦ rajadamnern.com. Bangkok's other main stadium is handily located next to the TAT office near Banglamphu (and handily surrounded by restaurants selling northeastern food), though the view from the B1000 section for foreigners is partially obscured. Usually Mon, Wed & Thurs 6.30pm, Sun 5pm & 8.30pm.

Sor Vorapin's Gym 13 Trok Kasap, off Thanon Chakrabongse in Banglamphu ☎02 282 3551, ⓦ thaiboxings.com. This gym holds *muay thai* classes twice daily (B500 per session). Sor Vorapin also offers extended training and a homestay at a second gym in Thonburi (B6500 all-in for 1 week) – see the website for details.

CINEMAS

Most Bangkok cinemas show recent American and European releases with their original dialogue and Thai subtitles, screening shows around four times a day. Several websites give showtimes of movies in Bangkok, including ⓦ moveedoo .com; cinema locations are printed on *Nancy Chandler's Map of Bangkok* (see p.32). Whatever cinema you're in, you're expected to stand for the king's anthem, which is played before every performance.

Alliance Française 179 Thanon Witthayu, opposite the east side of Lumpini Park behind the Japanese Embassy ☎02 670 4200, ⓦ afthailande.org. Movies at the French cultural centre (every Wed 7pm; free) are usually subtitled in English.

Apex Lido Thanon Rama I, Siam Square ☎02 252 6498, ⓦ apexsiam-square.com. Among half a dozen cinemas in and around Siam Square, this is your best bet for independent foreign films.

Goethe Institut 18/1 Soi Goethe, between Thanon Sathorn Tai and Soi Ngam Duphli ☎02 108 8231–2, ⓦ goethe.de/thailand. In the cool season (Dec–Feb), the German cultural centre screens an interesting free programme of recent movies from German-speaking countries, always subtitled in English, outdoors in the garden; check their website, which has a detailed map. Wed 7.30pm.

House Royal City Avenue (RCA) ☎02 641 5177, ⓦ houserama.com. Bangkok's only art-house cinema, well to the northeast of the centre. The nearest subway station, Phetchaburi, is a long walk away, so it's best to come by taxi.

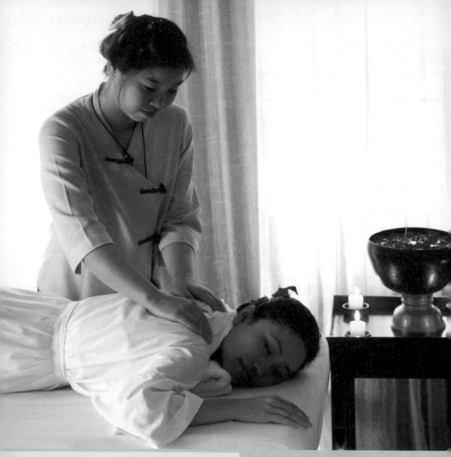

Mind and body

The last few years have seen an explosion in the number of spas opening in Bangkok – mainly inside the poshest hotels, but also as small, affordable walk-in centres around the city. With their focus on indulgent self-pampering, spas are usually associated with high-spending tourists, but the treatments on offer at Bangkok's five-star hotels are often little different from those used by traditional medical practitioners, who have long held that massage and herbs are the best way to restore physical and mental well-being. Even in the heart of the city, it's also possible to undergo a bit of highly traditional mental self-help by practising meditation.

SPAS AND MASSAGE CENTRES

Thais visit a masseur for many conditions, including fevers, colds and muscle strain, but bodies that are not sick are also considered to benefit from the restorative powers of a **massage**, and nearly every hotel and guesthouse will be able to put you in touch with a masseur. A session should ideally last at least one and a half hours and will cost B300–1500, or a lot more in the most exclusive spas. All **spas** in Bangkok feature traditional Thai massage and herbal therapies in their programmes, but most also offer dozens of other international treatments, including facials, aromatherapy, Swedish massage and various body wraps. Spa centres in upmarket hotels are usually open to non-guests but generally need to be booked in advance; day spas that are not attached to hotels may not require reservations.

14

Divana Massage and Spa 7 Soi 25, Thanon Sukhumvit ☎ 02 661 6784–5, ⓦ divanaspa.com. Delightful spa offering massages (Thai B1100/70min), foot, aromatherapy and herbal massages, facials and Ayurvedic treatments. Tues–Fri 11am–11pm, Sat, Sun & Mon 10am–11pm.

Health Land 55/5 Soi 1, Thanon Asok Montri (Sukhumvit Soi 21) ☎ 02 261 1110, ⓦ healthlandspa.com. Excellent Thai (B500/2hr) and other massages, reflexology, facials and body polishes, in swish surroundings, with several other locations around Bangkok. Daily 9am–11pm.

Nicolie Sun Square, a small shopping arcade on the south side of Thanon Silom between sois 21 and 23 ☎ 02 233 6957, ⓦ nicolie-th.com. Superb Thai (B1900/90min) and other massages, facials and scrubs, in an environment decorated with Asian objets d'art. Daily 11am–10pm.

Pian's Soi Susie Pub, which runs between the east end of Thanon Khao San and Thanon Ram Bhuttri ☎ 02 629 0924. Clinical-looking but highly rated a/c massage centre, offering Thai massages (B220/hr), foot, oil and herbal massages; you can study Thai massage here. Daily 8am–midnight.

Pimmalai Thanon Sukhumvit, 50m east of BTS On Nut, exit 1, between sois 81 and 83 ☎ 02 742 6452, ⓦ pimmalai.com. In a nice old wooden house, Thai massages (B250/1hr), plus foot, herbal and oil massages, herbal steam treatments, body scrubs, masks and facials. Mon–Fri 9.30am–10pm, Sat & Sun 9.30am–10.30pm.

THAI MASSAGE

Thai massage (*nuad boran*, "traditional massage") is based on the principle that many physical and emotional problems are caused by the blocking of vital energy channels within the body. The masseur uses his or her feet, heels, knees and elbows, as well as hands, to exert a gentle pressure on these channels, supplementing this acupressure-style technique by pulling and pushing the limbs into yogic stretches. This distinguishes Thai massage from most other massage styles, which are more concerned with tissue manipulation. One is supposed to emerge from a Thai massage feeling both relaxed and energized, and it is said that regular massages produce long-term benefits in muscles as well as stimulating the circulation and aiding natural detoxification.

The **science** behind Thai massage has its roots in Indian Ayurvedic medicine, which classifies each component of the body according to one of the four elements (earth, water, fire and air), and holds that balancing these elements within the body is crucial to good health. Many of the stretches and manipulations fundamental to Thai massage are thought to have derived from yogic practices introduced to Thailand from India by Buddhist missionaries in about the second century BC; Chinese acupuncture and reflexology have also had a strong influence. In the nineteenth century, King Rama III ordered a series of murals illustrating the principles of Thai massage to be painted around the courtyard of Bangkok's Wat Pho (see p.56), and they are still in place today, along with statues of ascetics depicted in typical massage poses. **Wat Pho** has been the leading school of Thai massage for hundreds of years, and it's possible to take courses there as well as to receive a massage. Masseurs who trained at Wat Pho are considered to be the best in the country and masseurs all across the city advertise this as a credential, whether it's true or not. Many Thais consider blind masseurs to be especially sensitive practitioners.

The same Indian missionaries who introduced yogic practices to Thailand are also credited with spreading the word about the therapeutic effects of herbal saunas and **herbal massages**, in which the masseur will knead you with a ball of herbs (*phrakop*) wrapped in a cloth and steam-heated; they're said to be particularly good for stiffness of the neck, shoulders and back. The **herbs** themselves, however, are resolutely Thai and feature in Thai cuisine as well as herbal treatments. Among these the most popular are tamarind, whose acidic content makes it a useful skin exfoliant, and turmeric, which is known for its disinfectant and healing properties; both are a common component of the scrubs and body wraps offered at many spas. The same places will also use lemon grass, probably Thailand's most distinctive herb, and the ubiquitous jasmine as soothing agents in aromatherapy treatments.

14

MASSAGE PRACTICALITIES

Thai masseurs do not use oils or lotions and the client is treated on a mat or mattress; you'll often be given loose-fitting trousers and a loose top to change into. English-speaking masseurs will often ask if there are any areas that you would like them to concentrate on, or if you have any problem areas that you want them to avoid; if your masseur doesn't speak English, the simplest way to signal the latter is to point at the area while saying *mai sabai* ("not well"). If you're in pain during a massage, wincing usually does the trick, perhaps adding *jep* ("it hurts"); if your masseur is pressing too hard, say *bao bao na khrap/kha* ("gently please"). If you're wary of submitting to the full works, try a **foot massage** first, which will apply the same techniques to just your feet and lower legs.

Ruen Nuad 42 Thanon Convent, near Thanon Sathon Nua ☎02 632 2662–3. Excellent Thai massages (B350/1hr, B600/2hr), as well as aromatherapy and foot massages and a juice bar, in an a/c, characterful wooden house, down an alley opposite the BNH Hospital and behind *Naj* restaurant. Daily 10am–9.30pm.

Wat Pho Wat Pho Compound (see p.56); 392/33–4 Soi Pen Phat 1, Thanon Maharat (the soi is unmarked but look for the Coconut Palm restaurant on the corner; ☎02 622 3533 or ☎02 622 3551, ⓦwatpomassage.com); map p.50. Excellent massages are available in two a/c buildings inside Wat Pho's main compound; allow 2hr for the full works (B420/hr; foot reflexology massage B420/hr). There are often long queues, however, so you might be better off heading over to the massage centre's other premises just outside the temple. Here you can also enrol on a 30hr massage training course in English, over five days (B9500), and foot-massage courses (B7500). Wat Pho daily 8am–5pm; 392/33–4 Soi Pen Phat 1 daily 8am–6pm.

MEDITATION SESSIONS AND RETREATS

Most of Thailand's retreats are out in the provinces, but a few temples and centres in Bangkok cater for foreigners by holding **meditation sessions** in English; novices and practised meditators alike are generally welcome. The meditation taught is mostly Vipassana, or "insight", which emphasizes the minute observation of internal sensations; the other main technique is Samatha, which aims to calm the mind and develop concentration (these two techniques are not entirely separate, since you cannot have insight without some degree of concentration). A **useful resource** is ⓦwanderingdhamma.org, a blog written by an American, with some fascinating articles, information on English-speaking retreats in Thailand and lots of good links. Meanwhile, Little Bangkok Sangha (ⓦlittlebang.org) is a handy blog maintained by a British-born monk, Phra Pandit, which gives details of talks in Bangkok and retreats. There are also retreats at Wat Mahathat (see p.59) and there are events for English-speakers at the Buddhadasa Indapanno Archives in Chatuchak Park (ⓦfacebook.com/suanmokkhbangkok/events).

House of Dhamma Insight Meditation Centre 26/9 Soi Lardprao 15, Chatuchak, Bangkok ☎02 511 0439, ⓦhouseofdhamma.com. Regular two-day courses in Vipassana, as well as day workshops in Metta (Loving Kindness) meditation. Courses in reiki and other subjects available.

Thailand Vipassana Centres ⓦdhamma.org. Frequent courses in a Burmese Vipassana tradition (ten days), in nine centres around Thailand, including Bangkok and nearby Chanthaburi, Kanchanaburi and Prachinburi.

World Fellowship of Buddhists (WFB) 616 Benjasiri Park, Soi Medhinivet off Soi 24, Thanon Sukhumvit, Bangkok ☎02 661 1284–7, ⓦwfbhq.org. Headquarters of an influential worldwide organization of (mostly Theravada) Buddhists, founded in Sri Lanka in 1950; its website carries information about meditation retreats in Thailand, though it's not updated very often.

LONG MEDITATION RETREATS

Longer retreats are for the serious-minded only. Strict segregation of the sexes is enforced and many places observe a vow of silence. Reading and writing are also discouraged, and you'll not be allowed to leave the retreat complex unless absolutely necessary, so try to bring whatever you'll need in with you. All retreats expect you to wear modest clothing, and some require you to wear white – check ahead whether there is a shop at the retreat complex or whether you are expected to bring this with you. An average day at any one of these monasteries starts with a **wake-up** call at around 4am and includes several hours of **group meditation** and chanting, as well as time put aside for chores and personal reflection. However long their stay, visitors are expected to keep the eight main Buddhist precepts, the most restrictive of these being the abstention from food after midday and from alcohol, tobacco, drugs and sex at all times. Most wats ask for a minimal daily **donation** (around B200) to cover the costs of the simple accommodation and food.

SILK, CHATUCHAK WEEKEND MARKET

Shopping

Bangkok has a good reputation for shopping, particularly for antiques, gems, contemporary interior design and fashion, where the range and quality are streets ahead of other Thai cities. Silk and handicrafts are good buys too. Watch out for fakes: cut glass masquerading as precious stones, damaged goods being passed off as antiques, counterfeit designer clothes and accessories, pirated CDs and DVDs, even mocked-up international driver's licences (Thai travel agents and other organizations aren't easily fooled). Bangkok also has Thailand's best English-language bookshops. Downtown is full of smart shopping plazas such as Embassy, Emporium and Siam Centre, which is where you'll find the majority of the city's fashion stores, designer lifestyle goods and bookshops. The plazas tend to be air-conditioned and thronging with trendy young Thais, but don't hold much interest for tourists.

Shopping centres, department stores and tourist-oriented shops in the city keep late **hours**, opening daily at 10 or 11am and closing at about 9pm; many small, upmarket boutiques, for example along Thanon Charoen Krung and Thanon Silom, close on Sundays, one or two even on Saturdays. Monday is meant to be no-street-vendor day throughout Bangkok, a chance for the pavements to get cleaned and for pedestrians to finally see where they're going, but plenty of stalls manage to flout the rule.

MARKETS

For travellers, spectating, not shopping, is apt to be the main draw of Bangkok's neighbourhood **markets** – notably the **bazaars of Chinatown** and the blooms and scents of **Pak Khlong Talat**, the flower and vegetable market just west of Memorial Bridge (see p.79). The massive **Chatuchak Weekend Market** is an exception, being both a tourist attraction and a marvellous shopping experience (see p.106). With the notable exception of Chatuchak, most markets operate daily from dawn till early afternoon; early morning is often the best time to go to beat the heat and crowds.

Asiatique About 2km south of Taksin Bridge, between the river and Thanon Charoen Krung ⓦwww .thaiasiatique.com. New night-time market for tourists in ten rebuilt 1930s warehouses and sawmills that belonged to the Danish East Asiatic Company. Several of them are given over to souvenirs and to clothes stalls, which tend to morph into bigger, more chic and expensive fashion outlets the closer to the river you get. Warehouse 1, devoted to furniture and home decor, is probably the most interesting section, featuring some creative contemporary designs. There's plenty to eat, of course, with the poshest restaurants, including a branch of *Baan Khanitha*, occupying the pleasant riverside boardwalk. Free ferries shuttle back and forth from Tha Sathorn pier, though the queues are often very long. Currently, the Chao Phraya Express tourist boats (see p.28) leaving Phra Arthit at 4pm, 4.30pm and 5pm are extending their route from Tha Sathorn to Asiatique. You could also catch an orange-flag express boat to Wat Rajsingkorn, leaving a 10min walk through the wat and down Thanon Charoen Krung to Asiatique. Daily 5pm–midnight.

HANDICRAFTS, TEXTILES AND CONTEMPORARY DESIGN

Samples of nearly all regionally produced **handicrafts** end up in Bangkok, so the selection is phenomenal. Many of the shopping plazas have at least one classy handicraft outlet, and competition keeps prices in the city at upcountry levels, with the main exception of household objects – particularly wickerware and tin bowls and basins – which get palmed off relatively expensively in Bangkok. Several places on and around Thanon Khao San sell reasonably priced triangular **"axe" pillows** (*mawn khwaan*) in traditional fabrics (see box below). The cheapest outlet for traditional northern and northeastern **textiles** is Chatuchak Weekend Market (see p.106), where you'll also be able to nose out some interesting handicrafts. Most Thai **silk**, which is noted for its thickness and sheen, comes from the northeast and the north, where shopping for it is probably more fun. However, there is a decent range of outlets in the capital, including many branches of Jim Thompson. Bangkok also has a good reputation for its **contemporary interior design**, fusing minimalist Western ideals with traditional Thai and other Asian craft elements.

AXE PILLOWS

Traditional triangular pillows (*mawn*) – so named because their shape supposedly resembles an axe head (*khwaan*) – are a lot more comfortable than they look and come in a range of sizes, fabrics and colours, both traditional and contemporary. **Axe pillows** have been used in Thai homes for centuries, where it's normal to sit on the floor and lean against a densely stuffed *mawn khwaan*; in wealthier homes one reclines on a polished teak chaise longue and props one's head against a *mawn khwaan*.

Pillows are made up of seven or more triangular pods, each of which is packed with kapok, although the cheaper (but longer-lasting) versions are bulked out with cardboard. The **design** has been slightly adapted over the years, so it's now also possible to get *mawn khwaan* with up to four flat cushions attached, making lying out more comfortable. The trademark *khit* fabric used in traditional-style pillows is characterized by stripes of (usually yellow) supplementary weft and is mostly woven in north and northeast Thailand. Pillows made from the multi-coloured red, blue and green nylon *khit* are the most durable, but those covered in muted shades of cotton *khit* are softer and more fashionable.

Axe pillows make fantastic souvenirs but are heavy to post home; some places sell unstuffed versions which are simple to mail home, but a pain to fill when you return.

SHOPPING FOR EVERYDAY STUFF

You're most likely to find useful everyday items in one of the city's numerous **department stores**: seven-storey Central Chidlom on Thanon Ploenchit (daily 10am–10pm), which boasts handy services like watch-, garment- and shoe-repair booths as well as a huge product selection (including large sizes), is probably the city's best. For **children's stuff**, Central Chidlom also has a branch of Mothercare, as do the Emporium, Central World and Siam Paragon shopping centres. Meanwhile, the British chain of **pharmacies**, Boots, has scores of branches across the city, including on Thanon Chakrabongse in Banglamphu, in Siam Paragon, in Central World, in Emporium and at the Thanon Suriwong end of Patpong 1.

The best place to buy anything to do with **mobile phones** (see p.46) is the scores of small booths on the third floor of Mah Boon Krong (MBK) Shopping Centre at the Rama I/Phrayathai intersection. For **computer** hardware and genuine and pirated software, as well as digital cameras, Panthip Plaza, at 604/3 Thanon Phetchaburi, is the best place; it's slightly off the main shopping routes, but handy for Khlong Saen Saeb boat stop Tha Pratunam, or a longer walk from BTS Ratchathevi. Mac-heads are catered for here, including authorized resellers, and there are dozens of repair and secondhand booths, especially towards the back of the shopping centre and on the upper floors.

15

RATANAKOSIN

Queen Sirikit Museum of Textiles Shop Grand Palace (on the right just inside the Gate of Glorious Victory) ⓦqsmtthailand.org/museum_shop; map p.50. Not-for-profit shop under the auspices of the Queen's Support Foundation, which is especially good for beautiful, top-quality *yan lipao*, traditional basketware made from delicately woven fern stems. Daily 9am–5pm (except when the Grand Palace is closed for royal events).

BANGLAMPHU AND THE DEMOCRACY MONUMENT AREA

Lofty Bamboo Buddy Hotel shopping complex, 265 Thanon Khao San; map pp.66–67; Floor 2, Mah Boon Krong (MBK) Centre, corner of Thanon Phrayathai and Thanon Rama I; map p.95; ⓦloftybamboo.com. Fair-trade outlet for Thai crafts, accessories, clothes and jewellery, including silver and bags made by Karen people and textiles and accessories by Lisu people from northern Thailand. Buddy Hotel shopping complex daily 10.30am–7.30pm; Mah Boon Krong (MBK) Centre daily 10.30am–8pm.

Taekee Taekon 118 Thanon Phra Arthit ☎02 629 1473, ⓦon.fb.me/1DzAOFb; map pp.66–67. Tasteful assortment of handicraft gifts, souvenirs and textiles, plus a selection of Thai art cards and black-and-white photocards. Mon–Sat 9am–6pm.

DOWNTOWN: AROUND SIAM SQUARE AND THANON PLOENCHIT

Alexander Lamont Floor 3, Gaysorn Plaza; map p.95; Central Embassy; map p.95; ⓦalexanderlamont.com. Beautiful lacquerware bowls, vases and boxes, as well as objects using bronze, glass, crystal, ceramic, parchment, gold leaf and petrified wood, all in imaginative contemporary, Asian-inspired styles. Daily 10am–8pm.

Chabatik Floor 4, Siam Paragon ⓦchabatik.com; map p.95. Gorgeous scarves, wraps and hangings in a rainbow of colours, made from soft Khon Kaen silk. Daily 10am–8pm.

Doi Tung Lifestyle Floor 2, Siam Discovery Centre ⓦwww.doitung.org; map p.95. Part of the late Princess Mother's development project based at Doi Tung, selling very striking and attractive cotton and linen in warm colours, made up into clothes, cushion covers, rugs and so on, as well as coffee and macadamia nuts from the Chiang Rai mountains. Mon–Thurs 11am–8pm, Fri–Sun 11am–9pm.

Exotique Thai Floor 4, Siam Paragon ⓦsiamparagon .co.th; map p.95. A collection of small outlets from around the city and the country – including silk-makers and designers from Chiang Mai – makes a good, upmarket one-stop shop that is much more interesting than Narai Phand (see below). There's everything from jewellery and beauty products to celadons and axe pillows. Daily 10am–10pm.

Narai Phand Ground floor, President Tower Arcade, just east of Gaysorn Plaza, Thanon Ploenchit ⓦnaraiphand.com; map p.95. This souvenir centre was set up to ensure the preservation of traditional crafts and to maintain standards of quality, as a joint venture with the Ministry of Industry in the 1930s, and has a duly institutional feel, though it makes a reasonable one-stop shop for last-minute presents. It offers a huge assortment of reasonably priced, good-quality goods from all over the country, including silk and cotton, *khon* masks, *bencharong*, celadon, woodcarving, lacquerware, silver, brass, bronze, *yan lipao* basketware and axe pillows. Daily 10am–8pm.

OTOP Central Embassy ⓦcentralembassy.com/brands /otop-heritage; map p.95. An attractive selection of the more high-end handicrafts made under the national OTOP (One Tambon, One Product) scheme. Daily 10am–8pm.

Propaganda Floor 4, Siam Discovery Centre ⓦpropagandaonline.com; map p.95. All sorts of poppy and playful stuff, often with a sexual or scatological theme,

ranging from bags to dental floss holders. Daily 10am–9pm.
Thann Floor 3, Gaysorn Plaza ⓦ thann.info; map p.95.
Striking contemporary rugs, cushion covers, vases and wooden objects, plus famous spa and beauty products (with a high-concept modern spa next door and a café outside). Daily 10am–8pm.

THANON SUKHUMVIT

Krishna's Just west of Soi 11 ⓦ krishnasianarts.com; map p.99. Large emporium of mostly mass-produced but good-quality household and decorative items in ceramic, brass, fibreglass and sandstone, especially figurines and Buddha statues. Mon–Sat 9am–7pm.

The Shop @ TCDC Thailand Creative and Design Centre, Floor 6, Emporium, Thanon Sukhumvit, between sois 22 and 24 ⓦ tcdc.or.th; map p.99. The retail outlet at Bangkok's design centre sells innovative products dreamt up by local creatives, mostly stocking-fillers, bags and household items, with more than a whiff of kitsch. Tues–Sun 10.30am–9pm.

Sop Moei Arts 8 Soi 49 ⓦ sopmoeiarts.com; map p.99. It's well worth checking out the lovely fabrics and basketware at this small branch of the Chiang Mai shop. Tues–Sat 9.30am–5pm.

Thai Craft Fairs Floor L, Jasmine City Building, corner of Thanon Sukhumvit and Soi 23 ⓦ thaicraft.org; map p.99. Roughly monthly craft sales and demonstrations, involving about seventy groups of artisans from all over the country, run on fair-trade principles by the Thai Craft Association, an independent development organization.

DOWNTOWN: SOUTH OF THANON RAMA IV

Jim Thompson 9 Thanon Suriwong, corner of Thanon Rama IV; map p.101; branches at the Jim Thompson

House Museum (see p.94), Don Muang Airport and many department stores, malls and hotels around the city; ⓦ jimthompson.com. A good place to start looking for traditional Thai fabric, or at least to get an idea of what's out there. Stocks silk, linen and cotton by the metre and ready-made items from shirts to cushion covers, which are well designed and of good quality, but pricey. They also have a home-furnishings section (daily 9am–7pm). If you're keen on a bargain, they have a factory outlet way out east of the centre on Soi 93, Thanon Sukhumvit (daily 9am–6pm). Daily 9am–9pm.

Khomapastr 56–58 Thanon Naret, between Suriwong and Si Phraya ⓦ khomapastrfabrics.com; map p.101. Branch of the famous Hua Hin shop, selling brightly coloured, hand-printed cotton in traditional Thai patterns. Mon–Sat 9am–5.30pm.

The Legend Floor 3, Thaniya Plaza, corner of Soi Thaniya and Thanon Silom ☎ 02 231 2170; map p.101. Stocks a small selection of well-made Thai handicrafts, from wood and wickerware to pretty fabrics and celadon and other ceramics, at reasonable prices. Daily 10am–7pm.

Silom Village 286/1 Thanon Silom ⓦ silomvillage .co.th; map p.101. An open-air complex of low-rise shops that attempts to create a relaxing, upcountry atmosphere as a backdrop for its diverse, fairly pricey handicrafts. Most shops daily 10am–9/10pm.

Tamnan Mingmuang Floor 3, Thaniya Plaza, corner of Soi Thaniya and Thanon Silom ☎ 02 231 2120; map p.101. Subsidiary of *The Legend* (see above), which sells clay figurines but concentrates on basketry from all over the country: among the unusual items on offer are trays and boxes for tobacco and betel nut made from *yan lipao* (intricately woven fern vines), and bambooware sticky-rice containers, baskets and lampshades. Daily 10am–7pm.

TAILORED CLOTHES

Inexpensive **tailoring shops** crowd Silom, Sukhumvit and Khao San roads, but the best single area to head for is the short stretch of Thanon Charoen Krung between Thanon Suriwong and Thanon Silom (near the Chao Phraya express-boat stops at Tha Oriental and Tha Wat Muang Kae, or a 10min walk from Saphan Taksin Skytrain station), where the recommended tailors below can be found. It's generally advisable to avoid tailors in tourist areas such as Thanon Khao San, shopping malls and Thanon Sukhumvit, although if you're lucky it's still possible to come up trumps here. For cheap and reasonable shirt and dress material other than silk, go for a browse around Pahurat market (see p.78), though the suit materials are mostly poor and best avoided.

A Song Tailor 8 Trok Chartered Bank, just round the corner from OP Place shopping centre off Thanon Charoen Krung, near the Oriental Hotel ☎ 02 630 9708; map p.101. Friendly, helpful small shop that's a good first port of call if you're on a budget. Men's and women's suits and shirts; ideally three to four days with two fittings, but can turn work around in two days. Mon–Sat 10am–7pm.

Ah Song Tailor 1203 Thanon Charoen Krung, opposite Soi 36 ☎ 02 233 7574; map p.101. Younger brother of the

above (neither of them should be confused with the nearby Ah Sun Tailor), a meticulous tailor who takes pride in his work. Men's and women's suits and shirts in around four days, with two fittings. Mon–Sat 10am–7pm.

Golden Wool 1340–2 Thanon Charoen Krung ☎ 02 233 0149; ⓦ golden-wool.com; map p.101. A larger operation than both of the above, which can turn around decent work for men and women in two days, though prices are slightly on the high side. Mon–Sat 9.30am–8pm.

OPPOSITE BUDDHA STATUETTE, CHATUCHAK WEEKEND MARKET >

15

HAVING CLOTHES TAILOR-MADE

Bangkok can be an excellent place to get tailor-made suits, dresses, shirts and trousers at a fraction of the price you'd pay in the West. Tailors here can copy a sample brought from home and will also work from any photographs you can provide; most also carry a good selection of catalogues. The bad news is that many tourist-oriented tailors aren't terribly good, often attempting to get away with poor work and shoddy materials (and sometimes trying to delay delivery until just before you leave the city, so that you don't have time to complain). However, with a little effort and thought, both men and women can get some fantastic clothes made to measure.

Choosing a tailor can be tricky, and unless you're particularly knowledgeable about material, shopping around won't necessarily tell you much. However, don't make a decision wholly on prices quoted – picking a tailor simply because they're the cheapest usually leads to poor work, and cheap suits don't last. Special deals offering two suits, two shirts, two ties and a kimono for US$99 should be left well alone. Above all, ignore recommendations by anyone with a vested interest in bringing your custom to a particular shop.

Prices vary widely depending on material and the tailor's skill. As a very rough guide, for labour alone expect to pay B5000–6000 for a two-piece suit, though some tailors will charge rather more (check whether or not the price you're quoted includes the lining). For middling **material**, expect to pay about B3000–5000, or anything up to B20,000 for top-class cloth. With the exception of silk, local materials are frequently of poor quality, and for suits in particular you're far better off using English or Italian cloth. Most tailors stock both imported and local fabrics, but bringing your own from home can work out significantly cheaper.

Give yourself as much **time** as possible. For suits, insist on two fittings. Most good tailors require around three days for a suit (some require ten days or more), although a few have enough staff to produce good work in a day or two. The more **detail** you can give the tailor the better. As well as deciding on the obvious features such as single- or double-breasted and number of buttons, think about the width of lapels, style of trousers, whether you want the jacket with vents or not, and so forth. Specifying factors like this will make all the difference as to whether you're happy with your suit, so it's worth discussing them with the tailor; a good tailor should be able to give good advice. Finally, don't be afraid to be an awkward customer until you're completely happy with the finished product – after all, the whole point of getting clothes tailor-made is to get exactly what you want.

FASHION

Thanon Khao San is lined with stalls selling **low-priced fashion clothing**: the baggy cotton fisherman's trousers, elephant pants and embroidered blouses are all aimed at backpackers, but they're supplemented by cheap contemporary fashions that appeal to urban Thais as well. Downtown, the most famous area for low-cost, low-quality casual clothes is the warren-like Pratunam Market and surrounding malls such as Platinum Fashion Mall around the junction of Phetchaburi and Ratchaprarop roads (see map, p.95), but for the best and latest trends from **Thai designers**, you should check out the shops in Siam Square and across the road in the more upmarket Siam Centre. Prices vary considerably: street gear in Siam Square is undoubtedly inexpensive (and look out for outlet stores such as Jaspal's in Amarin Plaza on Thanon Ploenchit), while genuine Western brand names are generally competitive but not breathtakingly cheaper than at home; larger sizes can be hard to find. **Shoes and leather** goods are good buys in Bangkok, being generally handmade from high-quality leather and quite a bargain.

Central Embassy Thanon Ploenchit ⓦ centralembassy .com; map p.95. This new mall, built on land sold off by the British Embassy, is bidding to become the most chic of the city's shopping plazas: here you'll find Gucci and Chanel – and gentlemen can get a very civilized haircut or shave at a branch of the London barber, Truefitt and Hill – while a few upmarket Thai names have made it to the party, notably Fly Now, which mounts dramatic displays of women's party and formal gear. Daily 10am–10pm.

Central World Ratchaprasong Intersection, corner of Rama I and Rajdamri ⓦ centralworld.co.th; map p.95.

This shopping centre – refurbished after it was torched during the suppression of the red-shirt street protests in 2010 – is so huge that it defies easy classification, but you'll find plenty of Thai and international fashions on its lower floors and in the attached Zen department store at its southern end. Daily 10am–9/10pm.

Emporium Thanon Sukhumvit, between sois 22 and 24 ⓦ emporiumthailand.com; map p.99. Large and rather glamorous shopping plaza, with its own department store and a good range of fashion outlets, from exclusive designer wear to trendy high-street gear. Genuine brand-name shops include Prada, Chanel, Louis Vuitton, as well as established local labels such as Soda and Asava. Two adjoining sister malls are being built, Emquartier and Emsphere. Daily 10am–8/10pm.

Mah Boon Krong (MBK) At the Rama I/Phrayathai intersection ⓦ mbk-center.co.th; map p.95. Vivacious, labyrinthine shopping centre which most closely resembles a traditional Thai market that's been rammed into a huge mall. It houses hundreds of small, mostly fairly inexpensive outlets, including plenty of high-street fashion shops. Daily 10am–9/10pm.

Siam Centre Thanon Rama I ⓦ siamcenter.co.th; map p.95. Particularly good for hip local labels (especially on Floor

3), many of which have made the step up from the booths of Siam Square across the road – look out for Greyhound, Baking Soda and Theatre – as well as international names like DKNY and Lacoste. Daily 10am–9pm.

Siam Square map p.95. It's worth poking around the alleys here and the "mini-malls" inside the blocks. All manner of inexpensive boutiques, some little more than booths, sell colourful street-gear to the capital's fashionable students and teenagers.

Viera by Ragazze Floor 2, Central World and in the attached Isetan and Zen department stores ⓦ ragazze .co.th; map p.95. Stylish, Italian-influenced leather goods. Daily 10am–9/9.30pm.

BOOKS

English-language **bookshops** in Bangkok are always well stocked with everything to do with Thailand, and most carry fiction classics and popular paperbacks as well. The capital's secondhand bookshops are not cheap, but you can usually part-exchange your unwanted titles.

Asia Books Flagship store in Central World on Thanon Rama I, plus dozens of other branches around town ⓦ asiabooks.com; map p.95. English-language bookshop (and publishing house) that's especially recommended for its books on Asia – everything from guidebooks to cookery books, novels to art. Also stocks bestselling novels and coffee-table books. Daily 10am–9.30pm.

B2S Floor 7, Central Chidlom, Thanon Ploenchit ⓦ b2s .co.th; map p.95. This shop sells a decent selection of English-language books, but is most notable for its huge selection of magazines, newspapers and stationery. There are dozens of branches around town. Daily 10am–10pm.

Books Kinokuniya 3rd Floor, Emporium Shopping Centre, Thanon Sukhumvit; map p.99; Floor 6, Isetan, in Central World, Thanon Rama I; map p.95; Floor 3, Siam Paragon, Thanon Rama I; map p.95; ⓦ thailand .kinokuniya.com. Huge, efficient, Japanese-owned, English-language bookshop with a wide selection of books ranging from bestsellers to travel literature and from

classics to sci-fi; not so hot on books about Asia, though. All daily 10am–10pm.

Dasa Book Cafe Between sois 26 and 28, Thanon Sukhumvit ⓦ dasabookcafe.com; map p.99. Bangkok's best secondhand bookshop, Dasa is appealingly calm and intelligently, and alphabetically, categorized, with sections on everything from Asia to chick lit, health to gay and lesbian interest. Browse its stock online, or enjoy coffee and cakes *in situ*. Daily 10am–8pm.

Shaman Books 71 Thanon Khao San, Banglamphu ☎ 02 629 0419; map pp.66–67. Well-stocked secondhand bookshop, with lots of books on Asia (travel, fiction, politics and history), as well as a decent range of novels and general-interest books. Daily 9am–10pm.

Ton's Booksellers 327/5 Thanon Ram Bhuttri, Banglamphu; map pp.66–67. Small bookshop where you're likely to find a bus map or *Nancy Chandler's map of Bangkok*, as well as books on Southeast Asia and a section of English literary classics. Daily 11am–8pm.

JEWELLERY AND GEMS

Bangkok boasts Thailand's best **gem and jewellery** shops, and some of the finest lapidaries in the world, making this *the* place to buy cut and uncut stones such as rubies, blue sapphires and diamonds. However, countless gem-buying tourists get badly ripped off, so remember to be extremely wary.

Asian Institute of Gemological Sciences Jewelry Trade Center, 919 Thanon Silom ☎ 02 267 4325 (laboratory) or ☎ 02 267 4315 (school), ⓦ aigsthailand.com; map p.101. Independent professional advice and precious stones certification from its laboratory. Also runs reputable courses, such as a five-day introduction to gems and gemology (US$700). Mon–Fri 8am–6pm.

Jewelry Trade Center West end of Thanon Silom ⓦ jewelrytradecenter.com; map p.101. Dozens of

members of the Thai Gem and Jewelry Traders Association have outlets in this shopping mall (and on the surrounding streets). Daily roughly 11am–8pm.

Lambert Floor 4, Silom Shanghai Building, Soi 17, 807–9 Thanon Silom ☎ 02 236 4343, ⓦ lambertgems .com; map p.101. Thoroughly reputable, thirty-year-old, American-owned outlet, offering a full service: loose stones and pearls, including collectors' stones, ready-made pieces, cutting, design, redesign and repairs. Mon–Fri 9am–5pm, Sat 9am–4pm.

15

15

GEM SCAMS

Gem scams are so common in Bangkok that TAT has published a brochure about it and there are lots of web pages on the subject, including ⓦen.wikipedia.org/wiki/Gem_scam and the very informative ⓦ2bangkok.com/2bangkok-scams-sapphire.html, which describes typical scams in detail. Never buy anything through a tout or from any shop recommended by a "government official"/"student"/"businessperson"/tuk-tuk driver who just happens to engage you in conversation on the street, and note that there are no government jewellery shops, despite any information you may be given to the contrary, and no special government promotions or sales on gems.

The basic **scam** is to charge a lot more than what the gem is worth based on its carat weight – at the very least, get it **tested** on the spot, ask for a written guarantee and receipt. Don't even consider **buying gems in bulk** to sell at a supposedly vast profit elsewhere: many a gullible traveller has invested thousands of dollars on a handful of worthless multicoloured stones, believing the vendor's reassurance that the goods will fetch at least a hundred percent more when resold at home.

If you're determined to buy precious stones, check that the shop is a member of the **Thai Gem and Jewelry Traders Association** by visiting their website, which has a directory of members (ⓦthaigemjewelry.or.th). To be doubly sure, you may want to seek out shops that also belong to the TGJTA's **Jewel Fest Club** (look for the window stickers), which guarantees quality and will offer refunds.

ANTIQUES

Bangkok is the entrepôt for the finest Thai, Burmese and Cambodian **antiques**, but the market has long been sewn up, so don't expect to happen upon any undiscovered treasure. Even experts admit that they sometimes find it hard to tell real antiques from fakes, so the best policy is just to buy on the grounds of attractiveness. The River City shopping complex (☎02 237 0077, ⓦrivercity.co.th) off Thanon Charoen Krung, which is near Si Phraya and Harbour Department express-boat piers, devotes its third, fourth and some of its second floors to a bewildering array of pricey treasures, ranging from Buddha images to tribal masks, as well as holding an auction on the first Saturday of every month (viewing during the preceding week). The other main area for antiques is the nearby section of Charoen Krung that runs down to the bottom of Thanon Silom, and the stretch of Silom running east from here up to and including the multistorey Jewelry Trade Center. Here you'll find a good selection of largely reputable individual businesses specializing in woodcarvings, ceramics, bronze statues and stone sculptures culled from all parts of Thailand and neighbouring countries as well. Remember that most antiques require an export permit (see p.42).

DREAM WORLD

Kids' Bangkok

Thais are very tolerant of children, so you can take them almost anywhere without restriction. The only drawback might be the constant attention lavished on your kids by complete strangers, which some adults and children might find tiring. Should you be in Thailand in January, your kids will be able to join in the free entertainments and activities staged all over the city on National Children's Day (Wan Dek), which is held on the second Saturday of January. They also get free entry to zoos that day and free rides on public buses.

ESSENTIALS

A **changing mat** may be worth bringing with you as, although there are public toilets in every shopping plaza and department store, few have baby facilities (toilets at posh hotels being a useful exception). International brands of powdered milk are available throughout the country, and brand-name baby food is sold in big towns and resorts, though some parents find restaurant-cooked rice and bananas go down just as well. Thai women do not **breastfeed** in public.

Getting around Child-carrier backpacks are ideal for getting around (though make sure that the child's head extends no higher than yours, as there are countless low-hanging obstacles on Thai streets). Opinions are divided on whether or not it's worth bringing a buggy or three-wheeled stroller. Bangkok's pavements are bumpy at best and there's an almost total absence of ramps. Buggies and strollers do, however, come in handy for feeding small children (and even for daytime naps), as highchairs are provided only in some restaurants (and then often without restraints for smaller toddlers). Taxis almost never provide baby car seats, and even if you bring your own you'll often find there are no seat belts to strap them in with; branches of international car-rental companies should be able to provide car seats.

Accommodation and discounts Many of Bangkok's expensive hotels offer special deals for families (see p.147), and an increasing number of guesthouses offer three-person rooms. Decent cots are available free in the bigger hotels as well as at some smaller ones (though cots in these places can be a bit grotty) and top- and mid-range rooms often come with a fridge. Many hotels can also provide a babysitting service. Kids get discounts at most of the theme parks and amusement centres listed below, though not at the majority of the city's museums, and there are no reductions on Bangkok buses and boats.

Shopping Although most Thai babies don't wear them, disposable nappies (diapers) are sold at supermarkets, department stores, pharmacies and convenience stores across the city – Mamy Poko is a reliable Japanese brand available in supermarkets. Should you need to buy a crucial piece of children's gear while you're in Bangkok, you should be able to find it in one of the department stores (see p.185), which all have children's sections selling bottles, slings and clothes. There are even several branches of Mothercare in the main shopping plazas, including in the Emporium (between Sukhumvit sois 22 and 24; BTS Phrom Pong; see map, p.99); in Central World on Thanon Rama I; BTS Chit Lom or Central; see p.95); in Central Chidlom on Thanon Ploenchit (BTS Chit Lom; see map, p.95); and in Siam Paragon at Siam Square (BTS Central; see map, p.95). Children's clothes are very cheap in Thailand.

Useful websites Bangkok Mothers and Babies International (⟨w⟩ bambiweb.org) is mostly for expat mothers and kids, but some of the information and advice on the website should be useful. Bkk Kids (⟨w⟩ bkkkids.com) is especially good on activities for kids in Bangkok, but also covers health matters and other services thoroughly. Thailand 4 Kids (⟨w⟩ thailand4kids.com) has lots of advice on the practicalities of family holidays in Thailand.

ACTIVITIES

The following theme parks and amusement centres are all designed for kids, the main drawbacks being that many are located a long way from the city centre. Other attractions kids should enjoy include the Museum of Siam (see p.58), feeding the turtles at Wat Prayoon (see p.85), Dusit Zoo (see p.90), Bangkok Ocean World aquarium (see p.97), the Snake Farm (see p.100), cycling around Muang Boran Ancient City (see p.112), taking a canal boat through Thonburi (see p.81) and pedal-boating in Lumphini Park (see p.100).

Bangkok Butterfly Garden and Insectarium Suan Rotfai (Railway Park), just north of Chatuchak Weekend Market; free; ☎ 02 272 4359. Over five hundred butterflies flutter within an enormous landscaped dome. There's also a study centre, plus family-oriented cycle routes and bikes (with infant seats) for rent in the adjacent park, which also has a kids' playground. The park is walkable from BTS Mo Chit or Chatuchak Park subway. Tues–Sun 8.30am–4.30pm.

HAZARDS

Even more than their parents, children need protecting from the sun, unsafe drinking water, heat and unfamiliar **food**. Consider packing a jar of a favourite spread so that you can always rely on toast if all else fails to please. As with adults, you should be careful about unwashed fruit and salads and about dishes that have been left uncovered for a long time. As diarrhoea can be dangerous for a child, rehydration solutions (see p.34) are vital if your child goes down with it. Avoiding **mosquitoes** is difficult, but low-strength DEET lotions should do the trick. You should also make sure, if possible, that your child is aware of the dangers of rabies; keep children away from **animals**, especially dogs and monkeys, and ask your medical adviser about rabies jabs.

Dream World Ten minutes' drive north of Don Muang Airport at kilometre-stone 7 Thanon Rangsit–Ongkarak; B1000/person including transfers; ⓦ dreamworld.co.th. Theme park with different areas such as Snow Town and Fairytale Land, including water rides, a hanging roller coaster and other amusements. Mon–Fri 10am–5pm, Sat & Sun 10am–7pm.

Funarium Soi 26, Thanon Sukhumvit, down towards Thanon Rama IV; B110–320, depending on height of visitor; ⓦ funarium.co.th. Huge indoor playground, with an arts and crafts room, cooking classes and a restaurant. Mon–Thurs 9am–6pm, Fri–Sun 9am–7pm.

KidZania Floor 5, Siam Paragon shopping centre, Thanon Rama I; B350–850, depending on age; ⓦ bangkok.kidzania.com. Imaginative and varied new activities centre, where kids can play at being doctors and nurses, Japanese chefs, and even fortune tellers. Mon–Fri 10am–5pm, Sat & Sun 10.30am–8.30pm.

Safari World On the northeastern outskirts at 99 Thanon Ramindra, Minburi; joint ticket to both parks B1200, children B650; ⓦ www.safariworld.com. Bus tours through a huge safari park, with monkeys, lions, giraffes and zebras, plus a separate marine park with dolphins and sea lions, as well as various animal shows (phone ☎ 02 914 4100–19 for times). Daily 9am–5pm.

Siam Park City On the far eastern edge of town at 101 Thanon Sukhapiban 2; B500, children 100–130cm B120, under 100cm free, with extra charges for some rides, or B900 for an unlimited day pass; ⓦ siamparkcity.com. Waterslides, whirlpools and artificial surf, plus roller coasters and other rides. Daily 10am–6pm.

16

THAI MANUSCRIPT SHOWING PARADE IN AYUTTHAYA

Contexts

History

Bangkok is a comparatively new capital, founded in 1782 after the previous capital of Ayutthaya, a short way upriver, had been razed by the Burmese, but it has established an overwhelming dominance in Thailand. Its history over the last two centuries directly mirrors that of the country as a whole, and the city has gathered to itself, in the National Museum and elsewhere, the major relics of Thailand's previous civilizations, principally from the eras of Ayutthaya and its precursor, Sukhothai.

Early history

The region's first distinctive civilization, **Dvaravati**, was established around two thousand years ago by an Austroasiatic-speaking people known as the Mon. One of its mainstays was Theravada Buddhism, which had been introduced to Thailand during the second or third century BC by Indian missionaries. From the discovery of monastery boundary stones (*sema*), clay votive tablets and Indian-influenced Buddhist sculpture, it's clear that the Dvaravati city-states (including **Nakhon Pathom**) had their greatest flourishing between the sixth and ninth centuries AD. Meanwhile, in the eighth century, peninsular Thailand to the south of Dvaravati came under the control of the **Srivijaya** empire, a Mahayana Buddhist state centred on Sumatra which had strong ties with India.

From the ninth century onwards, however, both Dvaravati and Srivijaya Thailand succumbed to invading **Khmers** from Cambodia, who consolidated their position during the watershed reign of **Jayavarman II** (802–50). To establish his authority, Jayavarman II had himself initiated as a *chakravartin* or universal ruler, the living embodiment of the **devaraja**, the divine essence of kingship – a concept which was adopted by later Thai rulers. From their capital at **Angkor**, Jayavarman's successors took control over northeastern, central and peninsular Thailand, thus mastering the most important trade routes between India and China. By the thirteenth century, however, the Khmers had overreached themselves and were in no position to resist the onslaught of a vibrant new force in Southeast Asia, the Thais.

The earliest Thais

The earliest traceable history of the **Thai people** picks them up in southern China around the fifth century AD, when they were squeezed by Chinese and Vietnamese expansionism into sparsely inhabited northeastern Laos. Their first significant entry into what is now Thailand seems to have happened in the north, where some time after the seventh century the Thais formed a state known as Yonok. Theravada Buddhism spread to **Yonok** via Dvaravati around the end of the tenth century, which served not only to unify the Thais themselves but also to link them to the wider community of Buddhists.

3rd century BC	6–9th centuries AD	Late 9th century
Theravada Buddhism probably first enters Thailand	Dvaravati civilization flourishes	Khmers, from Cambodia, begin to push into Thailand

By the end of the twelfth century they formed the majority of the population in Thailand, then under the control of the Khmer empire. The Khmers' main outpost, at Lopburi, was by this time regarded as the administrative capital of a land called **Syam** (possibly from the Sanskrit *syam*, meaning swarthy) – a mid-twelfth-century bas-relief at Angkor portraying the troops of Lopburi, preceded by a large group of self-confident Syam Kuk mercenaries, shows that the Thais were becoming a force to be reckoned with.

Sukhothai

At some time around 1238, Thais in the upper Chao Phraya valley captured the main Khmer outpost in the region at **Sukhothai** and established a kingdom there. For the first forty years it was merely a local power, but an attack by the ruler of the neighbouring principality of Mae Sot brought a dynamic new leader to the fore: the king's nineteen-year-old son, Rama, defeated the opposing commander, earning himself the name **Ramkhamhaeng**, "Rama the Bold". When Ramkhamhaeng himself came to the throne around 1278, he seized control of much of the Chao Phraya valley, and over the next twenty years, more by diplomacy than military action, gained the submission of most of Thailand under a complex tribute system.

Although the empire of Sukhothai extended Thai control over a vast area, its greatest contribution to the Thais' development was at home, in cultural and political matters. A famous **inscription** by Ramkhamhaeng, now housed in the Bangkok National Museum, describes a prosperous era of benevolent rule: "In the time of King Ramkhamhaeng this land of Sukhothai is thriving. There is fish in the water and rice in the fields… [The King] has hung a bell in the opening of the gate over there: if any commoner has a grievance which sickens his belly and gripes his heart… he goes and strikes the bell… [and King Ramkhamhaeng] questions the man, examines the case, and decides it justly for him."

Although this plainly smacks of self-promotion, it seems to contain at least a kernel of truth: in deliberate contrast to the Khmer god-kings (*devaraja*), Ramkhamhaeng styled himself as a **dhammaraja**, a king who ruled justly according to Theravada Buddhist doctrine and made himself accessible to his people. A further sign of the Thais' growing self-confidence was the invention of a new script to make their tonal language understood by the non-Thai inhabitants of the land.

The growth of Ayutthaya

After the death of Ramkhamhaeng around 1299, however, his empire quickly fell apart. By 1320 Sukhothai had regressed to being a kingdom of only local significance, though its mantle as the capital of a Thai empire was taken up shortly after at **Ayutthaya** to the south. Soon after founding the city in 1351, the ambitious king **Ramathibodi** united the principalities of the lower Chao Phraya valley, which had formed the western provinces of the Khmer empire. When he recruited his bureaucracy from the urban elite of Lopburi, Ramathibodi set the style of government at Ayutthaya, elements of which persisted into the Bangkok empire and up to the present day. The elaborate etiquette, language and rituals of Angkor were adopted, and, most importantly, the conception of the ruler as *devaraja*: when the king processed through the town, ordinary people were forbidden to look at him and had to be silent while he passed.

Mid-12th century	1238	1278	1299
Bas-relief at Angkor Wat depicting Thai mercenaries, a new force to be reckoned with in the region	The Thais seize the Khmer outpost of Sukhothai	Ramkhamhaeng "the Bold" comes to the throne of Sukhothai	With the death of Ramkhamhaeng, Sukhothai begins its decline

The site chosen by Ramathibodi was the best in the region for an international port, and so began Ayutthaya's rise to prosperity, based on exploiting the upswing in trade in the middle of the fourteenth century along the routes between India and China. By 1540, the Kingdom of Ayutthaya had grown to cover most of the area of modern-day Thailand. Despite a 1568 invasion by the Burmese, which led to twenty years of foreign rule, Ayutthaya made a spectacular comeback, and in the seventeenth century its **foreign trade** boomed. In 1511 the Portuguese had become the first Western power to trade with Ayutthaya, and a treaty with Spain was concluded in 1598; relations with Holland and England were initiated in 1608 and 1612 respectively. European merchants flocked to Thailand, not only to buy Thai products, but also to gain access to Chinese and Japanese goods on sale there.

The Burmese invasion

In the mid-eighteenth century, however, the rumbling in the Burmese jungle to the north began to make itself heard again. After an unsuccessful siege in 1760, in February 1766 the Burmese descended upon the city for the last time. The Thais held out for over a year, during which they were afflicted by famine, epidemics and a terrible fire which destroyed ten thousand houses. Finally, in April 1767, the walls were breached and the city taken. The Burmese savagely razed everything to the ground and led off tens of thousands of prisoners to Myanmar, including most of the royal family. The city was abandoned to the jungle, and Thailand descended into banditry.

Taksin and Thonburi

Out of this lawless mess, however, emerged **Phraya Taksin**, a charismatic and brave general, who had been unfairly blamed for a failed counterattack against the Burmese at Ayutthaya and had quietly slipped away from the besieged city. Taksin was crowned king in December 1768 at his new capital of **Thonburi**, on the opposite bank of the river from modern-day Bangkok. Within two years he had restored all of Ayutthaya's territories; more remarkably, by the end of the next decade Taksin had outdone his Ayutthayan predecessors by bringing Cambodia and much of Laos into a huge new empire.

However, by 1779 all was not well with the king. Taksin was becoming increasingly paranoid about plots against him, a delusion that drove him to imprison and torture even his wife and sons. At the same time he sank into religious excesses, demanding that the monkhood worship him as a god. By March 1782, public outrage at his sadism and dangerously irrational behaviour had reached such fervour that he was ousted in a coup.

Chao Phraya Chakri, Taksin's military commander, was invited to take power and had Taksin executed. In accordance with ancient etiquette, this had to be done without royal blood touching the earth: the mad king was duly wrapped in a black velvet sack and struck on the back of the neck with a sandalwood club. (Popular belief has it that even this form of execution was too much: an unfortunate substitute got the velvet sack treatment, while Taksin was whisked away to a palace in the hills near Nakhon Si Thammarat, where he is said to have lived until 1825.)

1351	1511	1767	1768
Ramathibodi founds the capital of Ayutthaya	The first Western power, Portugal, begins trading with Ayutthaya	Ayutthaya is razed to the ground by the Burmese	Taksin crowned king at the new capital, Thonburi

The early Bangkok empire: Rama I

With the support of the Ayutthayan aristocracy, Chakri – reigning as **Rama I** (1782–1809) – set about consolidating the Thai kingdom. His first act was to move the capital across the river to what we know as **Bangkok**, on the more defensible east bank where the French had built a grand but short-lived fort in the 1660s. Borrowing from the layout of Ayutthaya, he built a new royal palace and impressive monasteries in the area of **Ratanakosin** – which remains the city's spiritual heart – within a defensive ring of two (later expanded to three) canals. In the palace temple, Wat Phra Kaeo, he enshrined the talismanic Emerald Buddha, which he had snatched during his campaigns in Laos. Initially, as at Ayutthaya, the city was largely amphibious: only the temples and royal palaces were built on dry land, while ordinary residences floated on thick bamboo rafts on the river and canals, and even shops and warehouses were moored to the river bank.

During Rama I's reign, trade with China revived, and the style of government was put on a more modern footing: while retaining many of the features of a *devaraja*, he shared more responsibility with his courtiers, as a first among equals.

Rama II and Rama III

The peaceful accession of his son as **Rama II** (1809–24) signalled the establishment of the **Chakri dynasty**, which is still in place today. This Second Reign was a quiet interlude, best remembered as a fertile period for Thai literature. The king, himself one of the great Thai poets, gathered round him a group of writers including the famous Sunthorn Phu, who produced scores of masterly love poems, travel accounts and narrative songs.

In contrast, **Rama III** (1824–51) actively discouraged literary development and was a vigorous defender of conservative values. To this end, he embarked on an extraordinary redevelopment of **Wat Pho**, the oldest temple in Bangkok. Hundreds of educational inscriptions and mural paintings, on all manner of secular and religious subjects, were put on show, apparently to preserve traditional culture against the rapid change which the king saw as corroding the country.

The danger posed by Western influence became more apparent in the Third Reign. As early as 1825, the Thais were sufficiently alarmed by British colonialism to strengthen Bangkok's defences by stretching a great iron chain across the mouth of the Chao Phraya River, to which every blacksmith in the area had to donate a certain number of links. In 1826 Rama III was obliged to sign the **Burney Treaty**, a limited trade agreement with the British by which the Thais won some political security in return for reducing their taxes on goods passing through Bangkok.

Mongkut

Rama IV, commonly known to foreigners as **Mongkut** (in Thai, Phra Chom Klao; 1851–68), had been a Buddhist monk for 27 years when he succeeded his brother. But far from leading a cloistered life, Mongkut had travelled widely throughout Thailand, had maintained scholarly contacts with French and American missionaries, and had taken an interest in Western learning, studying English, Latin and the sciences.

When his kingship faced its first major test, in the form of a threatening British mission in 1855 led by **Sir John Bowring**, Mongkut dealt with it confidently. Realizing

1782–1809	1782	1826
Reign of Rama I, founder of the current Chakri dynasty	A grandiose new capital, Bangkok, is established, modelled on Ayutthaya	The signing of the Burney Treaty, a trade agreement between Thailand and Britain

that Thailand would be unable to resist the military might of the British, the king reduced import and export taxes, allowed British subjects to live and own land in Thailand and granted them freedom of trade. Furthermore, Mongkut quickly made it known that he would welcome diplomatic contacts from other Western countries: within a decade, agreements similar to the Bowring Treaty had been signed with France, the United States and a score of other nations.

Thus by skilful diplomacy the king avoided a close relationship with just one power, which could easily have led to Thailand's annexation. And as a result of the open-door policy, foreign trade boomed, financing the redevelopment of Bangkok's waterfront and, for the first time, the building of paved roads. However, Mongkut ran out of time for instituting the far-reaching domestic reforms which he saw were needed to drag Thailand into the modern world.

Chulalongkorn

Mongkut's son, **Chulalongkorn**, took the throne as Rama V (1868–1910) at the age of only fifteen, but he was well prepared by an excellent education which mixed traditional Thai and modern Western elements – provided by Mrs Anna Leonowens, subject of *The King and I*. When Chulalongkorn reached his majority after a five-year regency, he set to work on the reforms envisioned by his father.

One of his first acts was to scrap the custom by which subjects were required to prostrate themselves in the presence of the king. He constructed a new residential palace for the royal family in **Dusit**, north of Ratanakosin, and laid out that area's grand European-style boulevards. In the 1880s Chulalongkorn began to **restructure the government** to meet the country's needs, setting up a host of departments, for education, public health, the army and the like, and bringing in scores of foreign advisers to help with everything from foreign affairs to rail lines.

Throughout this period, however, the Western powers maintained their pressure on the region. The most serious threat to Thai sovereignty was the **Franco-Siamese Crisis** of 1893, which culminated in the French sending gunboats up the Chao Phraya River to Bangkok. Flouting numerous international laws, France claimed control over Laos and made other outrageous demands, to which Chulalongkorn had no option but to concede. During the course of his reign the country was obliged to cede almost half of its territory, and forewent huge sums of tax revenue, in order to preserve its independence; but by Chulalongkorn's death in 1910, the frontiers were fixed as they are today.

The end of absolute monarchy

Chulalongkorn was succeeded by a flamboyant, British-educated prince, **Vajiravudh** (Rama VI, 1910–25). However, in 1912 a group of young army lieutenants, disillusioned by the absolute monarchy, plotted a coup. The conspirators were easily broken up, but this was something new in Thai history: the country was used to infighting among the royal family, but not to military intrigue by men from comparatively ordinary backgrounds. By the time the young and inexperienced **Prajadhipok** – seventy-sixth child of Chulalongkorn – was catapulted to the throne as

1855	1874	1893
The Bowring Treaty exacts further trade concessions for the British	Beginning of the abolition of slavery in Thailand	Gunboats up the Chao Phraya: the Franco–Siamese Crisis obliges Thailand to give up its claims to Laos and Cambodia

Rama VII (1925–35), Vajiravudh's extravagance had created severe financial problems. The vigorous community of Western-educated intellectuals who had emerged in the lower echelons of the bureaucracy were becoming increasingly dissatisfied with monarchical government. The Great Depression, which ravaged the economy in the 1930s, came as the final shock to an already moribund system.

On June 24, 1932, a small group of middle-ranking officials, led by a lawyer, **Pridi Phanomyong**, and an army major, Luang Phibunsongkhram (**Phibun**), staged a **coup** with only a handful of troops. Prajadhipok weakly submitted to the conspirators, and 150 years of absolute monarchy in Bangkok came to a sudden end. The king was sidelined to a position of symbolic significance, and in 1935 he abdicated in favour of his ten-year-old nephew, **Ananda**, then a schoolboy living in Switzerland.

Up to World War II

The success of the 1932 coup was in large measure attributable to the army officers who gave the conspirators credibility, and it was they who were to dominate the constitutional governments that followed. Phibun emerged as prime minister after the decisive elections of 1938, and encouraged a wave of nationalistic feeling with such measures as the official institution of the name Thailand in 1939 – Siam, it was argued, was a name bestowed by external forces, and the new title made it clear that the country belonged to the Thais rather than the economically dominant Chinese.

The Thais were dragged into **World War II** on December 8, 1941, when, almost at the same time as the assault on Pearl Harbor, the Japanese invaded the east coast of peninsular Thailand, with their sights set on Singapore to the south. The Thais at first resisted fiercely, but realizing that the position was hopeless, Phibun quickly ordered a cease-fire.

The Thai government concluded a military alliance with Japan and declared war against the United States and Great Britain in January 1942, probably in the belief that the Japanese would win. However, the Thai minister in Washington, Seni Pramoj, refused to deliver the declaration of war against the US and, in cooperation with the Americans, began organizing a resistance movement called **Seri Thai**. Pridi Phanomyong, now acting as regent to the young king, furtively coordinated the movement under the noses of the occupying Japanese, smuggling in American agents and housing them in a European prison camp in Bangkok.

By 1944 Japan's defeat looked likely, and in July Phibun, who had been most closely associated with them, was forced to resign by the National Assembly. Once the war was over, American support prevented the British from imposing heavy punishments on the country for its alliance with Japan.

Postwar upheavals

With the fading of the military, the election of January 1946 was for the first time contested by organized political parties, resulting in Pridi becoming prime minister. A new constitution was drafted and the outlook for democratic, civilian government seemed bright. Hopes were shattered, however, on June 9, 1946, when King Ananda was found dead in his bed, with a bullet wound in his forehead. Three palace servants

1912	1932	1939
The first of many coup attempts in modern Thailand takes place	A coup brings the end of the absolute monarchy and introduces Thailand's first constitution	The country's name is changed from Siam to the more nationalistic Thailand

were hurriedly tried and executed, but the murder has never been satisfactorily explained. Pridi resigned as prime minister, and in April 1948 Phibun, playing on the threat of communism, took over the premiership.

As **communism** developed its hold in the region with the takeover of China in 1949 and the French defeat in Indochina in 1954, the US increasingly viewed Thailand as a bulwark against the red menace. Between 1951 and 1957, when its annual state budget was only about $200 million a year, Thailand received a total $149 million in American economic aid and $222 million in military aid. This strengthened Phibun's dictatorship, while enabling leading military figures to divert American money and other funds into their own pockets.

Phibun narrowly won a general election in 1957, but only by blatant vote rigging and coercion. Although there's a strong tradition of foul play in Thai elections, this is remembered as the dirtiest ever: after vehement public outcry, **General Sarit**, the commander-in-chief of the army, overthrew the new government in September 1957. Believing that Thailand would prosper best under a unifying authority, Sarit set about re-establishing the monarchy as the head of the social hierarchy and the source of legitimacy for the government. Ananda's successor, **Bhumibol (Rama IX)**, was pushed into an active role, while Sarit ruthlessly silenced critics and pressed ahead with a plan for economic development, achieving a large measure of stability and prosperity.

The Vietnam War

Sarit died in 1963, whereupon the military succession passed to **General Thanom**, closely aided by his deputy prime minister, General Praphas. Their most pressing problem was the **Vietnam War**. The Thais, with the backing of the US, quietly began to conduct military operations in Laos, to which North Vietnam and China responded by supporting anti-government insurgency in Thailand. The more the Thais felt threatened by the spread of communism, the more they looked to the Americans for help – by 1968 around 45,000 US military personnel were on Thai soil, which became the base for US bombing raids against North Vietnam and Laos.

The effects of the **American presence** were profound. The economy swelled with dollars, and hundreds of thousands of Thais became reliant on the Americans for a living, with a consequent proliferation of prostitution – centred on Bangkok's infamous Patpong district – and corruption. The sudden exposure to Western culture also led many to question traditional Thai values and the political status quo.

The democracy movement and civil unrest

Poor farmers in particular were becoming increasingly disillusioned with their lot, and many turned against the Bangkok government. At the end of 1964, the Communist Party of Thailand and other groups formed a broad left coalition which soon had the support of several thousand insurgents in remote areas of the northeast and the north. By 1967, a separate threat had arisen in southern Thailand, involving Muslim dissidents and the Chinese-dominated Communist Party of Malaya, as well as local Thais.

Thanom was now facing a major security crisis, especially as the war in Vietnam was going badly. In November 1971 he reimposed repressive military rule, under a

1941	1946	1957–63
The Japanese invade, and Thailand forms an alliance with them	Rama VIII is mysteriously shot dead; the present king, Rama IX (Bhumibol), accedes	Successful coup-maker and military strongman, General Sarit, brings Thailand ever closer to the US

triumvirate of himself, his son Colonel Narong and Praphas, who became known as the "Three Tyrants". However, the 1969 experiment with democracy had heightened expectations of power-sharing among the middle classes, especially in the universities. **Student demonstrations** began in June 1973, and in October as many as 500,000 people turned out at Thammasat University in Bangkok to demand a new constitution. King Bhumibol intervened with apparent success, and indeed the demonstrators were starting to disperse on the morning of October 14, when the police tried to control the flow of people away. Tensions quickly mounted and soon a full-scale riot was under way, during which over 350 people were reported killed. The army, however, refused to provide enough troops to suppress this massive uprising, and later the same day, Thanom, Narong and Praphas were forced to resign and leave the country.

In a new climate of openness, **Kukrit Pramoj** formed a coalition of seventeen elected parties and secured a promise of US withdrawal from Thailand, but his government was riven with feuding. In October 1976, the students demonstrated again, protesting against the return of Thanom to Bangkok to become a monk at Wat Bowonniwet. This time there was no restraint: supported by elements of the military and the government, the police and reactionary students launched a massive assault on **Thammasat University**. On October 6, hundreds of students were brutally beaten, scores were lynched and some even burned alive; the military took control and suspended the constitution.

"Premocracy"

Soon after the events of October 6, the military-appointed prime minister, **Thanin Kraivichien**, forced dissidents to undergo anti-communist indoctrination, but his measures seem to have been too repressive even for the military, who forced him to resign in October 1977. **General Kriangsak Chomanand** took over, and began to break up the insurgency with shrewd offers of amnesty. He in turn was displaced in February 1980 by **General Prem Tinsulanonda**, backed by a broad parliamentary coalition.

Untainted by corruption, Prem achieved widespread support, including that of the monarchy. Overseeing a period of rapid economic growth, Prem maintained the premiership until 1988, with a unique mixture of dictatorship and democracy sometimes called **Premocracy**: although never standing for parliament himself, Prem was asked by the legislature after every election to become prime minister. He eventually stepped down because, he said, it was time for the country's leader to be chosen from among its elected representatives.

The 1992 demonstrations and the 1997 constitution

The new prime minister was indeed an elected MP, **Chatichai Choonhavan**, a retired general with a long civilian career in public office. He pursued a vigorous policy of economic development, but this fostered widespread corruption, in which members of the government were often implicated. Following an economic downturn and Chatichai's attempts to downgrade the political role of the military, the armed forces staged a bloodless coup on February 23, 1991, led by Supreme Commander Sunthorn and General Suchinda, the army commander-in-chief, who became premier.

When Suchinda reneged on promises to make democratic amendments to the

1973	1976	1980–88
Bloody student demonstrations bring the downfall of Sarit's successor, General Thanom	The brutal suppression of further student demos ushers the military back in	Period of Premocracy, General Prem's hybrid of military rule and democracy

constitution, hundreds of thousands of ordinary Thais poured onto the streets around Bangkok's Democracy Monument in **mass demonstrations** between May 17 and 20, 1992. Hopelessly misjudging the mood of the country, Suchinda brutally crushed the protests, leaving hundreds dead or injured. Having justified the massacre on the grounds that he was protecting the king from communist agitators, Suchinda was forced to resign when King Bhumibol expressed his disapproval in a ticking-off that was broadcast on world television.

Elections were held in September, with the **Democrat Party**, led by Chuan Leekpai, a noted upholder of democracy and the rule of law, emerging victorious. Chuan was succeeded in turn by Banharn Silpa-archa – nicknamed by the local press "the walking ATM", a reference to his reputation for buying votes – and General Chavalit Yongchaiyudh. The most significant positive event of the latter's tenure was the approval of a **new constitution** in 1997. Drawn up by an independent drafting assembly, its main points included: direct elections to the senate, rather than appointment of senators by the prime minister; acceptance of the right of assembly as the basis of a democratic society and guarantees of individual rights and freedoms; greater public accountability; and increased popular participation in local administration. The eventual aim of the new charter was to end the traditional system of patronage, vested interests and vote-buying.

Tom yam kung: the 1997 economic crisis

In February 1997 foreign-exchange dealers began to mount speculative attacks on the **baht**, alarmed at the size of Thailand's private foreign debt – 250 billion baht in the unproductive property sector alone, much of it accrued through the proliferation of prestigious skyscrapers in Bangkok. Chavalit's government defended the pegged exchange rate, spending $23 billion of the country's formerly healthy foreign-exchange reserves, but at the beginning of July was forced to give up the ghost – the baht was floated and soon went into free-fall. Thailand was forced to seek help from the **IMF**, who in August put together a $17-billion **rescue package**, coupled with severe austerity measures.

In November, the inept Chavalit was replaced by Chuan Leekpai, who immediately took a hard line in following the IMF's advice, which involved maintaining cripplingly high interest rates to protect the baht and slashing government budgets. Although this played well abroad, at home the government encountered increasing hostility from its newly impoverished citizens – the downturn struck with such speed and severity that it was dubbed the **tom yam kung crisis**, after the searingly hot Thai soup. Chuan's tough stance paid off, however, with the baht stabilizing and inflation falling back, and in October 1999 he announced that he was forgoing almost $4 billion of the IMF's package.

Thaksin

The 2001 general election was won by a new party, **Thai Rak Thai** (Thai Loves Thai), led by one of Thailand's wealthiest men, **Thaksin Shinawatra**, an ex-policeman who had made a personal fortune from government telecommunications concessions. Instead of a move towards greater democracy, as envisioned by the new constitution, however, Thaksin began to apply commercial and legal pressure to try to silence critics in the media and parliament. As his standing became more firmly entrenched, he rejected constitutional

1997

A landmark new constitution aims to end corruption and guarantee individual rights and freedoms

1997

Tom yam kung: Thailand is ravaged by economic crisis

reforms designed to rein in his power – famously declaring that "democracy is only a tool" for achieving other goals. Thaksin did, however, live up to his billing as a reformer. In his first year of government, he issued a three-year loan moratorium for perennially indebted farmers and set up a one-million-baht development fund for each of the country's seventy thousand villages. To improve public health access, a standard charge of B30 per hospital visit was introduced nationwide.

In early 2004, politically and criminally motivated violence in the **Islamic southern provinces** escalated sharply, and since then, there has been on average nearly a death a day on both sides in the troubles. The insurgents have targeted any representative of central authority, including monks and teachers, as well as setting off bombs in marketplaces and near tourist hotels. The authorities have inflamed opinion in the south by reacting violently, notably in crushing protests at Tak Bai and the much-revered Krue Se Mosque in Pattani in 2004, in which a total of over two hundred alleged insurgents died. In 2005, the government imposed **martial law** in Pattani, Yala and Narathiwat provinces and in parts of Songkhla province – this, however, has exacerbated economic and unemployment problems in what is Thailand's poorest region. Facing a variety of shadowy groups, whose precise aims are unclear, the authorities' natural instinct has been to get tough – which so far has brought the problem no nearer to a solution.

Despite these problems, Thaksin breezed through the **February 2005 election**, becoming the first prime minister in Thai history to win an outright majority at the polls, but causing alarm among a wide spectrum of Thailand's elites. When Thaksin's relatives sold their shares in the family's Shin Corporation in January 2006 for £1.1 billion, without paying tax, tens of thousands of mostly middle-class Thais flocked to Bangkok to take part in protracted but peaceful demonstrations, under the umbrella of the **People's Alliance for Democracy (PAD)**. After further allegations of corruption and cronyism, in September Thaksin, while on official business in the United States, was ousted by a military government in a **coup**.

The spectre of Thaksin

Thaksin set up home in London, but his supporters, now the **People's Power Party (PPP)**, won the December 2007 general election. In response, the PAD – its nationalist and royalist credentials and its trademark yellow shirts (the colour of the king) now firmly established – restarted its mass protests. Meanwhile, there was a merry-go-round of tribunals and court cases, including Thaksin's conviction *in absentia* for corruption.

Matters came to a head in November and December 2008: the PAD seized and closed down Bangkok's Suvarnabhumi airport; the ruling People's Power Party was declared illegal by the courts; and **Pheu Thai** (sometimes "Peua Thai"; meaning "For Thais"), the PPP's swift reincarnation, found itself unable to form a new coalition government. Instead, led by the Eton- and Oxford-educated **Abhisit Vejjajiva**, the Democrat Party jumped into bed with the Bhumjaithai Party, formerly staunch supporters of Thaksin, to take the helm.

This in turn prompted Thaksin's supporters – now **red-shirted** and organized into the **UDD** (United Front for Democracy against Dictatorship) – to hold mass protest meetings. In March 2009, Thaksin claimed by video broadcast that Privy Council President, Prem Tinsulanonda, had masterminded the 2006 coup and Abhisit's

2001	2004	2006
Thaksin Shinawatra, loved and hated in roughly equal measure, wins the general election	The violence in the Islamic southern provinces sharply escalates	While in the US, Thaksin is ousted in a military coup and goes into exile

appointment as prime minister, and called for the overthrow of the *amat* (elite). Amid a clampdown by the Democrat government on free speech, including heavy-handed use of Article 112, the *lèse majesté* law, much more violent protests took place early the following year. Calling on Abhisit to hold new elections, thousands of red shirts set up a heavily defended camp around the **Ratchaprasong** intersection in central Bangkok in early April. On May 19, Abhisit sent in the army to break up the camp by force; altogether 91 people died on both sides in the two months of protests.

Mass popular support for Thaksin, however, did not wane, and in the general election of May 2011, Pheu Thai – now led by his younger sister, **Yingluck Shinawatra** – romped home with an absolute majority. Thailand's first woman prime minister, Yingluck proposed an amnesty bill for all those involved in the political turmoils of the last ten years, which would have included wiping out Thaksin's corruption convictions, thus allowing him to return to Thailand. However, in late 2013 this prompted further mass protests on the streets of Bangkok: led by Suthep Thaugsuban, who resigned his seat as a Democrat Party MP, thousands of nationalists – no longer wearing yellow shirts, but now blowing whistles as their trademark – occupied large areas of the city centre for several months, in an attempt to provoke the military into staging a coup.

In May 2014, this duly happened, Thailand's twelfth successful **coup d'état** in the period of constitutional monarchy since 1932 (not to mention seven failed attempts). The army chief, **General Prayut Chan-ocha**, installed himself as prime minister, at the head of a military junta known as the National Council for Peace and Order (NCPO). Political gatherings were banned, politicians, journalists, academics and activists were detained (most temporarily) and censorship of the media was tightened (which in turn fostered broad self-censorship). In January 2015, Yingluck Shinawatra was banned from politics for five years and may face a lengthy prison term. The NCPO has set up a committee to draft a new constitution, with the aim of reducing the powers of elected politicians, but at the time of writing, it's unclear when new elections will be held. Meanwhile, the 87-year-old king, now the world's longest-running head of state, is in failing health; and Thailand is expected to take a leading role in the formation of the ASEAN Economic Community, an integrated single market that's optimistically scheduled for the end of 2015.

2010	**2011**	**2014**
Red-shirted supporters of Thaksin set up a month-long protest camp in Bangkok, before being dispersed by force	Thaksin's sister, Yingluck, wins the general election with an outright majority	Thailand's twelfth military coup since 1932

Religion: Thai Buddhism

Over 85 percent of Thais consider themselves Theravada Buddhists, followers of the teachings of a holy man usually referred to as the Buddha (Enlightened One), though more precisely known as Gautama Buddha to distinguish him from lesser-known Buddhas who preceded him. Theravada Buddhism is one of the two main schools of Buddhism practised in Asia, and in Thailand it has absorbed an eclectic assortment of animist and Hindu elements. Islam is the biggest of the minority religions in Thailand, practised by between five and ten percent of the population. Most Muslims live in the south, along the Malaysian border. The rest of the Thai population comprises Mahayana Buddhists, Hindus, Sikhs, Christians and animists.

The Buddha: his life and beliefs

Gautama Buddha was born in Nepal as **Prince Gautama Siddhartha** in either the sixth or seventh century BC. At his birth, astrologers predicted that he would become either a famous king or a celebrated holy man, depending on which path he chose. Much preferring the former, the prince's father forbade the boy from leaving the palace grounds, and set about educating Gautama in all aspects of the high life. Most statues of the Buddha depict him with elongated earlobes, which is a reference to this early pampered existence, when he would have worn heavy precious stones in his ears.

The prince married and became a father, but at the age of 29 he flouted his father's authority and sneaked out into the world beyond the palace. On this fateful trip he encountered successively an old man, a sick man, a corpse and a hermit, and thus for the first time was made aware that pain and suffering were intrinsic to human life. Contemplation seemed the only means of discovering why this was so – and therefore Gautama decided to leave the palace and become a **Hindu ascetic**.

For several years he wandered the countryside leading a life of self-denial and self-mortification, but failed to come any closer to the answer. Eventually concluding that the best course of action must be to follow a "Middle Way" – neither indulgent nor overly ascetic – Gautama sat down beneath the famous riverside bodhi tree at **Bodh Gaya** in India, facing the rising sun, to **meditate** until he achieved enlightenment. For 49 days he sat cross-legged in the "lotus position", contemplating the causes of suffering and wrestling with temptations that materialized to distract him. Most of these were sent by **Mara**, the Evil One, who was finally subdued when Gautama summoned the earth goddess **Mae Toranee** by pointing the fingers of his right hand at the ground – the gesture known as **Calling the Earth to Witness**, or *Bhumisparsa Mudra*, which has been immortalized by thousands of Thai sculptors. Mae Toranee wrung torrents of water from her hair and engulfed Mara's demonic emissaries in a flood, an episode that's also commonly reproduced, most famously in the statue in Bangkok's Sanam Luang.

Temptations dealt with, Gautama soon came to attain **enlightenment** and so become a Buddha. As the place of his enlightenment, the **bodhi tree** (or bo tree) has assumed special significance for Buddhists: not only does it appear in many Buddhist paintings, but there's often a real bodhi tree (*Ficus religiosa*) planted in temple compounds as well. In addition, the bot is nearly always built facing either a body of water or facing east (preferably both).

The Buddha preached his **first sermon** in a deer park in India, where he characterized his doctrine, or **Dharma**, as a wheel. From this episode comes the early Buddhist symbol the **Dharmachakra**, known as the Wheel of Law, which is often accompanied by a statue of a deer. Thais celebrate this first sermon with a public holiday in July known as **Asanha Puja**. On another occasion 1250 people spontaneously gathered to hear the Buddha speak, an event remembered in Thailand as **Maha Puja** and marked by a public holiday in February.

For the next forty-odd years the Buddha travelled the region converting non-believers and performing miracles. One rainy season he even ascended into the **Tavatimsa heaven** (Heaven of the 33 Gods) to visit his mother and to preach the doctrine to her. His descent from this heaven is quite a common theme of paintings and sculptures, and the **Standing Buddha** pose of numerous Buddha statues comes from this story.

The Buddha "died" at the age of 80 on the banks of a river at Kusinari in India – an event often dated to 543 BC, which is why the **Thai calendar** is 543 years out of synch with the Western one, so that the year 2016 AD becomes 2559 BE (Buddhist Era). Lying on his side, propping up his head on his hand, the Buddha passed into **Nirvana** (giving rise to another classic pose, the **Reclining Buddha**), the unimaginable state of nothingness which knows no suffering and from which there is no reincarnation. Buddhists believe that the day the Buddha entered Nirvana was the same date on which he was born and on which he achieved enlightenment, a triply significant day that Thais honour with the **Visakha Puja** festival in May.

Buddhists believe that Gautama Buddha was the five-hundredth incarnation of a single being: the stories of these five hundred lives, collectively known as the **Jataka**, provide the inspiration for a lot of Thai art. Hindus also accept Gautama Buddha into their pantheon, perceiving him as the ninth manifestation of their god Vishnu.

The spread of Buddhism

After the Buddha entered Nirvana, his **doctrine** spread relatively quickly across India, and probably was first promulgated in Thailand in about the third century BC. His teachings, the *Tripitaka*, were written down in the Pali language – a derivative of Sanskrit – in a form that became known as **Theravada**, or "The Doctrine of the Elders".

By the beginning of the first millennium, a new movement called **Mahayana** (Great Vehicle) had emerged within the Theravada school, attempting to make Buddhism more accessible by introducing a pantheon of **bodhisattva**, or Buddhist saints, who, although they had achieved enlightenment, postponed entering Nirvana in order to inspire the populace. Mahayana Buddhism spread north into China, Korea, Vietnam and Japan, also entering southern Thailand via the Srivijayan empire around the eighth century and parts of Khmer Cambodia in about the eleventh century. Meanwhile, Theravada Buddhism (which the Mahayanists disparagingly renamed "Hinayana" or "Lesser Vehicle") established itself most significantly in Sri Lanka, northern and central Thailand and Myanmar.

Buddhist doctrine and practice

Central to Theravada Buddhism is a belief in **karma** – every action has a consequence – and **reincarnation**, along with an understanding that craving is at the root of human suffering. The ultimate aim for a Buddhist is to get off the cycle of perpetual reincarnation and suffering and instead to enter the blissful state of non-being that is **Nirvana**. This enlightened state can take many lifetimes to achieve so the more realistic goal for most is to be reborn slightly higher up the karmic ladder each time. As Thai Buddhists see it, animals are at the bottom of the karmic scale and monks at the top, with women on a lower rung than men.

Living a good life, specifically a life of "pure intention", creates good karma and Buddhist doctrine focuses a great deal on how to achieve this. Psychology and an understanding of human weaknesses play a big part. Key is the concept of **dukka**, which holds that craving is the cause of all suffering or, to put it simplistically, human unhappiness is caused by the unquenchable dissatisfaction experienced when one's sensual, spiritual or material desires are not met. Accepting the truth of this is known as the **Four Noble Truths** of Buddhism. The route to enlightenment depends on a person being sufficiently detached from earthly desires so that *dukka* can't take hold. One acknowledges that the physical world is impermanent and ever-changing, and that all things – including the self – are therefore not worth craving. A Buddhist works towards this realization by following the **Eightfold Path**, or **Middle Way**, that is by developing a set of highly moral personal qualities such as "right speech", "right action" and "right mindfulness". Meditation is particularly helpful in this.

A devout Thai Buddhist commits to the **five basic precepts**, namely not to kill or steal, to refrain from sexual misconduct and incorrect speech (lies, gossip and abuse) and to eschew intoxicating liquor and drugs. There are **three extra precepts** for special *wan phra* holy days and for those laypeople including foreign students who study meditation at Thai temples: no eating after noon, no entertainment (including TV and music) and no sleeping on a soft bed; in addition, the no sexual misconduct precept turns into no sex at all.

Making merit

Merit-making in popular Thai Buddhism has become slightly skewed, so that some people act on the assumption that they'll climb the karmic ladder faster if they make bigger and better offerings to the temple and its monks. However, it is of course the purity of the intention behind one's merit-making (*tham bun*) that's fundamental.

Merit can be made in many ways, from giving a monk his breakfast to attending a Buddhist service or donating money and gifts to the neighbourhood temple, and most **festivals** are essentially communal merit-making opportunities. Between the big festivals, the most common days for making merit and visiting the temple are **wan phra** (holy days), which are determined by the phase of the moon and occur four times a month. The simplest **offering** inside a temple consists of lotus buds, candles and three incense sticks (representing the three gems of Buddhism – the Buddha himself, the Dharma or doctrine, and the monkhood). One of the more bizarre but common merit-making activities involves **releasing caged birds**: worshippers buy tiny finches from vendors at wat compounds and, by liberating them from their cage, prove their Buddhist compassion towards all living things. The fact that the birds were free until netted earlier that morning doesn't seem to detract from the ritual. In riverside and seaside wats, fish or even baby turtles are released instead.

For an insightful introduction to the philosophy and practice of Thai Buddhism, see ⓦ thaibuddhism.net. A number of Thai temples welcome foreign students of Buddhism and meditation (see p.182).

The monkhood

It's the duty of Thailand's 200,000-strong **Sangha** (monkhood) to set an example to the Theravada Buddhist community by living a life as close to the Middle Way as possible and by preaching the Dharma to the people. The life of a monk (*bhikkhu*) is governed by 227 precepts that include celibacy and the rejection of all personal possessions except gifts.

Each day begins with an alms round in the neighbourhood so that the laity can donate food and thereby gain themselves merit, and then is chiefly spent in meditation, chanting, teaching and study. As the most respected members of any community, monks act as teachers, counsellors and arbiters in local disputes. They also perform rituals at cremations, weddings and other events, such as the launching of a new business or even the purchase of a new car. Many young boys from poor families find themselves almost obliged to become either a *dek wat* (temple boy) or a **novice monk** because that's the only way they can get accommodation, food and, crucially, an education. This is provided free in exchange for duties around the wat, and novices are required to adhere to ten rather than 227 Buddhist precepts.

Monkhood doesn't have to be for life: a man may leave the Sangha three times without stigma, and in fact every Thai male (including royalty) is expected to **enter the monkhood** for a short period, ideally between leaving school and marrying, as a rite of passage into adulthood. Thai government departments and some private companies grant their employees paid leave for their time as a monk, but the custom is in decline as young men increasingly have to consider the effect their absence may have on their career prospects. Instead, many men now enter the monkhood for a brief period after the death of a parent, to make merit both for the deceased and for the rest of the family. The most popular time for temporary ordination is the three-month Buddhist retreat period – **Pansa**, sometimes referred to as "Buddhist Lent" – which begins in July and lasts for the duration of the rainy season. The monks' confinement is said to originate from the earliest years of Buddhist history, when farmers complained that perambulating monks were squashing their sprouting rice crops.

Monks in contemporary society

In recent years, some monks have become influential activists in social and environmental issues, and some upcountry temples have established themselves as successful drug rehabilitation centres. Other monks have acquired such a reputation for giving wise counsel and bringing good fortune and prosperity to their followers that they have become national gurus; their temples now generate great wealth through the production of specially blessed amulets (see p.72) and photographs.

Though the increasing involvement of many monks in the secular world has not met with unanimous approval, far more disappointing to the laity are those monks who **flout the precepts** of the Sangha by succumbing to the temptations of a consumer society, flaunting Raybans, Rolexes and Mercedes (in some cases actually bought with temple funds), chain-smoking and flirting, even making pocket money from predicting lottery results and practising faith-healing. With so much national pride and integrity riding on the sanctity of the Sangha, any whiff of a deeper scandal is bound to strike deep into the national psyche. Cases of monks involved in drug-dealing, gun-running, even rape and murder have prompted a stream of editorials on the state of the Sangha and the collapse of spiritual values at the heart of Thai society. The inclusivity of the monkhood – which is open to just about any male who wants to join – has been highlighted as a particularly vulnerable aspect, not least because donning saffron robes has always been an accepted way for criminals, reformed or otherwise, to repent of their past deeds.

Interestingly, back in the late 1980s, the influential monk Phra Bodhirak (Photirak) was defrocked after criticizing what he saw as a tide of decadence infecting Thai Buddhism. He now preaches his ascetic code of anti-materialism through his breakaway **Santi Asoke** sect, famous across the country for its cheap vegetarian restaurants, its philosophy of self-sufficiency and for the simple blue farmers' shirts worn by many of its followers.

Women and the monkhood

Although the Theravada Buddhist hierarchy in some countries permits the ordination of **female monks**, or *bhikkhuni*, the Thai Sangha does not. Instead, Thai women are officially only allowed to become **nuns**, or *mae chii*, shaving their heads, donning white robes and keeping eight rather than 227 precepts. Their status is lower than that of the monks and they are chiefly occupied with temple upkeep rather than conducting religious ceremonies.

However, the progressives are becoming more vocal, and in 2002 a Thai woman became the first of several to break with the Buddhist authorities and get **ordained** as a novice *bhikkhuni* on Thai soil. Thailand's Sangha Council, however, still recognizes neither her ordination nor the temple, Watra Songdhammakalyani in Nakhon Pathom, where the ordination took place. The Watra (rather than Wat) is run by another Thai *bhikkuni*, Dhammananda Bhikkhuni, the author of several books in English about **women and Buddhism** and of an informative website, ⓦthaibhikkhunis.org.

Hindu deities and animist spirits

The complicated history of the area now known as Thailand has made Thai Buddhism a confusingly syncretic faith, as you'll realize when you enter a Buddhist temple compound to be confronted by a statue of a Hindu deity. While regular Buddhist merit-making insures a Thai for the next life, there are certain **Hindu gods and animist spirits** that many Thais – sophisticated city dwellers and illiterate farmers alike – also cultivate for help with more immediate problems; and as often as not it's a Buddhist monk who is called in to exorcise a malevolent spirit. Even the Buddhist King Bhumibol employs Brahmin priests and astrologers to determine auspicious days and officiate at certain royal ceremonies and, like his royal predecessors of the Chakri dynasty, he also associates himself with the Hindu god Vishnu by assuming the title Rama IX – Rama, hero of the Hindu epic the *Ramayana*, having been Vishnu's seventh manifestation on Earth.

If a Thai wants help in achieving a short-term goal, like passing an exam, becoming pregnant or winning the lottery, he or she will quite likely turn to the **Hindu pantheon**, visiting an enshrined statue of Brahma, Vishnu, Shiva or Ganesh, and making offerings of flowers, incense and maybe food. If the outcome is favourable, the devotee will probably come back to show thanks, bringing more offerings and maybe even hiring a dance troupe to perform a celebratory *lakhon chatri*. Built in honour of Brahma, Bangkok's Erawan Shrine is the most famous place of Hindu-inspired worship in the country.

Spirits and spirit houses

Whereas Hindu deities tend to be benevolent, **spirits** (or *phi*) are not nearly as reliable and need to be mollified more frequently. They come in hundreds of varieties, some more malign than others, and inhabit everything from trees, rivers and caves to public buildings and private homes – even taking over people if they feel like it.

So that these *phi* don't pester human inhabitants, each building has a special **spirit house** (*saan phra phum*) in its vicinity, as a dwelling for spirits ousted by the building's construction. Usually raised on a short column to set it at or above eye level, the spirit house must occupy an auspicious location – not, for example, in the shadow of the main building. It's generally about the size of a dolls' house and designed to look like a wat or a traditional Thai house, but its ornamentation is supposed to reflect the status of the humans' building, so if that building is enlarged or refurbished, the spirit house should be improved accordingly. And as architects become increasingly bold in their designs, so modernist spirit houses are also beginning to appear in Bangkok, where an eye-catching new skyscraper might be graced by a spirit house of glass or polished concrete. **Figurines** representing the relevant guardian spirit and his aides are sometimes put inside, and daily offerings of incense, lighted candles and garlands of jasmine are placed alongside them to keep the *phi* happy – a disgruntled spirit is a dangerous spirit, liable to cause sickness, accidents and even death.

Art and architecture

Aside from pockets of Hindu-inspired statuary and architecture, the vast majority of Thailand's cultural monuments take their inspiration from Theravada Buddhism, and so it is temples and religious images that constitute Bangkok's main sights. Artists, sculptors and architects have tended to see their work as a way of making spiritual merit rather than as a means of self-expression or self-promotion, so pre-twentieth-century Thai art history is all about evolving styles rather than individual artists. This section is designed to help make sense of the most common aspects of Thai art and architecture at their various stages of development. Though Bangkok's temples nearly all date from the eighteenth century or later, many of them display features that originate from a much earlier time. The National Museum (see p.60) is a good place to see some of Thailand's more ancient Hindu and Buddhist statues, and a visit to the fourteenth-century ruins at Ayutthaya (see p.115), less than two hours from Bangkok, is also recommended.

The wat

The **wat** or Buddhist temple complex has a great range of uses: as home to a monastic community, a place of public worship, a shrine for holy images and a shaded meeting place for townspeople and villagers. Wat architecture has evolved in ways as various as its functions, but there remain several essential components which have stayed constant for some fifteen centuries.

The most important wat building is the **bot** (sometimes known as the *ubosot*), a term most accurately translated as the "ordination hall". It usually stands at the heart of the compound and is the preserve of the monks: lay persons are rarely allowed inside and it's generally kept locked when not in use. There's only one bot in any wat complex, and often the only way to distinguish it from other temple buildings is by the eight **sema** or boundary stones which always surround it (sometimes in simpler temples, there are only four stones, at the corners of the building).

Often almost identical to the bot, the **viharn** or assembly hall is for the lay congregation, and as a tourist this is the building you're most likely to enter, since it usually contains the wat's principal **Buddha image**, and sometimes two or three minor images as well. Large wats may have several viharns, while strict meditation wats, which don't deal with the laity, may not have one at all.

Thirdly, there's the **chedi** or stupa, a tower which was originally conceived as a monument to enshrine relics of the Buddha, but which has since become a place to contain the ashes of royalty – and anyone else who can afford it.

Buddhist iconography

In the early days of Buddhism, image-making was considered inadequate to convey the faith's abstract philosophies, so the only approved iconography comprised doctrinal **symbols** such as the Dharmachakra (Wheel of Law, also known as Wheel of Doctrine or Wheel of Life). Gradually these symbols were displaced by **images of the Buddha**, construed chiefly as physical embodiments of the Buddha's teachings rather than as portraits of the man.

Of the four postures in which the Buddha is always depicted – sitting, standing, walking and reclining – the seated Buddha, which represents him in meditation, is the most common in Thailand. A popular variation shows the Buddha **seated** on a coiled serpent, protected by the serpent's hood – a reference to the story about the Buddha meditating during the rainy season, when a serpent offered to raise him off the wet ground and shelter him from the storms. The **reclining** pose symbolizes the Buddha entering Nirvana at his death, while the **standing** and **walking** images both represent his descent from Tavatimsa heaven.

Hindu iconography

Hindu images tend to be a lot livelier than Buddhist ones, partly because there is a panoply of gods to choose from, and partly because these gods have mischievous personalities and reappear in all sorts of bizarre incarnations.

The Hindu Trinity

Vishnu has always been a favourite god: in his role of "Preserver" he embodies the status quo, representing both stability and the notion of altruistic love. He is most often depicted as the deity, but has ten manifestations in all, of which **Rama** (number seven) is by far the most popular in Thailand. The epitome of ideal manhood, Rama is the superhero of the epic story the *Ramayana* – in Thai, the *Ramakien* (see box, p.55) – and appears in storytelling reliefs and murals in every Hindu temple in Thailand; in painted portraits you can usually recognize him by his green face. Manifestation number eight is **Krishna**, more widely known than Rama in the West, but slightly less common in Thailand. Krishna is usually characterized as a flirtatious, flute-playing, blue-skinned cowherd, but he is also a crucial moral figure in the lengthy moral epic poem, the *Mahabharata*. Confusingly, Vishnu's ninth avatar is the **Buddha** – a manifestation adopted many centuries ago to minimize defection to the Buddhist faith. When represented as **the deity**, Vishnu is generally shown sporting a crown and four arms, his hands holding a conch shell (whose music wards off demons), a discus (used as a weapon), a club (symbolizing the power of nature and time) and a lotus (symbol of joyful flowering and renewal). He is often depicted astride a **garuda**, a half-man, half-bird. Even without Vishnu on its back, the garuda is a very important beast: a symbol of strength, it's often shown "supporting" temple buildings.

Statues and representations of **Brahma** (the Creator) are rare. He too has four arms, but holds no objects; he has four faces (sometimes painted red), is generally borne by a goose-like creature called a *hamsa*, and is associated with the direction north.

Shiva (the Destroyer) is the most volatile member of the pantheon. He stands for extreme behaviour, for beginnings and endings, as enacted in his frenzied Dance of Destruction, and for fertility, and is a symbol of great energy and power. His godlike form typically has four, eight or ten arms, sometimes holding a trident (representing creation, protection and destruction) and a drum (to beat the rhythm of creation). In his most famous role, as **Nataraja**, or Lord of the Dance, he is usually shown in a stylized standing position with legs bent into a balletic position and the full complement of arms outstretched above his head. Three stripes on a figure's forehead also indicate Shiva, or one of his followers. In abstract form, he is represented by a **lingam** (once found at the heart of every Khmer temple in the northeast). Primarily a symbol of energy and godly power, the lingam also embodies fertility, particularly when set upright in a vulva-shaped vessel known as a **yoni**. The yoni doubles as a receptacle for the holy water that worshippers pour over the lingam.

Lesser gods

Close associates of Shiva include **Parvati**, his wife, and **Ganesh**, his elephant-headed son. As the god of knowledge and overcomer of obstacles (in the path of learning), Ganesh is used as the symbol of the Fine Arts Department, so his image features on all entrance tickets to national museums and historical parks.

Lesser mythological figures include the **yaksha** giants who ward off evil spirits (like the enormous freestanding ones guarding Bangkok's Wat Phra Kaeo); the graceful half-woman, half bird **kinnari**; and the ubiquitous **naga**, or serpent king of the underworld, often depicted with seven heads.

The schools

In the 1920s art historians and academics began compiling a classification system for Thai art and architecture that was modelled along the lines of the country's historical periods. The following brief overview starts in the sixth century, when Buddhism began to take a hold on the country.

Dvaravati (sixth to eleventh centuries)

Centred on the towns of Nakhon Pathom, U Thong, Lopburi and Haripunjaya (modern-day Lamphun), the Dvaravati state was populated by Theravada Buddhists who were strongly influenced by Indian culture.

In an effort to combat the defects inherent in the poor-quality limestone at their disposal, Dvaravati-era **sculptors** made their Buddhas quite stocky, cleverly dressing the figures in a sheet-like drape that dropped down to ankle level from each raised wrist, forming a U-shaped hemline – a style which they used when casting in bronze as well. Nonetheless many **statues** have cracked, leaving them headless or limbless. Where the faces have survived, Dvaravati statues display some of the most naturalistic features ever produced in Thailand, distinguished by their thick lips, flattened noses and wide cheekbones.

Srivijaya (eighth to thirteenth centuries)

While Dvaravati's Theravada Buddhists were influencing the central plains, southern Thailand was paying allegiance to the Mahayana Buddhists of the **Srivijayan** empire. Mahayanists believe that those who have achieved enlightenment should postpone their entry into Nirvana in order to help others along the way. These stay-behinds, revered like saints both during and after life, are called **bodhisattva**, and statues of them were the mainstay of Srivijayan art.

The finest Srivijayan *bodhisattva* statues were cast in bronze and show such grace and sinuosity that they rank among the finest sculptures ever produced in the country. Many are lavishly adorned and some were even bedecked in real jewels when first made. By far the most popular *bodhisattva* subject was *Avalokitesvara*, worshipped as compassion incarnate and generally shown with four or more arms and clad in an animal skin. Bangkok's National Museum holds a beautiful example.

Khmer and Lopburi (tenth to fourteenth centuries)

By the end of the ninth century the **Khmers** of Cambodia were starting to expand from their capital at Angkor into the Dvaravati states, bringing with them the Hindu faith and the cult of the god-king (*devaraja*). As lasting testaments to the sacred power of their kings, the Khmers built hundreds of imposing stone sanctuaries across their newly acquired territory.

Each magnificent castle-temple – known in Khmer as a **prasat** – was constructed primarily as a shrine for a shiva lingam, the phallic representation of the god Shiva. Almost every surface of the sanctuary was adorned with intricate **carvings**, usually gouged from sandstone, depicting Hindu deities – notably Vishnu Reclining on the Milky Sea of Eternity in the National Museum (see p.60) – and stories, especially episodes from the *Ramayana* (see p.55).

During the Khmer period the former Theravada Buddhist principality of Lopburi produced a distinctive style of Buddha statue. Broad-faced and muscular, the classic **Lopburi** Buddha wears a diadem or ornamental headband – a nod to the Khmers' ideological fusion of earthly and heavenly power – and the *ushnisha* (the sign of enlightenment) becomes distinctly conical rather than a mere bump on the head.

Sukhothai (thirteenth to fifteenth centuries)

Two Thai generals established the first real Thai kingdom in **Sukhothai** (some 400km north of modern-day Bangkok, in the northern plains) in 1238, and over the next two hundred years the artists of this realm produced some of Thailand's most refined art. Sukhothai's artistic reputation rests above all on its **sculpture**. More sinuous even than the Srivijayan images, Sukhothai Buddhas tend towards elegant androgyny, with slim oval faces and slender curvaceous bodies usually clad in a plain, skintight robe that fastens with a tassle close to the navel. Fine examples include the Phra Buddha Chinnarat image at Bangkok's Wat Benjamabophit, and the enormous Phra Sri Sakyamuni in Bangkok's Wat Suthat. Sukhothai sculptors were the first to represent the walking Buddha, a supremely graceful figure with his right leg poised to move forwards.

Sukhothai-era architects also devised a new type of chedi, as elegant in its way as the images their sculptor colleagues were producing. This was the **lotus-bud chedi**, a slender tower topped with a tapered finial that was to become a hallmark of the Sukhothai era.

Ancient Sukhothai is also renowned for the skill of its potters, who produced a **ceramic ware** known as Sawankhalok, after the name of one of the nearby kiln towns. It is distinguished by its grey-green celadon glazes and by the fish and chrysanthemum motifs used to decorate bowls and plates.

Ayutthaya (fourteenth to eighteenth centuries)

From 1351 Thailand's central plains came under the thrall of a new power centred on **Ayutthaya**, and over the next four centuries, the Ayutthayan rulers commissioned some four hundred grand wats as symbols of their wealth and power. Though essentially Theravada Buddhists, the kings also adopted some Hindu and Brahmin beliefs from the Khmers – most significantly the concept of *devaraja* or god-kingship, whereby the monarch became a mediator between the people and the Hindu gods.

Retaining the concentric layout of the typical Khmer **temple complex**, Ayutthayan builders refined and elongated the prang into a **corncob-shaped tower**, rounding it off at the top and introducing vertical incisions around its circumference. The most famous example is Bangkok's Wat Arun, which, though built during the subsequent Ratanakosin period, is a classic Ayutthayan structure.

Ayutthaya's architects also adapted the Sri Lankan **chedi** so favoured by their Sukhothai predecessors, stretching the bell-shaped base and tapering it into a very graceful conical spire, as at Wat Phra Sri Sanphet in Ayutthaya. The **viharns** of this era are characterized by walls pierced by slit-like windows, designed to foster a mysterious atmosphere by limiting the amount of light inside the building; Wat Yai Suwannaram in Phetchaburi (see p.134) has a particularly fine example.

From Sukhothai's Buddha **sculptures** the Ayutthayans copied the soft oval face, adding an earthlier demeanour to the features and imbuing them with a hauteur in tune with the *devaraja* ideology. Like the Lopburi images, early Ayutthayan statues wear crowns to associate kingship with Buddhahood; as the court became ever more lavish, so these figures became increasingly adorned, until – as in the monumental bronze at Wat Na Phra Mane – they appeared in earrings, armlets, anklets, bandoliers and coronets. The artists justified these luscious portraits of the Buddha – who was, after all, supposed to have given up worldly possessions – by pointing to an episode when the Buddha transformed himself into a well-dressed nobleman to gain the ear of an emperor, whereupon he scolded the man into entering the monkhood.

Ratanakosin (eighteenth century to the 1930s)

When **Bangkok** emerged as Ayutthaya's successor in 1782, the new capital's founder was determined to revive the old city's grandeur, and the **Ratanakosin** (or Bangkok) period began by aping what the Ayutthayans had done. Since then neither wat architecture nor religious sculpture has evolved much further.

The first **Ratanakosin building** was the bot of Bangkok's Wat Phra Kaeo, built to enshrine the Emerald Buddha. Designed to a typical Ayutthayan plan, it's coated in glittering mirrors and gold leaf, with roofs ranged in multiple tiers and tiled in green and orange. To this day, most newly built bots and viharns follow a more economical version of this paradigm, whitewashing the outside walls but decorating the pediment in gilded ornaments and mosaics of coloured glass. The result is that modern wats are often almost indistinguishable from each other, though Bangkok does have a few exceptions, including Wat Benjamabophit, which uses marble cladding for its walls and incorporates Victorian-style stained-glass windows, and Wat Rajapobhit, which is covered all over in Chinese ceramics. The most dramatic chedi of the Ratanakosin era – one of the tallest in the world – was constructed in the mid-nineteenth century in Nakhon Pathom (see p.125), to the original Sri Lankan style.

Early Ratanakosin sculptors produced adorned **Buddha images** very much in the Ayutthayan vein, sometimes adding real jewels to the figures; more modern images are notable for their ugliness rather than for any radical departure from type. The obsession with size, first apparent in the Sukhothai period, has plumbed new depths, with graceless concrete statues up to 60m high becoming the norm (as in Bangkok's Wat Indraviharn), a monumentalism made worse by the routine application of browns and dull yellows. Most small images are cast from or patterned on older models, mostly Sukhothai or Ayutthayan in origin.

Painting has fared much better, with the *Ramayana* murals in Bangkok's Wat Phra Kaeo (see p.54) a shining example of how Ayutthayan techniques and traditional subject matters could be adapted into something fantastic, imaginative and beautiful.

Contemporary

Following the democratization of Thailand in the 1930s, artists increasingly became recognized as individuals and took to signing their work for the first time. In 1933 the first school of fine art (now Bangkok's Silpakorn University) was established under the Italian sculptor **Silpa Bhirasri**, designer of the capital's Democracy Monument and, as the new generation experimented with secular themes and styles adapted from the West, Thai art began to look a lot more **"modern"**. As for subject matter, the leading artistic preoccupation of the past eighty years has been Thailand's spiritual heritage and its role in contemporary society. Since 1985, a number of Thailand's more established contemporary artists have earned the title **National Artist**, an honour that's bestowed annually on notable artists working in all disciplines, including fine art, performing arts, film and literature.

ART GALLERIES AND EXHIBITIONS

Bangkok has a near-monopoly on Thailand's **art galleries**. While the permanent collections at the capital's **National Gallery** (see p.63) are disappointing, regular exhibitions of more challenging contemporary work appear at the huge, ambitious **Bangkok Art and Cultural Centre** (see p.97); the main art school, **Silpakorn University Art Centre** (see p.59); the **Queen's Gallery** (see p.73); and at smaller gallery spaces around the city.

The excellent monthly **Bangkok Art Map** (Ⓦfacebook.com/bangkokartmap), an annotated map of the capital's galleries, carries exhibition listings and is available free from galleries. For a preview of works by Thailand's best modern artists, visit the virtual Rama IX Art Museum at Ⓦrama9art.org.

The artists

One of the first modern artists to adapt traditional styles and themes was **Angkarn Kalayanapongsa** (1926–2012), an early recipient of the title National Artist. He was employed as a temple muralist and many of his paintings, some of which are on show in Bangkok's National Gallery, reflect this experience, typically featuring casts of two-dimensional Ayutthayan-style figures and flying *thep* in a surreal setting laced with Buddhist symbols and nods to contemporary culture.

Taking this fusion a step further, one-time cinema billboard artist **Chalermchai Kositpipat** (b. 1955) specializes in temple murals with a modern, controversial, twist. Outside Thailand his most famous work enlivens the interior walls of London's Wat Buddhapadipa with strong colours and startling imagery. At home his latest project is the unconventional and highly ornate all-white Wat Rong Khun in his native Chiang Rai province.

Aiming for the more secular environments of the gallery and the private home, National Artist **Pichai Nirand** (b. 1936) rejects the traditional mural style and makes more selective choices of Buddhist imagery, appropriating religious objects and icons and reinterpreting their significance. He's particularly well known for his fine-detail canvases of Buddha footprints, many of which can be seen in Bangkok galleries and public spaces.

Pratuang Emjaroen (b. 1935) is famous for his social commentary, as epitomized by his huge and powerful canvas *Dharma and Adharma; The Days of Disaster*, which he painted in response to the vicious clashes between the military and students in 1973. The 5m x 2m picture depicts severed limbs, screaming faces and bloody gun barrels amid shadowy images of the Buddha's face, a spiked Dharmachakra and other religious symbols. Many of Pratuang's subsequent works have addressed the issue of social injustice, using his trademark strong shafts of light and bold colour in a mix of Buddhist iconography and abstract imagery.

Prolific traditionalist **Chakrabhand Posayakrit** (b. 1943) is also inspired by Thailand's Buddhist culture; he is famously proud of his country's cultural heritage, which infuses much of his work and has led to him being honoured as a National Artist. He is best known for his series of 33 *Life of the Buddha* paintings, and for his portraits, including many of members of the Thai royal family.

More controversial, and more of a household name, **Thawan Duchanee** (1939–2014) tended to examine the spiritual tensions of modern life. His surreal juxtaposition of religious icons with fantastical Bosch-like characters and explicitly sexual images prompted a group of outraged students to slash ten of his early paintings in 1971 – an unprecedented reaction to a work of Thai art. Nevertheless, Thawan continued to produce allegorical investigations into the individual's struggles against the obstacles that dog the Middle Way, prominent among them lust and violence, but after the 1980s his street cred waned as his saleability mushroomed. Critics questioned his integrity at accepting commissions from corporate clients, and his neo-conservative image cannot have been enhanced when he was honoured as a National Artist in 2001.

Complacency is not a criticism that could be levelled at **Vasan Sitthiket** (b. 1957), Thailand's most outspoken and iconoclastic artist, whose uncompromising pictures are shown at – and still occasionally banned from – large and small galleries around the capital. A persistent crusader against the hypocrisies of establishment figures such as monks, politicians, CEOs and military leaders, Vasan's is one of the loudest and most aggressive political voices on the contemporary art scene, expressed on canvas, in multimedia works and in performance art. His significance is well established and he was one of the seven artists to represent Thailand at the 2003 Venice Biennale, where Thailand had its own pavilion for the first time.

Equally confrontational is fellow Biennale exhibitor, the photographer, performance artist and social activist **Manit Sriwanichpoom** (b. 1961). Manit is best known for his "Pink Man" series of photographs in which he places a Thai man (his collaborator Sompong Thawee), dressed in a flashy pink suit and pushing a pink shopping trolley, into different scenes and situations in Thailand and elsewhere. The Pink Man represents thoughtless, dangerous consumerism and his backdrop might be an impoverished hill-tribe village (*Pink Man on Tour*; 1998), or black-and-white shots from the political violence of 1973, 1976 and 1992 (*Horror in Pink*; 2001).

Women artists tend to be less high profile in Thailand, but in 2007 **Pinaree Sanpitak** (b. 1961) became the first female recipient of the annual Silpathorn Awards for established artists, sharing the honour that year with, among others, notorious bad boy Vasan Sitthiket. Pinaree is known for her interest in gender issues and for her recurrent use of a female iconography in the form of vessels and mounds, often exploring the overlap with Buddhist stupa imagery. She works mainly in multimedia; her "Vessels and Mounds" show of 2001, for example, featured installations of huge, breast-shaped floor cushions, candles and bowls.

Among the younger faces on the Thai art scene, **Thaweesak Srithongdee** (b. 1970) blends surrealism and pop culture with the erotic and the figurative, to cartoon-like effect. He is preoccupied with popular culture, as is **Jirapat Tatsanasomboon** (b. 1971), whose work plays around with superheroes and cultural icons from East and West, pitting the *Ramayana*'s monkey king, Hanuman, against Spiderman in *Hanuman vs Spiderman*, and fusing mythologies in *The Transformation of Sita (after Botticelli)*.

Books

We have included publishers' details for books that may be hard to find outside Thailand, though some of them can be ordered online through ⓦ www.dcothai.com, which sells ebooks on ⓦ ebooks.dco.co.th. Other titles should be available worldwide. Titles marked ★ are particularly recommended. There's a good selection of Thai novels and short stories in translation, available to buy as ebooks, on ⓦ thaifiction.com.

TRAVEL

James O'Reilly and Larry Habegger (eds) *Travelers' Tales: Thailand*. Absorbing anthology of contemporary writings about Thailand, by Thailand experts, social commentators, travel writers and first-time visitors.

Steve Van Beek *Slithering South* (Wind and Water, Hong Kong). An expat writer tells how he single-handedly paddled his wooden boat down the entire 1100km course of the Chao Phraya River, and reveals a side of Thailand that's rarely written about in English.

William Warren *Bangkok*. An engaging portrait of the unwieldy capital, weaving together anecdotes and character sketches from Bangkok's past and present.

CULTURE AND SOCIETY

Michael Carrithers *The Buddha: A Very Short Introduction*. Accessible account of the life of the Buddha, and the development and significance of his thought.

★ **Philip Cornwel-Smith and John Goss** *Very Thai*. Why do Thais decant their soft drinks into plastic bags, and how does one sniff-kiss? Answers and insights aplenty in this intriguingly observant, fully illustrated guide to contemporary Thai culture. Look out also for Cornwel-Smith's *Very Bangkok*.

James Eckardt *Bangkok People*. The collected articles of a renowned expat journalist, whose encounters with a varied cast of Bangkok inhabitants – from construction-site workers and street vendors to boxers and political candidates – add texture and context to the city.

Sandra Gregory with Michael Tierney *Forget You Had A Daughter: Doing Time in the "Bangkok Hilton" – Sandra Gregory's Story*. The frank and shocking account of a young British woman's term in Bangkok's notorious Lard Yao prison after being caught trying to smuggle 89 grams of heroin out of Thailand.

Father Joe Maier *Welcome To The Bangkok Slaughterhouse: The Battle for Human Dignity in Bangkok's Bleakest Slums* and *The Open Gate of Mercy*. Catholic priest Father Joe shares the stories of some of the Bangkok street kids and slum-dwellers that his charitable foundation has been supporting since 1973 (see p.41).

Trilok Chandra Majupuria *Erawan Shrine and Brahma Worship in Thailand* (Tecpress, Bangkok). The most concise introduction to the complexities of Thai religion, with a much wider scope than the title implies.

Cleo Odzer *Patpong Sisters*. An American anthropologist's funny and touching account of her life with the prostitutes and bar girls of Bangkok's notorious red-light district.

★ **Phra Peter Pannapadipo** *Little Angels: The Real-Life Stories of Twelve Thai Novice Monks*. A dozen young boys, many of them from desperate backgrounds, tell the often-poignant stories of why they became novice monks. For some, funding from the Students Education Trust (see p.41) has changed their lives. Another book, *Phra Farang: An English Monk in Thailand*, gives the reader a glimpse behind the scenes in a Thai monastery: the frank, funny and illuminating account of a UK-born former businessman's life as a Thai monk.

★ **Pasuk Phongpaichit and Sungsidh Piriyarangsan** *Corruption and Democracy in Thailand*. Fascinating academic study, revealing the nuts and bolts of corruption in Thailand and its links with all levels of political life, and suggesting a route to a stronger society. Their sequel, a study of Thailand's illegal economy, *Guns, Girls, Gambling, Ganja*, co-written with Nualnoi Treerat, makes equally eye-opening and depressing reading.

Denis Segaller *Thai Ways*. Fascinating collection of short pieces on Thai customs and traditions written by a long-term English resident of Bangkok.

Richard Totman *The Third Sex: Kathoey – Thailand's Ladyboys*. As several *kathoey* share their life stories with him, social scientist Totman examines their place in modern Thai society and explores the theory, supported by Buddhist philosophy, that *kathoey* are members of a third sex whose transgendered make-up is predetermined from birth.

Tom Vater and Aroon Thaewchatturat *Sacred Skin*. Fascinating, beautifully photographed exploration of Thailand's spirit tattoos, *sak yant*.

Daniel Ziv and Guy Sharett *Bangkok Inside Out*. This A–Z of Bangkok quirks and cultural substrates is full of slick photography and sparky observations but was deemed offensive by Thailand's Ministry of Culture and so some Thai bookshops won't stock it.

HISTORY

Anna Leonowens *The English Governess at the Siamese Court*. The mendacious memoirs of the nineteenth-century English governess that inspired the infamous Yul Brynner film *The King and I*; low on accuracy, high on inside-palace gossip.

Chang Noi *Jungle Book: Thailand's Politics, Moral Panic and Plunder 1996–2008* (Silkworm Books, Chiang Mai). A fascinating, often humorous, selection of columns about Thailand's political and social jungle, by "Little Elephant", an anonymous foreign resident, which first appeared in *The Nation* newspaper.

Michael Smithies *Old Bangkok*. Brief, anecdotal history of the capital's early development, emphasizing what remains to be seen of bygone Bangkok.

William Stevenson *The Revolutionary King*. Fascinating biography of the normally secretive King Bhumibol, written by a British journalist who was given unprecedented access to the monarch and his family. The overall approach is fairly uncritical, but lots of revealing insights emerge along the way.

William Warren *Jim Thompson: the Legendary American of Thailand*. The engrossing biography of the ex-intelligence agent, art collector and Thai silk magnate whose disappearance in Malaysia in 1967 has never been satisfactorily resolved.

Thongchai Winichakul *Siam Mapped*. Intriguing, seminal account of how Rama V, under pressure on his borders from Britain and France at the turn of the twentieth century, in effect colonized his own country, which was then a loose hierarchy of city-states.

★ **David K. Wyatt** *Thailand: A Short History*. An excellent treatment, scholarly but highly readable, with a good eye for witty, telling details. Good chapters on the story of the Thais before they reached what's now Thailand, and on more recent developments.

ART, ARCHITECTURE AND FILM

★ **Susan Conway** *Thai Textiles*. A fascinating, richly illustrated work which draws on sculptures and temple murals to trace the evolution of Thai weaving techniques and costume styles, and to examine the functional and ceremonial uses of textiles.

★ **Sumet Jumsai** *Naga: Cultural Origins in Siam and the West Pacific*. Wide-ranging discussion of water symbols in Thailand and other parts of Asia, offering a stimulating mix of art, architecture, mythology and cosmology.

Bastian Meiresonne (ed) *Thai Cinema* (ⓦ asiexpo.com). Anthology of twenty short essays on Thai cinema, published to accompany a film festival in France, including pieces on arthouse, shorts and censorship. In French and English.

Steven Pettifor *Flavours: Thai Contemporary Art*. Takes up the baton from Poshyananda (see below) to look at the newly invigorated art scene in Thailand from 1992 to 2004, with profiles of 23 leading lights, including painters, multimedia and performance artists.

★ **Apinan Poshyananda** *Modern Art In Thailand*. Excellent introduction which extends up to the early 1990s, with very readable discussions on dozens of individual artists, and lots of colour plates.

Dome Sukwong and Sawasdi Suwannapak *A Century of Thai Cinema*. Full-colour history of the Thai film industry and the promotional artwork (billboards, posters, magazines and cigarette cards) associated with it.

★ **Steve Van Beek** *The Arts of Thailand*. Lavishly produced and perfectly pitched introduction to the history of Thai architecture, sculpture and painting, with superb photographs by Luca Invernizzi Tettoni.

LITERATURE

M.L. Manich Jumsai *Thai Ramayana* (Chalermnit, Bangkok). Slightly stilted abridged prose translation of King Rama I's version of the epic Hindu narrative, full of gleeful descriptions of bizarre mythological characters and supernatural battles. Essential reading for a full appreciation of Thai painting, carving and classical dance.

★ **Chart Korbjitti** *The Judgement* (Howling Books). Sobering modern-day tragedy about a good-hearted Thai villager who is ostracized by his hypocritical neighbours. Contains lots of interesting details on village life and traditions and thought-provoking passages on the stifling conservatism of rural communities. Winner of the Southeast Asian Writers Award in 1982.

★ **Rattawut Lapcharoensap** *Sightseeing*. This outstanding debut collection of short stories by a young Thai-born author now living overseas highlights big, pertinent themes – cruelty, corruption, racism, pride – in its neighbourhood tales of randy teenagers, bullyboys, a child's friendship with a Cambodian refugee, and a young man who uses family influence to dodge the draft.

Nitaya Masavisut (ed) *The S.E.A. Write Anthology of Thai Short Stories and Poems* (Silkworm Books, Chiang Mai). Interesting medley of short stories and poems by Thai writers who have won Southeast Asian Writers' Awards. The collection provides a good introduction to the contemporary literary scene.

Kukrit Pramoj *Si Phaendin: Four Reigns* (Silkworm Books, Chiang Mai). A kind of historical romance spanning the four reigns of Ramas V to VIII (1892–1946). Written by former prime minister Kukrit Pramoj, the story has become a modern classic in Thailand, made into films, plays and TV dramas, with heroine Ploi as the archetypal feminine role model.

S.P. Somtow *Jasmine Nights*. An engaging and humorous rites-of-passage tale of an upper-class boy learning what it is to be Thai. Another of his works, *Dragon's Fin Soup and Other Modern Siamese Fables*, is an imaginative and entertaining collection of often supernatural short stories, focusing on the collision of East and West.

★**Khamsing Srinawk** *The Politician and Other Stories*. A collection of brilliantly satirical short stories, full of pithy moral observation and biting irony, which capture the vulnerability of peasant farmers in the north and northeast as they try to come to grips with the modern world. Written by an insider from a peasant family, who was educated at Chulalongkorn University, became a hero of the left, and joined the communist insurgents after the 1976 clampdown.

Klaus Wenk *Thai Literature – An Introduction* (White Lotus, Bangkok). Dry, but useful, short overview of the last seven hundred years by a noted German scholar, with plenty of extracts.

THAILAND IN FOREIGN LITERATURE

Dean Barrett *Kingdom of Make-Believe*. Despite the clichéd ingredients – the Patpong go-go bar scene, opium smuggling in the Golden Triangle, Vietnam veterans – this novel about a return to Thailand following a twenty-year absence turns out to be a rewardingly multi-dimensional take on the farang experience.

★**Mischa Berlinski** *Fieldwork*. Anthropology versus evangelism, a battle played out over an imaginary hill tribe in the hills of northern Thailand by a fascinating cast of characters. Wryly and vividly told by an eponymous narrator.

Botan *Letters from Thailand*. Probably the best introduction to the Chinese community in Bangkok, presented in the form of letters written over a twenty-year period by a Chinese emigrant to his mother. Branded as both anti-Chinese and anti-Thai, this 1969 prizewinning book is now mandatory reading in school social studies' classes.

Pierre Boulle *The Bridge over the River Kwai*. The World War II novel that inspired the David Lean movie and kicked off the Kanchanaburi tourist industry.

John Burdett *Bangkok 8*. Riveting Bangkok thriller that takes in Buddhism, plastic surgery, police corruption, the

yaa baa drugs trade, hookers, jade-smuggling and the spirit world.

Alex Garland *The Beach*. Gripping cult thriller (later made into a film) that uses a Thai setting to explore the way in which travellers' ceaseless quests for "undiscovered" utopias inevitably lead to them despoiling the idyll.

Michel Houellebecq *Platform*. Sex tourism in Thailand provides the nucleus of this brilliantly provocative (some would say offensive) novel, in which Houellebecq presents a ferocious critique of Western decadence and cultural colonialism, and of radical Islam too.

Christopher G. Moore *God of Darkness*. Thailand's best-selling expat novelist sets his most intriguing thriller during the economic crisis of 1997 and includes plenty of meat on endemic corruption and the desperate struggle for power within family and society.

Darin Strauss *Chang & Eng*. An intriguing imagined autobiography of the famous nineteenth-century Siamese twins (see box, p.84), from their impoverished Thai childhood via the freak shows of New York and London to married life in smalltown North Carolina. Unfortunately marred by lazy research and a confused grasp of Thai geography and culture.

FOOD AND COOKERY

Vatcharin Bhumichitr *The Taste of Thailand*. Another glossy introduction to this eminently photogenic country, this time through its food. The author runs a Thai restaurant in London and provides background colour as well as about 150 recipes adapted for Western kitchens.

★**David Thompson** *Thai Food and Thai Street Food*. Comprehensive, impeccably researched celebrations of the cuisine, with hundreds of recipes, by the owner of the first Thai restaurant ever to earn a Michelin star.

Language

Thai belongs to one of the oldest families of languages in the world, Austro-Thai, and is radically different from most of the other tongues of Southeast Asia. Being tonal, Thai is very difficult for Westerners to master, but by building up from a small core of set phrases, you should soon have enough to get by. Most Thais who deal with tourists speak some English, but once you stray off the beaten track you'll probably need at least a little Thai. Anywhere you go, you'll impress and get better treatment if you at least make an effort to speak a few words.

Distinct dialects are spoken in the north, the northeast and the south, which can increase the difficulty of comprehending what's said to you. **Thai script** is even more of a problem to Westerners, with 44 consonants and 32 vowels. However, street signs in touristed areas are nearly always written in Roman script as well as Thai, and in other circumstances you're better off asking than trying to unscramble the swirling mess of letters and accents. For more information on transliteration into Roman script, see the box in this book's introduction (see box, p.4).

Probably the best pocket dictionary is Paiboon Publishing's (ⓦpaiboonpublishing .com) *Thai-English, English-Thai Dictionary* (also available as a CD and as an app), which lists words in phonetic Thai as well as Thai script, and features very useful examples of the Thai alphabet in different fonts.

The best **teach-yourself course** is the expensive *Linguaphone Thai* (including eight CDs and an alphabet book), which also has a shorter, cheaper beginner-level *PDQ* version (with four CDs or available as a downloadable coursebook and audio files). *Thai for Beginners* by Benjawan Poomsan Becker (book with CDs or app; Paiboon Publishing) is a cheaper, more manageable textbook and is especially good for getting to grips with the Thai writing system. For a more traditional textbook, try Stuart Campbell and Chuan Shaweevongse's *The Fundamentals of the Thai Language*, which is comprehensive, though hard going. The **website** ⓦthai-language.com is an amazing free resource, featuring a searchable dictionary with over sixty thousand entries, complete with Thai script and audio clips, plus lessons and forums; you can also browse and buy Thai language books and learning materials. There are also plenty of **language classes** available in Thailand (see p.45).

Pronunciation

Mastering **tones** is probably the most difficult part of learning Thai. Five different tones are used – low, middle, high, falling, and rising – by which the meaning of a single syllable can be altered in five different ways. Thus, using four of the five tones, you can make a sentence from just one syllable: "mái mài mâi măi" meaning "New wood burns, doesn't it?" As well as the natural difficulty in becoming attuned to speaking and listening to these different tones, Western efforts are complicated by our habit of denoting the overall meaning of a sentence by modulating our tones – for example, turning a statement into a question through a shift of stress and tone. Listen to native Thai speakers and you'll soon begin to pick up the different approach to tone.

The pitch of each tone is gauged in relation to your vocal range when speaking, but they should all lie within a narrow band, separated by gaps just big enough to differentiate them. The **low tones** (syllables marked `` ` ``), **middle tones** (unmarked syllables), and **high tones** (syllables marked ´) should each be pronounced evenly and with no inflection. The **falling tone** (syllables marked ˆ) is spoken with an obvious drop in pitch, as if you were sharply emphasizing a word in English. The **rising tone** (marked ˇ) is pronounced as if you were asking an exaggerated question in English.

As well as the unfamiliar tones, you'll find that, despite the best efforts of the transliterators, there is no precise English equivalent to many **vowel and consonant sounds** in the Thai language. The lists below give a simplified idea of pronunciation.

VOWELS

a as in dad

aa has no precise equivalent, but is pronounced as it looks, with the vowel elongated

ae as in there

ai as in buy

ao as in now

aw as in awe

ay as in pay

e as in pen

eu as in sir, but heavily nasalized

i as in tip

ii as in feet

o as in knock

oe as in hurt, but more closed

oh as in toe

u as in loot

uu as in pool

CONSONANTS

r as in rip, but with the tongue flapped quickly against the palate – in everyday speech, it's often pronounced like "l"

kh as in keep

ph as in put

th as in time

k is unaspirated and unvoiced, and closer to "g"

p is also unaspirated and unvoiced, and closer to "b"

t is also unaspirated and unvoiced, and closer to "d"

GENERAL WORDS AND PHRASES

GREETINGS AND BASIC PHRASES

When you speak to a stranger in Thailand, you should generally end your sentence in *khráp* if you're a man, *khâ* if you're a woman – these untranslatable politening syllables will gain goodwill, and are nearly always used after *sawàt dii* (hello/goodbye) and *khàwp khun* (thank you). *Khráp* and *khâ* are also often used to answer "yes" to a question, though the most common way is to repeat the verb of the question (precede it with *mâi* for "no"). *Châi* (yes) and *mâi châi* (no) are less frequently used than their English equivalents.

Hello	sawàt dii
Where are you going?	pai nǎi? (not always meant literally, but used as a general greeting)
I'm out having fun/ I'm travelling	pai thîaw (answer to pai nǎi, almost indefinable pleasantry)
Goodbye	sawàt dii/la kàwn
Good luck/cheers	chôhk dii
Excuse me	khǎw thâwt
Thank you	khàwp khun
It's nothing/ it doesn't matter	mâi pen rai
How are you?	sabai dii reǔ?
I'm fine	sabai dii
What's your name?	khun chêu arai?
My name is...	phǒm (men)/diichǎn (women) chêu...

I come from...	phǒm/diichǎn maa jàak...
I don't understand	mâi khâo jai
Do you speak English?	khun phûut phasǎa angkrìt dâi mǎi?
Do you have...?	mii...mǎi?
Is...possible?	...dâi mǎi?
Can you help me?	chûay phǒm/ diichǎn dâi mǎi?
(I) want...	ao...
(I) would like to...	yàak jà...
(I) like...	châwp...
What is this called in Thai?	nîi phasǎa thai rîak wâa arai?

GETTING AROUND

Where is the...?	...yùu thîi nǎi?
How far?	klai thâo rai?
I would like to go to...	yàak jà pai...
Where have you been?	pai nǎi maa?
Where is this bus going?	rót nîi pai nǎi?
When will the bus leave?	rót jà àwk mêua rai?
What time does the bus arrive in...?	rót theǔng...kìi mohng?
Stop here	jàwt thîi nîi
here	thîi nîi
there/over there	thîi nâan/thîi nôhn
right	khwǎa

left	sái
straight	trong
north	neŭa
south	tâi
east	tawan àwk
west	tawan tòk
near/far	klâi/klai
street	thanŏn
train station	sathàanii rót fai
bus station	sathàanii rót mae
airport	sanăam bin
ticket	tŭa
hotel	rohng raem
post office	praisanii
restaurant	raan ahăan
shop	raan
market	talàat
hospital	rohng pha-yaabaan
motorbike	rót mohtoesai
taxi	rót táksîi
boat	reua
bicycle	jàkràyaan

ACCOMMODATION AND SHOPPING

How much is…?	…thâo rai/kìi bàat?
I don't want a plastic bag, thanks	mâi ao thŭng khráp/khâ
How much is a room here per night?	hâwng thîi nîi kheun lá thâo rai?
Do you have a cheaper room?	mii hâwng thùuk kwàa măi?
Can I/we look at the room?	duu hâwng dâi măi?
I/We'll stay two nights	jà yùu săwng kheun
Can you reduce the price?	lót raakhaa dâi măi?
Can I store my bag here?	fàak krapăo wái thîi nîi dâi măi?
cheap/expensive	thùuk/phaeng
air-con room	hăwng ae
ordinary room	hăwng thammadaa
telephone	thohrásàp
laundry	sák phâa
blanket	phâa hòm
fan	phát lom

GENERAL ADJECTIVES

alone	khon diaw
another	ìik…nèung
bad	mâi dii
big	yài
clean	sa-àat
closed	pìt
cold (object)	yen
cold (person or weather)	năo

delicious	aròi
difficult	yâak
dirty	sokaprok
easy	ngâi
fun	sanùk
hot (temperature)	ráwn
hot (spicy)	phèt
hungry	hiŭ khâo
ill	mâi sabai
open	pòet
pretty	sŭay
small	lek
thirsty	hiŭ nám
tired	nèu-ay
very	mâak

GENERAL NOUNS

Nouns have no plurals or genders, and don't require an article.

bathroom/toilet	hăwng nám
boyfriend or girlfriend	faen
food	ahăan
foreigner	fàràng
friend	phêuan
money	ngoen
water/liquid	nám

GENERAL VERBS

Thai verbs do not conjugate at all, and also often double up as nouns and adjectives, which means that foreigners' most unidiomatic attempts to construct sentences are often readily understood.

come	maa
do	tham
eat	kin/thaan khâo
give	hâi
go	pai
sit	nâng
sleep	nawn làp
walk	doen pai

NUMBERS

zero	sŭun
one	nèung
two	săwng
three	săam
four	sìi
five	hâa
six	hòk
seven	jèt
eight	pàet
nine	kâo
ten	sìp
eleven	sìp èt

twelve, thirteen…	sìp săwng, sìp săam…	midnight	thîang kheun
twenty	yîi sìp/yiip	What time is it?	kìi mohng láew?
twenty-one	yîi sìp èt	How many hours?	kìi chûa mohng?
twenty-two,	yîi sìp săwng,	How long?	naan thâo rai?
twenty-three…	yîi sìp săam…	minute	naathii
thirty, forty, etc	săam sìp, sìi sìp…	hour	chûa mohng
one hundred,	nèung rói, săwng rói…	day	wan
two hundred…		week	aathít
one thousand	nèung phan	month	deuan
ten thousand	nèung mèun	year	pii
one hundred thousand	nèung săen	today	wan níi
one million	nèung lăan	tomorrow	phrûng níi
		yesterday	mêua wan níi

TIME

The most common system for telling the time, as outlined below, is actually a confusing mix of several different systems. The State Railway and government officials use the 24-hour clock (9am is *kâo naalikaa*, 10am *sìp naalikaa*, and so on), which is always worth trying if you get stuck.

1–5am	tii nèung–tii hâa
6–11am	hòk mohng cháo–sìp èt mohng cháo
noon	thîang
1pm	bài mohng
2–4pm	bài săwng mohng– bài sìi mohng
5–6pm	hâa mohng yen– hòk mohng yen
7–11pm	nèung thûm–hâa thûm

now	diăw níi
next week	aathít nâa
last week	aathít kàwn
morning	cháo
afternoon	bài
evening	yen
night	kheun

DAYS

Monday	wan jan
Tuesday	wan angkhaan
Wednesday	wan phút
Thursday	wan pháréuhàt
Friday	wan sùk
Saturday	wan săo
Sunday	wan aathít

FOOD AND DRINK

BASIC INGREDIENTS

kài	chicken	man faràng thâwt	chips
mŭu	pork	taeng kwaa	cucumber
néua	beef, meat	phrík yùak	green pepper
pèt	duck	krathiam	garlic
ahăan thalay	seafood	hèt	mushroom
plaa	fish	tùa	peas, beans or lentils
plaa dùk	catfish	tôn hŏrm	spring onions
plaa mèuk	squid		
kûng	prawn, shrimp	**NOODLES**	
hŏy	shellfish	ba mìi	egg noodles
hŏy nang rom	oyster	kwáy tiăw (sên yaì/ sên lék)	white rice noodles (wide/thin)
puu	crab		
khài	egg	khanŏm jiin nám yaa	noodles topped with fish curry
phàk	vegetables		
		kwáy tiăw/ba mìi haêng	rice noodle/egg noodles fried with egg, small pieces of meat and a few vegetables

VEGETABLES

makĕua	aubergine
makĕua thêt	tomato
nàw mái	bamboo shoots
tùa ngâwk	bean sprouts
phrík	chilli
man faràng	potato

kwáy tiăw/ba mìi nám (mŭu)	rice noodle/egg noodle soup, made with chicken broth (and pork balls)

kwáy tiăw/ba mìi	rice noodles/egg noodles
rât nâ (mǔu)	fried in gravy-like sauce with vegetables (and pork slices)
mìi kràwp	crisp fried egg noodles with small pieces of meat and a few vegetables
phàt thai	thin noodles fried with egg, bean sprouts and tofu, topped with ground peanuts
phàt siyú	wide or thin noodles fried with soy sauce, egg and meat

RICE

khâo	rice
khâo man kài	slices of chicken served over marinated rice
khâo mǔu daeng	red pork with rice
khâo nâ kài/pèt	chicken/duck served with sauce over rice
khâo niăw	sticky rice
khâo phàt	fried rice
khâo kaeng	curry over rice
khâo tôm	rice soup (usually for breakfast)

CURRIES AND SOUPS

kaeng phèt	hot, red curry
kaeng phánaeng	thick, savoury curry
kaeng khîaw wan	green curry
kaeng mátsàman	rich Muslim-style curry, usually with beef and potatoes
kaeng karìi	mild, Indian-style curry
hàw mòk thalay	seafood curry soufflé
kaeng liang	peppery vegetable soup
kaeng sôm	tamarind soup
tôm khà kài	chicken, coconut and galangal soup
tôm yam kûng	hot and sour prawn soup
kaeng jèut	mild soup with vegetables and usually pork

SALADS

lâap	spicy ground meat salad
nám tòk	grilled beef or pork salad
sôm tam	spicy papaya salad
yam hua plee	banana flower salad
yam néua	grilled beef salad
yam plaa mèuk	squid salad
yam sôm oh	pomelo salad
yam plaa dùk foo	crispy fried catfish salad
yam thùa phuu	wing-bean salad
yam wun sen	noodle and pork salad

OTHER DISHES

hâwy thâwt	omelette stuffed with mussels
kài phàt bai kraprao	chicken fried with holy basil leaves
kài phàt nàw mái	chicken with bamboo shoots
kài phàt mét mámûang	chicken with cashew nuts
kài phàt khǐng	chicken with ginger
kài yâang	grilled chicken
khài yát sài	omelette with pork and vegetables
kûng chúp paêng thâwt	prawns fried in batter
mǔu prîaw wǎn	sweet and sour pork
néua phàt krathiam phrík thai	beef fried with garlic and pepper
néua phàt nám man hâwy	beef in oyster sauce
phàt phàk bûng fai daeng	morning glory fried in garlic and bean sauce
phàt phàk ruam	stir-fried vegetables
pàw pía	spring rolls
plaa nêung páe sá	whole fish steamed with vegetables and ginger
plaa rât phrík	whole fish cooked with chillies
plaa thâwt	fried whole fish
sàté	satay
thâwt man plaa	fish cake

THAI DESSERTS (KHANǑM)

khanǒm beuang	small crispy pancake folded over with coconut cream and strands of sweet egg inside
khâo lǎam	sticky rice, coconut cream and black beans cooked and served in bamboo tubes
khâo niăw daeng	sticky red rice mixed with coconut cream
khâo niăw thúrian/ mámûang	sticky rice mixed with coconut cream and durian/mango
klûay khàek	fried banana
lûk taan chêum	sweet palm kernels served in syrup
sǎngkhayaa	coconut custard
tàkôh	squares of transparent jelly (jello) topped with coconut cream

DRINKS (KHREÛANG DEÙM)

bia	beer
chaa ráwn	hot tea
chaa yen	iced tea
kaafae ráwn	hot coffee
kâew	glass
khúat	bottle
mâekhŏng (or anglicized Mekong)	Thai brand-name rice whisky
klûay pan	banana shake
nám mánao/sôm	fresh, bottled or fizzy lemon/orange juice
nám plào	drinking water (boiled or filtered)
nám sŏdaa	soda water
nám taan	sugar
kleua	salt
nám yen	cold water
nom jeùd	milk
ohlíang	iced black coffee
thûay	cup

ORDERING

I am vegetarian/vegan	Phŏm (male)/diichăn (female) kin ahăan mangsàwirát/jeh
Can I see the menu?	Khăw duù menu nóy?
I would like…	Khăw…
with/without…	Saì/mâi saì…
Can I have the bill please?	Khăw check bin?

Glossary

Amphoe District.
Amphoe muang Provincial capital.
Ao Bay.
Apsara Female deity.
Avalokitesvara Bodhisattva representing compassion.
Avatar Earthly manifestation of a deity.
Ban Village or house.
Bang Village by a river or the sea.
Bencharong Polychromatic ceramics made in China for the Thai market.
Bhumisparsa mudra Most common gesture of Buddha images; symbolizes the Buddha's victory over temptation.
Bodhisattva In Mahayana Buddhism, an enlightened being who postpones his or her entry into Nirvana.
Bot Main sanctuary of a Buddhist temple.
Brahma One of the Hindu trinity – "The Creator". Usually depicted with four faces and four arms.
Celadon Porcelain with grey-green glaze.
Changwat Province.
Chao ley/chao nam "Sea gypsies" – nomadic fisherfolk of south Thailand.
Chedi Reliquary tower in Buddhist temple.
Chofa Finial on temple roof.
Deva Mythical deity.
Devaraja God-king.
Dharma The teachings or doctrine of the Buddha.
Dharmachakra Buddhist Wheel of Law (also known as Wheel of Doctrine or Wheel of Life).
Doi Mountain.
Erawan Mythical three-headed elephant; Indra's vehicle.
Farang Foreigner/foreign.
Ganesh Hindu elephant-headed deity, remover of obstacles and god of knowledge.
Garuda Mythical Hindu creature – half man, half bird; Vishnu's vehicle.

Gopura Entrance pavilion to temple precinct (especially Khmer).
Hamsa Sacred mythical goose; Brahma's vehicle.
Hanuman Monkey god and chief of the monkey army in the *Ramayana*; ally of Rama.
Hat Beach.
Hin Stone.
Hinayana Pejorative term for Theravada school of Buddhism, literally "Lesser Vehicle".
Ho trai A scripture library.
Indra Hindu king of the gods and, in Buddhism, devotee of the Buddha; usually carries a thunderbolt.
Isaan Northeast Thailand.
Jataka Stories of the Buddha's five hundred lives.
Khaen Reed and wood pipe; the characteristic musical instrument of Isaan.
Khao Hill, mountain.
Khlong Canal.
Khon Classical dance-drama.
Kinnari Mythical creature – half woman, half bird.
Kirtimukha Very powerful deity depicted as a lion-head.
Ko Island.
Ku The Lao word for *prang*; a tower in a temple complex.
Laem Headland or cape.
Lakhon Classical dance-drama.
Lak muang City pillar; revered home for the city's guardian spirit.
Lakshaman/Phra Lak Rama's younger brother.
Lakshana Auspicious signs or "marks of greatness" displayed by the Buddha.
Lanna Northern Thai kingdom that lasted from the thirteenth to the sixteenth century.
Likay Popular folk theatre.
Longyi Burmese sarong.

Luang Pho Abbot or especially revered monk.

Maenam River.

Mahathat Chedi containing relics of the Buddha.

Mahayana School of Buddhism now practised mainly in China, Japan and Korea; literally "the Great Vehicle".

Mara The Evil One; tempter of the Buddha.

Mawn khwaan Traditional triangular or "axe-head" pillow.

Meru/Sineru Mythical mountain at the centre of Hindu and Buddhist cosmologies.

Mondop Small, square temple building to house minor images or religious texts.

Moo/muu Neighbourhood.

Muang City or town.

Muay thai Thai boxing.

Mudra Symbolic gesture of the Buddha.

Mut mee Tie-dyed cotton or silk.

Naga Mythical dragon-headed serpent in Buddhism and Hinduism.

Nakhon Honorific title for a city.

Nam Water.

Nam tok Waterfall.

Nang thalung Shadow-puppet entertainment, found in southern Thailand.

Nielloware Engraved metalwork.

Nirvana Final liberation from the cycle of rebirths; state of non-being to which Buddhists aspire.

Pak Tai Southern Thailand.

Pali Language of ancient India; the script of the original Buddhist scriptures.

Pha sin Woman's sarong.

Phi Animist spirit.

Phra Honorific term – literally "excellent".

Phu Mountain.

Prang Central tower in a Khmer temple.

Prasat Khmer temple complex or central shrine.

Rama/Phra Ram Human manifestation of Hindu deity Vishnu; hero of the *Ramayana*.

Ramakien Thai version of the *Ramayana*.

Ramayana Hindu epic of good versus evil: chief characters include Rama, Sita, Ravana and Hanuman.

Ravana see Totsagan.

Reua hang yao Longtail boat.

Rishi Ascetic hermit.

Rot ae/rot tua Air-conditioned bus.

Rot thammadaa Ordinary bus.

Sala Meeting hall, pavilion, bus stop – or any open-sided structure.

Samlor Three-wheeled passenger tricycle.

Sanskrit Sacred language of Hinduism; also used in Buddhism.

Sanuk Fun.

Sema Boundary stone to mark consecrated ground within temple complex.

Shiva One of the Hindu trinity – "The Destroyer".

Shiva lingam Phallic representation of Shiva.

Soi Lane or side road.

Songkhran Thai New Year.

Songthaew Public transport pick-up vehicle; means "two rows", after its two facing benches.

Takraw Game played with a rattan ball.

Talat Market.

Talat nam Floating market.

Talat yen Night market.

Tambon Subdistrict.

Tavatimsa Buddhist heaven.

Tha Pier.

Thale Sea or lake.

Tham Cave.

Thanon Road.

That Chedi.

Thep A divinity.

Theravada Main school of Buddhist thought in Thailand; also known as Hinayana.

Totsagan Rama's evil rival in the *Ramayana*; also known as Ravana.

Tripitaka Buddhist scriptures.

Trok Alley.

Tuk-tuk Motorized three-wheeled taxi.

Uma Shiva's consort.

Ushnisha Cranial protuberance on Buddha images, signifying an enlightened being.

Viharn Temple assembly hall for the laity; usually contains the principal Buddha image.

Vipassana Buddhist meditation technique; literally "insight".

Vishnu One of the Hindu trinity – "The Preserver". Usually shown with four arms, holding a disc, a conch, a lotus and a club.

Wai Thai greeting expressed by a prayer-like gesture with the hands.

Wang Palace.

Wat Temple.

Wiang Fortified town.

Yaksha Mythical giant.

Yantra Magical combination of numbers and letters, used to ward off danger.

Small print and index

A ROUGH GUIDE TO ROUGH GUIDES

Published in 1982, the first Rough Guide – to Greece – was a student scheme that became a publishing phenomenon. Mark Ellingham, a recent graduate in English from Bristol University, had been travelling in Greece the previous summer and couldn't find the right guidebook. With a small group of friends he wrote his own guide, combining a highly contemporary, journalistic style with a thoroughly practical approach to travellers' needs.

The immediate success of the book spawned a series that rapidly covered dozens of destinations. And, in addition to impecunious backpackers, Rough Guides soon acquired a much broader readership that relished the guides' wit and inquisitiveness as much as their enthusiastic, critical approach and value-for-money ethos.

These days, Rough Guides include recommendations from budget to luxury and cover more than 120 destinations around the globe, as well as producing an ever-growing range of ebooks.

Visit **roughguides.com** to find all our latest books, read articles, get inspired and share travel tips with the Rough Guides community.

Rough Guide credits

Editor: Olivia Rawes
Layout: Jessica Subramanian
Cartography: Deshpal Dabas
Picture editor: Aude Vauconsant
Proofreader: Jan McCann
Managing editor: Andy Turner
Assistant editor: Sharon Sonam

Production: Jimmy Lao
Cover design: Nicole Newman, Jessica Subramanian
Editorial assistant: Freya Godfrey
Senior pre-press designer: Dan May
Programme manager: Gareth Lowe
Publisher: Keith Drew
Publishing director: Georgina Dee

Publishing information

This sixth edition published December 2015 by
Rough Guides Ltd,
80 Strand, London WC2R 0RL
11, Community Centre, Panchsheel Park,
New Delhi 110017, India
Distributed by Penguin Random House
Penguin Books Ltd,
80 Strand, London WC2R 0RL
Penguin Group (USA)
345 Hudson Street, NY 10014, USA
Penguin Group (Australia)
250 Camberwell Road, Camberwell,
Victoria 3124, Australia
Penguin Group (NZ)
67 Apollo Drive, Mairangi Bay, Auckland 1310,
New Zealand
Penguin Group (South Africa)
Block D, Rosebank Office Park, 181 Jan Smuts Avenue,
Parktown North, Gauteng, South Africa 2193
Rough Guides is represented in Canada by Tourmaline
Editions Inc. 662 King Street West, Suite 304, Toronto,
Ontario M5V 1M7
Printed in Singapore

MIX
Paper from
responsible sources
FSC
www.fsc.org   FSC™ C018179

Help us update

We've gone to a lot of effort to ensure that the sixth
edition of **The Rough Guide to Bangkok** is accurate
and up-to-date. However, things change – places get
"discovered", opening hours are notoriously fickle,
restaurants and rooms raise prices or lower standards. If
you feel we've got it wrong or left something out, we'd like
to know, and if you can remember the address, the price,
the hours, the phone number, so much the better.

Please send your comments with the subject
line "**Rough Guide Bangkok Update**" to mail@uk
.roughguides.com. We'll credit all contributions and
send a copy of the next edition (or any other Rough Guide
if you prefer) for the very best emails.
Find more travel information, connect with fellow
travellers and plan your trip on Ⓦ roughguides.com.

ABOUT THE AUTHOR

Paul Gray After twenty years of toing and froing, Paul has recently settled down in Thailand. He is co-author of the *Rough Guide to Thailand* and the *Rough Guide to Thailand's Beaches & Islands*, as well as the *Rough Guide to Ireland*, and has edited and contributed to many other guidebooks, including an update of his native Northeast for the *Rough Guide to England*.

Acknowledgements

The author would like to thank Kanokros Sakdanares, Marion Walsh-Hédouin and staff at the Bangkok Tourism Division office; and Olivia and Keith at Rough Guides.

Readers' updates

Thanks to all the readers who have taken the time to write in with comments and suggestions (and apologies if we've inadvertently omitted or misspelt anyone's name):

Angelika Becker, Hiroko Canning, Lucie Cluver and Rich, Steven Flintham, John Garratt, Eva Grimbergen, Alessa Hardwick, Dan Jacobs, Monica Mackaness, Gabriel Martinez, Alan McEvoy, Jo Murphy, Silke Nelis and Nicolaas, Chris Pitt, Barry Rice, Liz Talliss, Alina Vasile, Suzanne Verheij.

Photo credits

All photos © Rough Guides except the following:
(Key: t-top; c-centre; b-bottom; l-left; r-right)

p.1 Robert Harding Picture Library: Art Wolfe
p.2 Robert Harding Picture Library: Tibor Bognar
p.4 Getty Images: Prachanart
p.5 Getty Images: Gavin Gough
p.9 Robert Harding Picture Library: Martin Engelmann (t)
p.10 Dreamstime.com: Liorpt
p.11 Corbis: xPACIFICA (t); Robert Harding Picture Library: Ellen Rooney (c)
p.13 123RF.com: Atipan Khantalee (b)
p.14 Alamy Images: Bea Cooper (r)
p.15 Corbis: Michel Gounot/Godong (t); Robert Harding Picture Library: Ingolf Pompe (c); Alamy Images: Raquel Mogado (b)
p.16 Robert Harding Picture Library: Bernd Bieder (t); Corbis: Chaiwat Subprasom (c); Robert Harding Picture Library: Luca Tettoni (b)
p.17 Alamy Images: Blaine Harrington III (t); SuperStock: Luca Tettoni (cl); Robert Harding Picture Library: Gonzalo Azumendi (cr)
p.18 Corbis: Shaun Egan (bl); Yuna Yagi: Yuna Yagi (br)
p.19 Corbis: Jean-Pierre Lescourret (b)
p.20 Corbis: Bertrand Gardel/Hemis
p.48 Robert Harding Picture Library: Tim Graham

p.64 Alamy Images: Parkerphotography
p.74 Robert Harding Picture Library: XYZ PICTURES
p.80 iStockphoto.com: IlonaBudzbon
p.111 Corbis: Tuul & Bruno Morandi
p.126 Corbis: Stuart Black (bl)
p.146 Robert Harding Picture Library: Martin Kreuzer
p.156 Getty Images: Sylvain Sonnet
p.161 Robert Harding Picture Library: Jochen Tack (tl); AWL Images: Peter Adams (bl); 4Corners: Richard Taylor (br)
p.168 Getty Images: Visions Of Our Land
p.173 Alamy Images: Zoonar GmbH
p.176 Corbis: Jack Kurtz
p.183 Robert Harding Picture Library: Rod Porteous
p.187 Robert Harding Picture Library: Doug Scott/age fotostock
p.191 Dreamstime.com: Jimmyfitness
p.194 Corbis: Luca Tettoni

Front cover & spine Statue at Wat Phra Kaeo © AWL Images: Katie Garrod
Back cover Longtail boats © AWL Images: Alex Robinson (t); Tuk-tuk © Getty Images: Robert Harding World Imagery (bl); Wat benchamabophit © Shaun Egan (br)

Index

Maps are marked in grey

Map index

Listings key

■ Accommodation

● Restaurant/café

■ Bar/club

● Shop

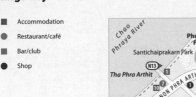

Map symbols

▬ ▬ ··	International boundary	♦	Point of interest	⌒	Arch
▬ ▬ ▬	Chapter division boundary	@	Internet access	⌂	Cave
▬▬▬	Expressway	ⓘ	Tourist information	⊙	Statue
═══	Pedestrianized road	ℂ	Telephone office	⚓	Boat stop
─────	Road	⊞	Hospital/clinic	♠	Museum
→	One-way street	✉	Post office	⚲	Temple
- - - -	Path	E	Embassy/consulate	⛩	Hindu temple
═■═■═	Railway	⊗	Airline office	⛩	Chinese temple/pagoda
── ──	Ferry route	✈	Airport	◯	Stadium
─────	River/canal	★	Transport stop	⊡	Church
▬▬▬▬	Wall	$	Bank/ATM	▨	Building
●----●	Cable car & station	▨	Market	⊡	Christian cemetery
⌣	Bridge	⊠	Gate	⬚	Park/forest
⋀⋀	Mountain				

City plan

The **city plan** on the pages that follow is divided as shown:

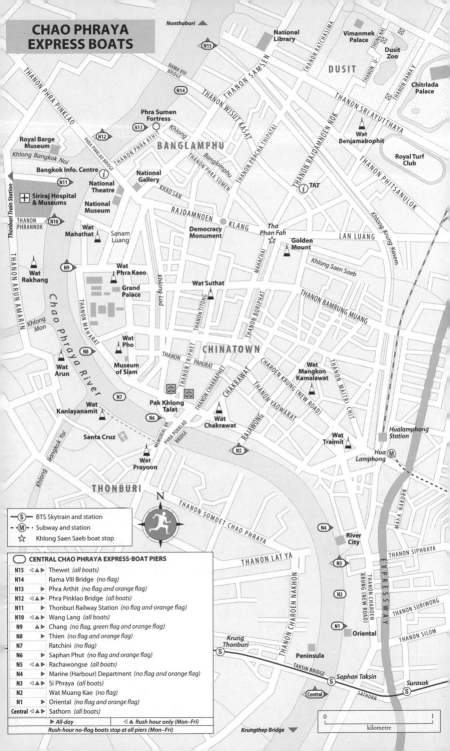

CHAO PHRAYA
EXPRESS BOATS

DUSIT

Nonthaburi

National Library
Vimanmek Palace
Dusit Zoo
Chitrlada Palace
THANON SRI AYUTTHAYA
Wat Benjamabophit
Royal Turf Club
THANON PHITSANULOK

RAMA VIII BRIDGE
N15
N14
THANON WISUT KASAT
THANON SAMSEN
THANON RATCHASIMA
THANON RATCHADAMNOEN NOK
THANON PHRA PINKLAO
PHRA PINKLAO BRIDGE
N12
N13
Phra Sumen Fortress
Khlong
THANON PHRA ATHIT
BANGLAMPHU
Banglamphu
THANON PHRA SUMEN
THANON RACHA THIPATAI
TAT

Royal Barge Museum
Khlong Bangkok Noi
Bangkok Info. Centre
N11
National Theatre
National Gallery
National Museum
KHAO SAN
RAJDAMNOEN KLANG
Tha Phan Fah
Golden Mount
LAN LUANG
Khlong Krung Kasem

Thonburi Train Station
Siriraj Hospital & Museums
THANON PHRANNOK
N10
Wat Mahathat
Sanam Luang
Democracy Monument
Khlong Saen Saeb
THANON BAMRUNG MUANG

THANON ARUN AMARIN
Wat Rakhang
N9
THANON MAHARAT
Wat Phra Kaeo
Grand Palace
Khlong Lod
Wat Suthat
MAHACHAI
BORIPHAT
THANON TITONG

Chao Phraya River
Khlong Mon
N8
Wat Pho
Museum of Siam
CHINATOWN
THANON PAHURAT
THANON TRIPHET
Wat Mangkon Kamalawat
THANON MAITRI CHIT

Wat Arun
N7
Pak Khlong Talat
THANON CHAKRAPHET
CHARAWAT
CHAROEN KRUNG (NEW ROAD)
Hualamphong Station

Wat Kanlayanamit
N6
Wat Chakrawat
THANON YAOWARAT
RAJWONG
Wat Traimit
Hua Lamphong
M

Khlong Bangkok Yai
Santa Cruz
MEMORIAL BR.
PHRA PINKLAO BRIDGE
N5

THONBURI
Wat Prayoon
N

MAHA NAKORN

THANON SOMDET CHAO PHRAYA
N4
River City
THANON SIPHRAYA

Legend

- (S) · BTS Skytrain and station
- (M) · Subway and station
- ☆ Khlong Saen Saeb boat stop

THANON LAT YA
N3
THANON CHAROEN KRUNG (NEW ROAD)
EXPRESSWAY
N2
THANON SURIWONG

Krung Thonburi
N1
Oriental
THANON SILOM

CENTRAL CHAO PHRAYA EXPRESS-BOAT PIERS

N15 ◁▲▷	Thewet	*(all boats)*
N14	Rama VIII Bridge	*(no flag)*
N13 ▷	Phra Arthit	*(no flag and orange flag)*
N12 ◁▲▷	Phra Pinklao Bridge	*(all boats)*
N11 ▷	Thonburi Railway Station	*(no flag and orange flag)*
N10 ◁▲▷	Wang Lang	*(all boats)*
N9 ▲▷	Chang	*(no flag, green flag and orange flag)*
N8 ▷	Thien	*(no flag and orange flag)*
N7	Ratchini	*(no flag)*
N6 ▷	Saphan Phut	*(no flag and orange flag)*
N5 ◁▲▷	Rachawongse	*(all boats)*
N4 ▷	Marine (Harbour) Department	*(no flag and orange flag)*
N3 ◁▲▷	Si Phraya	*(all boats)*
N2	Wat Muang Kae	*(no flag)*
N1 ▷	Oriental	*(no flag and orange flag)*
Central ◁▲▷	Sathorn	*(all boats)*

▷ All-day	◁▲ Rush hour only (Mon–Fri)

Rush-hour no-flag boats stop at all piers (Mon–Fri)

Peninsula
Krung Thonburi
(S)
TAKSIN BRIDGE
Saphan Taksin
(S)
Central
SATHORN
Surasak
(S)

Krungthep Bridge

0		1
	kilometre	

1

SOI CHARAN SANIT

SOI CHARAN SANIT WONG SOI 1

SOI C S W 37

SOI C S W 44

Khlong Bang Yikhan

BOROMMARAJCHONNEE

Khlong Bong Ramu

SOI CHARAN SANIT WONG

CHARANSANITWONG 49

SOI CHARAN SANIT WONG

SOI CHARAN SANIT WONG 42

SOI CHARAN SANIT WONG 44

LUKM

BANG PHLAT

SOI CHARAN SANITWONG 40

Central Development Store

CHARAN SANIT WONG

SOI CHARAN SANIT WONG 5

Pata Department Store

SOMDET PHRA PIN KLAO

SOI BOONPHONGSA 1

SOI SUJICHANDAMRI

Khlong Bang Yikhan

THANON ARUN AMARIN

THANON PHRA PINKLAO

SOI SAQLADA

Wat Suwannaram

Phra A

Thong

Khlong Bangkok Noi

N12

Tha Phra Pinklao

Suwannaram Market

Royal Barge Museum

PHRA PINKLAO BRIDGE

Bus stop 3

SOI CHARAN SANITWONG 32

Bangkok Noi/Thon Buri Station

BANGLAM

Bangkok Tourism (i)

THANON PHRA PINKLAO

Wat Song

Khlong

THANON NIKHOM BAHNPHAK ROTFAI

Siriraj Bimuksthan Museum

Bus stop 5

N

THANON ISARAPHAP

SOI WAT

KAN

SOI PHATTANA CHANG

THANON ARUN AMARIN

TROK WANG LANG

N11

Tha Bangkok Noi/Thonburi Train Station

National Theatre

Vo

Siriraj Hospital ✚

National Museum

Bangkok Noi Market

TROK WANG LANG

THANON PHRANNOK

N10

Tha Prachan

Thammasat University

THANON NA PHRA THAT

To

SOI WATTANA

SOI CHANG

SOI WAT RAKHANG

TROK WANG LANG

Tha Wang Lang (Siriraj)

THANON PHRA CHAN

THANON MAHARAT

s

SOI SALA TONCHAI

SOI WAT RAKHANG

Tha Maharat

Wat Mahathat ▲

Sanam Luang

THANON ISARAPHAP

SOI ITSARAPHAP 44

SOI WAT RAKANG KHOSITARAM

Wat Rakhang ▲

Tha Chang

N9

TROK SILLAPAKORN

Art Centre ✉ (i)

THANON NA PHRA LAN

THANON MAHARAT

(i)

THANON NA PHRA CHAN

THANON ISARAPHAP

SOI RATTANAKASING

SOI ITSARAPHAP 37

THANON ISARAPHAP

BANGKOK NOI

THANON ARUN AMARIN

SOI MATUM

Naval Department

Wat Phra Kaeo

Grand Palace

RATANAKOSIN

2

SOI SANGUAN SUK

THANON NAKHON CHAISI

Khlong Samsen

SUKOTHAI

PICHAI

THANON RAMA V

Rachawat
Market

SOI MIT ANAN

SOI SUTCHARIT NUA

SUKHOM

THARAM

SUKOTHAI

THANON SAMSEN

THANON SAMSEN

SUKOTHAI

PICHAI

THANON RAJWITHI

SOI SUTCHARIT 1

SOI SUTCHARIT 2

SOI SUKOTHAI 1

SOI SUKOTHAI 2

SOI SUKOTHAI 3

SOI SUKOTHAI 4

SOI SUKOTHAI 5

THANON SAWANKHALOK

Vimanmek
Palace

Support
Museum

Parliament

Elephant
Museum

U-THONG NAI

Dusit
Zoo

THANON RAJWITHI

DUSIT

TIMON

THANON RAMA V

Chitrlada
Palace

Suan
Amporn

Rama V Statue

Wat
Benjamabophit

THANON RAJDAMNOEN NOK

THANON RAMA V

PATHUM

THANON SRI AYUTTHAYA

THANON SAWANKHALOK

EXPRESSWAY

Government
House

MAHON

Royal
Turf Club

THANON LUK LUANG

THANON KRUNG KASEM

THANON PHITSANULOK

THANON SRI AYU

THANON SAWANKHALOK

NAKHORN SAWAN

THANON LUK LUANG

PHANANG

SUPPARAJ

Khlong Phadung Krung Kasem

THANON LUK LUANG

SOI 2

SOI MAN SIN 4

SOI 1

LAN LUANG

LAN LUANG

Bangkok
Mission

SOI MANSIN 3

SOI MANSIN 2

SOI MANSIN 1

S PEECH 4

S PEECH 5

SOI PETCHABURI 3

RAK

DAMRONG

SOI
URUPHONG 2

SOI URUPHONG 3

THANON PHETCHABURI

SOI PETCHABURI

POM PRAP
SATTRU
PHAI

Khlong Saen Saeb

THANON KRUNG KASEM

KHLONG LAM PAK

PHAYA NAK

SOI

RONGRIAN

SUDA

Khlong Saen Saeb

PHAYA NAK

Rong
Liang
Dek
Market

ANANTANAK

SOI PHRASI

RONGRIAN

THONG

BANTHAT

SOI SUAN MALI 1

SOI SUAN MALI 2

THANON BAMRUNG MUANG

TROK RONG LIANG DEK

SOI PHRAYA MAHA AMMAT

SOI WAT BODOMWAT

PHLAB PLACHAI

EXPRESSWAY

Jim
Thompson's
House

Tha
Hue

CHALOEM KHET 1

CHALOEM KHET 2

CHALOEM KHET 3

CHALOEM KHET 4

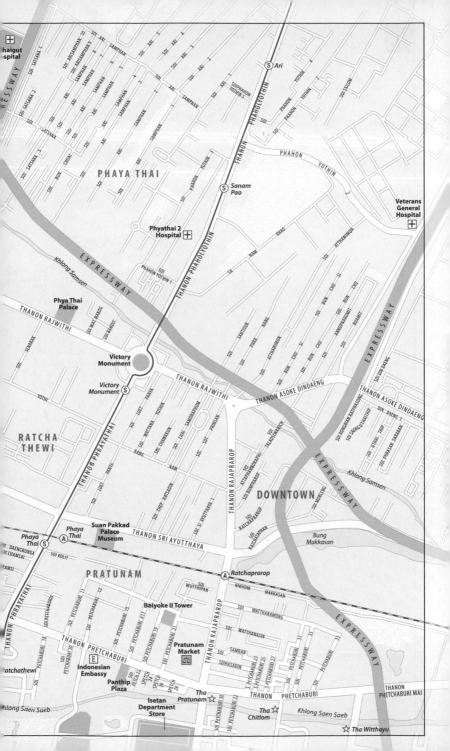

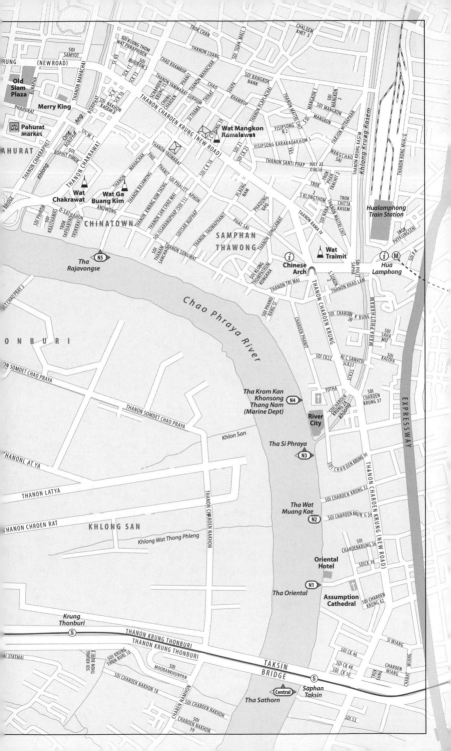

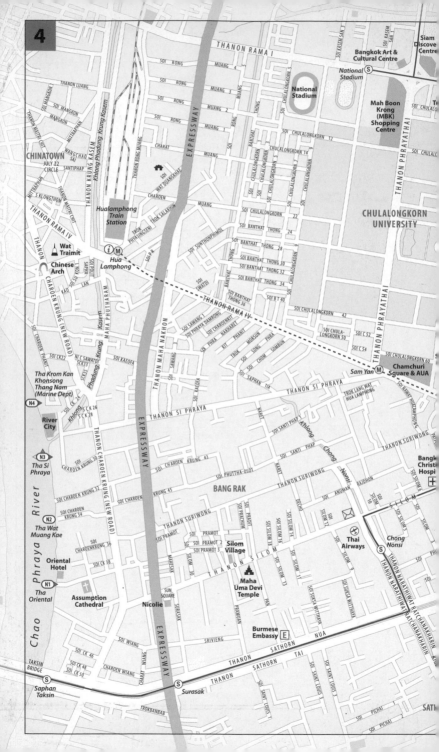

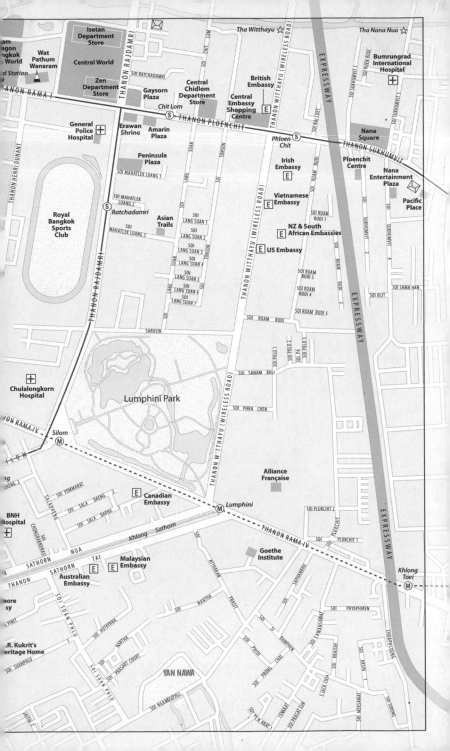

ROUGH GUIDES

SO NOW WE'VE TOLD YOU
HOW TO MAKE THE MOST
OF YOUR TIME, WE WANT
YOU TO STAY SAFE AND
COVERED WITH OUR
FAVOURITE TRAVEL INSURER

WorldNomads.com
keep travelling safely

GET AN ONLINE QUOTE
roughguides.com/travel-insurance

31901056724877

MAKE THE MOST OF YOUR TIME ON EARTH™